Modernism

Blackwell Guides to Criticism

Editor Michael O'Neill

The aim of this new series is to provide undergraduates pursuing literary studies with collections of key critical work from an historical perspective. At the same time emphasis is placed upon recent and current work. In general, historic responses of importance are described, and represented by short excerpts, in an introductory narrative chapter. Thereafter landmark pieces and cutting edge contemporary work are extracted or provided in their entirety according to their potential value to the student. Each volume seeks to enhance enjoyment of literature and to widen the individual student's critical repertoire. Critical approaches are treated as 'tools', and not articles of faith, to enhance the pursuit of reading and study. At a time when critical bibliographies seem to swell by the hour and library holdings to wither year by year, the *Blackwell Guides to Criticism* series offers students privileged access to and careful guidance through those writings that have most conditioned the historic current of discussion and debate as it now informs contemporary scholarship.

Published volumes

Roger Dalrymple	*Middle English*
Corinne Saunders	*Chaucer*
Emma Smith	*Shakespeare's Comedies*
Emma Smith	*Shakespeare's Histories*
Emma Smith	*Shakespeare's Tragedies*
Francis O'Gorman	*The Victorian Novel*
Michael Whitworth	*Modernism*

Forthcoming

Uttara Natarajan	*The Romantic Poets*

Modernism

Edited by Michael H. Whitworth

Blackwell
Publishing

Editorial material and organization © 2007 by Blackwell Publishing Ltd

BLACKWELL PUBLISHING
350 Main Street, Malden, MA 02148-5020, USA
9600 Garsington Road, Oxford OX4 2DQ, UK
550 Swanston Street, Carlton, Victoria 3053, Australia

First published 2007 by Blackwell Publishing Ltd

1   2007

Library of Congress Cataloging-in-Publication Data

Modernism / edited by Michael H. Whitworth.
    p. cm. — (Blackwell guides to criticism)
    Includes bibliographical references and index.
    ISBN-13: 978-0-631-23077-9 (hardcover : alk. paper)
    ISBN-10: 0-631-23077-7 (hardcover : alk. paper)
    ISBN-13: 978-0-631-23078-6 (pbk. : alk. paper)
    ISBN-10: 0-631-23078-5 (pbk. : alk. paper) 1. Modernism (Literature)
I. Whitworth, Michael H. II Series.

    PN56.M54M598 2007
    809'.9112—dc22

                                                                2006009535

A catalogue record for this title is available from the British Library.

Set in 10/12.5pt Caslon
by Newgen Imaging Systems (P) Ltd., Chennai, India
Printed and bound in Singapore
by Markono Print Media Pte Ltd

The publisher's policy is to use permanent paper from mills that operate a sustainable
forestry policy, and which has been manufactured from pulp processed using acid-free
and elementary chlorine-free practices. Furthermore, the publisher ensures that the
text paper and cover board used have met acceptable environmental accreditation
standards.

For further information on
Blackwell Publishing, visit our website:
www.blackwellpublishing.com

Contents

Acknowledgements   vii

Note on the Texts   x

Part I   **1**

Introduction   **3**

Part II   **61**

1 Modernism and Romanticism   **63**

Romantic Image   67
Frank Kermode

Pound/Stevens: Whose Era?   81
Marjorie Perloff

2 Realism and Formalism   **99**

The Ideology of Modernism   102
Georg Lukács

Reconciliation Under Duress   114
Theodor Adorno

3 Modernism and the Avant-Garde   **122**

Adorno: A Critical Introduction   123
Simon Jarvis

Theory of the Avant-Garde   131
Peter Bürger

4 Modernism, the Masses, and the Culture Industry   **141**

Mass Culture as Woman   144
Andreas Huyssen

T. S. Eliot and the Cultural Divide: A 'Black and Grinning Muse'   160
David E. Chinitz

T. S. Eliot and the Cultural Divide: Down at Tom's Place   164
David E. Chinitz

T. S. Eliot and the Cultural Divide: An 'Avant-Garde' Program   173
David E. Chinitz

5 Modernity and the City   **181**

The Metropolis and Mental Life   182
Georg Simmel

The Mire of the Macadam   190
Marshall Berman

The Invisible Flâneuse: Women and the Literature of Modernity   199
Janet Wolff

6 Regendering Modernism   **216**

'A Tangled Mesh of Modernists' (diagram)   218
Bonnie Kime Scott

'Beyond the Reaches of Feminist Criticism: A Letter from Paris'   220
Shari Benstock

'Modernism and Modernity: Engendering Literary History'   228
Rita Felski

7 Publishing Modernism   **244**

The Price of Modernism   247
Lawrence Rainey

8 Late Modernism   **272**

The Epistemology of Late Modernism   276
Alan Wilde

Late Modernist Poetics   281
Anthony Mellors

Late Modernist Poetics   288
Anthony Mellors

Further Reading   297

Index   303

Acknowledgements

Much of the work on this book was undertaken while I was a lecturer in the English Department, University of Wales, Bangor. I would like to thank the Department and the Library for their support, as well as the staff of the British Library, and, in Oxford, the Bodleian Library, the English Faculty Library, Balliol College Library, and Merton College Library. I would like to record my gratitude to the students at Bangor who took the module '*Ulysses*, Modernism, and Modernity', and who gave me the opportunity to see some of the texts included in this collection from a student's point of view. I am grateful to Jessica Maynard for discussions of modernism over many years, which have suggested important lines of enquiry. I would also like to thank the organizers of, and participants in, the London Modernism Seminar and Northern Modernism Seminar, both of which have been stimulating forums. Andrew McNeillie first approached me to edit this volume while at Blackwell, and I would like to thank him for suggestions that helped to shape it. Needless to say, responsibility for the selection of texts and for the editorial matter is mine alone.

For their patience in awaiting this volume, and their efforts in producing it, thanks to Emma Bennett, Jennifer Hunt, Astrid Wind, and Karen Wilson. Thanks too to Roxanne Selby for giving me a publisher's perspective on authorial procrastination.

The editor and publisher gratefully acknowledge the permission granted to reproduce the copyright material in this book:

1. Frank Kermode, pp. 109–13, 121–32 from *Romantic Image*. London: Routledge and Kegan Paul, 1957. Extracts from *The Romantic Image* by Frank Kermode (Copyright © Frank Kermode 1957) are reproduced by permission of PFD (www.pfd.co.uk) on behalf of Professor Sir Frank Kermode.

2. Marjorie Perloff, "Pound/Stevens: Whose Era?," pp. 485–95, 504–6 from *New Literary History* 13, 1982. Reprinted by permission of Marjorie Perloff.

3. Simon Jarvis, pp. 116 from *Adorno: A Critical Introduction.* Cambridge: Polity, 1998. Reprinted by permission of Polity Press Ltd. Copyright ©1998 from *Adorno: A Critical Introduction*, by Simon Jarvis. Reproduced by permission of Routledge/Taylor & Francis Group, LLC and reprinted by permission of the author Simon Jarvis.

4. Peter Bürger, pp. 47–53 from *Theory of the Avant-Garde.* Minneapolis: University of Minneapolis Press, 1984. Originally published in German as *Theorie der Avantgarde*, copyright © 1974, 1980 by Suhrkamp Verlag. English translation copyright © 1984 by the University of Minnesota.

5. Georg Lukács, "The Ideology of Modernism," pp. 17–26, 30–35 from *The Meaning of Contemporary Realism*, John and Necke Mander. London: Merlin Press, 1963. Reprinted by permission of the Merlin Press, Suite 4, 96 Monnow Street, Monmouth NP25 3EQ.

6. Theodor Adorno, "Reconciliation Under Duress," pp. 157–63 from Ernest Bloch et al., *Aesthetics and Politics.* London: Verso, 1977. Reprinted by permission of Verso.

7. Andreas Huyssen, "Mass Culture as Woman," pp. 44–58 from *After the Great Divide*, parts I–V. Basingstoke: Macmillan/Indiana University Press, 1986 (US)/1988 (UK). Reprinted by permission of the publisher Indiana University Press and with permission of Palgrave Macmillan.

8. David Chinitz, pp. 28–32, 41–9, 80–4 from *T. S. Eliot and the Cultural Divide.* London and Chicago: University of Chicago Press, 2003. Reprinted by permission of the publisher The University of Chicago Press and by the author David E. Chinitz.

9. George Simmel, "The Metropolis and Mental Life," pp. 409–24 from Kurt H. Wolff, *The Sociology of Georg Simmel*, Kurt H. Wolff. New York: Free Press of Glencoe, 1964. Reprinted and edited with the permission of The Free Press, a Division of Simon & Schuster Adult Publishing Group, from *The Sociology of Georg Simmel*, translated and edited by Kurt H. Wolff. Copyright © 1950 by The Free Press. Copyright © renewed 1978 by The Free Press. All rights reserved.

10. Marshall Berman, "The Mire of Macadam," pp. 155–64 from *All that is Solid Melts Into Air.* London: Verso, 1983. Reprinted by permission of Verso.

11. Janet Wolff, "The Invisible Flâneuse: Women and the Literature of Modernity," pp. 141–56 from Andrew Benjamin, *The Problems of Modernity: Adorno and Benjamin.* London: Routledge and Kegan Paul, 1988. Copyright © 1988, Routledge and Kegan Paul. Reproduced by permission of Taylor & Francis Books UK and reprinted by permission of Roger Trigg.

This volume appeared in the series Warwick Studies in Philosophy and Literature

12. Bonnie Kime Scott, diagram "A Tangled Mesh of Modernists," p. 10 from Bonnie Kime Scott, *The Gender of Modernism*. Bloomington: Indiana University Press, 1990. Reprinted by permission of the publisher Indiana University Press.

13. Shari Benstock, "Beyond the Reaches of Feminist Criticism: A Letter from Paris," pp. 42–48 from S. Benstock, *Feminist Issues in Literary Scholarship*. Bloomington: Indiana University Press, 1987. Reprinted by permission of the publisher Indiana University Press.

14. Rita Felski, "Modernism and Modernity: Engendering Literary History," pp. 191-208 from Lisa Rado, *Rereading Modernism*. New York: Garland Press, 1994. Copyright © 1994. Reproduced by permission of Routledge/ Taylor & Francis Group, LLC and by permission of the author Rita Felski.

15. Lawrence Rainey, "The Price of Modernism," pp. 77–91, 98–106 from *Institutions of Modernism*. New Haven, CT: Yale University Press, 1998. Reprinted by permission of the publisher Yale University Press.

16. Alan Wilde, "The Epistemology of Late Modernism," pp. 106–9 from *Horizons of Assent: Modernism, Postmodernism, and the Ironic Imagination*. Baltimore and London: Johns Hopkins University Press, 1981. Reprinted by permission of the author.

17. Anthony Mellors, pp. 19–24, 41–5 from *Late Modernist Poetics*. Manchester: Manchester University Press, 2005. From *Late Modernist Poetics: From Pound to Prynne*, by Anthony Mellors, January 2005, Manchester University Press, Manchester UK.

Every effort has been made to trace copyright holders and to obtain their permission for the use of copyright material. The publisher apologizes for any errors or omissions in the above list and would be grateful if notified of any corrections that should be incorporated in future reprints or editions of this book.

Note on the Texts

While I have tried as far as possible to present continuous arguments, most of the texts included here have had sections removed. Moreover, discursive footnotes have been reduced or removed. Readers are advised to consult the original texts for full information.

Part I

Introduction

According to some critics, this book should not exist: it concerns a wholly illusory topic. The argument has been put most forcefully by Perry Anderson:

> Modernism as a notion is the emptiest of all cultural categories. Unlike the terms Gothic, Renaissance, Baroque, Mannerist, Romantic, or Neo-Classical, it designates no describable object in its own right: it is completely lacking in positive content. In fact, [...] what is concealed beneath the label is a wide variety of very diverse – indeed incompatible – aesthetic practices: symbolism, constructivism, expressionism, surrealism. These, which do spell out specific programmes, were unified post hoc in a portmanteau concept whose only referent is the blank passage of time itself. There is no other aesthetic marker so vacant or vitiated. For what once was modern is soon obsolete. The futility of the term, and its attendant ideology, can be seen all too clearly from current attempts to cling to its wreckage and yet swim with the tide still further beyond it, in the coinage 'post-modernism': one void chasing another in a serial regression of self-congratulatory chronology.[1]

There are several respects in which this criticism is true, but there are also good reasons, as Anderson himself recognises, for continuing to use the term 'modernism' as one of a set of mutually dependent concepts. Though the movements that are commonly grouped under the term were diverse in their practices, and though the underlying justifications for those practices often draw on incompatible ideas about art, psychology, and society, a fragile unity may be found in the idea that all of them respond to a shared set of social and ideological conditions. 'Modernism' is not so much a thing as a set of responses to problems posed by the conditions of modernity. The recognition that modernism and modernity are related but not identical is crucial to most recent work in the area. At one time it was possible to write of there being 'two modernities', one being the modernity of technology and social life, and the other being aesthetic modernity;[2] more recently, critics have used 'modernism' for the second of these, reserving 'modernity' for the social and ideological context. 'Social and ideological context' requires more careful definition: for some critics, the city and the comfort of modern life are at the forefront; for others, the dominance of 'instrumental reason', an inflexible form of rationality which threatens to enslave us; for others, historical events such as the First World War or the holocaust are more significant. Exactly which factors are included within modernity, and the relative importance of each, is something over which there is little critical agreement, and is one reason for the diversity in the accounts of modernism found in the present collection.

Part I of this guide aims to introduce modernism by surveying how 'modernist' writers understood their own newness and their relation to their social context. (The extent to which the labels 'modernist' and 'modernism' are anachronistic is something to which we shall return.) Many of the critical questions that have come to dominate later criticism have their roots in the modernists' self-conception. However, modernist writers articulated these questions in a vocabulary that now seems unfamiliar. In some cases, the questions were half-buried, implicit in other aspects of their work. Part I begins by outlining eight major problems posed by modernity, in the light of which the stylistic experiments and formal difficulties of modernist texts become more significant. The following section defines modernism in terms of twelve visible features of modernist texts. Such definitions can be restrictive, and in the past have had the effect of excluding some 'modern' works from the 'modernist' canon, but they have the advantage of connecting directly to textual evidence. When the visible features are set in the perspective offered by the underlying problems, the qualities of modernist texts acquire an interest that is historical as well as aesthetic.

As Perry Anderson's remarks make clear, 'modernism' is a fragile category. The section on the Victorians asks to what extent they differed from the modernists, while the next section, 'Modernist Self-Construction', examines the ways in which modernists sought to emphasise their difference. One of their methods was to set out a clear aesthetic programme through manifestos, reviews, and essays. These texts form the beginning of the critical tradition on modernism, though their emphasis on technique also sets them apart from more recent literary criticism. As the critical tradition developed, the terms 'modernist' and 'modernism' began to dominate, and their emergence is traced in the following section. The penultimate section in Part I examines the construction of modernism by the most significant critical school of the mid-twentieth century, The New Criticism; the final section briefly surveys later developments.

Although this guide frequently questions the definition of 'modernism', the selection of texts proceeds from a working definition: this guide concentrates on English-language writers active from 1910 to 1939. The chronological limits of modernism are questioned, however. In Part I the section on the Victorian questions the starting date of modernism, while in Part II the chapter on

'Late Modernism' reconsiders its terminal date. The concentration on English-language writers means that this guide does not address the full geographical range of European modernism. In consequence, Expressionism and Surrealism play a smaller part than they would in a work oriented towards continental Europe. However, the critical works gathered in Part II draw on a wide range of European, and particularly German-language, theorisations of modernism, and are thus relevant to readers with a linguistically wider range of interests.

Part II of the guide aims to introduce eight main debates surrounding literary modernism. It examines the relation of modernism to earlier movements and modes of writing, such as Romanticism, symbolism, and realism, and its relation to contemporaneous cultural formations, particularly the avant-garde and popular culture; it examines modernism's relation to the city, not simply as subject matter, but as an influence on the form of modern consciousness and modernist writing; it examines modernism's relation to questions of gender, both in the chapter on 'Regendering Modernism', and in the chapters on the Culture Industry and the City; it examines factors that affected the publication of modernist texts; and it asks how critics have approached variants of modernism that have flourished beyond its conventional chronological limits. Though Part II begins with one of the earliest pieces (dating from 1957) and concludes with one of the most recent (from 2005), the sequence is not a narrative of progress: many of the earliest debates continue to inform current work, albeit in transformed guises. The earliest piece in Part II, 'The Metropolis and Mental Life' (1903), predates many of the classic works of modernism, but has much in common with Marxist-influenced criticism from the late twentieth century.

Defining modernism need not mean laying finite limits to it, either in terms of a canon or a period. A more subtle definition defines not the material, but the processes that produced it: processes involving reactions to modernity that were sometimes aggressive, sometimes defensive, sometimes ambivalent. Such a definition is productive rather than restrictive, flexible rather than rigid, and capable of developing as it encounters new material.

Not Definitions, but Questions

In a valuable overview essay, Richard Sheppard has suggested that critics trying to understand modernism have adopted three main strategies. The first consists of trying to define key features of modernism, and it may be subdivided into attempts to define a modernist worldview, such as nihilism or authoritarianism, and attempts to define formal features of modernist works, such as the use of myth or of metaphor. The second approach tries to place modernism in 'a one-dimensional historical, literary-historical, or sociological context'. For example, it might try, in the historical dimension, to understand modernism as a product of the First World War, in the literary-historical dimension to understand the continuities or discontinuities between modernism and Romanticism, or in the sociological dimension, to understand it as a result of the 'megalopolitan experience'. The third approach is also contextual, and could validly employ the language of cause and effect (e.g. of the 'products' and 'results' of historical moments), but in doing so attributes a more active role to modernist writing. Modernism's response to its historical context is to try to understand it. Sheppard, summarising Fredric Jameson, says that modernist works 'are not just reflexes, transcriptions or symptoms of a profound cultural upheaval, but, *simultaneously*, responses through which the authors of those works try to pictorialise their understanding and so make sense of that upheaval'.[3]

The three approaches are not mutually exclusive – Sheppard notes that the second is often a development of the first – and more than one will often co-exist in a single piece of criticism. Sheppard offers the third as the most refined and subtle, but the other two approaches need not be rejected; rather, they should be subsumed into the third. A theory of modernism that could not make reference to the formal features of the work would be an impoverished one. However, a theory which comprehends the relation between those formal features and the deeper cultural upheaval is richer than a theory which acknowledges both aspects without relating them.

As an approach to the question of how English-language modernist writers understood and constructed their identities, I would like to suggest eight fundamental problems that motivated them to become modernist. For the sake of clarity, these problems are best posed as questions, but this should not be taken to imply that the writers were fully conscious of them. Moreover, some questions are most easily and clearly posed in terminology that was not available to the writers in question. In saying that these problems 'motivated' them to become modernist, I wish to imply that the problems gave them an incentive for developments in that direction, without implying a strictly deterministic logic; there were other factors impelling them. These fundamental problems become particularly valuable once we understand their relation to the immediately visible aspects of modernist texts.

(1) How can we justify art in a world dominated by commerce, quantification, and instrumental rationality? No modernist would have put the question in exactly this way, because 'instrumental reason' is a phrase indebted to Adorno and Horkheimer's *Dialectic of Enlightenment* (1944, tr. 1972). However, at least as early as 1922, writers were characterising their age as 'the machine age', and by the 1930s they were talking of the relation of the poet to the age of 'big business'. The centrality of this question explains why the philosophy of Henri Bergson was so attractive to some modernists, because it seemed to vindicate qualitative knowledge in a world of quantification. Another way of posing this question (to which my formula is indebted) is that of Andrew Brighton, who proposes that the 'inaugurating problem' of modernism is 'the issue of the status and possibility of imaginative and ethical consciousness in a culture dominated by modern rationality'.[4] Brighton's distinction of imaginative, ethical, and 'modern' rationality echoes Max Weber's argument that reason had become divided into the spheres of art, morality, and science, and in this light 'imaginative and ethical consciousness' should be understood as two distinct forms of knowledge. However, Brighton's coupling of the two terms raises the additional problem of whether imaginative consciousness is possible without its ethical complement, and vice versa. This too, it must be said, was a pressing question for modernist writers and critics, and one that appeared most explicitly in the debate between T. S. Eliot and I. A. Richards over whether it was possible to achieve 'a complete severance' between poetry and '*all* beliefs',[5] and again in the 1930s in debates over the relation of politics and literature.

(2) What model of the self is adequate to modern life? There are two aspects to this question. One asks what model of the self can accommodate scientific discoveries about human beings, primarily Darwin's recognition that humans are descended from apes, and the claims of psychologists and psychoanalysts about the more primitive aspects of the brain and the psyche. The other aspect is concerned with the experience of modernity, but – explicitly in Georg Simmel's essay in Part II – it overlaps with psychological questions about perception and cognition. The modern self is overwhelmed with sensations: the city is full of signs drawn from various codes, and full of fast and unpredictable movement. The question about the self is also a question about competing forms of knowledge. A self fully in touch with sense data does not have the capacity to reflect on what it perceives; a self that attempts to think about that sense data filters it, and so becomes detached from the empirical world. T. S. Eliot's phrase 'We had the experience but missed the meaning' ('The Dry Salvages', part II) gestures towards this idea, though in that poem Eliot is more optimistic than some about the possibility of uniting meaning and experience. Importantly, the question motivates the production of new modernist styles that attempt to place the reader in a characteristically modern subject position. Joseph Conrad's impressionistic style is one of the earliest forms: Conrad subjects the reader to a process of 'delayed decoding',[6] in which sense-impressions are reported before the described object is given its conventional name. The reader is made to feel the different competencies (and inadequacies) of each form of knowledge.

(3) What is the relation of an art-work to its creator? Should a poem express its author's feelings? If we allow a text to be non-expressive, and *impersonal*, does that mean that it is no longer *individual*? While many modernist writers were willing to accept that a text should be impersonal, the possibility of authorship becoming deindividualised was rather more threatening, as it implied a wholly mechanical process disturbingly consonant with the values of commerce and

mass culture. The novel-writing machines imagined by George Orwell in *Nineteen Eighty Four* (1949) embody this fear. If, on the other hand, it is granted that a text can be individual while at the same time being impersonal, we must ask where its individuality can be located.

(4) What makes a work of art valuable? In some respects this question is a restatement of the first and third, but there are other new questions under this general heading. There is a conflict between referentialism or formalism: is a work of art to be valued for its ability to refer to something beyond itself, or for its qualities of beautiful and subtle internal organisation? The question goes back to the aesthetic movement, and particularly Walter Pater's pronouncement that 'All art constantly aspires towards the condition of music':[7] that is, with certain limited exceptions, music cannot refer to anything beyond itself; notes are valued for their harmonic and melodic relations to each other (and of course for discordant and anti-melodic relations), but they cannot refer to anything; thus, the matter and the form cannot be distinguished. However, Pater advances the argument for one side only. As the existence of literary impressionism implies, other modern writers were aiming to get closer to reality. M. K. Spears summarised the conflict thus:

> there are two primary impulses in modern literature, both always present but one or the other dominating. The first is the drive toward aestheticism, toward the purification of form, its refinement and exploration, the development of those features that are most distinctive. The illusion becomes more convincing and self-sufficient; there is a tendency for the art-world to become separate and independent from life. This is countered by the opposing impulse, to break through art, destroy any possibility of escape to illusion, to insist that the immediate experience, the heightening of life is the important thing. Both elements co-exist from the beginning: *Ulysses* is a world of art, but with elements of raw and deliberately unassimilated reality, like the *collage* materials [...] used in so many early modern paintings.[8]

Significantly, Spears does not attempt to identify one element or the other as the true modernism: modernism is born from the tension between them.

The question comes with political concomitants. One of the attractions of the formalist position is that the work of art, if it ceases to become accountable to anything beyond itself, seems to have escaped the instrumental rationality of the modern world. However, in escaping instrumental rationality, the work of art becomes politically impotent. As Terry Eagleton says, by 'establishing a critical, negating distance between itself and the ruling social order, modernism must simultaneously bracket off the political forces which seek to transform that order'.[9]

(5) What is the relation between art and criticism? In the literary sphere the question is particularly vexed, because both are produced in the same verbal medium: any attempt to establish a difference between literary language and

a critical meta-language is doomed to deconstruction. This question has a similar outline to (4): the dilemma of referentiality and aestheticism is repeated in the dilemma of allying art with criticism and maintaining a clear separation. To ground art in critical discourse is potentially as destructive of its artistic status as would be the act of grounding it in referentiality. If the discourse of art differs from that of criticism, there nevertheless arises the question of whether to value that which cannot be accommodated within the established critical discourse. Like (4), this question ultimately relates back to (1): critical explication can be seen as the handmaiden of instrumental rationality, capturing autotelic works of art and tethering them to conventional concepts.

(6) What grand narratives best explain the recent course of human history? Should recent history be seen in conservative terms, as a narrative of decline (inevitable or otherwise), or in liberal terms as a narrative of increasing freedom and intellectual progress? Should it be seen in Marxist terms, as a class conflict? Though modernist writers were unaware of the terminology of 'grand narratives' – the phrase is a translation of 'grand récit' in Jean-François Lyotard's *The Postmodern Condition* (1979, tr. 1984) – they were familiar with this way of thinking about history; the emergence of Darwinian and Marxist theories in the nineteenth century made it inevitable. The question about grand narratives relates to questions about the self: is man, as T. E. Hulme and others would have had it, fundamentally 'fallen' and imperfect, and in need of discipline from a higher authority? Or is he fundamentally good, and held back only by outmoded customs, 'born free but everywhere in chains', as Jean-Jacques Rousseau would have had it?[10] These questions are literary questions because grand narratives are fundamentally ideological: they affect the value system through which a writer views the world. They can also, by means of various mediating arguments, be used by writers to justify their sense of what is proper in matters of literary form. If a writer believes, with Hulme, that it is only through 'tradition and organisation'[11] that humans can be made productive, that writer might be inclined to adopt traditional poetic forms. Traditionalism comes in many different guises, however, as T. S. Eliot's 'Tradition and the Individual Talent' (1919) makes clear, and another writer might be inclined to innovate in poetic form while working within the larger constraints of the tradition. For another writer, poetic qualities of 'hardness' and 'dryness' might be the necessary correlate of the conservative grand narrative, as they were for Hulme. While there is no simple one-to-one mapping of grand narratives onto literary forms, most modernist writers felt that the two were related. The disagreements about how they were related are one reason for the variety of modernist practices.

(7) What is the relation of art in the present moment to the art of the past? One extreme answer to this question was offered by the Italian futurists: 'We intend to destroy museums, libraries, academies of every sort […]'.[12] The opposite extreme is more difficult to pin down, because established tradition does not need to assert itself, and, when it does, does not usually employ a loud-hailer; however, it can be located in the more reactionary reviews of modern works, usually as a gesture towards a vaguely defined standard of moral and aesthetic decency thought to be under threat. T. S. Eliot's 'Tradition and the Individual Talent' represented a more reconciliatory position, arguing that innovation can occur only in the context of accepted norms. The answers that writers reach about this relationship often derive from their views on the grand narratives of human history, though how logical the relationship is between the two depends on many factors. What are posed here as questions were in many cases unconsciously incorporated into the writing practices of modern authors.

(8) What is the position of the writer in contemporary society? This question gives rise to one more immediately on the minds of most writers, namely, 'what is the relation between the writer and his/her readers?' The response that a writer makes to the latter will affect matters of content, tone, style, diction, structure, and range of reference. The former, superordinate question is closely connected to that of the justification of art in the modern world. Does the writer stand outside social and ideological conventions, and, if so, which conventions is the writer most widely separated from? Is the writer's attitude towards those conventions to be sympathetic or satirical? In pursuing the subordinate question, we must also ask where the reader is situated, and whether readers are also understood to be situated outside social convention.

It might be remarked that there ought to be a ninth question about the relation of art to politics, but I would argue that all of these questions have political dimensions. Even apparently pure aesthetic questions about impersonality imply things about the writer's position in society and about the dominant idea of the self.

Understanding Modernist Styles

These fundamental questions need to be placed in dialogue with the immediately visible aspect of literary modernism, its distinctive experiments in form, style, and subject matter. A formalist approach to modernism is most closely associated with the New Criticism, dominant in the 1950s and 1960s, but still influential into the 1970s. Harriet Davidson has summarised the kind of modernism that the New Criticism found in *The Waste Land*: the movement 'powerfully depicts and rejects modern life, valorising myth over history, spatial form over time, an orderly past over a chaotic present, and the transcendence of art over the pain of life – what I would call the proper over the improper'.[13] Marjorie Perloff has also listed fourteen main features of modernism in its institutionalised form from about 1965 onwards.[14] The following twelve points are indebted to their work, and to other works where noted.

(1) Modernist literature depicts modern life, especially urban life, and shows ambivalence towards it. In depicting modern life, modernist literature appears to be addressing the fundamental problem of the justification of art in the modern world: it is attempting to demonstrate that it is equal to the conditions around it, and is not retreating into pastoral. In so far as urban life was not conventionally deemed beautiful, the depiction of it also implicitly answers the question of what makes a work of art valuable: if the value of *Dubliners* or *The Waste Land* does not inhere in the subject matter, it must lie in the form or treatment. Many reviewers, however, felt that there was value in neither, and roundly condemned such works on both aesthetic and moral grounds. To some it seemed that modernism (in all media) was a 'cult of ugliness'.[15] This is in part due to its subject matter, and in part to its treatment.

(2) It is difficult: it makes use of a wide and sometimes unexpected range of reference (literary, cultural, and linguistic); it removes many of the devices that would conventionally have helped the reader to make sense of the text; it is verbally ambiguous and paradoxical. In consequence, the modernist text appears fragmentary. T. S. Eliot's remarks in 'The Metaphysical Poets' (1921) were a common point of reference in the 1920s and beyond:

> [P]oets in our civilisation, as it exists at present, must be *difficult*. Our civilisa-
> tion comprehends great variety and complexity, and this variety and complexity,
> playing upon a refined sensibility, must produce various and complex results. The
> poet must become more and more comprehensive, more allusive, more indirect,
> in order to force, to dislocate if necessary, language into his meaning.[16]

His remarks on St John Perse's poem *Anabase* are relevant to his work and modernist literature generally: 'any obscurity of the poem, on first readings, is due to the suppression of "links in the chain", of explanatory and connecting matter, and not to incoherence, or to the love of cryptogram'.[17] Where writers allude to the literature of the past, they are implicitly addressing the more fundamental question about the relation of the present to the past, though the value they answer their work gives will depend on the context of their allusion. The 'difficulty' created by allusion and fragmentation also implicitly supplies an answer to the question of the artist's relationship to the audience: the audience is expected to collaborate actively in the production of meaning.

(3) It contrasts an orderly past with a chaotic present. This characteristic of modernism was articulated early in its critical history: Stephen Spender wrote in 1935 that writers after Henry James 'are all conscious of the present as chaotic [...] and of the past as an altogether more solid ground'.[18] The contrast emerges not only in direct depictions of the past, but also in allusions to its literature.

The classic instance is *The Waste Land*'s allusion to Spenser's 'Prothalamion', in which the Thames of Spenser's sixteenth-century poem is contrasted with the river in the present day, filled with the detritus of modern life. Such contrasts implicitly answer the fundamental question about grand narratives: history is a story of decline. However, for some modernist writers, the chaos of the present is invigorating and liberating. As Shari Benstock notes in 'Beyond the Reaches of Feminist Criticism', at the start of the twentieth century many women writers were not at all disappointed to see the stable values of the past called into question and rejected.

(4) Where modernist literature displays the pessimistic contrast seen above, it often also includes the compensatory idea that art can transcend the disorder of the present. Yeats's poetry offers many clear examples. In 'Paudeen' (written 1913), the 'sweet crystalline cry' of the curlew, symbolising poetry, stands in contrast to the debased world of shopkeepers. In 'Sailing to Byzantium' (written 1926), the mechanical bird 'Of hammered gold and gold enamelling' symbolises an art which transcends the pain of old age. A variant on this characteristic is the idea that art is superior to nature: nature is inherently messy; art is orderly.[19]

(5) It experiments with time, implying a larger philosophy in which time is non-linear. This is true not only of narrative works, but also of poetry. It has been argued that modernist literature possesses 'spatial form': that is, we are forced to read it as if every part of the text were simultaneously present, even when, with texts as long as *Ulysses* or *The Cantos*, the feat is impossible to achieve on a single reading.

The most readily apparent consequence of this characteristic is that it requires the reader to be an active constructor of meaning, for example, by rearranging narrative events into their chronological sequence. As a self-conscious display of formal mastery, it again implicitly states that what makes a work of art valuable is its form rather than its subject matter. The idea that all moments are simultaneously present also implies a grand narrative of history in which there is neither progress nor decline, but simply eternal recurrence.

(6) It employs mythic allusion and mythic patterning as an 'organising structure'.[20] This characteristic was articulated early by T. S. Eliot, in '*Ulysses*, Order and Myth' (1923), and although the essay was less immediately influential on accounts of modernism than those included in *The Sacred Wood* (1920) and *Selected Essays* (1932), it has proved significant in the longer term.[21] In looking at *Ulysses*, Eliot makes remarks that are equally applicable to *The Waste Land*:

> In using the myth, in manipulating a continuous parallel between contemporaneity and antiquity, Mr Joyce is pursuing a method which others must pursue after him. [...] It is simply a way of controlling, of ordering, of giving a shape and a significance to the immense panorama of futility and anarchy which is contemporary history. It is a method already adumbrated by Mr Yeats, and of the need for

which I believe Mr Yeats to have been the first contemporary to be conscious. [...] Instead of narrative method, we may now use the mythical method.[22]

As a reading of *Ulysses*, the essay is partial and flawed: it overemphasises the extent to which 'myth' sits in judgement on the contemporary lives of Stephen Daedalus and Leopold Bloom, and overlooks the respects in which their lives, presented in a sympathetic manner, highlight the inadequacies of the heroic ideals of epic literature; it overemphasises the degree of order in the text, and overemphasises the importance of myth in creating the patterns of the text.

The connotations of classical mythology carried by the term 'myth' may obscure other organising principles that work similarly. The classics are relevant for *Ulysses*, for poems by Yeats such as 'Leda and the Swan', and for parts of *The Waste Land*, but are less immediately relevant to other modernist works. The concept can be generalised to an idea of recurrent deep structures. The narrative of a father and son searching for each other is not a specific myth, but a deep structure that informs numerous narratives, several of which *Ulysses* draws upon. In either form, the use of myth, like the use of spatial form, suggests an answer to the fundamental question about the grand narratives of human history: there is no narrative; we continually repeat the same mythic patterns.

(7) Modernist literature (and modernist art more generally) often takes man in his primitive state as a point of reference. Sometimes it does this through the medium of myth, but the two aspects of modernism are not identical. In colonial narratives of Europeans 'going native' – *Heart of Darkness* being the best-known example – the primitive state is feared. Elsewhere, most notably in D. H. Lawrence's writing, the primitive is welcomed as offering 'relief from enervating rationality'.[23] Clearly, the use of the primitive addresses the question of which model of the self is most relevant to modern life, though the actual answer depends on the value ascribed to primitive states. Likewise, reference to the primitive addresses the fundamental question of the grand narratives of human existence, but can be used to produce both narratives of decline and narratives of progress.

(8) Modernist literature displays an awareness of the complexity of the mind and the self. It is aware of the 'fluidity of consciousness', of the force of the unconscious, and of a division between the social and the personal self, between 'conduct' and 'consciousness'.[24] It embodies this awareness through the use of free direct or free indirect discourse, and through the employment of multiple linguistic registers to signal different levels or centres of consciousness. (The term 'stream of consciousness' is problematic primarily because it is a psychological hypothesis rather than a formal stylistic description, and secondarily because it does not distinguish between the different levels of consciousness, and because it does not by itself indicate whether individual or collective consciousness is being referred to.)[25] Most obviously, this feature of modernist literature stands in a significant relation to the underlying problem of which model of the self is best suited to modern life, but the complexity of self that is apparent in much modernist literature indicates a profound uncertainty about the right answer. Likewise, the complexity of self can be read as a symptom of uncertainty about grand narratives of human history. Indeed, if we cannot decide what it means to be human, then we will never readily know how to tell the story of human existence.

(9) A contrast between the individual and the 'herd' or 'mass' is commonly a feature of modernist literature; another version is a contrast between the elite and the masses. John Carey's *The Intellectuals and the Masses* (1992) provides the most extensive account of these structures, though, being polemical in intent, it gives little consideration to counter-arguments, and is sometimes reductive. Carey argues that the difficulty of modernist literature came about because modernist writers wished to exclude mass audiences. I would argue that they did not wish to exclude the mass audience, but wished to escape the homogenisation and trivialisation of literature that characterised the mass market. The circulating library system, for example, encouraged readers to think of literary works as interchangeable.[26] Literature, to modernist writers, was not a form of entertainment, but a form of knowledge. In working to sustain distinctions of value within the literary marketplace, modernist writers often defended the aesthetic values and ideological positions of their own class as if they were universal, and thus excluded many readers, but this is not a direct result of their modernism.

(10) Modernist writers distinguish between abstraction and empathy, often claiming to prefer the former. In the novel, the means by which earlier generations of writers would have allowed readers to identify with a character are eschewed or radically revised; in poetry, the identifiable speaking voice of lyric poetry is avoided, or is framed in unfamiliar contexts. For example, in narrative, the use of complex time schemes tends to disrupt continuity and thus disrupt our identification with a character. If events which belong late in the chronological sequence are presented earlier in the narrative, then the reader views the chronologically earlier events with ironic detachment, knowing more than the participants. In some writers, notably Wyndham Lewis, the narrator's language may also block empathy, presenting the characters as cultural constructs rather than as free agents.

Among English-speaking modernists, an important source for the distinction of abstraction and empathy was T. E. Hulme, particularly 'Modern Art and its Philosophy', a lecture delivered in 1914, and published posthumously in 1924; Hulme also used the ideas in articles published around 1914 in *The New Age*. The ideas in 'Modern Art and its Philosophy' was derived from the German aesthetician Wilhelm Worringer (1881–1965), but Worringer's *Abstraktion und Einfühlung* (1908) was not translated into English until 1953 (as *Abstraction and Empathy*). Hulme constructed the distinction in gendered terms, seeing empathetic art as sentimental and therefore feminine, and abstract art as hard and therefore masculine. The gendering of the distinction was widespread, but may have led to some writers being suspicious of it as masculinist posturing.

(11) It prefers the concrete to the abstract: Pound's imagist manifesto, calling upon writers to 'go in fear of abstractions', is the classic starting point. As we shall see, New Criticism further embedded this preference. In Perloff's elaboration, it prefers 'the particular as opposed to the general, the perceptual as opposed to the conceptual'. In order to reconcile this feature with the previous one, it is necessary to recognise that 'abstraction' is not the same as 'the abstract'. Abstraction is a process; abstractions are the stale products of previous generations. Through abstraction, the artist asserts control over the materials of his or her art; by employing abstractions, the weak writer betrays that he or she has failed to assert control, and is merely repeating old ideas. However, although we can distinguish the two concepts, the differences are not entirely stable. The modernist preference for the particular always has the potential to lapse into the passive reproduction of the real.

(12) The subject matter of modernist texts is sometimes controversial. It is possible to overstate this aspect, given that only a small minority of modernist writers suffered the effects of censorship. Nevertheless, the texts officially censored include two that have become central to the canon, *The Rainbow* (1915) and *Ulysses* (1922), as well as Wyndham Lewis's 'Cantleman's Spring Mate' (1917). Moreover, many other texts were heavily revised to overcome the objections of publishers or printers, notably *Dubliners* (1914) and *Sons and Lovers* (1912). While prose works were affected more often than poetry, Ezra Pound's *Lustra* (1916) appeared in a reduced, privately printed edition after the printers and publishers objected to four poems; the public edition was shorn of nine further poems.[27] Modernists found themselves in trouble with the censors because they wished to represent the body and sexuality as fully as possible, and, more generally, wished to depict the full range of human behaviour without having to place it in a moral frame. It is possible to trace this aspect of modernism back to mid-nineteenth century France where, in 1857, both Gustave Flaubert's *Madame Bovary* and Charles Baudelaire's *Les Fleurs du Mal* met with legal objections. It has been suggested that, in the case of *Madame Bovary*, the combination of the adultery theme with Flaubert's formal innovations was the root of the problem: 'the new formal structures of free indirect discourse and impersonal narration denied the possibility of a stable narrative position from which the heroine could be judged'.[28] Censorship was also sometimes an indirect consequence of other politically radical aspects of the texts: the individualism of certain characters in *The Rainbow* is an implicit indictment of militarism; the war-time authorities almost certainly recognised this, but chose prosecution for obscenity as the legally simpler option.

I have omitted two characteristics included in Perloff's list: that modernism has a concept of 'the artist as hero', and that modernism is *international*. The first is one of several possible answers to the question of the position of the writer in contemporary society, but not the only possible answer; or rather, we must stretch 'hero' to include 'anti-hero', 'outcast', and 'wanderer'. However, the idea of the artist as hero enters into the preference for the individual over the crowd, and into the ideal of the strong shaping consciousness seen in the preference for abstraction. I do not disagree with Perloff as to the internationalism of modernism, but would admit it to my list only in so far as it manifests itself in modernist texts: for example, in the range of languages used in any given text.

By considering both the visible characteristics of modernism and the underlying questions which motivated it, we can grasp both its unity and its diversity. The two lists presented here derive from a range of sources through the history of criticism of modernism. The remainder of Part I takes a broadly chronological approach to modernism and modernity, to reconstruct the ways that modernism was initially constructed. It begins before the conventional beginning of modernism, by considering modernity in the Victorian era.

The Victorians and Modernity

To define modernism as a reaction to modernity has the advantage of producing flexible and non-reductive approaches to the range of modernisms, but it raises the problem of modernism's relation to the Victorian era. Many modernist writers explicitly differentiated their movement from the norms of their predecessors. Even when their target was the immediately preceding generation, as in Woolf's distinction between the Edwardians and the Georgians in 'Mr Bennett and Mrs Brown' (1923), the older generation were very often taken to task for their uncritical adoption of Victorian norms and values. Yet the Victorian age was also an age marked by self-consciousness of modernity. If the Victorians could also be said to be reacting to modernity, and particularly if they could be said to be reacting ambivalently to it, then it might seem that they too are to be understood as modernists. If that were to be the case, 'modernism' as a period term might lose its usefulness.

Wyndham Lewis argued in 1914 that the British relation to modernity differed from that of its continental neighbours; he stated his case in characteristically abrasive terms, aiming to undermine the aesthetic credentials of the Italian futurists: 'While Italy was still a Borgia-haunted swamp of intrigue, England was buckling on the brilliant electric armour of the modern world, and sending out her inventions and new spirit across Europe and America'.[29] The fact that nineteenth-century writers had been responding to the 'brilliant electric armour' raises difficult questions for a theory of modernism that would define it as a response to modernity. Such responses can be traced across all modes of nineteenth-century writing, but for present purposes the non-fictional prose of the 'sage' writers must suffice. Writing in 1829, Thomas Carlyle (1795–1881) identified the characteristics of the age:

> Were we required to characterise this age of ours by any single epithet, we should be tempted to call it, not an Heroical, Devotional, Philosophical, or Moral Age, but above all others, the Mechanical Age. It is the Age of Machinery in every outward and inward sense of that word; the age which, with its whole undivided might, forwards, teaches and practises the great art of adapting means to ends. Nothing is now done directly, or by hand; all is by rule and calculated contrivance. For the simplest operation, some helps and accompaniments, some cunning abbreviating process is in readiness. Our old modes of exertion are all discredited, and thrown aside. On every hand, the living artisan is driven from his workshop, to make room for a speedier, inanimate one. The shuttle drops from the fingers of the weaver, and falls into iron fingers that ply it faster [...].
>
> But leaving these matters for the present, let us observe how the mechanical genius of our time has diffused itself into quite other provinces. Not the external and physical alone is now managed by machinery, but the internal and spiritual also. Here too nothing follows its spontaneous course, nothing is left to be accomplished by old natural methods. Everything has its cunningly devised implements, its preëstablished apparatus; it is not done by hand, but by machinery.[30]

Carlyle's diagnosis of his age anticipates the early twentieth century's conception of itself as 'the machine age'. Moreover, his emphasis on the 'inward' sense of 'machinery', meaning rational calculation and self-consciousness, anticipates the late twentieth century idea of modernity being characterised by instrumental rationality. Carlyle's conclusion to his related essay, 'Characteristics', also anticipates the Frankfurt School's recognition that rationality had come to enslave man, and that, by the same token, it might be turned once again to man's service: Carlyle sees the spirit of mechanism as something sitting 'like a choking incubus' on the soul of contemporary man, but also as something which could be transformed into 'our slave'.[31] John Ruskin developed a similar line of argument with more direct application to aesthetics, arguing in *Modern Painters* (5 vols., 1843–60) and *The Stones of Venice* (3 vols., 1851–3) against painting and architecture dominated by rational design.

Though the relation of Carlyle to modernism has most often been considered in relation to particular writers, notably D. H. Lawrence, the extent to which Ruskin anticipated or influenced later developments has been considered more extensively and in more general terms. The recognition that modernity was a crucial concern for the Victorians has also been important in several recent studies.[32] That studies of modernism have not embraced a chronologically wider definition of the movement is because of the residual importance of formalist definitions of modernism: the Victorian writers did not experiment with narrative time, the personal lyric voice, or the coherent self in the ways that writers did in the period 1890–1939. Though they wrote of modernity, the texture of their writing bore little sign of its effects. Stephen Spender recognised this in 1963:

> I would not call Tennyson, Ruskin, Carlyle moderns because although they were aware of the effects of science, and most contemporary in their interest, they remained within the tradition of rationalism, unshaken in the powers of what Lawrence called the 'conscious ego'. They had the Voltairean 'I', the confidence that they stood outside a world of injustices and irrationality which they judged clearly with their powers of reason and imagination. They regarded themselves as in a line of writer-prophets. Their sensibility was not the product of the times that they deplored.[33]

Though one might dispute the idea that the sage writers were rationalist, particularly given Carlyle's admiration for instinct and for irrational force, Spender's characterisation of their subject position is consonant with the idea of the sage or prophet as one who 'positions himself in conscious opposition to his audience or entire society'.[34]

A more difficult intermediate category comes with the writers of the aesthetic movement, beginning with Walter Pater. Pater's 'Conclusion' to *The Renaissance* grapples with the consequences of a materialist worldview in which the world is constantly in flux. Pater invites his reader to imagine a typical, simple physical sensation, the moment 'of delicious recoil from the flood of water in summer heat'. (The 'typical' moment recalls Heraclitus's dictum that one can never put one's foot twice in the same river; the material of which the river is composed will have flowed onwards.) Pater's analysis is materialist:

> What is the whole physical life in that moment but a combination of natural elements to which science gives their names? But those elements, phosphorus and lime and delicate fibres, are present not in the human body alone: we detect them in places most remote from it. Our physical life is a perpetual motion of them – the passage of the blood, the waste and repairing of the lenses of the eye, the modification of the tissues of the brain under every ray of light and sound – processes which science reduces to simpler and more elementary forces. [...] That clear, perpetual outline of face and limb is but an image of ours, under which we group them – a design in a web, the actual threads of which pass out beyond it.[35]

Pater in 1873 anticipates Saussure's idea that thought, in itself, is just a swirling cloud, divided arbitrarily by human conventions of thought. We choose to distinguish 'face' and 'limb' from the material that surrounds them, although they are fundamentally undifferentiated. When Pater comes to consider the mind, conventional certainties are similarly dissolved:

> And if we continue to dwell in thought on this world, not of objects in the solidity with which language invests them, but of impressions, unstable, flickering,

inconsistent, which burn and are extinguished with our consciousness of them, it contracts still further: the whole scope of observation is dwarfed into the narrow chamber of the individual mind. Experience, already reduced to a group of impressions, is ringed round for each one of us by that thick wall of personality through which no real voice has ever pierced on its way to us, or from us to that which we can only conjecture to be without.[36]

The outside world is only a conjecture, a convenient fiction. Though Ruskin and Carlyle may have had confidence in the stable 'I', in Pater's writing it dissolves, creating a distinctly modern sense of imprisonment and solipsism.

Modernist Self-Construction

As the case of Walter Pater demonstrates, there are many intermediate positions between 'modernism' and 'Victorianism'; the clarity of each category is an illusion constructed by early twentieth-century writers and mid-twentieth-century critics. This section outlines the means by which modernist writers constructed an identity distinct from writers of earlier periods and from other contemporary groups.

Modernist writers were conscious of themselves as a distinct generation, within which three subdivisions can be identified. Most of the canonical English-language modernist writers were born in the 1880s. They were followed by a distinct younger generation of lesser-known modernist writers and associates of modernists, including Richard Aldington, Rebecca West, and Djuna Barnes (born in 1892), Herbert Read and I. A. Richards (1893), and Aldous Huxley (1894). The works of this generation have never held a firm place in the high modernist canon, but it produced critical work which eased the acceptance of modernist writing, and novels which exemplified a modern outlook without being formally modernist. The first decade of the twentieth century saw the births of a distinct generation which became prominent in the 1930s, including Michael Roberts (born 1902), George Orwell (1903), W. H. Auden (1907), and Stephen Spender (1909). By deliberately drawing on the techniques of the first generation, the poets among them confirmed the importance of the pioneers of modernism.

The sense of belonging to a distinct generation (or two successive generations) was an enabling condition for the creation of modernism. The sense of a generational gap was sharpened by the First World War, in which it appeared that an older generation of generals had sent a younger generation to their deaths. Though many of the modernist writers were non-combatants, Wyndham Lewis, Richard Aldington, and Herbert Read all saw active service and returned; T. E. Hulme and the sculptor Henri Gaudier-Brzeska (b. 1891) went to the front line and were killed. The General in charge of the British Expeditionary Force at the start of the First World War, John French, was born in 1852; his successor, Douglas Haig, was born in 1861.

However, the generational divide was not clear-cut. The modernists sought precedents for what they were doing. The 1880s generation recruited allies from among the older writers: W. B. Yeats (b. 1865) is the most prominent example; Ford Madox Ford (b. 1873) was an influential editor. Both Yeats and Ford knew the central modernists personally. Writers such as Henry James (b. 1843) and Joseph Conrad (b. 1857) were identified by modernists as significant forerunners, but were not so closely part of their networks. The partnership between the canonical modernists and the earlier generation may serve to remind that there is no inevitable connection between date of birth and aesthetic orientation. The three writers chosen by Virginia Woolf as her antitypes in several of her essays, Arnold Bennett, John Galsworthy, and H. G. Wells, were one or two years younger than Yeats. The difference was that Yeats had appeared to modernise himself, while they had not. Similarly J. C. Squire, a literary editor and minor poet, came to embody for many the conservatism of Georgian poetry, yet his date of birth was 1884. Although the moderns defined themselves in terms of a generational conflict, the correspondence to actual dates of birth was only partial.

Current definitions of modernism originated in the period when these writers formed themselves into groups. The most clearly identifiable are those which named themselves at the time and were self-consciously 'movements', the Imagists and the Vorticists. However, such groups were relatively short lived, and less important in the long term than the groups created through social networks and named in retrospect (of which the Bloomsbury Group is the best known) and the groups associated with various periodicals. Without the ability to get itself into print, a literary group is nothing. Of course, these processes were not mutually exclusive: the Vorticists were also a social network, and in *BLAST* they had their own journal, albeit briefly; the *Athenaeum* was an important critical journal in the period 1919–21, but it also formed the basis for a social network, and many of its contributors were drawn from Bloomsbury. One of the first acts of a self-conscious artistic group is to issue a manifesto. The Italian futurists set the pattern with their 1909 text, 'The Founding and the Manifesto of Futurism'. The Imagists issued their principles and Ezra Pound's prohibitions ('A Few Don'ts by an Imagiste') through the journal *Poetry* in 1913, while the later Vorticist movement issued two manifestos in the first issue of *BLAST* (1914).[37] A survey of these and other manifestos will not produce a single coherent picture of 'modernism': no group produced a 'Modernist Manifesto'. Many groups defined themselves in opposition to each other: the Vorticists against the futurists, for example. For some critics, the diversity of artistic groups is an argument against the existence of 'modernism'. While the diversity of responses to modernity needs to be acknowledged, it is possible to see each of these groups as offering different answers to the more fundamental problems outlined earlier, and it is the fundamental problems that unite them. The Vorticists internalised such self-division, making a tension between opposing points of view fundamental to their movement. Their Manifesto stated 'Between Action and Reaction we would establish ourselves', and 'We fight first on one side, then on the other, but always for the SAME cause, which is neither side or both sides and ours'.[38]

Both manifestos and informal groupings create a sense of community and fellow feeling. Both create a sense of distinction between 'us' and 'them'. While the content of manifestos cannot be overlooked, the speech act that brings a new 'we' into existence is as important as the actual programme to which it is attached. Certainly, the creation of a first-person plural pronoun is common to both manifestos and to communities of writers surrounding a journal. Many critics of modernism have given special emphasis to the 'little magazine', a small-circulation periodical 'with a limited but distinctive readership, specialised and usually advanced in taste'; it was 'the logical obverse' to the 'solemn, serious, debating' reviews of the Victorian era. Bradbury and McFarlane, the source of these definitions, argue that the little magazine was often 'an analogue or extension of the manifesto formula', with *BLAST* as the clearest point of convergence: the very publication of the little magazine is an announcement of the presence of a new artistic force.[39] They also note that the earlier, more confrontational publications were succeeded by more sober and respectable titles, of which Eliot's *The Criterion* (1922–39) is the best known in the English-speaking world. Though this account is broadly fair, the emphasis on the little magazine and the narrative of growing respectability have tended to overshadow sober critical reviews such as *The Athenaeum* under the editorship (1919–21) of John Middleton Murry. Even the *Times Literary Supplement*, conservative in its format and typography, provided employment to writers such as Eliot and Woolf, and was receptive to new thinking in literature and science. Eliot's assertion that the modern poet 'must be *difficult*' first appeared in its pages. The awareness among innovative writers that a journal is wholly sympathetic to their work, as was *The Athenaeum*, or even partially sympathetic, as was the *TLS*, creates an environment in which they can flourish.

The Athenaeum under Middleton Murry provides clear evidence of the creation of a community. Murry had taken over the editorship in April 1919 and had revived what had been a dull political weekly, turning it into a review of the arts and of science. Though Murry was not fully part of 'Bloomsbury', he was well connected with it and with Lady Ottoline Morrell's salon in London and at Garsington Manor. From this network he recruited contributors including T. S. Eliot, Virginia Woolf, and Aldous Huxley; D. H. Lawrence and Ezra Pound also appeared in his journal. When, later in 1919, J. C. Squire launched a new periodical, *The London Mercury*, Murry saw it as a competitor. His feelings of opposition were sharply focused by a talk T. S. Eliot gave on 'Modern Tendencies in Poetry' (a variant of 'Tradition and the Individual Talent') in October 1919. He reported on the audience to Katherine Mansfield, his wife: 'The anti-*Athenaeums* – Munro, Jack Squire etc – present in force. There's no doubt it's a fight to finish between us & Them – them is the "Georgians" *en masse*. It's a queer feeling I begin to have now: that we're making literary history'.[40] The name of Murry's movement is not a periodising name equivalent to 'Georgians', but rather is one associated with a literary journal and its literary community. Murry's pronouncement also calls into question the thesis (to which we shall return shortly) that modernism was a retrospective formation. By 1919 at least, certain self-consciously modern writers were aware of the movement's importance *prospectively*.

Such oppositional tactics are one way of creating a group identity. Another is the construction of a genealogy and a reading list. In 1926, setting out the purpose of his critical review, T. S. Eliot defined the 'modern tendency' as being towards 'classicism', and listed six books that exemplified the tendency. Such definitions are a non-confrontational form of manifesto: they define a worldview. Waldo Frank's 'For a Declaration of War' is closer to a conventional manifesto (as its title suggests), but includes a more academic outline of the intellectual assumptions of the old and the new worldviews. In outlining how the old worldview broke up, Frank lists the eighteenth- and nineteenth-century thinkers who brought old certainties into question: 'Kant, Schopenhauer, Darwin, Kelvin, Freud, the Non-Euclidean and n-dimensional mathematicians'.[41] The urge to find precedents and to construct a genealogy for modernism is common to both modernists and to later critics. For Richard Kain in 1947, the forefathers were 'Marx, Darwin, Freud, and Einstein'. In 1967, we find Irving Howe naming Frazer, Marx, Freud, and Nietzsche, while suggesting that they will already be familiar. In 1970 Monroe Spears listed 'Nietzsche, Freud, and Frazer', and, as if by afterthought, '[p]robably Karl Marx'. In 1976, Bradbury and McFarlane suggest that Modernism responds to 'the world changed and reinterpreted by Marx, Freud and Darwin'.[42] Any reader of introductions to modernism will be familiar with many other examples of such catalogues, and may have been frustrated at the slender explanations of why these great men are important. More recent critics have become more critical of what Christopher Herbert terms 'the pantheon': Peter Nicholls in 1995 wisely chose not to 'bombard the reader with great names'.[43] My point in gathering the examples above is not simply to note one of the more frustrating features of modernist criticism, but to draw attention to a long-standing anxiety about the legitimacy of modernism. The anxiety is rooted in a paradox: if the forefather appears to have anticipated the works of 'modern' writers, then their claim to be modern is undermined; yet, if cultural legitimacy depends upon a connection to previous generations, such a search for forefathers cannot be avoided.

Modernist writers themselves were as much concerned to find literary as intellectual precedents for their innovations: hence Eliot's interest in Baudelaire, and in Herbert Grierson's *Metaphysical Lyrics and Poems of the Seventeenth Century* (1921); hence the interest among other modernists in the posthumous publication of Gerard Manley Hopkins's poetry in 1918. Interest in Baudelaire has continued to the present day, but the focus of the interest has been substantially altered by Walter Benjamin's essays on him. While for Eliot the focus was evil and Original Sin, for post-Benjaminian critics, the focus has been the city, the *flâneur*, and modernist irony. The metaphysical poets offered to Eliot and to Herbert Read a model for an ambitious poetry that was open to the full range of contemporary thought and experience.[44] When Michael Roberts placed Hopkins at the beginning of his canon-defining anthology, *The Faber Book of Modern Verse* (1936), he offered a complex mesh of justifications: Hopkins was a stylistic innovator whose innovations had been misunderstood by the majority, but accepted by a minority; his innovations expressed an inner conflict which nevertheless related to 'an outer social and intellectual conflict'.[45] In these respects, his work and its reception were taken to have anticipated modernism.

As the modern movement began to become established, various author-critics attempted to secure its group identity by writing first drafts of its history, and, in particular, by defining epochal dates or moments at which 'the modern' was born. Best-known among these is 1910, thanks to Virginia Woolf's suggestion that 'on or about December 1910 human character changed'.[46] Woolf's remark is atypical in that, with the magnitude of its claim being so far out of key with the precision of the date, it seems to parody the usual mode of historical boundary-marking. Nevertheless, there is some seriousness behind its claim. Most critics note that December 1910 was the point at which Roger Fry's exhibition of post-impressionist painting became the focus of media attention, much of it outraged; the death of King Edward VII in May 1910 seemed to have prepared the country for a transition, as had the two General Elections in January and December. Commentators at the time wrote of the 'era of Victoria' being over, and a new epoch beginning.[47] However, although there is real substance behind Woolf's claim, other modern writers and later critics have made similar claims for different dates: the actual date is less important than the act of definition. T. S. Eliot's identification of the seventeenth century as a period in which a 'dissociation of sensibility' set into English poetry also defines an epochal point, but in his case, the beginning of a modernity against which modernism was to define itself.[48] Ezra Pound in 1918 noted 'the spring or early summer of 1912' as the date at which he, H. D., and Richard Aldington had set down the principles of Imagism, and several later critics have followed his lead in identifying this as the crucial year.[49] The 1913 exhibition known as the Armory Show – an exhibition of impressionist, post-impressionist, and cubist painting at the 69th Regiment Armory in New York – has led many critics to identify that year as the crucial one in the development of American modernism. The year 1914 has also been seen as a defining moment, primarily because of the outbreak of the First World War. June of that year had seen the publication of the first issue of the Vorticist journal *BLAST*, and one of the prime movers of vorticism, Wyndham Lewis, was later to identify himself, Pound, Eliot, and Joyce as 'the men of 1914'. The influence of the phrase on the shape of the modernist canon is seen most strongly in Hugh Kenner's *The Pound Era* (1971).[50] In 1924, D. H. Lawrence identified 1915 as the year in which, because of the war, 'the old world' had ended. The identification of the war as the crucial event is problematic, however. Firstly, it overlooks earlier moments in the emergence of modernism. Secondly, as Janet Wolff has noted, it 'privileges the masculine experience'.[51]

The tactic of defining epochal dates is one that has survived from modern writers through to later critics of modernism. Not only have later critics made choices between 1910, 1912, 1913, and 1914, but many have identified 1922 as the high point or the *annus mirabilis* of modernism: the year in which *The Waste Land* and *Ulysses* were published, as well as *Jacob's Room* and the first issue of *The Criterion*. Bonnie Kime Scott has suggested that 1928 marked a similar important moment for modernist writing by women: it was the year in which women in Britain were granted the vote on complete equality with men, the year of *Orlando*, and the year of the prosecution of *The Well of Loneliness*.

Modernist Reviews and Essays

Modernist writers defined their artistic aims not only through manifestos and editorials in literary journals, but also through essays and reviews of each other's work and through reassessments of earlier generations. Many modernist narrative works explicitly concern writers and artists – *A Portrait of the Artist as a Young Man*, for example, or *To the Lighthouse* – while many modernist poems either explicitly concern poetry (e.g. Yeats's 'Adam's Curse') or can be read as reflections on issues of creativity. More privately, many modernist writers set out their principles in lectures and in letters to editors, patrons, and friends. When book reviews are taken into consideration, the full corpus of texts is immense. This section considers some of the key documents.

Imagism

The three principles of Imagism were published in 1913 under the name of F. S. Flint, though Pound was the author, and he reprinted them in his 1918 retrospect. The Imagists had agreed that their rules were:

1. Direct treatment of the 'thing', whether subjective or objective.
2. To use absolutely no word that did not contribute to the presentation.
3. As regarding rhythm: to compose in the sequence of the musical phrase, not in sequence of a metronome.[52]

Pound established a formalist agenda: the Imagists were to be judged by their poetic technique, not their subject matter. Their modernity is marked by their breaking with a previous generation which, Pound believed, had padded their verse with superfluous poeticisms and had unthinkingly adopted rigid metres, regardless of their suitability to the task in hand. The Imagist, he said in 'A Few Don'ts by an Imagiste', should '[u]se no superfluous word, no adjective which does not reveal something'.[53] Their modernity is signalled too by the emphasis on economy: contemporary society valued efficiency.

The issue of rhythm was more complex. The principle of composing in musical phrases was taken by many to be an endorsement of *vers libre*, but it is possible to write *vers libre* without being musical, and Eliot and Pound soon felt that it had become a new cliché. Eliot in 1917 recommended that 'the ghost of some simple metre should lurk behind the arras in even the "freest" verse; to advance menacingly as we doze, and withdraw as we rouse'. The issue was not simply aesthetic: Eliot, certainly, was out of sympathy with a liberal ideology of individual freedom. There is a sharp contrast between Eliot's views and those of D. H. Lawrence, expressed in the following year: 'free verse is, or should be, direct utterance from the instant, whole man. It is the soul and the mind and body surging at once, nothing left out'. The free verse movement was, for Lawrence, a matter of breaking 'the stiff neck of habit'.[54] '[T]here is no freedom in art', wrote Eliot; the life of verse came from a 'contrast between fixity and flux'. Similarly, Eliot justified the rejection of rhyme not as 'a leap at facility' but as something that imposed 'a much severer strain' upon the language.[55] Though Eliot's idea of discipline and tradition concurs with T. E. Hulme's, and was dominant within modernist conceptions of poetry, it would be a mistake to identify modernism exclusively with Eliot's idea. Eliot and Pound's pronouncements in 1917–18 were a reaction against an earlier position. The truth is more complex: modernism exists as a dialogue between individualistic innovation and the dominant traditions.

Definitions of Imagism also established questions of temporality as central to modernism. Pound defined the image as

that which presents an intellectual and emotional complex in an instant of time. [...] It is the presentation of such a 'complex' instantaneously which gives that sense of sudden liberation; that sense of freedom from time limits and space limits;

that sense of sudden growth, which we experience in the presence of the greatest works of art.[56]

Lawrence contrasts free verse with restricted verse in terms of their relation to time, free verse being associated with the present moment. Later discussions of modernism and time, such as Georg Lukács's 'The Ideology of Modernism', build on these early definitions.

Character and the self

Modernist writers reappraised the idea of the self, in relation both to the artist and to the idea of character in fiction and drama. As the names in the 'pantheon' suggest, they were spurred to it by Darwin's discovery that humans are related to animals, by the arguments of anthropologists such as J. G. Frazer that supposedly civilised patterns of behaviour were related to supposedly 'primitive' rituals, and the theories of Freud concerning the unconscious mind. Nietzsche's distinction between Apolline and Dionysiac forms of art and, more fundamentally, modes of cognition, also suggested new ways of thinking about the self. Many writers were drawn to a self which can be described as 'inhuman' or 'dehumanised', but which can also be seen as more fundamentally human. The rational and self-determining subject of humanism seemed inadequate to the conditions of modernity. However, this 'profound' self needs to be understood in relation to a fragmented subjectivity which is composed of a kaleidoscope of sense impressions and memories: each complements the other.

Nietzsche in *The Birth of Tragedy* (1872, tr. 1909) distinguished between the arts appropriate to the gods Apollo and Dionysus. Apollo is the god of light, of sculpture, of clearly delineated rational boundaries; Dionysus is the god of intoxication, of music, of the dissolution of boundaries. Nietzsche's distinctions inform the binaries of many later critics, though in many cases elements are reversed: for example, when it becomes abstract, sculptural form has the ability to transport us beyond the rational.

T. E. Hulme's 'Modern Art and its Philosophy' began as a lecture delivered in London in January 1914, and was first published in 1924. It should thus be seen both as an influence on a small coterie of early, pre-war modernists, and as part of the conceptual framework through which post-war modernists justified their achievement. As Hulme used concepts from this essay in his contemporaneous art criticism for *The New Age*, they were available to more than the small number who heard his lecture. His fundamental distinction, following Wilhelm Worringer, is between 'geometrical' and 'vital' art. Each form of art satisfies different aspects of the mind, and so corresponds to different conceptions of the self.

You have these two different kinds of art. You have first the art which is natural to you, Greek art and modern art since the Renaissance. In these arts the lines are soft and vital. You have other arts like Egyptian, Indian and Byzantine, where everything tends to be angular, where curves tend to be hard and geometrical, where the representation of the human body, for example, is often entirely non-vital, and distorted to fit into stiff lines and cubical shapes of various kinds.

Hulme goes on to ask why there exist such widely divergent forms of art. He refutes the suggestion that the angular forms of geometrical art are due to technical deficiencies on the part of the artists. Rather, it is due to fundamentally different mentalities: 'While a naturalistic art is the result of a happy pantheistic relation between man and the outside world, the tendency to abstraction, on the contrary, occurs in races whose attitude to the outside world is the exact contrary of this'. He develops this point:

Take first, the case of more primitive people. They live in a world whose lack of order and seeming arbitrariness must inspire them with a certain fear. One may perhaps get a better description of what must be their state of mind by comparing it to the fear which makes certain people unable to cross open spaces. The fear I mean here is mental, however, not physical. They are dominated by what Worringer calls a kind of spiritual 'space-shyness' in face of the varied confusion and arbitrariness of existence. In art this state of mind results in a desire to create a certain abstract geometrical shape, which, being durable and permanent shall be a refuge from the flux and impermanence of outside nature. The need which art satisfies here, is not the delight in the forms of nature, which is a characteristic of all vital arts, but the exact contrary. In the reproduction of natural objects there is an attempt to purify them of their characteristically living qualities in order to make them necessary and immovable. The changing is translated into something fixed and necessary. This leads to rigid lines and dead crystalline forms, for pure geometrical regularity gives a certain pleasure to men troubled by the obscurity of outside appearance. The geometrical line is something absolutely distinct from the messiness, the confusion, and the accidental details of existing things.[57]

The distinction is not merely historical: Hulme argues that the geometrical mode, far from being an historical relic, is the mode of his contemporaries, Picasso, Jacob Epstein, and Wyndham Lewis. It is not the mode of all contemporary art, however, and Hulme argues specifically that futurism is an outmoded 'vital' art, 'the deification of the flux, the last efflorescence of impressionism'.[58]

Though 'Modern Art and its Philosophy' does not explicitly concern literature, the distinction between geometrical and vital arts broadly corresponds with the distinction in Hulme's literary essays between the classical and the romantic attitudes. (The terminology is, however, inconsistent, as the vital curves of classical Greek art correspond to the empathetic or 'romantic' mindset.) Hulme's 'classical' mindset acknowledges the post-lapsarian imperfection of man, and responds by imposing rigid rules and traditions upon him; these are equivalent to the geometrical artist's imposition of abstraction onto the confusion of nature. 'Modern Art and its Philosophy' also licenses literary experiments in representation and expression: caricature becomes as valid a means of characterisation as psychological depth; the poetic voice need not correspond to the natural speaking voice, and the vocabulary of the poet need not correspond to the Wordsworthian ideal of 'the language really used by men'. Wyndham Lewis's defamiliarisation of language, referred to earlier, similarly breaks the empathetic bond between the reader and the object of representation.

Though Hulme identified a similarity between futurism and impressionism, and hence with the empathetic strain of art, F. T. Marinetti's 'Technical Manifesto of Futurist Literature' (1912) had already proposed a distinctly antihumanist view of the self. While the early part of the manifesto is directed towards specific verbal prescriptions, such as the destruction of syntax, the abolition of adjectives, and the use of verbs in the imperative, its eleventh commandment is more fundamental:

> *Destroy the 'I' in literature*: that is, all psychology. The sort of man who has been damaged by libraries and museums, subjected to a logic and wisdom of fear, is absolutely of no interest anymore. We must abolish him in literature and replace him once and for all with matter, whose essence must be seized by strokes of intuition, something which physicists and chemists can never achieve.
>
> To capture the breath, the sensibility, and the instincts of metals, stones, woods, and so on, through the medium of free objects and capricious motors. To substitute, for human psychology, now exhausted, *the lyrical obsession with matter*.
>
> Be careful not to assign human sentiments to matter, but instead to divine its different governing impulses, its forces of compression, dilation, cohesion, disaggregation, its heaps of molecules massed together or its electrons whirling like turbines. There is no point in creating a drama of matter that has been humanised. It is the solidity of a steel plate which interests us as something in itself, with its incomprehensible and inhuman cohesion of molecules or electrons which can resist penetration by a howitzer. The heat of a piece of iron or wood leaves us more impassioned than the smile or tears of a woman.[59]

Marinetti's desire to avoid anthropomorphism suggests the influence of Nietzsche, who had argued that the truth that we 'find' in nature is simply a reflection of ourselves, and is 'anthropomorphic through and through'.[60] The technical innovations advocated would, Marinetti claimed, enable the futurists to develop 'an intuitive psychology of matter'. Marinetti is apparently drawn to the supposed objectivity of scientific knowledge, while claiming that his intuitive method will provide something that surpasses it. Both this aspect of the manifesto and its fixation with technology reflect the modernist concern with the place of art in a world dominated by science and instrumental rationality.

Marinetti's manifesto was read by D. H. Lawrence, as he was writing *The Rainbow* and *Women in Love*. He took it as a starting point in his defence of his method to Edward Garnett, who was acting as an informal literary agent.

Though he mistranslated Marinetti's 'psychology of matter' as 'physiology of matter', he understood the futurist's deeper argument.

> when I read Marinetti [...] I see something of what I am after. I translate him clumsily, and his Italian is obfuscated – and I don't care about physiology of matter – but somehow – that which is physic – non-human, in humanity, is more interesting to me than the old-fashioned human element – which causes one to conceive a character in a certain moral scheme and make him consistent. The certain moral scheme is what I object to. In Turguenev, and in Tolstoi, and in Dostoievski, the moral scheme into which all the characters fit – and it is nearly the same scheme – is, whatever the extraordinariness of the characters themselves, dull, old, dead. When Marinetti writes: 'it is the solidity of a blade of steel that is interesting by itself, that is, the incomprehending and inhuman alliance of its molecules in resistance to, let us say, a bullet. The heat of a piece of wood or iron is in fact more passionate, for us, than the laughter or tears of a woman' – then I know what he means. He is stupid, as an artist, for contrasting the heat of the iron and the laugh of the woman. Because what is interesting in the laugh of the woman is the same as the binding of the molecules of steel or their action in heat: it is the inhuman will, call it physiology – or like Marinetti – physiology of matter, that fascinates me. I don't care so much about what the woman *feels* – in the ordinary usage of the word. That presumes an *ego* to feel with. I only care about what the woman *is* – what she *is* – inhumanly, physiologically, materially – according to the use of the word: but for me, what she *is* as a phenomenon (or as representing some greater, inhuman will), instead of what she feels according to the human conception. That is where the futurists are stupid. Instead of looking for the new human phenomenon, they will only look for the phenomena of the science of physics to be found in human being. They are crassly stupid. But if anyone would give them eyes, they would pull the right apples off the tree, for their stomachs are true in appetite. You mustn't look in my novel for the old stable ego of the character. There is another ego, according to whose action the individual is unrecognisable, and passes through, as it were, allotropic states which it needs a deeper sense than any we've been used to exercise, to discover are states of the same single radically-unchanged element. (Like as diamond and coal are the same pure single element of carbon. The ordinary novel would trace the history of the diamond – but I say 'diamond, what! This is carbon'. And my diamond might be coal or soot, and my theme is carbon.)
>
> You must not say my novel is shaky – It is not perfect, because I am not expert in what I do. [...] Again I say, don't look for the development of the novel to follow the lines of certain characters: the characters fall into the form of some other rhythmic form, like when one draws a fiddle-bow across a fine tray delicately sanded, the sand takes lines unknown.[61]

In taking Marinetti's proposal that poems be written about inert matter, and finding an application for it within the traditional mode of the novel, Lawrence could be accused of blunting the radical edge of the futurist project. Yet in the depth of its revision of the conventional humanist idea of subjectivity, Lawrence's project is more daring. Though Lawrence does not speculate more widely on whether human character has changed, his remark about 'the new human phenomenon' suggests that he believes there has been a fundamental alteration. In attempting to articulate what has changed, he draws both upon science (the allotropic states of carbon) and upon occultist traditions: the image of sand forming into a pattern due to vibrations in the metal tray, known as Chladni figures, had been used in an influential theosophical book.[62] Both metaphors imply that there are two selves, one empirically observable (coal or diamonds, or individual grains of sand), and the other deeper but inaccessible to ordinary human perception: the deeper self of carbon can be seen only in the forms of coal or diamonds; the force that organises the sand into patterns can be observed only through its effects.

The latter metaphor was widespread among modernist writers and their critics, particularly in the variant of a magnet organising iron filings into patterns. While it was most frequently used to describe the form of a modernist work of art, in which the fragmented surface details retained their individual qualities while participating in a larger order, it could also be used as a new model of the self, in which the diverse aspects of a single individual were held together in all their contradictoriness. Ezra Pound used it in 1915:

> An organization of forms expresses a confluence of forces. These forces may be the 'love of God', the 'life-force', emotions, passions, what you will. For example: if you clap a strong magnet beneath a plateful of iron filings, the energies of the magnet will proceed to organise form. It is only by applying a particular and suitable force that you can bring order and vitality and thence beauty into a plate of iron filings, which are otherwise as 'ugly' as anything under heaven. The design in the magnetised iron filings expresses a confluence of energy. It is not 'meaningless' or 'inexpressive'.[63]

In 1922, the image of the fiddle bow and the sanded tray appeared in a novel by Lawrence's friend John Middleton Murry: the central character, escaping his life as a city broker, spends time in a country inn, and is impressed by the striking beauty of a pregnant mare, around which 'all life' seems to order itself 'like a pattern of sand on a glass touched by a bow'.[64] Whether Murry derived the image directly from Lawrence or Garnett, or from the same theosophical book, is less important than the fact that he too was searching for new ways of describing the self, albeit in this case an equine self. Lawrence's letter, published in 1932, was available to critics as modernism itself began to take a definite shape.

The techniques of caricature were often suggested as a means of representing the non-human aspects of humanity. T. S. Eliot found this quality in Wyndham Lewis's *Tarr* in 1918, praising Lewis as a 'deliberate', 'frigid', and 'inhuman' writer. This might suggest a very modern pseudo-scientific detachment, but Eliot in conclusion found a more complex blend:

> The artist, I believe, is more primitive, as well as more civilized, than his contemporaries, his experience is deeper than civilization, and he only uses the phenomena of civilization in expressing it. Primitive instincts and the acquired habits of ages are confounded in the ordinary man. In the work of Mr Lewis we recognize the thought of the modern and the energy of the cave man.[65]

Eliot also compared Lewis's form of humour to that of Ben Jonson, and he was to develop his idea of the 'inhuman' self in an essay on Jonson in November 1919. Jonson's art was, for Eliot, an art 'of the surface', in contrast to Shakespeare's, which had a 'third dimension'. However, an art 'of the surface' was not superficial. Jonson's simplification of his characters was not a weakness, but the key to his success:

> The simplification consists largely in reduction of detail, in the seizing of aspects relevant to the relief of an emotional impulse which remains the same for that character, in making the character conform to a particular setting. This stripping is essential to the art, to which is also essential a flat distortion in the drawing; it is an art of caricature, of great caricature, like Marlowe's. It is a great caricature, which is beautiful; and a great humour, which is serious.[66]

Though Eliot would not have known Hulme's 'Modern Art and its Philosophy' at this date, his account suggests that Jonson's is an abstractionist rather than an empathetic art.

As the foregoing quotation suggests, Jonson's idea of the self is fundamentally contextual: that is to say, the self has no existence beyond its dramatic context, nor, in terms of the real world, beyond its social context. Shakespeare's characters, said Eliot, 'are such as might exist in different circumstances than those in which Shakespeare sets them'. In Jonson's *Volpone*, by contrast, 'Volpone's life [...] is bounded by the scene in which it is played; in fact the life is the life of the scene and derivatively the life of Volpone; the life of the character is inseparable from the life of the drama'.[67] To expand on Eliot's contrast: Shakespeare's characterisation is humanist, while Jonson's is pre-humanist; Shakespeare's is outmoded, while Jonson's offers a model for a post-humanist aesthetics. Shakespeare's characterisation produces the illusion of autonomous human subjects with a life of their own; Jonson's suggests that subjectivity exists only by virtue of its context. One consequence is that the worlds of Shakespeare's plays seem continuous with our own, whereas Jonson's seem independent. Eliot took as an analogy the non-Euclidean geometries, which, although they break rules that had long been thought to be fundamental to geometry, are mathematically self-consistent.[68] The analogy allowed Eliot to distinguish an 'art of the surface' from a 'superficial art'. The verse of Beaumont and Fletcher was, he said, 'hollow', 'superficial with a vacuum behind it', whereas 'the superficies of Jonson is solid'.

> We cannot call a man's work superficial when it is the creation of a world; a man cannot be accused of dealing superficially with the world which he himself has created; the superficies *is* the world. Jonson's characters conform to the logic of the emotions of their world. It is a world like Lobatchevsky's; the worlds created by artists like Jonson are like systems of non-Euclidean geometry. They are not fancy, because they have a logic of their own; and this logic illuminates the actual world, because it gives us a new point of view from which to inspect it.[69]

The comparison of works of art to mathematics suggests a form of aestheticism: aestheticist art, like mathematics, is valid because of its internal coherence, not its ability to refer to the world. By saying that Jonson's logic illuminates the actual world, Eliot draws back from a thoroughgoing aestheticism, suggesting that the conventional world is the final arbiter of value; the three-dimensional self retains a degree of normative force. What remains, however, is the suggestion of impersonality about Jonson's work, something that Eliot was writing about in his other important essay of 1919, 'Tradition and the Individual Talent': 'Poetry is not a turning loose of emotion, but an escape from emotion; it is not the expression of personality, but an escape from personality'.[70] To compare a play to a work of mathematical logic is to characterise it as impersonal in the extreme.

As I have suggested throughout, Eliot's essay is an oblique manifesto for modernist art and an oblique account of the modern conditions of subjectivity. Though Eliot does not make these issues explicit, towards the conclusion he commends Jonson to his contemporary readers. 'Of all the dramatists of his time, Jonson is probably the one whom the present age would find the most sympathetic, if it knew him. There is a brutality, a lack of sentiment, a polished surface, a handling of large bold designs in brilliant colours, which ought to attract about three thousand people in London and elsewhere'.[71] The combination of brutality and polish recalls Eliot's oxymoronic account of Lewis as a contemporary caveman. The caricatural simplicity of Jonson's personae coexists with the sophistication of the non-Euclidean geometer.

Hulme, Lawrence, and Eliot all identify an inhuman element in modern subjectivity, defined by its opposition to empathy. Hulme gives the clearest account of why this should be so: empathy is impossible because the external world has become too threatening. For Lawrence, empathy would appear to be tainted by association with inflexible moral schemes. Eliot's remarks are restricted in their scope to aesthetic matters, so that qualities of expressiveness, empathy, and three-dimensionality are to be assessed only in so far as they help to create good or bad literary works. Eliot does not reject Shakespeare's three-dimensional selves, but makes a case for the equal validity of other aesthetic modes. If he believes that modern subjects are really like Jonson's caricatures, he does not say so explicitly.

Literary impressionism and reality

Between 1919 and 1925, Virginia Woolf wrote several related essays which question the nature of reality and the relation of novelistic form to it.[72] She describes the Edwardian novelists Bennett, Galsworthy, and Wells, as materialists, implying both that they have a mistaken view of reality as consisting only of material objects, and that they have a mistaken view of the novelist's responsibility towards that reality. Moreover, she argues that they write within novelistic conventions that prevent them from capturing the true, evanescent nature of reality. The 'essential thing' that novelists wish to capture has moved on, but '[n]evertheless we go on perseveringly, conscientiously, constructing our thirty-two chapters after a design which more and more ceases to resemble the vision in our minds. So much of the enormous labour of proving the solidity, the likeness to life, of the story is not merely labour thrown away but labour misplaced to the extent of obscuring and blotting out the light of the conception'. Novelists should ask themselves whether life is really like this:

> Is it not possible that the accent falls a little differently, that the moment of importance came before or after, that, if one were free and could set down what one chose, there would be no plot, little probability, and a vague general confusion in which the clear-cut features of the tragic, the comic, the passionate, and the lyrical were dissolved beyond the possibility of separate recognition? The mind exposed to the ordinary course of life, receives upon its surface a myriad impressions – trivial, fantastic, evanescent, or engraved with the sharpness of steel. From all sides they come, an incessant shower of innumerable atoms, composing in their sum what we might venture to call life itself; and to figure further as the semi-transparent envelope, or luminous halo, surrounding us from the beginning of consciousness to the end. Is it not perhaps the chief task of the novelist to convey this incessantly varying spirit with whatever stress or sudden deviation it may display, and as little admixture of the alien and external as possible? We are not pleading merely for courage and sincerity; but suggesting that the proper stuff of fiction is a little other than custom would have us believe it.[73]

Reality is more chaotic than the 'materialist' novelists will allow. Woolf's account of a shower of sense impressions is, in its own way, materialist, but her version of the material world is in constant flux; it is not characterised by the stultifying solidity of the worlds of Bennett, Galsworthy, and Wells. In a later essay the object of fiction, personified as Mrs Brown, becomes magically intangible as soon as fictional conventions are set aside: 'In the first place, her solidity disappears; her features crumble; the house in which she has lived so long (and a very substantial house it was) topples to the ground. She becomes a will-o'-the-wisp, a dancing light, an illumination gliding up the wall and out of the window [...]'.[74] The absence of solidity licenses the rejection of realist narrative conventions. Woolf took James Joyce as the best available exemplar of the new approach to fiction. The 'Cemetery scene' of *Ulysses* ('Hades'), which she had read in *The Little Review*, contained much 'that, in its restless scintillations, in its irrelevance, its flashes of deep significance succeeded by incoherent inanities, seems to be life itself'.[75]

'Modern Novels' is ambiguous on two points. Firstly, it is unclear whether Woolf believes that reality has a structure, and, relatedly, whether a novel should have a structure. She speaks of there being 'moment[s] of importance' in novels, points of 'accent' and 'emphasis', but also speaks of the novelist, liberated from convention, producing works characterised by 'a vague general confusion'. Woolf is aware of the difficulty faced by readers in adapting to new conventions. She comments, in relation to a short story by Anton Chekhov, that

> The emphasis is laid upon such unexpected places that at first it seems as if there were no emphasis at all; and then, as the eyes accustom themselves to twilight and discern the shapes of things in a room, we see how complete the story is, how profound, and how truly in obedience to his vision Tchehov has chosen this, that, and the other and placed them together to compose something new.[76]

If this passage suggests that a novel should have a structure, albeit an unconventional one, it nevertheless leaves open the question of whether that structure is imposed upon reality, or discerned within it. This question leads to the second ambiguity, which concerns the agency of creation. Woolf says that the shower of atoms composes 'life itself'. In the better-known formulation of the revised essay, she says that the atoms 'shape themselves into the life of Monday or Tuesday'. It is the task of the novelist 'to convey' the 'varying', 'unknown', and 'uncircumscribed' spirit of life in all its complexity,[77] but to convey is not to shape. This view of literature contrasts sharply with the view advanced by Pound in 1915: 'Vorticism means that one is interested in the creative faculty as opposed to the mimetic. We believe that it is harder to make than to copy'.[78] Woolf's criticism of the Edwardians shares with them the assumption that the value of the novel lies in mimesis. In their purest forms, the impressionist and expressionist schools of modernism take widely differing views of the artist's role in relation to reality.

However, the model of the subject passively receiving an incessant shower of atoms is not the only one in 'Modern Novels', nor the only one in Woolf's work. Her contrast between the outmoded 'design' of the thirty-two-chapter novel and 'the vision in our minds' suggests that the writer does impose a vision onto reality, that she does make rather than copy. If one takes the distinction between impressionism and expressionism to be fundamental, then 'Modern Novels' is inconsistent, containing elements of both theories. If, however, one accepts that both 'making' and 'copying' were significant for modernist literary art, then Woolf's essay may be commended for including both activities, though criticised for failing to articulate the relation between them. Elsewhere in her writing, Woolf also advances the idea of the modern artist as a maker rather than a copier. The fullest version appears not in an essay, but in *To the Lighthouse*, where Lily Briscoe wishes to achieve her vision, and is happy to adopt non-mimetic means, for example, by reducing a mother and child to the abstract form of a triangle.[79]

Modernism and tradition

One of the better anagrammatical accidents of English is the possibility of taking 'idiot rant' and producing 'tradition'.[80] 'Idiot' shares its roots with 'idiom' in a classical Greek word meaning 'own, private, peculiar'. The anagrammatic accident that is 'tradition' nicely illustrates the tensions that presented themselves to modern writers: how far should writing be impersonal, public, and founded on shared norms, and how far should it be private and idiosyncratic? The question is closely related to that posed earlier (pp. 9–10), concerning the relation of the art of the present to that of the past, but more specifically concerns the relation of the innovative individual in the present to the potentially conservative weight of tradition.

We have already seen the futurists' answer to this problem: burn the museums. It was this form of modernism which the architectural critic Sir Reginald Blomfield criticised in 1934. Blomfield feared that modernism 'could lead to 'the bankruptcy of Literature and the Arts', but he was prepared to distinguish 'the Modernism which deliberately turns its back on the past' and a traditionalism which was not static, a 'Traditionalism which recognises the past, and advances on technical lines which have hitherto been followed as a matter of course'.[81] Marinetti's futurist manifesto provoked many modernists to think more subtly about the relation of the present to the past, and to find definitions of tradition that would reconcile some critics to innovation. Ezra Pound in 1913 proposed that the aspiring poet take the scientist as his model: the scientist 'begins by learning what has been discovered already. He goes from that point onward'.[82] The idea that knowledge of the tradition was a prerequisite for even the most modern artistic production was a crucial one over the following ten years.[83] Presenting it as scientific gave it a sheen of modernity and rigour.

In 1916, A. E. Randall, a regular contributor to *The New Age*, reflected on the legacy of the futurists as a group who had perversely rejected 'the works of their forbears'. Randall argued that the value of new work lay in the light it shone on the old:

> For we sharpen our minds on new works only to look back and discover the new beauty in the old work. He was a mere cynic who said: 'When a new book comes out, read an old one': the proper course would be to read the new one first, and then to discover that what you have seen in it could have been seen in the old one if only you could have lent to it that part of your mind which you gave to the consideration of the new work. 'Things are because we see them, and what we see, and how we see it, depends on the Arts that have influenced us'. That only the trained modern mind can really enjoy the works of the ancients would probably be too violent a statement of the idea; but the fact remains that the judgment of posterity seldom agrees with that of a man's contemporaries, that, for example, we see everything in 'Hamlet', while the Elizabethans thought 'Timon of Athens' the better work. And the more masterpieces we enjoy, the more surely shall we believe that everything is in everything.[84]

Randall recognises that the new does not simply accumulate on top of the old like so much archaeological rubble; it has the potential to clarify our perceptions of the old. However, Randall stops short of suggesting that reading new works can radically transform our perception of the old: he implies that the supposedly new beauty had always existed potentially in the old work, had the reader been educated enough to recognise it; his model of interpretation ultimately puts the reader in a passive position. He also implies that the reading of contemporary work might be viewed not as a simple, transient pleasure, but as a *training* for further reading. The idea of training had been implicit in Pound's scientist analogy, but the idea of an active reinterpretation of the past was not.

In the following year Edwin Muir tried to discriminate between mere novelty and true modernity in the latest movements. He did so on the basis that truly modern movements 'are movements in the direction of emancipation, "the elevation of the type man"'.[85] Muir proposes the paradox that what is most modern is that which is most rooted in the past:

> If modernism be a vital thing it must needs have roots in the past and be an essential expression of humanity, to be traced, therefore, in the history of humanity: in short, it can only be a tradition. The true modern is a continuator of tradition as much as the Christian or the conservative: the true fight between progress and stagnation is always a fight between antagonistic *traditions*.[86]

Muir's starting point for this argument is the failure, as he saw it, of futurism. Later in the article, he mocks the futurists for having proposed 'that works of art should not endure'; their creations were, by their own principles, 'true works of art'. He laments the present-day lack of tradition:

> The sentiment of transiency is our *most deeply rooted* sentiment: it is the very spirit of the age. But by its essential nature it cannot hope to endure, to be

known by future generations; for we shall not produce immortal works until we become interested in some idea long enough to be inspired by it, and to write monumentally and surely of it. We hold our ideas by the day; but for a masterpiece to be born, an idea must have taken root and defied time. Permanence of form, moreover, would seriously embarrass a modern writer, who wishes to change with the hour, and does not want his crotchets of yesterday to live to be refutations of his fads of to-day. Thus we are too fleeting to make even our transitoriness eternal.[87]

Though Muir was not part of the Vorticist movement, his views concur with the Vorticist criticism of futurist work for lacking form and for being 'accelerated impressionism'. The passage also uncovers one of the rationales for the modernist valorisation of form: the belief that the monumental, well-formed work was more durable than the ill-formed, perhaps even to the extent of being immortal. The underlying assumption is that the well-formed work achieves the same status as Platonic forms, existing in a realm beyond ordinary transient matter.

The classic statement of the dialectical relationship between modern artistic innovation and tradition is T. S. Eliot's essay 'Tradition and the Individual Talent'. In 1918 Eliot had adopted the analogy of the artist as scientist to express part of the relationship between the individual and his discipline: 'A poet, like a scientist, is contributing toward the organic development of a culture: it is just as absurd for him not to know the work of his predecessors or of men writing in other languages as it would for a biologist to be ignorant of Mendel or De Vries'.[88] The idea of the culture developing organically is taken up in the later essay:

if the only form of tradition, of handing down, consisted in following the ways of the immediate generation before us in a blind or timid adherence to its successes, 'tradition' should positively be discouraged. We have seen many such simple currents soon lost in the sand; and novelty is better than repetition. Tradition is a matter of much wider significance. It cannot be inherited, and if you want it you must obtain it by great labour. It involves, in the first place, the historical sense, which we may call nearly indispensable to anyone who would continue to be a poet beyond his twenty-fifth year; and the historical sense involves a perception, not only of the pastness of the past, but of its presence; the historical sense compels a man to write not merely with his own generation in his bones, but with a feeling that the whole of the literature of Europe from Homer and within it the whole of the literature of his own country has a simultaneous existence and composes a simultaneous order. This historical sense, which is a sense of the timeless as well as of the temporal and of the timeless and of the temporal together, is what makes a writer traditional. And it is at the same time what makes a writer most acutely conscious of his place in time, of his own contemporaneity.[89]

Modernism, as Muir had said, has its roots in the past. In this model of the relation of the past and present, the past is still relatively immovable. But in the following paragraph, Eliot develops the model into something more complex.

> No poet, no artist of any sort, has his complete meaning alone. His significance, his appreciation is the appreciation of his relation to the dead poets and artists. You cannot value him alone; you must set him, for contrast and comparison, among the dead. I mean this as a principle of aesthetic, not merely historical, criticism. The necessity that he shall conform, that he shall cohere, is not onesided; what happens when a new work of art is created is something that happens simultaneously to all the works of art which preceded it. The existing monuments form an ideal order among themselves, which is modified by the introduction of the new (the really new) work of art among them. The existing order is complete before the new work arrives; for order to persist after the supervention of novelty, the *whole* existing order must be, if ever so slightly, altered; and so the relations, proportions, values of each work of art toward the whole are readjusted; and this is conformity between the old and the new. Whoever has approved this idea of order, of the form of European, of English literature will not find it preposterous that the past should be altered by the present as much as the present is directed by the past.

Like A. E. Randall, Eliot acknowledges the potential for the new work to change the meaning of the old. However, while Randall had been interested in the intrinsic qualities of the work, Eliot is concerned with its significance in relation to other works. Eliot's half-expressed metaphor of a museum curator rearranging massive sculptures would appear to respond to Muir's accusation that contemporary writers were not writing 'monumentally'; it implies that the works themselves were sufficiently durable as to be fundamentally unaltered. Though Eliot's idea of change does not suggest that the meaning of the works will change, it is more radical than Randall's, in that it envisages the work belonging to a new order which its creator could never have envisaged.

The metaphor of monuments is a misleading one in many respects. Eliot imagines adjustments of the monuments, but he does not suggest that the curator might consign one to a basement or storeroom. We might imagine that a literary work will endure permanently, like a monument protected from damaging environmental conditions. In practice, to endure, literary works need to remain in print and available, need to remain interesting to new writers, and need to remain interesting to critics; above all, they need to be read. The revival of interest in the metaphysical poets that followed Grierson's edition and Eliot's review of it is a case in point.

Eliot defined tradition not as a static product of past cultures, but as an active process linking the present with the past. It was a process that made room for individual innovation ('idiotic' or otherwise) and for accumulated norms and values. Had Sir Reginald Blomfield known it, Eliot's was a definition of modernism that would have fitted very comfortably with his 'traditionalism', and might have tempered some of his irritation with *Modernismus*.

'Modernism' and 'Modernist'

Modernists defined themselves by creating distinctive groups and by contrasting their practices with those of a previous generation. In their critical writings, they emphasised the technical innovations necessary to realise their vision of modernity. As was noted earlier, however, they did not consistently refer to themselves as 'modernists' nor to their movement as 'modernism'. How these terms came to dominate requires some attention.

For many years critics used the term 'modernism' without reflection on its origins. In 1976, Bradbury and McFarlane expressed regret that a historical period had come to be labelled with a term that should always be relative to the present moment, but they did not stop to ask whether the modernists themselves would have recognised the label.[90] In 1977, Calinescu noted that the 'notion' of modernism 'gained wider acceptance and legitimacy only after the 1920s'.[91] His point has been repeated with stronger emphasis by many critics since. Stan Smith's *The Origins of Modernism* (1994) has been particularly influential. While many have adopted Smith's observation that 'modernism' is 'an epithet applied in hindsight to a disparate collection of writers', fewer have tested it against the available evidence, or have considered the implications of his remark that it was 'also a real element in their discourse of themselves'.[92] One critic writes that ' "modernism" was not bandied about by the actual artists, writers and "agitators" ' of the late 1910s and 1920s, another that 'modernism' is 'a term coined in retrospect', and another still that it 'has always been a retrospective formation'.[93] While it is reasonable to say that the signifieds of 'modernism' and 'modernist' have changed, some of these statements imply that even the signifiers were unknown. While it is true that the term 'high modernism' did not appear until the 1970s (the chapter on 'Late Modernism' in Part II gives a brief history), 'modernism' and 'modernist' were available and in use from 1908 onwards. Moreover, there are continuities between the signs employed in the 1910s and 1920s and those employed by later critics. A more balanced view is given by Chris Baldick, who notes that 'The appearance of the terms "modernist" and "modernism" in literary discussion before 1940 is something of a rarity', and that critics in that period more often referred to 'the modern movement'.[94]

Both 'modernism' and 'modernist' were used widely at the start of the twentieth century in relation to theology. The modernist movement within Roman Catholicism was condemned by Pope Pius X in 1907. Though the dual reference of the signifier can cause some incidental amusement, it very rarely leads to genuine ambiguities. Smith's observation that a book titled *Postmodernism and Other Essays* predated Laura Riding and Robert Graves's *A Survey of Modernist Poetry* (1927) by one year becomes rather less interesting when one discovers that its author wrote on theological matters.[95] It is diverting to speculate whether the prominence of the theological meaning of the word inhibited its adoption in aesthetic matters, but it would be difficult to bring evidence to bear on such a hypothesis.

In their aesthetic senses, 'modernism' and 'modernist' were used by actual artists and writers in the 1910s and 1920s, and were used increasingly in the 1930s. 'Modernist', my own impressionistic records would suggest, appeared more frequently than 'modernism'. The *OED* gives an instance of 'modernism' from 1879, but 1908 is the watershed year. The *OED* cites R. A. Scott-James's critical study *Modernism and Romance* (1908), but far more significant is T. E. Hulme's 'Lecture on Modern Poetry', dated by its editor to November 1908, in which Hulme summarises Imagist technique, and describes his viewpoint as one of 'extreme modernism'.[96] As early as 1911 there is a reference to the 'modernist art movement' in a little magazine.[97] A complete roll call of later instances would be out of place in the present work, but between 1911 and 1922 the two terms may be found in both little magazines and in more conservatively formatted journals, for example *Rhythm*, *The New Age*, *The Freewoman*, *The New Statesman*, *The Egoist*, *Art and Letters*, *Secession* and *Broom*. Between 1923 and 1939 there are further examples in *The Criterion*, *The Fugitive*, *the transatlantic review*, as well as in more mainstream journals, newspapers, and books. A significant number of these references appear in connection with painting, sculpture, and architecture, and it seems possible that the terms were adopted into literary criticism by analogy with those disciplines; or at least, if the earliest uses could be shown to be literary, that their widespread adoption within literary criticism was due to their acceptance in other disciplines.

Many of the examples mentioned above treat 'modernism' as a movement to be welcomed, or at least treated open-mindedly. However, by the mid-1930s the two terms were frequently adopted by reactionary critics. In *Modernismus* (1934), Blomfield directed his ire principally towards modernists in architecture and sculpture. In the following year, Ronald Fuller gave a conservative sketch of the recent history of poetry: the abandonment of formal technique had begun a period of chaos, against which there had been a reaction. Fuller, however, was more ambivalent about nomenclature: the values of clarity, balance, and judgement that he valued were to be found in 'young modernist poets' but were absent in their predecessors, whom Fuller presumably considered to be mature modernist poets. In the following year, taking *The Waste Land* as his reference point for modern poetry, Fuller referred to 'the modernist poet of yesterday', and again found a young new alternative.[98] In their desire to bury certain modern tendencies in art and poetry, and in their desire to find a suitable name for the headstone, Blomfield and Fuller seem inadvertently to have unified and christened the experimental movements of the 1920s. The common currents among 'modernist' writers were more apparent to those who opposed them than to the writers themselves. Blomfield makes reference to Herbert Read's *Art Now* as an intelligible account 'of what the Modernists think they are doing in painting and sculpture'. The summary is interesting because, although Read uses the term 'modernists' once, he far more commonly refers to 'the modern artist' and 'the modern movement', and is as much concerned to identify the differences between the constituent movements (such as cubism and surrealism) as to give a unified account.[99] In literary criticism, anti-modernist works such as John Sparrow's *Sense and Poetry* (1934) gave the next generation of defenders of modernism an identifiable argument against which to define the movement. In defending it, the next generation drew upon the emerging critical principles of the 'new criticism', and redefined the signified of 'modernism' more narrowly. However, the signifier 'modernism' was not wholly new, and the concept had already become established as something with a contentious relation to concepts such as tradition and form.

The idea that modernism was a retrospective construction is a myth: not in the sense of being a complete falsehood, but in the sense of being a partial, ideological truth. Modernism has been constructed retrospectively, but not completely so, nor at a single stroke; it has accumulated on foundations laid down by the writers now known as modernists. The myth served a useful purpose in the 1980s and 1990s, reminding critics that modernism could be reconstructed in other ways, and particularly reminding them of the plurality of modernist movements, each of which often contradicted others.

The New Criticism

To the extent that modernism was a retrospective construction, its most significant constructors were working under the influence of the New Criticism. The earliest members of the school were Allen Tate, John Crowe Ransom, and Cleanth Brooks; the name derived from a 1941 book by Ransom. Though this triumvirate were American, they derived their principles from critics based in England, particularly T. S. Eliot, I. A. Richards, and William Empson. Their influence was transatlantic. Many other critics working in the period from the 1930s to 1950s shared assumptions with the New Criticism, while differing on certain principles.

It is possible to overstate the extent to which New Criticism was chronologically separate from modernism. Because the height of its institutional influence came in the 1940s and 1950s, it is easy to forget that the main New

Critics were active from the 1920s onwards. Vincent Leitch has identified a first phase in the 1920s, in which the foundational texts were written, and a second in the 1930s and 1940s in which the movement grew and found a sympathetic reception in literary and academic journals.[100] The first issue of *The Fugitive*, the journal in which New Critics such as Allen Tate and John Crowe Ransom began their careers, was published in 1922. While New Criticism was not contemporaneous with the pre-1914 impressionist and Imagist periods of modernism, it was not wholly separate from what we now call 'high modernism'.

Whereas modernist writers couched their criticisms in manifesto-like terms of what literature should or ought to do, or at least in terms of tentative proposals of what it might do, the new critics more often spoke in terms of what literature 'is' and what a poet 'is'; the present tense implied a confidence that the values of good literature were eternal. (Where they used modal verbs such as 'should', it was in relation to the correct conduct of literary criticism.) The shift from 'should' to 'is' in relation to literature marks the institutionalisation of certain aspects of modernism.

The New Critics did not consciously elaborate a theory of modernism, and much of what they said about modernist texts they held to be true for other valued texts from other periods. Their accounts of modernism as such emerge in scraps and fragments. At the heart of New Criticism was the practice of close reading of poetry, and the New Critics did not greatly alter their approach according to the period in which the poem was written. Eliot's 'The Metaphysical Poets' (1921) gave them licence to identify modernist poetry with the work of Donne and other seventeenth-century forebears. However, modernism was important to them. As Mark Jancovich remarks, 'the attempt to get to grips with modernist poetry [...] was of crucial significance in the development of the New Criticism'.[101]

Earlier generations of scholarly critics had approached texts philologically, or biographically, or with the aim of identifying literary sources. Such approaches, the New Critics felt, directed attention away from the literary value of the text itself. Two well-known essays of the 1940s, 'The Intentional Fallacy' and 'The Affective Fallacy', summarised the principles that attention to the author's intentions or the poem's effects distracted from proper literary criticism. The New Critics' view of the relation of literature to politics was more complex: they rejected art which appeared to have a propagandistic intent, but they did not wholly detach culture from society. Their view of poetry was informed by a reactionary politics which rejected modernity.

A distinction of poetic language from the language of science was central to the New Critical view of literature. As early as 1923, in a review of *The Waste Land*, Ransom was contrasting science, understood as 'abstraction', with the qualities of literature.[102] Robert Graves's writings further reinforced the distinction, but the strongest support came from I. A. Richards's *The Principles of Literary Criticism* (1924).[103] Richards wrote that

> A statement may be used for the sake of the *reference*, true or false, which it causes. This is the *scientific* use of language. But it may also be used for the sake of the effects in emotion and attitude produced by the reference it occasions. This is the *emotive* use of language.[104]

However, the New Critical distinction of scientific and poetic language was not identical to Richards's distinction: 'poetic language' included far more than the emotive. T. S. Eliot's remark that Donne's sensibility was modified by intellectual experience made possible the important development: poetic language was not simply emotive, but was felt thought. Eliot's remarks that the poet must 'dislocate' language and must be 'difficult' were also highly influential. Science and ordinary language made statements directly; poetry, on the other hand, made them obliquely, through the use of metaphor, paradox, and irony.[105] Such tropes can be used for emotive purposes, but also for intellectual ones. Because poetic language was oblique, and because the meaning of any given phrase was dependent on its context in the whole, the meaning of a poem could not be paraphrased: to do so would be to subscribe to the 'Heresy of Paraphrase'.[106] The New Critics disdained poetry with a propagandistic intent on a similar basis: poetry with a paraphraseable message was not poetry. This view of poetic discourse as transcending rational meaning was also to be found in the symbolist theory of the magical properties of poetry.

The relation of the poet to the poem was important to the New Critical understanding of poetry in all eras. Firstly, poetry was impersonal. In this the New Critics were following Eliot's view, already quoted, that poetry was not an expression of emotion but 'an escape from emotion'. Secondly, the poet is a maker, not merely a copyist of nature.[107] This view echoes Pound in 1915 – 'We believe that it is harder to make than to copy' – but was also influenced by Eliot's remark that the modern poet 'must be *difficult*' and must 'dislocate' language. The dislocator of language is a maker of language, not a passive inheritor. In *The Fugitive* in 1925, Donald Davidson recognised that in 'The Metaphysical Poets', Eliot was 'defending [...] the complexity, or obscurity, or difficulty of much modern poetry'. 'A better *apologia* for a great part of modern poetry [...] could hardly be devised', he continued.[108] The points about impersonality and the poet's creativity were concisely stated by Brooks and Wimsatt in 1957: 'The business of the poet is not personal expression but craft'.[109] The New Critics' view of the poet's role is closely intermeshed with their belief that there is no inherently 'poetic' subject matter, and with the view that the poem is not a 'statement about experience', but must *be* an experience in itself.[110] The poet has not copied reality, but created an independent reality.

The view that nothing is 'intrinsically unpoetic'[111] has consequences both for subject matter and style. Eliot's 'The Metaphysical Poets' is again the source:

> When a poet's mind is perfectly equipped for its work, it is constantly amalgamating disparate experience; the ordinary man's experience is chaotic, irregular, fragmentary. The latter falls in love, or reads Spinoza, and these two experiences have nothing to do with each other, or with the noise of the typewriter or the smell of cooking; in the mind of the poet these experiences are always forming new wholes.[112]

Tate articulated the consequences:

> Certain modern poets offer no inherently poetical objects, and they fail to instruct the reader in the ways he must feel about the objects. All experience, then, becomes potentially the material of poetry – not merely the pretty and the agreeable – and the modern poet makes it possible for us to 'respond' to this material in all the ways in which men everywhere may feel and think.[113]

The most obvious consequence is the turn away from nature as subject matter and locus of value to the city as subject matter, with value being located in the manner of the treatment. However, Tate also implies that there is no inherently poetic vocabulary, and that metaphors may be drawn from any possible source. In 1936 Michael Roberts – not a New Critic, but a poet-critic working in the same tradition – wrote that, to modern poets, 'a certain amount of chemistry and physics' was as familiar as Greek mythology: 'they find it natural to refer to ideas which are ingrained in their thought but foreign to readers brought up on a different curriculum'.[114] This may seem contradictory to the New Critical rejection of science, but, once recruited as poetic material, ideas from chemistry and physics become poetic and indirect.

Metaphor was highly prized by the New Critics. Its centrality to their theory was a logical consequence of their distinction of scientific and poetic language, and of an assumption underlying it, that scientific language is never metaphoric. Metaphor in poetry has a cognitive, not a decorative function: it does not dress up a thought that could be explained more plainly, but rather it articulates a new thought that could be expressed in no other way. The serious use of metaphor was seen as feature common to both the metaphysicals and the moderns. The New Critical valorisation has its roots in Imagism, particularly Pound's instruction to 'Go in fear of abstractions',[115] but whereas Pound's phrase was practical advice as to poetic craft, the New Critical view was more explicitly meshed into an ideological and metaphysical system.

The New Critics saw poetic *structure* as fundamentally important. As early as 1922, Allen Tate spoke of the fusion of form and content in *The Waste Land* as a commonplace of criticism.[116] Brooks elaborated on this idea in *The Well Wrought Urn*: 'Unless one asserts the primacy of the pattern, a poem becomes merely a bouquet of intrinsically beautiful items'. The 'pattern', however, is not to be equated with form in the sense of metrical and rhyme form, nor the arrangement of stanzas, nor genre. Rather, it is 'a structure of meanings, evaluations, and interpretations; and the principle of unity which informs it seems to be one of balancing and harmonising connotations, attitudes, and meanings'.[117] The New Critical emphasis on structure does not mean that poems have no content; rather, they have no content that is detachable from structure. The sorts of epigrammatic 'truths' that are often extracted from poems should properly be seen as meaningless when isolated from their poetic context. The New Critics traced this idea back to the early days of modernism: Wimsatt and Brooks quoted Hulme on the idea of an 'organic' complexity in which each part of a work 'is modified by the other's presence'.[118]

The other crucial idea concerning structure was Joseph Frank's idea of *spatial form*, first advanced in 1945. As language unfolds in a consecutive sequence, literature might be seen as a fundamentally temporal art, but Frank argued that both poets and narrative writers (Eliot, Pound, Proust, Joyce, and Barnes) 'ideally intend the reader to apprehend their work spatially, in a moment of time, rather than as a sequence'.[119] Frank took his cue from Imagist theory. As we have seen, Pound had defined 'the image' as presenting a complex 'in an instant of time'. Instantaneity was essential to its creating a 'sense of freedom from time limits and space limits'.[120] Pound's Imagist theory raised the problem of what happens in longer poems containing several images. Does the succession of images compromise the atemporal power of Imagism? Or is the poem itself to be understood as 'one vast image'? Frank argued that, in order to achieve the latter, Eliot and Pound work to 'undermine the inherent consecutiveness of language, frustrating the reader's normal expectation of a sequence and forcing him to perceive the elements of the poem as juxtaposed in space rather than unrolling in time'.[121] They achieved this through fragmentation and through the suppression of regular metres. In *The Cantos*, an anecdote begun in one place might be continued in another. In *The Waste Land*, 'syntactical sequence is given up for a structure depending on the perception of relationships between disconnected word-groups. To be properly understood, these word-groups must be juxtaposed with one another and perceived simultaneously'.[122] Frank traces the difficulty of much modernist literature to the contradiction between the inherent temporality of language (its 'time logic') and the 'space logic' of the modernist writers.

Aesthetic form in modern poetry, then, is based on a space-logic that demands a complete reorientation in the reader's attitude towards language. Since the primary reference of any word-group is to something inside the poem itself, language in modern poetry is really reflexive. The meaning-relationship is completed only by the simultaneous perception in space of word-groups that have no comprehensible relation to each other when read consecutively in time. Instead of the instinctive and immediate reference of words and word-groups to the objects or events they symbolize and the construction of meaning from the sequence of these references, modern poetry asks its readers to suspend the process of individual reference temporarily until the entire pattern of internal references can be apprehended as a unity.[123]

Although Frank is not always counted as a New Critic, his emphasis on pattern and structure is classically New Critical; so too is his assumption that the elements of the poem combine into an organic unity. He diverges from the mass of New Critics in his inclusion of narrative. By doing so, he expanded the range of the modernist canon, and created a critical environment in which prose and poetry could be discussed together.

Frank's account of spatial form implies something articulated in more general terms by Allen Tate: modern poetry requires 'the direct and active participation' of the reader. If modern poetry, or forebears such as metaphysical poetry, appeared difficult, it was because the modern reader 'expects to lie down and be passive when he is reading poetry'.[124] This view of the reader is implicit also in Brooks's view, already quoted, of the poem being not a statement about experience, but an experience in itself: it follows that poem can be as difficult and as baffling as real experience. There is a cultural politics underlying the New Critical view of the reader which has some similarities to the Frankfurt School. The culture industry creates passive consumers who expect their cultural experiences to be easily digestible.

The distinction between scientific and poetic language is rooted in a deeper antipathy to science, and a tendency to take science as a token of all that is wrong with modernity. The New Critics were little interested in the internal variety of science, and tended to view it all as a mechanistic attitude that supported 'the practical will', or what we might now call instrumental reason. There was some variety in their receptiveness to science, with Ransom and Tate being more strongly antipathetic than most.[125] For Tate, the scene in *The Waste Land* of the typist seduced by the clerk was, properly interpreted, concerned with science: 'The seduction scene is the picture of modern and dominating man. The arrogance and pride of conquest of the "small house agent's clerk" are the badge of science, bumptious practicality, overweening secular faith'.[126] For Brooks, the proper role of the poet is defined by contrast with the methods of science: 'It is not enough for the poet to analyse his experience as the scientist does, breaking it up into parts, distinguishing part from part, classifying the various parts. His task is finally to unify experience'.[127] It goes without saying that this is a very partial view of science, one that emphasises empirical data collection, but says nothing about the role of imagination and intelligence in the formation of theories. Whereas the modernist poets themselves sometimes took science as positive point of reference, the New Critics presented it in an unfavourable light.

The idea that art can transcend the chaos of life, discussed earlier, was largely systematised by the New Critics. As early as 1922, John Crowe Ransom cited Robert Graves's account of poets as 'men of repressions and inner conflicts'. Poetry has a therapeutic function: 'these conflicts come to the surface in poetry and there is peace again'.[128] Cleanth Brooks's reading of *The Waste Land* emphasises the redemptive power of the poem, against Edmund Wilson's view of it as a 'statement of despair and disillusionment'. The use of parallelism creates a sense of 'the oneness of all experience' and 'the unity of all periods': Brooks's thinking here anticipates Frank's concept of spatial form. Eliot's theme is 'the rehabilitation of a system of beliefs': through his method of ironic juxtaposition, Eliot rescues the Christian symbols from the status of cliché.[129] More generally, the New Critical model of the poem as a harmonious reconciliation of tensions implies that it has the ability to incorporate and transcend chaos.

The New Critics' account of modernism placed a great deal of emphasis on the forms and techniques of poetry. Their division of language into scientific and poetic meant that metaphor and the structure of the poem were crucial to their understanding of it. Subject matter was subordinated to structure, and the skilled poet was capable of rendering any subject matter meaningful and beautiful. The meaning of a poem was likewise inseparable from its structure. Though their formalist emphasis appears to exclude social issues from consideration, their view of poetry was informed by a rejection of modernity, particularly in the guise of science, and by a belief that poetry had a redemptive ability. In many of its beliefs the New Criticism drew upon Imagist manifestos and on Eliot's essays of 1919–23, but its tendency was to rework those fragmentary suggestions within a more systematic and universal theory of poetry.

The New Critics' work on modernism provides useful tools for interpretative criticism, but in other areas it is deficient. It suggests how to deal with metaphors that, to critics like John Sparrow, did not make sense; it suggests that the fragmentation of modernist poems is not an obstacle to meaning, but part of their way of making meaning. It is much weaker when one begins to ask questions about history, politics, and culture. The New Critics themselves were conscious of the accusation that they neglected history: Tate argued in 1949 that Empson and Brooks did not exclude it, but used it in such a way that 'it no longer devours the literary text; it survives as contributory knowledge'.[130] However, what it contributes to is an interpretation of the individual text; this excludes any analysis of the cultural conditions which made it possible for the text to exist. In so far as the New Critics have a wider sense of history, it relates to literary history. It elaborates T. S. Eliot's story of the 'dissociation of sensibility' that began after the metaphysical poets. In the New Critical version, science becomes explicitly the villain of the piece, and science accounts for the weakness of romantic poetry. It goes without saying that this leaves out a great deal: class, gender, and imperialism, to give some of the most obvious headings. Even as an account of modernity, it leaves out much: modernity is identified with a mechanistic mindset and a will to control nature. There is no space in the New Critical account for modernisation in the sense of intellectual specialisation. The city is there, but only as the locus of soul-destroying modern experience; it is not a complex space of clashing cultural codes. The loss of faith is there, but is understood as essentially an unwelcome process, rather than a liberating one.

The view of history to be found in the New Critics' works mostly concerns literary history, but even in this narrow sphere it is deficient. Although the New Critics did not wholly reject romantic poetry, giving praise to Keats's Odes in particular, they tended to repress modernism's debts to it. As we shall see, Edmund Wilson had already in 1930s essayed a new genealogy of modernism that included Romanticism, and Frank Kermode was to develop it further in 1957. Because their basic unit is 'the poem', the New Critics show little interest in differences between literary periods: thus the modernists and the meta-physicals are treated as if they were fundamentally the same. Given that they homogenise literary history, it is unsurprising that they show little interest in distinctions within modernism. The distinctions between impressionists and expressionists, or between the avant-garde and modernism, which have been so productive for later critics, did not interest the New Critics. Their ahistorical tendency also means that they show no interest in the circulation and reception of the literary text. There is no indication that Donne's lyrics were produced in very different social circumstances from those of Eliot, and distributed dif-ferently. The New Critics had consciously reacted against a positivist textual scholarship of annotation and source hunting, but this led to certain limitations in their method. Above all, they speak predominantly of 'the poem', and, with a few honourable exceptions such as Joseph Frank, have little to say about prose narrative.

Though the New Critics certainly had a political position – broadly speaking, a conservatism defined in reaction against modernity – there is no place for polit-ics within their hermeneutics. Their fascination with the internal organisation of the poem, and their metaphysical reference to categories such as 'the unity of experience', excludes the politics of poetry. Their exclusion of the reader, codi-fied in 'The Affective Fallacy', means that they do not fully imagine a plurality of readers, some of whom might legitimately feel excluded by a certain poem or a certain poetics. In so far as they do imagine other readers, it is to lament the reader 'pampered by bad education' who will not make the effort to understand modern poetry.[131] Later accounts of modernism have seen it as evolving within a particular social fraction, whose experiences of education and modernity were by no means universal. The New Critical tendency to reintegrate all dishar-monious elements through the tool of 'irony' also closes off the interpretative strategy of symptomatic reading, in which contradictions or fault-lines in the text are seen as socially significant.

As the foregoing paragraphs imply, the concept of *culture* was relatively unproblematic for the New Critics. While they understood that there was a variety of different cultures, and acknowledged the existence of what we would call 'mass culture' or 'the culture industry', it did not intrude upon the world of the modernist poet, except as an antitype. More recent critics have envisaged a more complex, turbulent boundary between cultures, characterised by movements of absorption and expulsion. The New Critical concept of culture also places the poet in an authoritative position, controlling his or her cultural inheritance, deploying it at will in the form of allusion. The poet is a maker not only of poems, but also of culture. Later literary theories have tended to reduce the author's authority, seeing language (and hence culture) as something that speaks through the author. This later view exists in embryo in 'Tradition and the Individual Talent', particularly in the Eliot's talk of 'surrender' and 'self-sacrifice', but was not adopted by the New Critics. While the later view is not without its weaknesses, especially if the individual author becomes nothing more than a mouthpiece for the ideological tendencies of the age, it does at least allow a different kind of self-contradiction to enter in to the poem, one not wholly controlled by the poet, one in which 'a variety of writings, none of them original, blend and clash'.[132] The New Critical view valorises literary allusion, operating within a tightly controlled literary canon, but it cannot comprehend intertextuality.

After the New Criticism

The depth and range of the New Criticism's influence was so great that it is no easy task to state when it ceased to be a current school of criticism: dates between 1957 and 1980 have been proposed. W. K. Wimsatt and Cleanth Brooks's *Literary Criticism: A Short History* (1957) has been seen as a summation of the movement after which it began to ossify; the publication of Northrop Frye's *Anatomy of Criticism* in the same year has been seen as marking a new movement. However, one has only to note the revised and paperback editions of key New Critical texts (e.g. the 1968 edition of *The Well Wrought Urn*) to realise that, in practical terms, the New Criticism persisted long after. Its relative simplicity as a pedagogical method meant that critical schools demanding a higher level of abstract thought could not easily displace it. As late as 1976 one can find a critical reading of *The Waste Land* using the characteristic vocabulary: it seeks to demonstrate that there is an underlying plan that brings coherence and consistency, and that resolves ambiguities. However, this particular instance comes to mind because in 1979 Alan Wilde notes the traditionalism of its approach.[133] In the following year the title of Frank Lentricchia's volume of essays, *After the New Criticism*, suggested that the end had really come, though as Lentricchia argues, like a father-figure, the New Criticism continued to exert an influence after its death.

The New Criticism was succeeded by many movements. The impact of structuralism on the English-speaking world was relatively late, so that in practice it was indistinguishable from post-structuralist psychoanalytic, Marxist, and feminist criticism. In so far as there was a distinct structuralist phase, it was particularly oriented towards tropological readings, in which literary tropes such as synecdoche, metaphor, and metonymy were used both in close reading, and, more problematically, to characterise writers and movements. Roman Jakobson's 1956 essay 'Two Aspects of Language and Two Types of Aphasic Disturbances' was highly influential, as was Hayden White's *Metahistory* (1973). In *Ezra Pound: The Image and the Real* (1969), Herbert Schneidau relates Pound's work to the trope of synecdoche; in a 1976 essay, however, influenced by Jakobson, Schneidau related the difficulties of Pound's texts to the form of aphasia associated with metonymy.[134] In David Lodge's *The Modes of Modern Writing* (1977), metaphor and metonymy are used to map the representational methods of twentieth-century literary movements. However, tropological readings are not exclusively structuralist: a similar abstraction of rhetorical terms can be seen in Paul de Man's deconstructionist work from the late 1960s onwards, and tropology has also been influential on post-structuralist psychoanalytic readings.

There is no easily identifiable post-structuralist model of modernism to match that evolved by the New Critics. Many of the early books employing post-structuralist theory re-examined single authors, without reference to conventional period labels such as 'modernism'. The earliest by some distance was Colin MacCabe's *James Joyce and the Revolution of the Word* (1979). By the mid- to late 1980s, series such as Blackwell's 'Rereading Literature' (1985–8) and Harvester's 'Feminist Readings' (1987–91) made use of theory to propose revisionist readings of canonical writers. The impact of 'theory' was felt as much as anything else in subtle shifts in the canon. Most notably, James Joyce's linguistically experimental and 'open' texts (particularly *Finnegans Wake*) became more interesting than Eliot's allusive and supposedly 'closed' style.[135] A revival of interest in Gertrude Stein was also due in part to post-structuralism, and in part to feminist work.

Though the structuralist concept of intertextuality might seem particularly well suited to allusive modernist texts, there is a crucial difference between intertextuality and allusion, in that the concept of allusion implies intention on the part of the author, and is also stabilised by the idea of a limited canon on which the author draws. For structuralists, all writing is intertextual and 'the author' is only a critical fiction. *Finnegans Wake* is better adapted than *The Waste Land* to such models. Dennis Brown's *Intertextual Dynamics within the Literary Group* (1990) is a relatively rare example of an attempt to bring theory to bear on a group of modernist authors, striking a balance between granting agency to the text and to the author.

The period after New Criticism also saw the politics of modernism come into the foreground. Frank Kermode's discussion of modernist authoritarianism in *The Sense of an Ending* (1967) is often cited as a starting point, though as we shall see in Part II, chapter 4, such concerns have an intermittent history stretching back at least to the 1950s. In *Fables of Aggression: Wyndham Lewis, the Modernist as Fascist* (1979), Fredric Jameson developed an approach to reading 'reactionary modernism' that recognised the complexity of modernist texts, and which moved criticism of them beyond simple condemnation. In Part II, political approaches to modernism are most explicit in chapters 4 (the culture industry), and 6 (feminism), but political questions also emerge in chapters 2 (realism), 3 (the avant-garde), 5 (the city), and 8 (late modernism), and they are not altogether absent from the other two chapters. Indeed, the major change that has occurred in modernist studies since the end of the reign of the New Criticism has been the emergence of the political question. Criticism, in consequence, has had to adopt new tools and adapt old ones.

What Perry Anderson calls the 'portmanteau concept' of modernism is capacious, but is not without structure. It is internally structured by questions about the relation of the writer to modernity, and about the ways in which technique can best express that relation. The attitudes of writers to modernity have varied widely, as have their exact definitions of it, and in consequence the concept is more open than those of other aesthetic movements. Moreover, the modernist movement has a long critical history extending across specific historical traumas (most significantly the holocaust and the threat of global nuclear war) and rapid economic changes in the industrialised world. Within the realm of aesthetics, since 1945 there has been a succession of postmodernisms. Approaches to modernism have had to situate themselves within these shifting horizons. Though 'modernism' was in circulation during the 1920s and 1930s, the phrase 'the modern movement' has the advantage of reminding us that modernist writing is perpetually restless.

Chapter Notes

1. Perry Anderson, 'Modernity and Revolution', *New Left Review*, no.144 (Mar.–Apr. 1984), 112–13.
2. Matei Calinescu, *Faces of Modernity* (Bloomington: Indiana University Press, 1977), 5.

3. Richard Sheppard, 'The Problematics of European Modernism', in Steve Giles, ed., *Theorizing Modernism: Essays in Critical Theory* (London: Routledge, 1993), 1–51 (pp.2–5).

4. Andrew Brighton, 'Post-War Establishment Distaste for Wyndham Lewis: Some Origins', in Paul Edwards, ed., *Volcanic Heaven: Essays on Wyndham Lewis's Painting and Writing* (Santa Rosa: Black Sparrow Press, 1996), 169–83 (p.180).

5. I. A. Richards, *Science and Poetry* (London: Kegan Paul, Trench, Trubner, and Co., 1926), 64–5, n.1; T. S. Eliot, *The Use of Poetry and the Use of Criticism* (London: Faber and Faber, 1933), 130.

6. Ian Watt, *Conrad in the Nineteenth Century* (London: Chatto and Windus, 1980), 175–9.

7. Walter Pater, 'The School of Giorgione', in A. Phillips, ed., *The Renaissance*, (Oxford: Oxford University Press, 1986), 86.

8. M. K. Spears, *Dionysus and the City: Modernism in Twentieth-century Poetry* (New York: Oxford University Press, 1970), 62.

9. Terry Eagleton, 'Capitalism, Modernism and Postmodernism' (1985), in David Lodge, ed., *Modern Theory and Criticism: A Reader* (Harlow: Longman, 1988), 392.

10. T. E. Hulme, 'Romanticism and Classicism', in Karen Csengeri, ed., *Collected Writings of T. E. Hulme* (Oxford: Clarendon Press, 1994), 61.

11. Hulme 'Romanticism and Classicism', 61.

12. F. T. Marinetti, 'The Founding and the Manifesto of Futurism' [1912], tr. Lawrence Rainey, in Rainey, ed., *Modernism: An Anthology* (Oxford: Blackwell, 2005), 5.

13. Harriet Davidson, 'Improper Desire: Reading *The Waste Land*', in A. David Moody, ed., *Cambridge Companion to T. S. Eliot* (Cambridge: Cambridge University Press, 1994), 121–31.

14. Marjorie Perloff, 'Modernist Studies', in Stephen Greenblatt and Giles B. Gunn, eds., *Redrawing the Boundaries* (New York: Modern Language Association of America, 1992), 154–78 (p.158).

15. Unattributed phrase quoted by E. E. Cummings, 'Gaston Lachaise' [Feb. 1920], in George J. Firmage, ed., *E. E. Cummings: A Miscellany* (London: Peter Owen, 1966), 21.

16. T. S. Eliot, 'The Metaphysical Poets' [1921], in Frank Kermode, ed., *Selected Prose of T.S. Eliot* (London: Faber and Faber, 1975), 65.

17. T. S. Eliot, 'Preface to *Anabasis*' [1930], *Selected Prose* 77.

18. Stephen Spender, *The Destructive Element* (London: Jonathan Cape, 1935), p.12.

19. Item 2 in Perloff's list ('Modernist Studies', 158).

20. Item 11 in Perloff's list ('Modernist Studies', 158).

21. 'Ulysses, Order and Myth' was first published in *The Dial* in 1923, but was not reprinted until 1948. It was next reprinted in 1965, in Richard Ellmann and Charles Feidelson's influential anthology *The Modern Tradition*.

22. T. S. Eliot, 'Ulysses, Order and Myth' [1923], in Kermode, ed., *Selected Prose*, 177–8.

23. Irving Howe, 'Introduction: The Idea of the Modern', in I. Howe, ed., *Literary Modernism* (Greenwich, Conn.: Fawcett Publications, 1967), 11–40 (p.32).

24. Items 9, 10, and 12 in Perloff's list ('Modernist Studies', 158).

25. Lawrence Edward Bowling, 'What is the Stream of Consciousness Technique?' *PMLA*, 65, no.4 (1950), 333–45; Derek Bickerton, 'Modes of Interior Monologue: A Formal Definition', *Modern Language Quarterly*, 28 (1967) 229–39. Bowling partially endorses the use of 'stream of consciousnesss' as term, but his article nevertheless makes some valuable discriminations.

26. M. H. Whitworth, *Virginia Woolf* (Oxford: Oxford University Press, 2005), 82.

27. A. Parkes, *Modernism and the Theater of Censorship* (New York: Oxford University Press, 1996), 69–70.

28. Dominick LaCapra, qtd. Parkes, 5.

29. Wyndham Lewis, 'Automobilism' [1914], in Paul Edwards, ed., *Creatures of Habit and Creatures of Change* (Santa Rosa: Black Sparrow Press, 1989), 33–4.

30. Thomas Carlyle, 'Signs of the Times' [1829], in G. B. Tennyson, ed., *A Carlyle Reader* (1969; Cambridge: Cambridge University Press, 1984), 34–5.

31. Thomas Carlyle, 'Characteristics' [1831], in Tennyson, ed., *A Carlyle Reader*, 103.

32. Giovanni Cianci and Peter Nicholls, eds., *Ruskin and Modernism* (Basingstoke: Palgrave, 2001); Jessica R. Feldman, *Victorian Modernism* (Cambridge: Cambridge University Press, 2002); Helen Groth, *Victorian Photography and Literary Nostalgia* (Oxford: Oxford University Press, 2003).

33. Stephen Spender, *The Struggle of the Modern* (London: Hamish Hamilton, 1963), 71.

34. George Landow, *Elegant Jeremiahs* (Ithaca: Cornell University Press, 1986), 51.

35. Walter Pater, 'Conclusion', in A. Phillips, ed., *The Renaissance* (1873), (Oxford: Oxford University Press, 1985), 150.

36. Walter Pater, 'Conclusion', 151.

37. Lawrence Rainey, ed., *Modernism: An Anthology* (Oxford: Blackwell, 2005), 3–6, 94–7, 201–6.

38. Lawrence Rainey, ed., *Modernism*, 201.

39. Malcolm Bradbury and James McFarlane, 'Movements, Magazines and Manifestoes', in Bradbury and McFarlane, eds., *Modernism 1890–1930* (Harmondsworth: Penguin, 1976), 203.

40. J. M. Murry, letter of 29 Oct. 1919, in C. A. Hankin, ed., *The Letters of John Middleton Murry to Katherine Mansfield* (London: Constable, 1983), 199, n.2.

41. Waldo Frank, 'For a Declaration of War', *Secession*, 7 (Winter 1924), 9.

42. Richard Kain, *Fabulous Voyager: James Joyce's Ulysses* (Chicago: University of Chicago Press, 1947), 9; Irving Howe, 'The Idea of the Modern', in I. Howe, ed., *Literary Modernism* (1967), 23; Monroe K. Spears, *Dionysos and the City* (New York: Oxford University Press, 1970) 41; Malcolm Bradbury and James McFarlane, 'The Name and Nature of Modernism', in Bradbury and McFarlane, eds., *Modernism 1890–1930* (Harmondsworth: Penguin, 1976), 27.

43. Christopher Herbert, *Victorian Relativity* (Chicago: University of Chicago Press, 2001), 50; Peter Nicholls, *Modernisms* (Basingstoke: Macmillan, 1995), viii.

44. T. S. Eliot, 'The Metaphysical Poets' [1921], in Kermode, ed., *Selected Prose*, 59–67; Herbert Read, 'The Nature of Metaphysical Poetry' [1923], *Collected Essays in Literary Criticism* (London: Faber and Faber, 1938), 69–88.

45. Michael Roberts, 'Introduction', *The Faber Book of Modern Verse* (London: Faber and Faber, 1936), 3.

46. V. Woolf, 'Character in Fiction [1924], in Andrew McNeillie, ed., *Essays of Virginia Woolf*, to be 6 vols. (London: Hogarth Press, 1986 onwards), 4. 421.

47. 'Notes of the Week', *The New Age*, 7, no.2 (12 May 1910), 26; Huntly Carter, 'Editorial Notes', *The New Age*, 7, no.5 (2 June 1910), supplement, 1.

48. T. S. Eliot, 'The Metaphysical Poets', 64.

49. Ezra Pound, 'A Retrospect' [1918], in T. S. Eliot, ed., *Literary Essays of Ezra Pound* (London: Faber and Faber, 1954), 3; Richard Chase, 'The Fate of the Avant-Garde' [1957], in I. Howe, ed., *Literary Modernism* (1967) 148–9.

50. Wyndham Lewis, *Blasting and Bombardiering* (London: Eyre and Spottiswoode, 1937), 251–2.

51. Janet Wolff, *Feminine Sentences* (Cambridge: Polity, 1990), 56.

52. Ezra Pound, 'Imagisme' [1913], in L. Rainey, ed., *Modernism: An Anthology* (Oxford: Blackwell, 2005), 94.

53. Ezra Pound, 'A Few Don'ts by an Imagiste' [1913], in L. Rainey, ed., *Modernism: An Anthology*, 95.

54. D. H. Lawrence, 'Poetry of the Present' [1918], in V. de S. Pinto and W. Roberts, eds., *The Complete Poems*, (1964; London: Penguin, 1971), 184.

55. T. S. Eliot, 'Reflections on vers libre' [1917], *Selected Prose*, 32, 33, 36.

56. Ezra Pound, 'A Few Don'ts', 95.

57. T. E. Hulme, 'Modern Art and its Philosophy', 273–4.

58. T. E. Hulme, 'Modern Art and its Philosophy', 277.

59. F. T. Marinetti, 'Technical Manifesto of Futurist Literature' [1912], in Lawrence Rainey, ed., and trans., *Modernism: An Anthology*, 17–18.

60. Friedrich Nietzsche, 'On Truth and Lying in an Extra-Moral Sense' [1873], in C. Blair, S. L. Gilman, and D. J. Parent, eds., *Friedrich Nietzsche on Rhetoric and Language*, (New York: Oxford University Press, 1989), 251.

61. D. H. Lawrence, letter of 5 June 1914, in George J. Zytaruk, Andrew Robertson, Warren Roberts, et al., eds., *Letters*, 8 vols. (Cambridge: Cambridge University Press, 1979–2000), 2. 182–3.

62. A. Besant and C. Leadbetter, *Thought Forms* (London: Theosophical Publishing Co, 1905), 27–8; T. Gibbons, '"Allotropic States" and "Fiddlebow": D. H. Lawrence's Occult Sources', *Notes and Queries*, n.s. 35 (1988), 338–40.

63. E. Pound, 'Affirmations, II: Vorticism', *The New Age*, 16, no.11 (14 Jan. 1915), 277.

64. J. M. Murry, *The Things We Are* (London: Constable, 1922), 183.

65. T. S. Eliot, 'Tarr', *The Egoist*, 5, no.8 (Sept. 1918), 105–6.

66. T. S. Eliot, 'Ben Jonson', in *The Sacred Wood* (1920; London: Faber and Faber, 1997), 102.

67. Eliot, 'Ben Jonson', 95.

68. The analogy was topical, as Einstein had recently demonstrated that non-Euclidean geometry provided a good explanation of gravitation. I have explored the historical context of the analogy in Michael H. Whitworth, *Einstein's*

Wake: Relativity, Metaphor, and Modernist Literature (Oxford: Oxford University Press, 2001), 214–20.

69. Eliot, 'Ben Jonson', 98–9.

70. Eliot, 'Tradition and the Individual Talent' [1919], *Selected Prose* (1975), 43.

71. Eliot, 'Ben Jonson', 102.

72. 'Modern Novels' [Apr. 1919] was revised in 1925, as 'Modern Fiction', for her collection of essays *The Common Reader*. Meanwhile she had resumed the same questions in the essay 'Mr Bennett and Mrs Brown' [Nov. 1923], which was revised and expanded as 'Character in Fiction' [July 1924]; the Hogarth Press then published the latter essay, with minor revisions, as the pamphlet *Mr Bennett and Mrs Brown* [Oct. 1924].

73. Virginia Woolf, 'Modern Novels', *Essays of Virginia Woolf*, 3. 33.

74. Woolf, 'Mr Bennett and Mrs Brown', *Essays*, 3. 387.

75. Woolf, 'Modern Novels', *Essays*, 3. 34.

76. Woolf, 'Modern Novels', *Essays*, 3. 35.

77. Woolf, 'Modern Fiction', *Essays*, 4. 160.

78. Ezra Pound, 'Affirmations, II: Vorticism', 277.

79. Virginia Woolf, in M. Drabble, ed., *To the Lighthouse* (1927), (Oxford: Oxford University Press, 1992), 72.

80. The anagram is suggested in Virginia Woolf's *Between the Acts* (1941), where, with reference to a village pageant, a character announces that 'the idiot' is 'in the tradition'.

81. Reginald Blomfield, *Modernismus* (London: Macmillan, 1934), p.v.

82. Ezra Pound, 'A Few Don'ts', 96.

83. For a full account of Pound's use of the scientist metaphor, see Ian F. A. Bell, *Critic as Scientist: The Modernist Poetics of Ezra Pound* (London: Methuen, 1981).

84. A. E. R[andall], 'The New Job', *The New Age*, 19, no.21 (21 Sept. 1916), 497.

85. E. Muir (as 'Edward Moore'), 'We Moderns', *The New Age*, 21, no.10 (5 July 1917), 232. Muir is quoting Nietzsche, who writes that 'Every elevation of the type "man" has hitherto been the work of an aristocratic society – and so it will always be'. See *Beyond Good and Evil*, tr. R. J. Hollingdale (London: Penguin, 1990), 192 (§257).

86. E. Muir, 'We Moderns', 232.

87. E. Muir, 'We Moderns', 232.

88. T. S. Eliot, 'Contemporanea', *The Egoist*, 5, no.6 (Jun.–July 1918), 84–5.

89. T. S. Eliot, 'Tradition and the Individual Talent', 38.

90. Malcolm Bradbury and James McFarlane, 'The Name and Nature of Modernism', in Bradbury and McFarlane, eds., *Modernism 1890–1930* (1976), 22.

91. Matei Calinescu, *Faces of Modernity* (Bloomington: Indiana University Press, 1977), 69.

92. Stan Smith, *The Origins of Modernism* (New York, London: Harvester Wheatsheaf, 1994), 11.

93. Jean-Michel Rabaté, *The Ghosts of Modernity* (Gainesville: University Press of Florida, 1996), 203; Helen McNeil, 'Vortex Marsden: A Little Magazine and the Making of Modernity', in Kate Campbell, ed., *Journalism, Literature and*

Modernity (Edinburgh: Edinburgh University Press, 2000), 142; Peter Brooker and Simon Perril, 'Modernist Poetry and its Precursors', in Neil Roberts, ed., *A Companion to Twentieth-Century Poetry* (Oxford: Blackwell, 2001), 21.

94. Chris Baldick, *The Modern Movement* (Oxford: Oxford University Press, 2004), 4.

95. Stan Smith, *The Origins of Modernism*, 14.

96. T. E. Hulme, 'A Lecture on Modern Poetry', *Collected Writings*, 54.

97. Holbrook Jackson, 'A Plea for a Revolt in Attitude', *Rhythm*, 1, no.3 (Winter 1911), 6–10 (p.6).

98. Ronald Fuller, 'The Poetry of A. S. J. Tessimond, '*Poetry Review*, 26, no.6 (Nov.–Dec. 1935), 443–8; Ronald Fuller, 'The Poetry of John Lehmann', *Poetry Review*, 27, no.1 (Jan.–Feb. 1936), 15–21.

99. Reginald Blomfield, *Modernismus* (London: Macmillan, 1934), 62, note; H. Read, *Art Now* (London: Faber and Faber, 1933), 138.

100. Vincent B. Leitch, *American Literary Criticism from the Thirties to the Eighties* (New York: Columbia University Press, 1988), 24–59.

101. Mark Jancovich, 'The Southern New Critics', in A. Walton Litz, Louis Menand, and Lawrence Rainey, eds., *Modernism and the New Criticism* (The Cambridge History of Literary Criticism, vol. 7) (Cambridge: Cambridge University Press, 2000), 200–18 (p.202).

102. John Crowe Ransom, 'Waste Lands' [1923], in Michael Grant, ed., *T. S. Eliot: The Critical Heritage* (London: Routledge and Kegan Paul, 1982), 174.

103. For Graves, see John Crowe Ransom, 'A Doctrine of Relativity', *The Fugitive*, 4, no.3 (Sept. 1925), 93–4, which cites Graves's *On English Poetry* (1922).

104. I. A. Richards, *Principles of Literary Criticism*, 2nd ed. (London: Routledge and Kegan Paul, 1926), 267.

105. Cleanth Brooks, *The Well Wrought Urn* (1947; revised ed., London: Methuen, 1968), 6–7.

106. Brooks, *The Well Wrought Urn*, 157–75.

107. Cleanth Brooks, *Modern Poetry and the Tradition* (1939; London: Editions Poetry London, 1948), 22–3.

108. Donald Davidson, [review of *Homage to John Dryden* by T. S. Eliot], *The Fugitive*, 4, no.2 (June 1925), 61–2.

109. W. K. Wimsatt, Jr., and C. Brooks, *Literary Criticism: A Short History* (New York: Knopf, 1957), 661.

110. Brooks, *The Well Wrought Urn*, 173.

111. Brooks, *Modern Poetry and the Tradition*, 22. See also Wimsatt and Brooks, *Literary Criticism*, 661.

112. T. S. Eliot, 'The Metaphysical Poets' [1921], *Selected Prose*, 64.

113. Allen Tate, 'Understanding Modern Poetry' [1940], in *Essays of Four Decades* (London: Oxford University Press, 1970), 156.

114. Michael Roberts, 'Aunt Eudora and the Poets' [letter], *The Spectator* (21 February 1936), 302.

115. Ezra Pound, 'A Few Don'ts', *Modernism*, 95.

116. Allen Tate, 'Whose Ox', *The Fugitive*, 1, no.4 (Dec. 1922), 99–100.

117. Cleanth Brooks, *The Well Wrought Urn*, 158–9.

118. T. E. Hulme, 'Romanticism and Classicism' [c.1912], quoted by Wimsatt and Brooks, *Literary Criticism, A Short History* (New York: Knopf, 1957), 662.

119. Joseph Frank, 'Spatial Form in Modern Literature', *The Widening Gyre* (New Brunswick, NJ: Rutgers University Press, 1963), 9.

120. Ezra Pound, 'A Few Don'ts', 95.

121. Frank, 'Spatial Form', 10.

122. Frank, 'Spatial Form', 12.

123. Frank, 'Spatial Form', 13.

124. Allen Tate, 'Understanding Modern Poetry', 163.

125. René Wellek, *A History of Modern Criticism: 1750–1950*, 8 vols. (London: Jonathan Cape, 1955–92), 6. 151–2, 163–4.

126. Allen Tate, 'T. S. Eliot's Ash Wednesday' [1931], *Essays of Four Decades* (London: Oxford University Press, 1970), 467.

127. Brooks, *Well Wrought Urn*, 173.

128. John Crowe Ransom, 'Editorial', *The Fugitive*, 1, no.1 (Oct. 1922), 66–8 (p.67).

129. Brooks, *Modern Poetry and the Tradition*, 164, 167, 169.

130. Allen Tate, 'A Note on Critical "Autotelism"' [1949], *Essays of Four Decades* (London: Oxford University Press, 1970), 169.

131. Allen Tate, 'Understanding Modern Poetry', 163.

132. Roland Barthes, 'The Death of the Author' [1968], in David Lodge, ed., *Modern Criticism and Theory* (Harlow: Longman, 1988), 170.

133. F. C. McGrath, 'The Plan of *The Waste Land*', *Modern British Literature*, 1 (1976), 22–34; Alan Wilde, 'Modernism and the Aesthetics of Crisis', *Contemporary Literature*, 20 (1979), 13–50 (p.15).

134. Herbert Schneidau, 'Wisdom Past Metaphor: Another View of Pound, Fenollosa, and Objective Verse', *Paideuma*, 5, no.1 (Spring–Summer 1976), 15–29. For a summary of tropological readings of Pound, see Mary Ellis Gibson, *Epic Reinvented* (Ithaca, NY: Cornell University Press, 1995), ch. 4.

135. Raphaël Ingelbien, 'Intertextuality, Critical Politics and the Modernist Canon: The Case of Virginia Woolf', *Paragraph*, 22 (1999), 278–92 (p.280).

Further Reading

Modernists (and their Contemporaries) on Modernism

Aiken, Conrad. *Collected Criticism* (London: Oxford University Press, 1968). First published in 1958 as *A Reviewer's ABC*. Includes a checklist of other reviews by Aiken.

Eliot, T. S. *The Sacred Wood* (1920; London: Faber and Faber, 1997).

——. *Selected Prose*, ed. Frank Kermode (London: Faber and Faber, 1975).

Faulkner, Peter, ed. *A Modernist Reader: Modernism in England 1910–1930* (London: Batsford, 1987). Though not as comprehensive as the Kolocotroni (et al.) collection, it contains many useful documents.

Hulme, T. E. *Collected Writings*, ed. K. Csengeri (Oxford: Oxford University Press, 1994). During the 1920s, Hulme was known mostly through the posthumous collection *Speculations* (1924), edited by Herbert Read. Though imperfect as a scholarly edition, Csengeri's collection includes everything from *Speculations* and a great deal more besides, and dates the essays.

———. *Selected Essays*, ed. Patrick McGuinness (Manchester: Carcanet, 2003). A more affordable selection.

Kolocotroni, Vassiliki, Jane Goldman, and Olga Taxidou, eds. *Modernism: An Anthology of Sources and Documents* (Edinburgh: Edinburgh University Press, 1998). Particularly good on the politically radical side of modernism.

Lewis, Wyndham. *Creatures of Habit and Creatures of Change: Essays on Art, Literature and Society, 1914–56*, ed. Paul Edwards (Santa Rosa: Black Sparrow Press, 1989).

———. *Men without Art* (1934), ed. Seamus Cooney (Santa Rosa: Black Sparrow Press, 1987).

Muir, Edwin (as 'Edward Moore'). *We Moderns* (London: George Allen and Unwin, 1918). Brief Nietzschean essays on 'the modern' in all its forms, first printed in *The New Age* between 1916 and 1917.

Pound, Ezra. *Literary Essays of Ezra Pound*, ed. T. S. Eliot (London: Faber and Faber, 1951). A deliberately de-politicized account of Pound's literary output.

Rainey, Lawrence, ed. *Modernism: An Anthology* (Oxford: Blackwell, 2005). Includes critical writings alongside poems and prose.

Roberts, Michael. *Critique of Poetry* (London: Jonathan Cape, 1934).

Sitwell, Edith. *Aspects of Modern Poetry* (London: Duckworth, 1934).

Spender, Stephen. *The Destructive Element: A Study of Modern Writers and Beliefs* (London: Jonathan Cape, 1935).

Woolf, Virginia. *Essays of Virginia Woolf*, ed. Andrew McNeillie (London: Chatto and Windus, 1986 onwards).

In addition to these, the *Critical Heritage* (Routledge), *Critical Thought* (Scolar), and *Critical Assessments* (Helm Information) series reprint a host of contemporary reviews. The literary journals and little magazines of the time make for fascinating reading, but most are relatively inaccessible for most readers. The exceptions are the texts digitized by the Modernist Journals Project, currently (Nov. 2005) at http://www.modjourn. brown.edu/

Anti-Modernists (1934–60)

Blomfield, Reginald. *Modernismus* (London: Macmillan, 1934). Concerned primarily with modernism in the arts and architecture.

Brooks, Van Wyck. *Opinions of Oliver Allston* (London: J. M. Dent and Sons, 1941). Particularly 'What is Primary Literature' and 'Coterie Literature'.

MacLeish, Archibald. *The Irresponsibles* (New York: Duell, Sloan and Pearce, 1940). Criticizes modernist writers for evading their political responsibilities. Along with the essays by Van Wyck Brooks noted above, MacLeish's criticism was known as the

'Brooks–MacLeish thesis'. For responses, see *Partisan Review*, 8, no.6 (Nov.–Dec. 1941), and 9 no.1 (Jan.–Feb. 1942).

Shapiro, Karl. *In Defense of Ignorance* (New York: Random House, 1960). Kicking against the new orthodoxy of modernism.

Sparrow, John. *Sense and Poetry: Essays on the Place of Meaning in Contemporary Verse* (London: Constable, 1934). Argues that much modern verse is meaningless.

The New Critics

Brooks, Cleanth. *Modern Poetry and the Tradition* (1939; London: Editions Poetry London, 1948).

——. 'T. S. Eliot as a "Modernist" Poet', in Frank Brady, John Palmer, and Martin Price, eds., *Literary Theory and Structure: Essays in Honor of William K. Wimsatt* (New Haven and London: Yale University Press, 1973), 353–77.

——. *The Well-Wrought Urn* (1947; London: Dobson, 1949; revised, London: Dobson, 1968).

Empson, William. *Seven Types of Ambiguity* (London: Chatto and Windus, 1930).

Grant, Michael, ed. *T. S. Eliot: The Critical Heritage* (London: Routledge and Kegan Paul, 1982). Includes relatively inaccessible criticism on *The Waste Land* by Ransom and Tate.

Graves, Robert. *Poetic Unreason* (London: C. Palmer, 1925). Graves's influence on the New Criticism is less frequently acknowledged than that of Empson or Richards.

Jarrell, Randall. *Poetry and the Age* (1953; London: Faber and Faber, 1955).

Ransom, John Crowe. *The World's Body* (New York: C. Scribner's Sons, 1938). Poetry criticism. See particularly 'Poets without Laurels' (1935).

Richards, I. A. *Principles of Literary Criticism* (London: Kegan Paul, Trench, Trübner, 1925). With Empson, one of the main influences on the American New Critics.

Tate, Allen. *Essays of Four Decades* (1969; London: Oxford University Press, 1970). Particularly important are 'T. S. Eliot's Ash Wednesday' (1931), 'Three Types of Poetry' (1934), and 'Understanding Modern Poetry' (1940).

Secondary Texts on the New Critics

Burt, Stephen, and Jennifer Lewin. 'Poetry and the New Criticism', in Neil Roberts, ed., *Companion to Twentieth Century Poetry* (Oxford: Blackwell, 2001), 153–67. A brief and clear introduction, oriented towards a discussion of poetry by Tate, Ransom, and other New Critics, and others influenced by the New Criticism.

Jancovich, Mark. *The Cultural Politics of the New Criticism* (Cambridge: Cambridge University Press, 1993).

Leitch, Vincent. *American Literary Criticism from the Thirties to the Eighties* (New York: Columbia University Press, 1988), 24–59.

Perl, Jeffrey M. 'Passing the Time: Modernism versus New Criticism', in Hugh Witemeyer, ed., *The Future of Modernism* (Ann Arbor: University of Michigan Press, 1997), 33–48.

Wellek, René. *A History of Modern Criticism: 1750–1950* (Cambridge: Cambridge University Press, 1955 onwards), vol. 6. An insider's view.

After the New Criticism (1960–70, approx.)

Ellmann, Richard, and Charles Feidelson, eds. *The Modern Tradition* (New York: Oxford University Press, 1965). A major anthology of modern writers, including major philosophical forebears; highly influential in shaping views of modernism in the 1970s.

Fiedler, Leslie. 'The New Mutants', *Partisan Review*, 32, no.4 (1965): 505–25. Repr. in *A Fiedler Reader* (New York: Stein and Day, 1977), 189–210.

Harrison, John. *The Reactionaries* (London: Gollancz, 1967). Anticipates John Carey's *The Intellectuals and the Masses* (1992) in several respects.

Howe, Irving. *The Decline of the New* (London: Gollancz, 1971).

——. ed. *Literary Modernism* (Greenwich, CT: Fawcett Publications, 1967). An anthology of criticism, mostly from the post-war period, with the New York/*Partisan Review* school generously generously represented. Includes Howe's 'The Idea of the Modern', revised and reprinted elsewhere as 'The Culture of Modernism'.

Kermode, Frank. *Continuities* (London: Routledge and Kegan Paul, 1968). Includes Kermode's often-cited essay 'The Modern', also reprinted in his *Modern Essays* (1971).

Part II

1

Modernism and Romanticism

While some modernists wished to distinguish themselves from the Edwardian generation, and others from the Victorians, for many poets the dividing line was between Romanticism and the modern movement. Modernist criticisms of the *Georgian Poetry* anthologies (1912–22) were on account of their belated Romanticism. The New Criticism followed T. S. Eliot in criticising romantic poetry, particularly that of Shelley. The impersonality of modernist poetry was contrasted with the supposed personal, expressive quality of the romantic lyric, its precise use of metaphor with the supposed vagueness of romantic thinking. It has fallen to later critics to clarify the extent to which modernist writers were indebted to Romanticism, and the extent to which they were engaged in a distinctive project. Frank Kermode's and Marjorie Perloff's works on this topic have both proved influential. Kermode reminded critics of assumptions about the status of poetry and the poet that modernism inherited from Romanticism, via the late nineteenth-century symbolist movement, while Perloff recognized that there were several distinct strands within modernism, each with different relations to nineteenth-century precedents.

T. E. Hulme set down the clearest and most profound criticism of Romanticism for modernist writers and the earliest generation of critics. His lecture 'Romanticism and Classicism' was probably delivered in 1911 or 1912,[1] but did not receive wider circulation until it was posthumously published in *Speculations* (1924). Hulme's definition is fundamentally political: Romanticism for Hulme derives from the philosophy of Jean-Jacques Rousseau and from the French revolution. Rousseau taught (says Hulme) 'that man was by nature good, that it was only bad laws and customs that had suppressed him'. The opposing 'classical' view held that 'Man is an extraordinarily fixed and limited animal whose nature is absolutely constant. It is only by tradition and organisation that anything decent can be got out of him'.[2] Hulme notes that the classical view is supported by the theological dogma of Original Sin. He views Romanticism as an improper transposition of theological beliefs to the realm of the human – 'You don't believe in a God, so you begin to believe that man is a god' – and this leads to his often-quoted definition of Romanticism as being like a pot of treacle poured over the dinner table, or 'spilt religion'.[3]

Hulme traces the effects of the Romantic and classical philosophies primarily to imagery and vocabulary in poetry. 'The romantic, because he thinks man infinite, must always be talking about the infinite; and as there is always the bitter contrast between what you think you ought to be able to do and what man actually can, it always tends, in its later stages at any rate, to be gloomy'.[4] The romantic poet's belief in the infinite capacity of man 'seems to crystallise in verse round metaphors of flight'. The French poet Victor Hugo, for example, 'is always flying, flying over abysses, flying up into the eternal gases. The word infinite in every other line'.[5] By contrast, the 'classical' poet never forgets the finiteness of man, and so 'even in the most imaginative flights there is always a holding back, a reservation'.[6] The long predominance of Romantic views of poetry has blinded critics to the merits of classical poems. Hulme argues less carefully when defining the relevant qualities of a romantic poem, preferring emotive language and impressionistic metaphors: critics raised on Romanticism expect poems always to be 'moaning or whining about something'; the romantic poem is 'damp' and vague, while the classical poem is, by contrast, 'dry and hard'.[7]

T. S. Eliot endorsed Hulme's position on several occasions, most explicitly in *The Criterion* in January 1926, when he defined 'the modern tendency' as being towards 'classicism'. In Eliot's definition, this was a tendency 'toward a higher and clearer conception of Reason, and a more severe and serene control of the emotions by Reason'; he listed Hulme's *Speculations* among six books which exemplified the tendency. In 1928 Eliot defined his point of view as being, as well as royalist in politics and anglo-catholic in religion, classicist in literature. In 1929 he quoted approvingly from another essay in which Hulme had advanced his view of man as fallen and imperfect, and Hulme's categories also influence Eliot's 1930 essay on Baudelaire. His attachment to the distinction of Romanticism and classicism did however wane by the time he delivered the Page-Barbour lectures in 1933.[8]

In highlighting the anti-Romantic strain in modernism, Eliot was consolidating an attitude which had been apparent among many (though not all) modernist writers for many years. Eliot's critical writings on poetry and dramatic verse had tended to demote the Romantics relative to early seventeenth-century writers, as much by neglect as by positive critical statements. The doctrine of impersonality in literary art was constructed in opposition to a Romantic aesthetic of expression. James Joyce's Stephen Daedalus argues that:

> The personality of the artist, at first a cry or a cadence or a mood and then a fluid and lambent narrative, finally refines itself out of existence, impersonalises itself,

so to speak. … The artist, like the God of the creation, remains within or behind or beyond or above his handiwork, invisible, refined out of existence, indifferent, paring his fingernails.[9]

T. S. Eliot's essay 'Tradition and the Individual Talent' (1919) explicitly rejected Wordsworth's definition of poetry as 'emotion recollected in tranquillity', and argued that poetry should be impersonal: 'Poetry is not a turning loose of emotion, but an escape from emotion; it is not the expression of personality, but an escape from personality'.[10]

Romanticism was also rejected by describing it in the same value-laden metaphors of hardness versus softness, and dryness versus dampness, that Hulme had employed. The imagist movement in poetry had, from the outset, cast itself in 'classicist' terms. Ezra Pound in 'A Few Don'ts for Imagists' warned the poet to 'go in fear of abstractions', with the implication that hard and solid imagery was to be preferred. Pound's essay 'The Hard and Soft in French Poetry' (Feb. 1918) apologized for using such 'semi-metaphorical' terms, and accepted that writers such as Jules Romains could succeed without 'hardness' in their writing, but nevertheless implied that 'hardness' was normally a virtue.[11] In Pound's 'Hugh Selwyn Mauberley' (1920), it is taken as a matter of regret that the 'age demanded' work in malleable 'plaster', not the harder medium of 'alabaster'.

The modern movement was not simple or singular: it contained within it elements that were considered 'romantic' as well as 'classical'. In a 1932 retrospect, Pound recalled how he and Eliot had, in about 1919, decided that 'the dilutation' of vers libre and of Amy Lowell's brand of Imagism ('Amygism') had 'gone too far', reaching a state of 'general floppiness'. The prescribed remedy was the style of verse exemplified by Théophile Gautier's *Emaux et Camées* (1852): 'Rhyme and regular strophes'. That such a corrective remedy was required indicates that modernist writers defined themselves not only in contrast to a Romanticism of the past, but to a Romantic tendency existing within the movement itself. Kermode's *Romantic Image* retrieves one aspect of the Romantic inheritance concealed by polemicists such as Pound.

A significant precedent for Frank Kermode's argument comes in Edmund Wilson's pioneering study, *Axel's Castle* (1931). Wilson sees Romanticism as an assertion of 'the rights of the individual against the claims of society as a whole', and to this extent is in agreement with Hulme.[12] However, he also draws on A. N. Whitehead's influential intellectual history, *Science and the Modern World* (1926), and sees Romanticism as a reaction against the rationalism of the eighteenth century, and the physicists' 'mechanical' view of the universe. Furthermore, he argues that in the mid-nineteenth century, partly under the influence of Darwinism, there was a counter-reaction: the theory

of evolution reduced man from his heroic stature, and made him 'a helpless animal, again very small in the universe and at the mercy of the forces
about him'.[13] The literary counterpart of the counter-reaction was naturalism.
There were, however, survivals of Romanticism against the prevailing trend, and
for some poets, particularly in France, the deterministic and mechanistic view
taken by naturalism was inadequate to their understanding of the world. They
believed in perceptions that lay beyond the scope of ordinary language. This
further counter-reaction formed the symbolist movement. Wilson summarizes
its underlying assumptions thus:

> Every feeling or sensation we have, every moment of consciousness, is different
> from every other; and it is, in consequence, impossible to render our sensations
> as we actually experience them through the conventional and universal language
> of ordinary literature. Each poet has his unique personality; each of his moments
> has its special tone, its special combination of elements. And it is the poet's task
> to find, to invent, the special language which will alone be capable of expressing
> his personality and feelings. Such a language must make use of symbols: what
> is so special, so fleeting and so vague cannot be conveyed by direct statement
> or description, but only by a succession of words, of images, which will serve to
> suggest it to the reader.[14]

If Hulme's Romantics were always dragging in the infinite, Wilson's symbolists
were always attempting to drag in the inexpressible. Unlike Hulme, Wilson
believed that there had already been a reaction against Romanticism, and a
counter-reaction, and that in France the counter-reaction – Symbolism – had
produced an aesthetics close to that of the six English and French authors
studied in *Axel's Castle*: W. B. Yeats, Paul Valéry, T. S. Eliot, Marcel Proust,
James Joyce, and Gertrude Stein.

Though Wilson's view of poetry was not greatly different from that of the
New Critics, his contribution was greeted by them with indifference at best,
and scepticism at worst. They were uncomfortable with both the content and
the mode of his argument. Cleanth Brooks, in his account of *Axel's Castle*,
was concerned to undo the connection that Wilson had forged between the
symbolists and the Romantics.[15] Wilson's concern with contextualization was
not to the taste of the New Critics, who claimed to be interested only in the work
itself. The New Critic René Wellek, in his history of literary criticism, spoke of
Wilson's contextualizing methods disapprovingly, and regretted Wilson's lack
of technical skill in critical analysis.[16] It was not until Kermode's study of 1957
that Wilson's ideas were given serious consideration.

Kermode's study builds on Wilson's in that it identifies a distinctive conception of poetic knowledge, and a corresponding conception of the status of
the poetic. The Image is a 'radiant truth' existing 'out of space and time'; it

comes to the artist as a revelation or, in Joyce's terminology, an 'epiphany'. The ability to apprehend the Image is so peculiar that the artist 'has to pay a heavy price' to achieve it, most usually a state of isolation or estrangement from ordinary men.[17] The idea that poetic knowledge is beyond the reach of ordinary reason, and the idea that the poet is an isolated and specially gifted individual, are shared, argues Kermode, by Romanticism and modernism.

The similarities between symbolism and what we now call modernism were not accidental. The first extract from *Romantic Image* concerns Arthur Symons, whose *The Symbolist Movement in Literature* (1899) had done much to publicize the French poets in Britain. T. S. Eliot remarked on several occasions on its importance, not so much for the theories it advanced, as for its having brought certain poets to his attention.[18] In the second extract, Kermode turns his attention to Hulme.

Extracts from Frank Kermode, *Romantic Image* (London: Routledge and Kegan Paul, 1957), pp.109–14, 121–32.

For Symons, the Movement is essentially a revolution against 'the contemplation and rearrangement of material things' considered as normal art. He cites Carlyle's definition of the Symbol – a definition which had been widely circulated in France, where Taine had reported the relevant chapter in *Sartor Resartus* – as 'an embodiment and revelation of the infinite', 'concealment yet revelation'. The Decadence he regards simply as an inferior forerunner of Symbolism, calling attention to the predominantly philological metaphor implied by the term: it applies mainly to style, to 'that ingenious deformation of language' by which Mallarmé and the rest enter into competition with 'the Greek and Latin of the Decadence'. (Earlier, in a paper of 1893, he had given a different definition, calling Decadence 'oversubtilising refinement upon refinement, a spiritual and moral perversity'. 'Ces chers poèmes,' said Mallarmé of the literature of Rome's last agony, 'dont les plaques de fard ont plus de charme sur moi que l'incarnat de la jeunesse'.) But in any case Symbolism was much more, nothing less than 'an attempt to spiritualise literature, to evade the old bondage of rhetoric, the old bondage of exteriority ... Description is banished that beautiful things may be evoked, magically'. It is by the Symbol that 'the soul of things can be made visible'.

The main psychological assumption of Symbolism (from which it derives an audience for itself) is essentially that of early Romantic aesthetic: that the human mind is so constituted as to be able to recognize images of which it can have no perceived knowledge – the magic assumption, or the assumption that makes so much of dreams. That the whole work of art should be regarded as such an image would not have surprised Coleridge, nor, for that matter, Blake, though he might have put it very differently. Symons, indeed, saw that, although Blake's 'whole mental attitude was opposed to that of the practisers of magic', he had nevertheless the root of this matter in him: 'To Blake, to be "myself alone, shut up in myself" was to be in no merely individual but in a universal world, that world of imagination whose gates seemes to him to be open to every human being'. This is what Symons, using his new critical language, was after. But he was emphasising the magical analogy, giving the Symbol the same relation to spiritual reality as the daemonic 'sign' of the mage. It has the same qualities, on his view, of absolute revelation (it is the concrete embodiment of a supernatural entity) and arcane concealment (it is in no sense representational) that the sign has. And misty as all this may sound, I do not think the commonplace modern conception of the work of art as some sort of complex image, autotelic, liberated from discourse, with coincident form and meaning, could have evolved — as it clearly did — from Symbolist aesthetic if there had not been such a *rapprochement* between poet and occultist. Magic came, in an age of science, to the defence of poetry. In fact Symons, on grounds that Arnold might not have fully approved, calls the literature of the movement 'a new kind of religion, with all the duties and responsibilities of the sacred ritual'. Others spoke of poets as a third order of priesthood.

Some of this Symons got from Yeats, who regarded his magical studies as essential to his poetry — his essay on 'Magic' in *Ideas of Good and Evil*, with its emphasis on the power of the Image not only to wake analogies but also to penetrate to the Great Memory, has long been regarded as fundamental to his work. But Symons was also indebted directly to his French sources. He shows great interest in Nerval's *Le Rêve et la Vie*, particularly in a passage which deals with the doctrines of synaesthesia and *correspondance* — characteristic Symbolist preoccupations — and comments thus:

> To have realised that central secret of the mystics, from Pythagoras onwards, the secret which the Smaragdine Tablet of Hermes betrays in its 'As things are below, so they are above'; which Boehme has classed in his teaching of 'signatures' and Swedenborg has systematised in his doctrine of 'correspondences'; does it matter very much that he arrived at it by way of the obscure and fatal initiation of madness?

For to Nerval (whose madness is of so little account) this revelation brought the celebrity of having 'divined, before all the world, that poetry should be a miracle; not a hymn to beauty, not the description of beauty, nor beauty's mirror; but beauty itself, the colour, fragrance and form of the imagined flower, as it blossoms again out of the page'. Here the hermetic tradition and Symbolism become almost indistinguishable; and the truth is that the whole poetic movement was to a striking degree hermetic; the occult tradition, notably as mediated by Boehme and Swedenborg, lies behind it as it lies behind Blake and some seventeenth-century poetry. When Yeats wrote his long commentary on 'correspondence' in Blake, for the edition, he made the same distinction between 'perpendicular' and 'longitudinal' correspondences in his author that recent scholars (like M. Georges Blin) have introduced into the study of Baudelaire. The connexions at which I am here hinting were perfectly familiar to Yeats and Symons in the 'nineties, and although they have been partly forgotten, their effects are still to be detected in some of the assumptions of modern poetic, most of all in its persistent attempts to produce the equivalent of the 'metaphysical' conceit, which contemporary criticism justified by arguments drawn from a metaphysic of correspondence.

This metaphysic descended in a tenuous but unbroken line from the Renaissance to the Romantic movement, and emerged in a form significant for poetry as early as Blake and Novalis. In early nineteenth-century France there was considerable interest in the occult, though apparently with little attempt to discriminate between the genuine practitioner and the quack (a recurring feature of the history of magic). Baudelaire must have known about the various kinds of Illuminisme and masonry, and he greatly admired de Maistre; he was also aware of Nerval's curious effort, worthy of the Florentine Platonists, to gather together and use the occult potentialities of all religions. Balzac's story *Séraphîtâ*, a work much read by Symbolists, tells of men who understood 'the invisible bonds by which the material worlds are attached to the spiritual', and who found 'le principe des melodies en entendant les chants du ciel qui donnaient les sensations des couleurs, des parfums, de la pensée'. Here is both longitudinal (synaesthetic) and perpendicular (hermetic) correspondence. This aspect of occultism goes hand in hand with the Romantic movement in France, and might have done in England if Blake had had his due. To Yeats and Symons it was clear that the magic element must be re-introduced, in order to affirm, or re-affirm, the status of the Image as a means of tapping 'l'inépuisable fonds de l'universelle analogie'. The French had made this a central doctrine, after Baudelaire had affirmed that the imagination was the faculty which grasped the analogies and rendered them as symbols. Symbols are, simply, images with this essential magical power.

Now this makes the modern symbol resemble, in some ways, kinds of image used in seventeenth-century poetry. For example, it seems certain that behind the emblems so fashionable in that period – they are best known to us in the pietistic forms which came to exert, through Jesuit propaganda, a direct influence on Baroque art and poetry – was a justification in pure Neo-Platonic terms of the aniconic image presented as the only possible representative of some reality imperceptible to the senses and without phenomenal equivalent. This kind of image, as it appears in poetry, is something quite different from allegory; and the easiest way of distinguishing it is, interestingly enough, in Blake's terms. As Yeats put it,

> William Blake was the first writer of modern times to preach the indissoluble marriage of all great art with symbol. There had been allegorists and teachers of allegory in plenty, but the symbolic imagination, or, as Blake preferred to call it, 'vision', is not allegory, being 'a representation of what actually exists really and unchangeably'. A symbol is indeed the only possible expression of some invisible essence, a transparent lamp about a spiritual flame; while allegory is one of many possible representations of an embodied thing or familiar principle, and belongs to fancy, and not to imagination: the one is a revelation, the other an amusement.

The reference is to Blake's *Vision of the Last Judgment*, and a passage of greater import than Yeats suggests, since it expressly excludes allegory as 'Form'd by the daughters of Memory' and argues that 'Vision or Imagination' is the highest knowledge. 'Plato has made Socrates say that Poets & Prophets do not know or Understand what they write or Utter; this is a most Pernicious Falshood. If they do not, pray is an inferior kind to be call'd Knowing?' To this straightforward (and very Symbolist) way of putting it, Yeats has preferred a manner that incorporates the formulae of Coleridge. But the point is that Blake's position on allegory and symbol would have been acceptable to many seventeenth-century poets, who were also perfectly familiar with the doctrine of correspondence used as metaphysical support for image-theory. Their magic (for that is what it amounts to) is virtually the same as that which lay behind the later movement; the theory of correspondences enabled the aestheticians of the nineteenth-century to revive, as if they were new things, doctrines commonplace in 1600. Of course there are accidental differences, and the later poets made a formidable body of German philosophy support the traditional metaphysic, but the similarities are none the less substantial. And this is why I have allowed myself to digress from the consideration of Symons's book: these similarities are important. The development of Symbolist thought in England could not have proceeded far before somebody saw that there was matter for thought in seventeenth-century poetry. Symons did see this, and had a lively interest in Donne and the drama of that period, as any Symbolist historian of literature would. And, as the present century has so strongly associated its poetic with the Donne revival, it seems important, and this seems the place, to sketch very briefly the reason why it ever became possible to think of Laforgue and Donne, Webster and Villiers de l'Isle Adam, as poets of the same sort. Symons, in fact, makes intelligible a habit that came to dominate twentieth-century criticism in its historical phase. [. . .]

Hulme hands over to the English tradition a modernised, but essentially traditional, aesthetic of Symbolism. It would have made ground here in any case, but Hulme gave it a form which has persisted into modern thought, a form which for various reasons offers an acceptable version of the magic Image, or Romantic anti-positivism, and of the excluded artist. The hostility of Pound (his insistence that Ford rather than Hulme was the dominant figure of the pre-war group) is explained by Pound's dislike of the metaphysics adhering to the Hulmian theory – a metaphysics which has had its own considerable success, and in fact grew up side by side with Symbolist aesthetics. Pound's own aesthetic is not fundamentally different from Hulme's, though he is quite right to insist that it was available to him without Hulme's mediation.

The easiest way to explain Hulme is to follow, for a while at any rate, in his own wake. This means putting the metaphysics first, and the general theory of the history of art, though it is tolerably certain that he must have worked out a theory of the Image first and put together the rest of his theory afterwards. Hulme was not, we are told, a Roman Catholic; but he had strong Catholic sympathies. He was a devoted admirer of Bergson, whose *Introduction to Metaphysics* he translated. He had a great veneration for Pascal; and when we name Pascal and Bergson and add the name of Worringer, we have the triple source of Hulme's philosophy at any rate in so far as it affects his views on art.

To consider Bergson first: we are so accustomed (largely on the strength of the extraordinary celebrity of the paper called 'Romanticism and Classicism') to regard Hulme as a classicising, anti-Romantic thinker, that we incline to ignore his strong affiliation to that organicist, anti-positivist stream of ideas that stems from the Romantic movement. From Bergson Hulme derives the concept of discontinuity in nature, the notion of the 'intensive manifold' which is the philosophical justification of his theory of the image; and also his view of the artist as a man deficient in the normal human orientation to action. In Bergson the concept of discontinuity relates to the absolute lack of commerce between the mechanical and the vital, the former being the concern of the 'exact' sciences, against which art in the modern world is always more or less on the defensive; the second, not available to the intellect but only to 'intuition', is the business of a special class of enquirers, and these are artists. To these two discontinuous zones of truth Hulme adds another, borrowed from an earlier anti-naturalist, Pascal. The third order is a realm of absolute ethical and religious values, and it assumes a considerable though occasionally ambiguous importance in Hulme's theories. By definition it is utterly dissimilar to the other two realms, mechanical and vital, though Hulme himself held (and there are apparent contradictions in his thought on the point) that it was, if possible, more like the mechanical than the vital in at least one respect; it was absolutely unrelated to the vital, completely abstract. At this point Hulme professes his pleasure at having the support of Husserl and G. E. Moore, whom he treats as virtually neo-scholastic philosophers.

The second creditor is the German aesthetician Worringer. His thesis, *Abstraktion und Einfühlung*, was published in 1908 (a belated English translation is now available, published by Messrs. Routledge and Kegan Paul in 1953) and Hulme must have been one of its earliest English readers. Its basic ideas, which are all reported in *Speculations*, stem from a sudden perception that the theory of empathy as formulated by Theodor Lipps applies only to some kinds of art. 'Just as the urge to empathy as a pre-assumption of aesthetic experience finds its gratification in the beauty of the organic, so the urge to abstraction finds its beauty in the life-denying organic'. 'Life-denying' and 'life-alien' are key-words in Worringer. They apply to the kind of art produced by primitive peoples and in all phases of civilisation characterised by a fear of the world, by spiritual agoraphobia. Of the primitive he says 'it is because he stands so lost and spiritually helpless amidst the things of the eternal world, because he experiences only obscurity and caprice in the inter-connection and flux of the phenomena of the external world, that the urge is so strong in him to divest the things of the external world of their caprice and obscurity and to impart to them a value of necessity and a value of regularity'. So the primitive makes an abstract quasi-geometrical art, emancipated 'from all the contingency and temporality of the world-picture'. If you compare Egyptian art with Greek you find the first life-alien and the second life-worshipping, the first abstract and the other dependent on empathy. Compare Byzantine with Renaissance art and you have the same polarity. The Renaissance was pantheistic life-worship, it had an 'unproblematical sense of being at home in the world'; man had mastered nature, and there was no mystery to be afraid of, so that art became a means of 'objectified self-enjoyment'. It therefore replaced an art that was abstract (in Worringer's very wide sense) and non-organic. Worringer does not deny 'joy at the new possibilities of felicity' created by the Renaissance, but laments 'the great values hallowed by an immense tradition that were lost forever with this victory of the organic, of the natural'.

Hulme was more uncompromising. Accepting the view that the Renaissance represents a prime historical crisis, he claimed also that the *Weltanschauung* it introduced had remained dominant until his own time (for both he and Worringer, like nearly all serious Romantic thinkers, imagined themselves to be living at a moment of historical crisis, after which, in their case, a more primitive, more abstract art was to replace the Renaissance tradition of humanism and empathy) and that this *Weltanschauung* was entirely bad. The typical philosophical decision of the Renaissance for Hulme was the exclusion from serious consideration of the dogma of Original Sin; this gone (as Pascal saw) the whole third estate of value was closed, because perfection had to be conceived in entirely human terms; from this follows a radical change in art (for Hulme the Renaissance had no religious art at all) and in philosophy (which becomes consistently anthropocentric and anti-religious). If life, specifically human life, is at the centre, any attempt to think ethically must result in a confusion of the human and the divine. This confusion is the direct cause of relativism in ethics, modernism in religion, and Romanticism in literature. Romanticism is merely a phase of Renaissance Pelagianism, a humanistic sham religion ('spilt religion' in his most famous phrase, because of its weakness and shapelessness by comparison with the categorical form of absolute ethics).

Hulme set great store by his historical theories, holding that the main object of such speculations was the important one of destroying false categories in modern thought: a proposition which the author of a study like this, aimed ultimately at the same object, must heartily endorse. He undertook to make good this theory of the Renaissance by an elaborate examination of the philosophies of the period; and it is clear that had he had time to do so he must have modified his general theory with some severity; like the Romantics he so fiercely assailed, he did not know enough. A critique of this aspect of his historical theory would be irrelevant to the present purpose; it is sufficient for the moment to insist that Hulme was one of the first of the English to discover, what was later to become a dominating concept in modern criticism, some kind of disastrous psychical shift, some original moral catastrophe, in human history about the time of the Renaissance, and to couple it with a belief that another crisis, another major alteration of sensibility, was at hand.

For Hulme, the epoch of humanism, anti-religious in every department of life, but visibly so in art, was ending. He lavishes his contempt upon it; with a sort of doctrinaire fury he eliminates as bad and anti-religious (because on the side of life) even Michelangelo. Nor does he care for the kind of thing other Roman Catholics like – Fra Angelico, for instance. His Catholicism is intellectual in the extreme, almost to the point of being a dogmatic abstract from the religion; without its support he cannot have the world-picture he wants, but he will have none of its tenderness and sentiment. The art he cares for is that of the period which the Renaissance ended, an epoch which believed in Original Sin and produced, at its best, a geometric art quite distinct from the vitalism of Renaissance art, which ministered to the spectator's pleasure in being alive, his desire to be *acting*. The art of Byzantium abhors all this, being concerned with absolute non-human values; being life-alien, remote from organic life and even detesting it. This art resembled not that humanist art which began in Athens, but Egyptian religious sculpture and the art of primitive peoples. Geometrical abstraction is a characteristic of cultures which understand the human lot as tragic, and distinguish sharply between the human and the divine, never confusing them, as the 'vitalist' art he hated did. Hulme applies to philosophies and art alike what he calls his *critique of satisfaction*. Never mind what the philosophers say, he advises; ask instead, what emotional requirement in themselves are they trying to satisfy. And all post-Renaissance philosophy is the same, so considered; it satisfies only the need for an assurance of human centrality. But new needs are now, he adds, appearing, and we are beginning, with Epstein and Wyndham Lewis, to get that anti-vitalist, geometric art of which the beginnings were to be perceived in Cézanne.

Whenever Hulme generalises about historical periods he goes wrong. The critique of satisfaction apparently fails to distinguish between Descartes and Schopenhauer, and it tells us that Hartley and the later Coleridge were seeking the same answers. It is impossible to understand how anybody who had read the *Essay on Man* could possibly regard Pope as exempt from the heresy (which Hulme called 'Romantic') of denying the *absolute* inaccessibility of ethics to the reason; Pope's trace of scepticism has very little to do with the chilly fideism of Hulme, and he has far more of Montaigne than Pascal in him. Much more important than the numerous minor objections of this sort that one could bring against Hulme is the well-established fact (ably presented in Michael Roberts's book) that he disastrously misrepresents Romantic philosophy. For Hulme, as we have seen, Romanticism was a calamity however you looked at it: politically, philosophically, aesthetically. It was the anthropocentric assumption of the Renaissance at the stage of mania, all Rousseauistic rubbish about personality, progress and freedom, all a denial of human limit and imperfection. (In fact it would be truer to say that the movement was obsessed by Original Sin than to say, as Hulme does, that it completely ignored it, and made life the measure of all values). For Hulme, as for all seers, the moment at which he was thinking was the perfect one for seeing the whole matter in perspective, and so breaking history into two parts (Augustine to the Renaissance, the Renaissance to Hulme). He did not even see how inconsistent he was about Coleridge, whose 'vital' he sometimes uses in its original Coleridgean sense, and sometimes in Worringer's sense, with great confusion – a confusion, incidentally, which reflects the Paterian life-and-death ambiguity which we have already looked at, and which turns up again in the aesthetic of Vortex. Nor did he see how dependent he was upon the tradition he was attacking, despite his avowed and enormous debt to Bergson. In so far as he was merely doing propaganda for a new abstract art which had already got under way he was primarily a reporter of Worringer, and that is consistent and defensible as far as it goes, which is not so far as the main historical generalisation; but in so far as he was introducing a new 'classical' poetry – anti-humanist poetry he means, which is a pretty paradox in itself – his position is complex and unsatisfactory, because he has not found out what it really is. We shall see more clearly where he stood if we consider the theory of the image which is central to his whole aesthetic. It is closely related to the concept of discontinuity, with its attendant rejection of empathic, *vital* art; but, as we shall see, it fits much more neatly into the old Romantic-Symbolist theory with its dualist implication (*two* discontinuous orders related to reason and imagination) than into the triplex structure of his own Bergsonian-Pascalian hypothesis.

Let us, then, look at Hulme's requirements for good poetry. Negatively, it must not be concerned with the myth of human perfection or perfectibility in any form; it must accept the strict limitations of human powers, be life-alien. (Note that Hulme is evasive and inconsistent about Coleridge's Imagination, fearing that there is some connection between it and the hated divinisation of human intellect that denies limit; he seems to have been unaware of the controlling force over Coleridge's thought of his refusal to give up the doctrine of Original Sin, whatever metaphysical labour this refusal might involve him in. In fact Hulme's 'intellect' is much the same as the Coleridgean and Wordsworthian 'reason', the reflective faculty that partakes of death.) The acceptance of limit will at once cut out the ecstatic meaning and hysterical aspiration Hulme regards as characteristic of Romantic poetry. The first positive requirement is for *precise description* (Hulme might have reflected that it is also the first requirement of Wordsworth's *Preface* of 1815). For Hulme, however, this precision concerns the recording of images; and here we are at the core of Hulmian aesthetics.

Without pausing to comment upon its deficiencies, let us look at Hulme's distinction between prose and verse.

> In prose as in algebra concrete things are embodied in signs or counters which are moved about according to the rules, without being visualised at all in the process. There are in prose certain type situations and arrangements of words, which move as automatically into certain other arrangements as do functions in algebra. One only changes the X's and the Y's back into physical things at the end of the process. Poetry, in one aspect at any rate, may be considered as an effort to avoid this characteristic of prose. It is not a counter language, but a visible concrete one. It is a compromise for a language of intuition which would hand over sensations bodily. It always endeavours to arrest you, and to make you continuously see a physical thing, to prevent you gliding through an abstract process. It chooses fresh epithets and fresh metaphors, not so much because they are new, and we are tired of the old, but because the old cease to convey a physical thing and become abstract counters. A poet says a ship 'coursed the seas' to get a physical image, instead of the counter word 'sailed'. Visual meanings can only be transferred by the new bowl of metaphor; prose is an old pot that lets them leak out. Images in verse are not mere decoration, but the very essence of an intuitive language.

Presumably no one would now accept this as it is put; the semantics is, to say the least, naive, and Hulme's emphasis on the visual quality of all images (though not his insistence on their physical quality) has been outgrown. But that 'images are the very essence of an intuitive language' is as much an assumption of modern criticism as of Coleridge's. Poetry, by virtue of the image, *is*; prose merely describes. One is end, the other means. What poetry seems to be *about* is therefore irrelevant to its value. 'Subject doesn't matter'. Poetry is bad when it directs the attention away from the physical uniqueness and oneness of the image (the poem itself of course is an image, if it is good) and enables the reader 'to glide through an abstract process'. It is concrete, because the Image can be represented only as concrete, and entirely devoid of discursive meanings and appeals to the intellect; it is the direct representation of what is intuited. Whether the poem is good or not depends upon the accuracy of the representation, and upon that alone.

> I always think that the fundamental process at the back of all the arts might be represented by the following metaphor. You know what I call architect's curves – flat pieces of wood with all different kinds of curvature. By a suitable selection from these you can draw approximately any curve you like. The artist I take to be a man who simply can't bear the idea of that 'approximately'. He will get the exact curve of what he sees whether it be an object or an idea in the mind.

Poems are concerned with intuited truth, not with what is discursively explicable by the reason. The mechanical can be measured in its own way, but the approximations which are all that way can offer in the aesthetic sphere are intolerable to the artist.

But this does not mean that good poems are about 'the infinite' or 'the ineffable' – that would be to fall into the Romantic heresy in a slightly different form. We return to Bergson's two orders. What *is* intuited in terms of the Image? In what circumstances does this act of intuition occur? Hulme's answer is Bergson's. The sphere in which intuition operates is that reality which is conceived 'as a flux of interpenetrated elements unseizable by the intellect'. What normally debars our entry into this sphere is the usual orientation of the human mind towards action. If that were not so we should have easy commerce with it, and there would be no need for art at all; as it is, the artist is 'a man who is emancipated from the ways of perception engendered by action'.

At this stage in the book it is hardly necessary to point out how richly 'Romantic' this formulation of the artist's function is, but it is worth emphasising that the twin concepts of isolation and image occur in Hulme as surely as in the poetry he despised. But we must return to the question of the intuited image.

Hulme's metaphysical justification of his image-theory is borrowed from Bergson. The human intellect tends to explain (*explico*, unfold) everything in a manner fitting its limitations; it analyses, because 'that is the only way in which the intellect can deal with things'; 'we reduce everything to extensive manifolds'. We unfold everything out in space, and we tend to think that everything that cannot be so unfolded must be unknowable. But of course this is not so, and anybody can think of things which are somehow known but resist this form of knowing them. How do such things differ from the others which allow themselves to be treated as extensive manifolds? Bergson argues that such things, 'while incomprehensible by our ordinary standards', are nevertheless finite. The nature of their complexity is qualitative, not quantitative; they simply do not yield to explanation, to discursive methods of analysis; they resist the intellect. Their parts are 'interpenetrated in such a manner that they could not be separated or analysed out'. And yet one should not even speak of parts, because the complex thing is a continuous whole, and it is impossible to conceive of its parts as having a separate existence. This is the intensive manifold, by the very terms of the argument impossible to define; it is accessible only to intuition, belonging to a different order of reality. It is 'indescribable but not unknowable'. The artist knows it; it is his Image. It is finite; hence the need for precision. Its meaning is the same thing as its form, and the artist is absolved from participation with the discursive powers of the intellect.

This theory, as Hulme explains it, makes a show of being in opposition to Romantic imprecision – hence the emphasis on finiteness, and the lack of reference to the third, Pascalian order – but in fact it is fundamentally a new statement of the old defence of poetry against positivism and the universe of death. It is a revised form of the old proclamation that poetry has special access to truth, and is not merely light entertainment for minds tired out by physics. Poets, excluded from action, are enabled to achieve the special form of cognition and pierce the veil and intuit truth; this is communicated in the Image.

And yet 'new' is certainly the wrong word for all this. Hulme himself recognises the essential similarity between his intuited manifold and Schopenhauer's Idea, arguing reasonably for the technical superiority of the later conception. And this similarity, from which Hulme draws no conclusion, is in a sense the key to a proper historical appraisal of Hulme on poetry. Bergson himself is the almost inevitable result of the nineteenth-century effort to find room for art amid the encroachments of science; and the aesthetic of the Symbolists is predominantly the artists's version of such anti-intellectualist concepts as the Idea of Schopenhauer. Hulme knew de Gourmont, but avoided his conclusion that the alternative to intellect was something more primitive; he avoids anything remotely resembling surrealism, and for the *rêve* so dear to Symbolism he substitutes his rather austere version, a higher but finite order of truth. To this extent there is justice in his claim that he is at war with Romantic imprecision; but it must be said that the term *rêve* covers many meanings, including that of a means of access to realms of truth habitually inaccessible, and Hulme's artist is really the Romantic *voyant* expressed in terms more agreeable to a man who disliked some kinds of philosophical language. Insist as he might on the *finite* nature of his intuited truth, it is only another version of that truth unavailable to science which was part of the whole protest against eighteenth-century 'uniformitarianism' (whether expressed as German 'organicism' or as something more characteristically English in the thought of Blake and Coleridge). To get the exact curve of the thing, insisting upon the imperviousness to paraphrase of the symbolic work of art (the 'aesthetic monad') was Mallarmé's business as much as Hulme's; in fact Mallarmé anticipates Hulme in various particulars, such as the theory that a poem must be read silently, and both writers were driven (Hulme in *Cinders*, his 'Notes for a new *Weltanschauung*') to the dance as a necessary emblem of the symbol. In short, the Hulmian Image – precise, orderly, anti-discursive, the product of intuition – is the Symbol of the French poets given a new philosophical suit. As a matter of aesthetic decency it may be that this was needed; but once it is granted that Hulme was trying to do much the same thing as Mallarmé, it becomes evident that he did not do it very well.

As I have said, Hulme falls instinctively into the image of the Dancer, and to complete the pattern he writes in 'Notes on Language and Style' of 'the beauty of the feminine form ...as a typical vesture or symbol of beauty herself', adding that

> Rossetti saw the spiritual element in face and form, and desired the spirit through his desire for the body, and at last did not know the one desire from the other, and pressed on, true mystic that he was, in ever-narrowing circles, to some third thing that seemed to lie behind both desires. 'Soul is form and doth the body make'.

The prose here is in the Paterian tradition, quite unlike Hulme's usual colloquial brightness; it could be Yeats. The quotation from a Renaissance poet (Spenser) is a borrowing from the enemy; Hulme must have realised, with his predecessors and successors, that there was matter in such poetry made to his hand (compare the vogue for Donne's passage on Elizabeth Drury). And the reference to Rossetti is surely significant. In matter and manner this short passage is pure Romantic. And Hulme was certainly sufficiently informed by *l'âme romantique* to see the affinity of his kind of thinking about poetry for mysticism and magic. He calls the Christian mystics 'analogous to his own temper' (he would have been interested in the modern theory that much seventeenth-century poetry is technically based on prescribed methods of meditation) and he admires the 'physical analogies' of the Neo-Platonists, which are in the end the *correspondance* of Baudelaire and the Magic of Yeats. Something of the sort is, of course, necessary to any Symbolist theory of poetry, for if you insist on calling paraphrase a heresy, if you insist that the common language of reason cannot achieve knowledge of the thing that the Image is, then you are forced to guard against the absolute surrender of the power of communicating by some theory explaining how your supra-rational knowledge can be shared. Hulme has not the Great Memory, and he has no theory of shared subliminal symbolisms; nor has he the modern veneration for the magic underworld of language, to be visited by all who can achieve the golden bough of a pun or an irony. Instead he has the Bergsonian Veil which the artist can pierce, to show what everybody could see if only they were likewise equipped. It is a High Dream perhaps, but a dream all the same; and the view that under certain conditions everybody can dream it is a magical view.

* * *

By the standards of present-day historicist criticism, *Romantic Image* is limited in its scope to questions of aesthetics. Though it acknowledges that literary philosophers such as Hulme were conversant with the works of aestheticians such as Wilhelm Worringer, it does not attempt to trace the changes in aesthetics to wider historical changes. Raymond Williams's *Culture and Society*, published in the following year, revived a different set of questions about the relations of aesthetics and society. Kermode's account of the relations of modernism and Romanticism tends to overlook the conservative politics at the heart of Hulme's theorizing.

Although his study is now dated in its approach, the idea of poetry identified in Kermode's study is consonant with questions raised by later influential critics and theorists. The idea that poetic language has 'magical' qualities suggests that symbolist theory was a response to the loss of 'aura' identified by Walter Benjamin as one of the effects of the existence of art in an age of commodification and mechanical reproduction.[19] Moreover, the autonomy of art, its separation from society and social concerns, has been a central question for theorists following in the path of Theodor Adorno: their work has aimed to understand how the ideal of autonomy is covertly a response to larger social and cultural pressures. Artworks may 'seal themselves off' from the outside world, but Adorno interprets such non-communication as a form of communication; aesthetic form, which opposes referentiality, nevertheless contains its own hidden referentiality; aesthetic form must be recognized as 'sedimented content'.[20]

The currency of Kermode's thesis was affected by developments both in poetry and criticism. In poetry, the 'projectivist' school developed a form of poetry that drew its life primarily from the modernism of Ezra Pound and William Carlos Williams, but very much less from Eliot and Yeats. The poetry of poets such as Charles Olson (seen by many as the leader of the school), Robert Duncan, and Robert Creeley demanded a new understanding of terms such as metaphor and symbol, and a new understanding of the place of literal statement within poetry. In Charles Altieri's summary, Olson distinguishes himself from 'the symbolist proponents of the Romantic image' by 'insisting on the image as the intensification of objective reality, not a transcending of it'.[21] However, this is not to say that projectivism was anti-Romantic as such: because of the centrality it accorded to breath, Olson's poetics was recognized as being 'a fully fledged Romantic theory'.[22] A new account of Romanticism was called for, and a new account of its relation to modernism.

In criticism, the validity of Kermode's thesis was affected by revisionary views of Romanticism. In 'The Rhetoric of Temporality' (1969) Paul de Man argued against the long-held orthodoxy which placed the *symbol* (and with it, imagination) at the centre of Romantic poetics.[23] The symbol had become central, he argued, only by the suppression of the role of *allegory* in Romantic texts. The doctrine of symbol insisted upon there being continuity between part and whole, while allegory had been condemned by Romantic poets for its discontinuity and 'thinness'. The orthodoxy had established, in Jonathan Culler's words, 'a simple and questionable historical scheme that opposes an ambitious and deluded Romanticism, committed to an organic theory of imagination and to the possibility of continuity between form and meaning, with an ironic, self-conscious Modernism that arises by questioning these assumptions'.[24] Critics after de Man had shown that it was possible to read Romantic poets as being as ironic, self-conscious, and allegorical as their modernist successors. It was difficult, after de Man, for critics to use the term 'symbol' unselfconsciously.[25]

Marjorie Perloff's 1982 essay 'Pound/Stevens: Whose Era?' is informed directly by the question of projectivist poetics, and by tropological readings such as that by Herbert Schneidau; though de Man is not an explicit presence, his work offers a significant context for a critical reading of Perloff's account of modernism. In her 1981 collection of essays *The Poetics of Indeterminacy*, Perloff had argued for the existence of an 'anti-symbolist' tradition which had always been part of modernism, and which the development of the new poetics had made increasingly relevant. The shift from symbolist to anti-symbolist aesthetics was closely connected to the revaluation of Ezra Pound: Pound's rising reputation was both cause, in that a new theory of poetry was required to explain his work and that of his followers, and effect, in that new theories of poetry made sense of him for the first time.

When Kermode was writing *Romantic Image*, Pound's centrality to modernism was not so assured as it is at the present day. His support for Italian Fascism was a recent memory. The materials that would help critics to reassess his significance, such as T. S. Eliot's edition of his *Literary Essays* (1954), had not been fully absorbed. Though Pound had been central to the imagist movement, Kermode suggested that the aesthetics of Pound's later *Cantos* were a dead end. Pound, like Hulme and Mallarmé, seemed obscurely to wish that poetry could be made of something non-discursive, something 'other than words' (p.136). Pound's difficulty arose when he tried to construct a long poem on principles derived from Imagism. Kermode concedes that the whole of *The Cantos* might be understood as 'one vast image' (p.136), but argues that a long poem needs discursive 'binding matter' (p.137). In the absence of such linking, explanatory material, the long poem 'may be nothing but a confused heap of words'; in a long poem, the 'purgation of discourse' can produce only 'a disaster' (p.118).

By 1982 Pound's position was more secure. As Perloff's subtitle indicates, this was largely due to Hugh Kenner's massive study of Pound's literary works and networks, *The Pound Era* (1971), though Donald Davie's *Pound* (1975), more modest in scale, was also significant. However, Perloff's discussion takes as its starting point a continuing uncertainty about the status of both Pound and Stevens within modernism, and about the nature of modernism itself.

Extract from Marjorie Perloff, 'Pound/Stevens: Whose Era?' *New Literary History*, 13 (1982), pp.485–95.

On 26 October 1955 William Carlos Williams wrote to Ezra Pound at St Elizabeth's, asking him if he would care to comment on the obituary essay he had just written on Wallace Stevens, then two months dead, for *Poetry* magazine. Pound replied:

> … as to yr/ pal/ Wally S/…. it wd/ be highly improper for
> me to have opinions of yr/ opinion of a bloke I haven't read
>   and DOUBT like all hell
> that yu will be able to PURR-suade me to venture on
>   with such a
> hellUVAlot I don't know and WANT to find out.[1]

If this sounds unnecessarily dismissive, compare it to Stevens's curiously similar response to Pound. In 1947 Theodore Weiss invited Stevens to write something for a special Pound issue of the fledgling *Quarterly Review of Literature*. Stevens replied curtly: 'Nothing doing about Pound. I should have to saturate myself with the work and I have not the time'.[2]

Time for you and time for me – it seems that neither Pound nor Stevens could allow for it. We, reading these two great Modernists in the late decades of the twentieth century, tend to ignore such mutual distrust, positing that *of course* Pound and Stevens are among the four or five great American poets of the century. Literary historians and anthologists continue to give them roughly equal time, thus following the practice established by the New Criticism in the forties and fifties: Randall Jarrell, R. P. Blackmur, Allen Tate, and such of their followers as William Van O'Connor, Babette Deutsch, and Sr. Bernetta Quinn wrote respectfully – if also quite critically – about both poets. So, for that matter, did the great counter-critic of this period, Yvor Winters.[3] Yet by the late sixties, the very real gap between Pound and Stevens – a gap that perhaps no inclusive definition of Modernism can quite close – had become apparent; the alliance posited by the critics but never by the poets themselves was falling apart. 'The Pound Era', Hugh Kenner called the first half of our century, dismissing Stevens in 2 of his almost 600 pages as having created 'an Edward Lear poetic pushed toward all limits'. Kenner wrote: 'The gods have never left us.[4] Nothing we know the mind to have known has ever left us. Quickened by hints, the mind can know it again, and make it new. Romantic Time no longer thickens our sight, time receding, bearing visions away. Our books of cave paintings are the emblems of its abolition, perhaps the Pound Era's chief theme, and the literary consolidation of that theme stands as the era's achievement'.[5] *The Pound Era* appeared in 1971; in *A Map of Misreading* (1975), Harold Bloom retorted: 'Modernism in literature has not passed; rather, it has been exposed as never having been there. Gossip grows old and becomes myth; myth grows older and becomes dogma. Wyndham Lewis, Eliot and Pound gossiped with one another; the New Criticism aged them into a myth of Modernism; now the antiquarian Hugh Kenner has dogmatized this myth into the Pound Era, a canon of accepted titans. Pretenders to godhood Kenner roughly reduces to their mortality; the grand triumph of Kenner is his judgement that Wallace Stevens represented the culmination of the poetics of Edward Lear'.[6] And in *Wallace Stevens: The Poems of Our Climate* (1977), Bloom suggests that it is high time to call the period in question 'the Age of Stevens (or shall we say the Stevens Era?)'.[7]

This is neither an idle quarrel nor a narrow sectarian war between rival academics (e.g., Bloom, Hillis Miller, Helen Vendler, Frank Kermode in the Stevens camp; Kenner, Donald Davie, Guy Davenport, Christine Brooke-Rose among Poundians) who just happen to have different literary and political allegiances. The split goes deep, and its very existence raises what I take to be central questions about the meaning of Modernism – indeed about the meaning of poetry itself in current literary history and theory.

What prompts those who believe in the Stevens Era to ignore or dismiss Pound? In a recent study of Stevens, Lucy Beckett gives us a neatly reductive version of the anti-Pound myth. The *Cantos*, she argues, are a failure because Pound does not sufficiently resist what Stevens calls 'the pressure of reality': 'The fragments of [Pound's] own experience and of the civilizations, literatures and histories that have caught his attention remain a shifting heap of splinters. ... Aware of technique only, not of the poet's responsibility to the disciplined use of language, he is hardly aware at all of the poet's responsibility in respect of thought. ... The problems of belief and value in a world without established systems of truth, the search for 'what will suffice', the poet's task envisaged by such as Arnold and Santayana, concern him very little. In this sense he is a most unmodern poet'.[8] A 'modern poet', it seems, is one who understands his responsibilities to 'thought' rather than to 'technique', and 'thought' somehow has to do with the examination of 'belief and value in a world without established systems of truth'. Accordingly, 'the *Cantos*, that colossal attempt to master reality with *persistence of method* rather than with *persistence of thought*, remains the saddest of modern defeats'.[9]

Naively put as is this argument, Lucy Beckett's assumptions are quite in keeping with, say, Harold Bloom's repeated insistence that, in Emerson's words, 'it is not meter but a meter-making argument that makes a poem'. And not just any meter-making argument but especially one that entails the search for 'what will suffice' in a world 'without established systems of truth'. 'Pound's *Cantos*,' writes Geoffrey Hartman, 'remain a nostalgic montage without unity, a picaresque of styles'. By contrast, in Stevens 'the music left in the wake of the gods' demise is a great poetry, though limited by its very power to console'.[10] In a similar vein, Helen Vendler concludes her important book on Stevens by praising 'the short late poems ... those liquid lingerings in which the angel of reality transforms, for a moment, the bleak continuo of life's tragic drone'.[11] And Walton Litz observes: 'Unlike Ezra Pound's *Cantos* ... Stevens' final *mundo* is neither eccentric nor private. It is built upon the central reality of our age, the death of the gods and of the great coordinating mythologies, and in their place it offers the austere satisfactions of a 'self' dependent on the pure poetry of the physical world, a 'self' whose terrifying lack of belief is turned into a source of freedom. The final achievement of Wallace Stevens is a poetry of exclusions and denials which makes a sustaining fiction out of the search for irreducible reality'.[12] Carried one step further, we get this formulation from Harold Bloom: '[Stevens's] major phase, from 1942 to his death in 1955, gave us a canon of poems themselves more advanced as *interpretation* than our criticism as yet has gotten to be'.[13]

But Poundians have never claimed that their poet is great because his work constitutes an advanced form of 'interpretation'. Indeed, *poetry*, not to speak of *modern poetry*, is defined quite differently in discussions of Pound. Let me begin by comparing the ways critics have talked about two famous texts: Stevens's *Notes toward a Supreme Fiction* (1942), specifically the Canon Aspirin poems (Pt. III, cantos 5–8), and Pound's Canto LXXXI (1945), specifically the first ninety-five lines.[14] In confronting the Canon Aspirin with the Padré José Elizondo of the *Pisan Cantos*, we may come to a clearer sense of why the division between Pound and Stevens continues to haunt our own sense of Modernism.

II

Notes toward a Supreme Fiction is often called Stevens's greatest poem. Of Part III, 'It Must Give Pleasure,' Frank Kermode wrote in 1960: 'These two hundred lines of verse seem to me to give continuously a higher delight than anything of comparable length written in this century'. And more specifically, 'The complex and majestic Canon Aspirin poems ... raise the temperature of the whole work and justify not only the sober ecstasies of the conclusion but the immense and beautiful claims for poetry made in III. viii: if the poet creates an angel (and he has just done so) is not his joy equal to the angel's?' Kermode now quotes the entire eighth canto ('What am I to believe? ...') and concludes, 'The power of this is great in isolation; in its context, as sequel to the previous poem, it is overwhelming. ... the whole work exists in a radiant and productive atmosphere, saying the words of the world that are the life of the world'.[15]

'The words of the world that are the life of the world' – in his first major study of *Notes toward a Supreme Fiction* in 1963, Harold Bloom echoes this judgment: 'The Supreme Fiction ... enters the poem in the exhilarating person of the Canon Aspirin, Stevens' finest invention. The Canon is the cure for our current headache of unreality. ... In his activity the Canon first becomes the angel of reality, then is tempted too far in his benevolent impositions, and finally is surpassed by the poet himself, who discovers an order that his created angel could only impose'.[16] The opening of canto 5 ('We drank Meursault, ate lobster Bombay with mango / Chutney') is praised for its 'deceptive inconsequence', deceptive because the poem's vision is 'fiercely Romantic'. Bloom goes on to explain the symbolism of this canto: the Canon's sister stands for 'seeing the very thing itself and nothing else'; as such, her limited vision must be transcended, as it is in canto 6, whose 'thesis' (Bloom's word) is 'the Canon's quest toward an integration of all reality, fact and thought together'. Further, 'Section VII is the antithesis, presenting the Canon's surrender of his quest to the angelic impatience that imposes rather than discovers order. The synthesis is in Section VIII, which one does not hesitate to call Stevens' finest poem, where the poet's discovery of reality is both given and celebrated' (Borroff, p. 92).

The Canon's choice between reality and imagination in canto 6 is, according to Bloom, 'heroic', because he ultimately refuses to 'reject either order':

> He had to choose. But it was not a choice
> Between excluding things. It was not a choice
> Between, but of. He chose to include the things
> That in each other are included, the whole,
> The complicate, the amassing harmony.
>
> 　　　　　　　　　　[*Notes*, Pt. III, canto 6]

This choice, says Bloom, is 'Wordsworthian rather than Blakean, for it insists that the context of fact or nature can be harmonized with the more exuberant context of the poet's apocalyptic desires'. Thus after the 'extraordinary emotional progression' that leads the poet to the desperation of canto 7 ('It is possible, possible, possible. It must / Be possible'), Stevens 'gives us his ultimate poem, the supreme achievement of post-Romanticism and the culmination of Coleridgean and Blakean poetic theory'. The angel poem (canto 8) surpasses the *Prelude* in its courage 'to cross into this desperately triumphant poetic humanism' (Borroff, p. 94).

When Bloom returns to *Notes* more than a decade later in his *Poems of Our Climate*, he reads the poem according to the revisionary ratios and the theory of crossings he has formulated in the interim, but his response to it remains essentially unchanged; indeed, he now goes further in relating the Canon Aspirin to 'a high Romantic fallen angel, a morning star', and argues that 'the name "Aspirin" probably plays upon the archaic meaning of "aspires," the *andersstreben* of Pater's *"All art constantly aspires toward the condition of music,"* or the upward-rising of Blake's "On what wings dare he aspire"'. Further, '"Aspire" goes back to the Latin for "breaking upon, desiring, favoring," and ...we can translate "the Canon Aspirin" as the self-defining, self-describing human desire for a beyond, even if that beyond turns out to be an abyss' (p. 205).

Whether or not we agree with Bloom's interpretation of the Canon Aspirin poems is, I think, less important than what that interpretation tells us about Bloom's central assumptions about poetry. We might note, to begin with, that Bloom's value judgments – his use, for example, of such adjectives as 'exhilarating', 'moving', 'strenuously heroic', 'supreme', 'splendid', and 'extraordinarily emotional' – refer always to what the poet is saying rather than to how he says it. The poem's sound structure, for example, is treated as a mere irrelevancy, as is the syntax of Stevens's cantos and even, to a large extent, their diction. Would it matter, say, if we substituted 'poor' or 'paler' for 'pauvred' in Part V, canto 6? If 'closelier' in line 12 of the same canto became 'closer'? What is the effect of repeating 'paint' three times in the lines, 'The way a painter of pauvred colors paints. / But still she painted them'? Such questions are never raised because they have no real bearing on what Bloom takes to be the only question a Great Questioner should ask, namely, what is it that Stevens tells us in this poem? In the Coda to *Poems of Our Climate*, he says: 'Why do we read one poet rather than another? We believe the lies we want to believe because they help us to survive. Similarly, we read (reread) the poems that keep our discourse with ourselves going. Strong poems strengthen us by teaching us *how to talk to ourselves*, rather than how to talk to others' (p. 387; italics are Bloom's). Which is to say that the greatness of Stevens's poetry is a function of the 'desperately triumphant ... humanism' that Bloom believes in. *Notes* teaches us 'how to talk to ourselves', provided that we happen to share its sense of strenuous quest for the 'Supreme Fiction'.

There are two corollaries. First, Stevens's poetic truth is a 'late plural of Romantic tradition' – a condition assumed to be the only proper one for modern poets. To call *Notes toward a Supreme Fiction* Wordsworthian or Blakean or Keatsian is equivalent to calling the poem Good or True or Beautiful. Secondly, in its belatedness, *Notes* paradoxically betters Blake and Wordsworth and the Keats of *The Fall of Hyperion*, for it 'cultivates the highly anti-apocalyptic virtue of patience'.[17] We might restate Bloom's doctrine and its corollaries in the language of *Notes:* (1) It must be Romantic. (2) It must question Romantic premises. (3) It must be Visionary Humanist.

When we turn from Bloom's reading of Stevens to the powerful ones of, say, Hillis Miller or Helen Vendler, we find that, despite a number of conflicting interpretations (Vendler regards Part III, canto 7 of *Notes* as more pessimistic than does Bloom, referring to the 'repetitive, accumulative and hysterical affirmations [that] mount in a crescendo conveying the fear which is their origin'),[18] the central assumptions remain essentially the same. When Miller traces Stevens's gradual evolution from metaphysical dualism and 'representational thinking' to the recognition of the late poems that 'man's spiritual height and depth are available here and now or nowhere', he is reading Stevens along Bloomian lines, although he is much less inclined than Bloom to attribute value to Stevens's particular truths.[19] Again, although Helen Vendler does pay close attention to the linguistic and syntactic strategies of *Notes*, her emphasis, like Bloom's, is on the poem's final refusal 'to resolve theoretical difficulties', its 'strenuous exploration of every possible escape from … self-pity and its literary forms – nostalgia and elegy'.[20] Indeed, in a recent essay on Stevens, Vendler has made her personal predilection for his particular vision quite clear:

> Many of Stevens' poems – read from one angle, most of the best poems – spring from catastrophic disappointment, bitter solitude, or personal sadness. It is understandable that Stevens, a man of chilling reticence, should illustrate his suffering in its largest possible terms. That practice does not obscure the nature of the suffering, which concerns the collapse of early hopeful fantasies of love, companionship, success, and self-transformation. As self and beloved alike become, with greater or lesser velocity, the final dwarfs of themselves, and as social awareness diminishes dreams of self-transcendence, the poet sees dream, hope, love, and trust – those activities of the most august imagination – crippled, contradicted, dissolved, called into question, embittered. This history is the history of every intelligent and receptive human creature as the illimitable claims on existence made by each one of us are checked, baffled, frustrated, and reproved.[21]

What begins as loving description of the poetry, drawing upon Stevens's own vocabulary of final dwarfs and the august imagination, abruptly shifts, in the final sentence, to a statement of moral truth not everyone would endorse. For *is* Stevens's 'history', however accurately Vendler describes it, synonymous with 'the history of every intelligent and receptive human creature'? And, more important, is a given poet's *oeuvre* better for conveying such a history?

I am persuaded that those who regard Stevens as the great poet of the twentieth century would say yes to both questions. Indeed, in adopting such an Arnoldian, which is to say an essentially Romantic, view of poetry, they are, after all, merely giving tacit assent to Stevens's own definition of poetry as 'an unofficial view of being'.[22] In 'The Figure of Youth as a Virile Poet,' Stevens observes: 'In philosophy we attempt to approach truth through the reason. Obviously this is a statement of convenience. If we say that in poetry we attempt to approach truth through the imagination, this, too, is a statement of convenience. We must conceive of poetry as at least the equal of philosophy' (*NA*, p. 41). Despite the modest disclaimers with which he couches this familiar Romantic distinction, Stevens obviously means it. 'The poet's role,' he suggests, 'is to help people to live their lives' (*NA*, p. 28); 'he gives to life the supreme fictions without which we are unable to conceive of it' (*NA*, p. 31). As such, the poet is obviously set apart from all others: 'There is a life apart from politics. It is this life that the youth as virile poet lives, in a kind of radiant and productive atmosphere' (*NA*, p. 57). And, most tellingly, 'Poetry is a part of the structure of reality' (*NA*, p. 81).

These are aphorisms to which Pound would have taken strong exception, opposed as he was to the belief that 'there is a life apart from politics', a special 'radiant and productive atmosphere' in which the 'youth as virile poet' can retreat when he longs to have a final soliloquy with his interior paramour. Poetry must, on the contrary, relate to the whole of a man's life in the real world, which is not to say that it is 'a part of the structure of reality'. For how could it be, given that 'the medium of poetry' is not thoughts but 'WORDS'?[23] Or so Pound construed it.

'The poet,' says Stevens, 'is the priest of the invisible'.[24] It follows that certain discriminations must be made. In 'The Relation of Poetry to Painting', we read: 'Let me divide modern poetry into two classes, one that is modern in respect to what it says, the other that is modern in respect to form. ... The first kind is interested in form but it accepts a banality of form as incidental to its language. Its justification is that in expressing thought or feeling in poetry the purpose of the poet must be to subordinate the mode of expression, that while the value of the poem as a poem depends on expression, it depends primarily on what is expressed' (*NA*, p. 168). In the second class we find, says Stevens, too many poems 'in which the exploitation of form involves nothing more than the use of small letters for capitals, eccentric line-endings, too little or too much punctuation and similar aberrations. These have nothing to do with being alive. They have nothing to do with the conflict between the poet and that of which his poems are made'. And, in casting about for an example, Stevens refers to 'the division, say, between Valéry and Apollinaire' (*NA*, pp. 168–9).

Or, we might say, the division between Stevens himself and Pound, a poet more than fond of 'eccentric line-endings', 'too little punctuation', and 'similar aberrations', a poet in many ways similar to Apollinaire and certainly unlike a late Symboliste like Valéry. Stevens applies the same distinction between matter and manner to himself and Williams in a letter of 1946 to José Rodriguez Feo: 'I have not read Paterson. I have the greatest respect for [Williams], although there is the constant difficulty that he is more interested in the way of saying things than in what he has to say. The fact remains that we are always fundamentally interested in what a writer has to say. When we are sure of that, we pay attention

to the way in which he says it, not often before'.[25] Hugh Kenner, who cites
this passage in his chapter on Stevens and Williams in *A Homemade World*,
comments laconically: 'This is one of the most extraordinary misunderstandings
in literary history'.[26]

If so, it is a misunderstanding that Stevens scholars from Robert Buttel
to Adelaide Kirby Morris have been eager to perpetrate.[27] A concordance of
Stevens criticism, if there were such a thing, would probably show that the
following words had a very high incidence: *being, consciousness, fiction, reality,
self, truth*. These are, of course, Stevens's own words, and the poet's advocates
have adopted them quite naturally. But it does not follow that they have some
sort of absolute value as nodes of critical discourse. Certainly they are not the
words we meet in discussions of the *Cantos*.

III

One of the most interesting treatments of Canto LXXXI is that of
D. S. Carne-Ross, who submits the Canto's first twelve lines to a patient analysis, in dialogue with the students in his Pound seminar. The discussion makes
three main points: (1) the seemingly random elements in the Canto do have
necessary connections: thus line 12, 'and Dolores said, "Come pan, niño," eat
bread me lad', relates back to the divine marriage of sky and earth in line 1,
'Zeus lies in Ceres' bosom', the eating of bread (cereal) being for Pound not
just symbolic as in the Christian sacrament but a *real* part of the Eleusinian
mystery; (2) such connections are curiously elusive just because Pound 'leaves it
to us to put the elements together with the force of a personal discovery'; and
(3) it is incorrect to assume, as does one student in the class, that 'Pound makes
this Elizondo say' such and such, for: 'We are to suppose that Padre Elizondo
really did say this. He is a real man who on two occasions said something to
Pound in his own Castilian Spanish. It is a cardinal principle of the poem that
the materials it presents must be presented exactly as they are or were. A man's
actual words, and as far as possible even the sound of his words, must be reported, the date, location, etc. must be given. As Pound sees it, this is part of the
evidence'.[28]

In other words, the stress is always on what Pound called 'constatation of
fact', however disjunctively those 'facts' are structured in a given Canto. Indeed,
as Carne-Ross concludes:

> What is difficult about Pound's poetry is its 'simplicity' ... the whole reverberating
> dimension of inwardness is missing. There is no murmurous echo chamber where
> deeps supposedly answer to deeps. Not merely does the thing, in Pound's best
> verse, not point beyond itself: *it doesn't point to us*. The green tip that pushes

through the earth in spring does not stand for or symbolize man's power of spiritual renewal. ... Pound's whole effort is *not* to be polysemous but to give back to the literal first level its full significance, its old significance. ... That green thrust is itself the divine event, the fruit of the marriage at Eleusis. Persephone is in that thrusting tip, and if man matters it is because he too has a share in that same power, he too is a part of the seasonal, sacred life of nature. But only a part.[29]

A similar emphasis on what Carne-Ross calls 'Pound's offense against the great principle of inwardness, of internalisation that has put us at the center of things and laid waste the visible world' is to be found in the criticism of Guy Davenport, Donald Davie, and Hugh Kenner. Davenport, like Carne-Ross a classical scholar, argues that, unlike nineteenth-century poets 'who put everything against the scale of time and discovered that all behavior within time's monolinear progress was evolutionary. ... It was Pound's determination ... to treat what had become a world of ghosts as a world eternally present'. The first line of Canto LXXXI is, accordingly, meant quite literally: 'The myth of Persephone is here and now, in civilization's rhythm of inevitable decay and conscious renewal'.[30] Donald Davie, commenting on the 'wasp' passage in the neighboring Canto LXXXIII, makes a related case: 'At no point does the wasp become a symbol for something in Pound's predicament, or for his ethical and other programs, or for his personality. The wasp retains its otherness, as an independent form of life. ... Pound's repeated assertion that the paradisal is *real*, out there in the real world, is a conscious challenge to the whole symbolist aesthetic'.[31] And Hugh Kenner refers repeatedly to what he calls Pound's 'move out of Symbolism':[32] 'In shifting his interest ... from the articulation of personae to the observation of epiphanic events, Pound was participating in the major intellectual *peripeteia* of the past eighty years, the desertion of the windowless monadic world of pigeonholed 'subjects' for a lively explorer's interest in particulars, that one can grasp simultaneously, as from a moving ship, the relative and the continuous'.[33]

Which is to say that Padre José Elizondo (whose wise words about the difference between 'catoli*th*ismo' and 'ReliHion' and about the probable demise of 'los reyes' pick up key motifs from earlier Cantos) cannot be translated into something else in the sense that Harold Bloom speaks of 'translat[ing] the Canon Aspirin as the self-defining, self-describing human desire for a beyond, even if that beyond turns out to be an abyss'. As Stevens himself sums up the difference, 'The bare image and the image as symbol are the contrast' (*OP*, p. 161). For Stevens, as for Stevensian critics, 'Poetry as an imaginative thing consists of more than lies on the surface' (*OP*, p. 161). Poundians, on the other hand, are reluctant to generalize about *poetry;* rather, they want to show how *modern* poetry gives renewed attention precisely to what 'lies on the surface'.

The first step in dealing with that surface is, of course, to track down Pound's endlessly teasing allusions. Why does 'Taishan' appear in line 2 of Canto LXXXI? Because the high peak seen from his prison cell at Pisa reminds the poet of the sacred mountain of China, the home of the Great Emperor.[34] And where does the Mount Taishan motif reappear? Some sixty lines later, when 'Benin' (the friendly Black soldier whose face reminds Pound of a Benin bronze) supplies him with a 'table ex packing box', a gift 'light as the branch of Kuanon'. Kuanon is the daughter of the Emperor, the Chinese goddess of mercy. To make connections between these references is to discover, not a cluster of possible meanings as in the case of the Canon Aspirin and his sister, but rather the way the *structure* of Pound's long poem works.

Notes

1. Pound to Williams, 27 October 1955. Previously unpublished letter by Ezra Pound, Copyright © 1982 by the Trustees of the Ezra Pound Literary Property Trust. Reprinted by permission of the Collection of American Literature, Beinecke Rare Book and Manuscript Library, Yale University. The obituary essay appeared in *Poetry*, 87, No. 4 (January 1956), 234–9.
2. *Letters of Wallace Stevens*, ed. Holly Stevens (New York, 1966), p. 565.
3. In *Forms of Discovery* (Denver, 1967), Winters criticized Pound's 'associational' method but declared that 'eccentric for eccentric, I would rather read the Pound of the early *Cantos* than the Spenser of *The Faerie Queene*'. As for Stevens, Winters argued (in *Primitivism and Decadence* [New York, 1937] and in *The Anatomy of Nonsense* [Norfolk, Conn., 1943]) that 'Sunday Morning' is one of the great poems written in English, but that after 'Sunday Morning' Stevens's style declined into obscurantism and the emotional confusions of Romantic irony.
4. Hugh Kenner's phrase 'the gods' derives from *The Cantos* 113/787:17. Geoffrey Hartman's reference to 'the gods' demise' is a more general reference to an era of unbelief.
5. *The Pound Era* (Berkeley and Los Angeles, 1971), pp. 516–17, 554.
6. *A Map of Misreading* (New York, 1975), p. 28.
7. *Wallace Stevens: The Poems of Our Climate* (Ithaca and London, 1977), p. 152.
8. Lucy Beckett, *Wallace Stevens* (Cambridge, 1974), pp. 62–4.
9. Beckett, p. 64; italics mine.
10. 'Toward Literary History,' in *Beyond Formalism: Literary Essays 1958–1970* (New Haven and London, 1970), p. 358, and 'Spectral Symbolism,' in *The Fate of Reading and Other Essays* (Chicago and London, 1975), p. 59.
11. *On Extended Wings: Wallace Stevens' Longer Poems* (Cambridge, Mass., 1969), p. 314.
12. *Introspective Voyager: The Poetic Development of Wallace Stevens* (New York, 1972), p. vi.
13. *Poems of Our Climate*, p. 168.

14. The texts used are *The Collected Poems of Wallace Stevens* (New York, 1954), pp. 401–5, subsequently cited as *CP*, and *The Cantos of Ezra Pound* (New York, 1971), pp. 517–19.

15. *Wallace Stevens* (Edinburgh and London, 1967), pp. 117–19.

16. 'Notes toward a Supreme Fiction: A Commentary,' in *Wallace Stevens: A Collection of Critical Essays*, ed. Marie Borroff (Englewood Cliffs, N.J., 1963), p. 19.

17. 'Notes toward a Supreme Fiction,' Borroff, p. 19.

18. *On Extended Wings*, p. 197.

19. *Poets of Reality: Six Twentieth-Century Writers* (1965; rpt. New York, 1969), p. 283. Such distrust of thematics has become more marked in Miller's more recent deconstructionist essays on Stevens. See, e.g., 'Stevens' *Rock* and Criticism as Cure,' *Georgia Review*, 30 (1976), 330–48.

20. *On Extended Wings*, p. 205.

21. 'Apollo's Harsher Songs' (1979), in her *Part of Nature, Part of Us: Modern American Poets* (Cambridge, Mass., 1980), pp. 41–2.

22. *The Necessary Angel: Essays on Reality and the Imagination* (1951; rpt. New York, 1965), p. 40, subsequently cited as *NA*.

23. *ABC of Reading* (1934; rpt. New York, 1960), p. 46, subsequently cited as *ABC*.

24. *Adagia*, in *Opus Posthumous* (New York, 1957), p. 169, subsequently cited as *OP*.

25. *Letters of Wallace Stevens*, p. 544.

26. *A Homemade World* (New York, 1975), p. 55.

27. Buttel, *Wallace Stevens: The Making of Harmonium* (Princeton, 1967), p. x; Adelaide Kirby Morris, *Wallace Stevens: Imagination and Faith* (Princeton, 1974).

28. 'The Music of a Lost Dynasty: Pound in the Classroom,' *Boston University Journal*, 21 (Winter 1973), 26–7.

29. 'Music of a Lost Dynasty,' pp. 38–9; italics are Carne-Ross's.

30. 'Persephone's Ezra,' in *New Approaches to Ezra Pound*, ed. Eva Hesse (Berkeley and Los Angeles, 1969), pp. 157, 161.

31. *Ezra Pound: Poet as Sculptor* (New York, 1964), pp. 176–7, 181.

32. See *The Pound Era*, pp. 133, 136.

33. *The Poetry of Ezra Pound* (New York, 1951), p. 105.

34. See George Kearns, *Guide to Ezra Pound's Selected Cantos* (New Brunswick, N.J., 1980), p. 168.

* * *

Perloff goes on to survey the ways in which critics have understood Pound's use of structure as a meaningful element in itself. She notes that whereas in Stevens criticism, the key words are '*imagination, consciousness, being* and *self*', for Poundians, they are 'terms like *precision, particularity, image, technique, structure, invention*' (p.496). Stevens's poems are valued by their admirers for stating a 'chastened, qualified, and ironic form, of the Romantic position' (p.498). Even Stevens's long poems such as 'Notes toward a Supreme Fiction' employ the conventions of lyric: 'a solitary voice speaks out of a single moment in time, interiorizing as ambiguity conflicts that would, in fiction or drama, be allocated to discrete characters' (pp.498–9). The collage form of *The Cantos*, on the other hand, departs radically from such assumptions.

Extract from Marjorie Perloff, 'Pound/Stevens: Whose Era?', pp.504–6.

V

Let me now return to my original questions: What do we mean when we talk of Modernism in poetry? And, more important, what are our present norms for the 'great poem'?

To posit that ours is, in Harold Bloom's words, the Age of Stevens is to believe that, as he puts it, 'Modernism in literature has not passed; rather it has been exposed as never having been there'. The best twentieth-century poetry, in other words, carries on the great tradition of Romantic visionary humanism, a tradition Anglo-American to its roots, with a slight influx of French Symbolisme to add piquancy. Such poetry takes the lyric paradigm for granted; it answers to the demand for organic unity and symbolic structure, avoiding all contact with the language of ordinary prose and therefore with the prose discourses of the novel and of historical writing. Despite this emphasis on the poem as a special kind of discourse, as sacred text whose language is inherently different from, say, such texts as Stevens's own letters and diaries, the Stevens text subordinates such traditional lyric features as meter and qualitative sound repetition to the articulation of complex and ambiguous meanings. In keeping with the Romantic model, the 'I' of Stevens is a Solitary Singer; his voice, even at its most whimsical or ironic, is never less than serious about the truths for which it searches; the tone is meditative and subdued; the addressee is always the poet himself. For Stevens, 'Poetry and materia poetica are interchangeable terms', and so the emphasis, both of the poet and of his critics, is on the creation of the Supreme Fiction, the poet's evolving consciousness as it comes to terms with what Bloom calls the 'three crossings' central to the Romantic 'crisis-poem' – the loss of the creative gift (am I still a poet?), the loss of love (am I still capable of loving another beside myself?), and the loss of life itself (am I capable of resisting the death instinct?).[1] These are 'crossings' that, according to Bloom as well as to Helen Vendler and other Stevensians, all intelligent and receptive human creatures experience. In this sense, poetry clearly *matters;* it teaches us 'how to talk to ourselves'.

Poundians, of course, also believe that poetry *matters*, but in a very different sense. They regard Modernism less as a continuation of Romanticism than as a very real rupture with it. 'Keatsian', an honorific word for Bloom or Kermode or Hartman or Vendler, is, as we have seen in the case of Davie's essay on Stevens, a derogatory term. Instead – and perhaps curiously – we meet in Pound criticism such words as 'Augustan' and 'Enlightenment'. Thus Kenner compares Pound's Confucian sense of history, with its 'reconciliation of a loving feeling for detail with a search for eternal, archetypal situations', to that of the Augustans,[2] and Davie argues that Pound's America is 'the America of the Founding Fathers, Jefferson and John Adams ... specifically an Enlightenment product, a transplanting to American soil of the noblest values of that French eighteenth century which had also as a matter of historical record first introduced Europe to the experience of Confucian and pre-Confucian China'.[3]

The point, in any case, is to bypass Romanticism, to get back to something *prior* in time even as one is MAKING IT NEW. Surely it is no coincidence that Pound scholars have so often been classicists – D. S. Carne-Ross, J. P. Sullivan, Guy Davenport – or trained in medieval studies like Eva Hesse and Christine Brooke-Rose, or in Augustan literature like Davie and Kenner in their different ways. For all these critics, the Pound Era is the era when the norms of the Romantic crisis poem as of the Symbolist lyric were exploded, when poetry found that it could once again incorporate the seemingly alien discourses of prose without losing its identity. It is curious, in this regard, to compare Pound's prose to that of Stevens. From *Gaudier-Brzeska* (1916) to *Guide to Kulchur* (1938) and beyond, Pound's critical prose is closely allied to his poetry by its structural properties: collage, fragmentation, parataxis. Again, the letters of the later years adopt all the stylistic oddities of the *Cantos:* phonetic spelling, the insertion of foreign phrases, documentary evidence, puns and other jokes, the juxtaposition of disjunctive images. The Romantic and Symbolist distinction between literary and ordinary language is thus blurred: the rule is that anything goes as long as the poet knows, in Charles Olson's words, how to 'keep it moving', how to make the poem an energy discharge, a field of action. The *how*, for Poundians, thus becomes more interesting than the *what:* if poetry teaches us how to talk to ourselves, it is not because it provides us with a vision of Reality but because its processes imitate the processes of the external world as we have come to know it.

The Pound critics do not, then, equate poetry with lyric; rather, they return to the Aristotelian definition of *poiesis* as *mimesis praxeos*, the imitation of an action. The eclectic nature of the *Cantos*, their capacity to assimilate all kinds of material and to incorporate many voices, makes more sense when we read Pound's text against, say, the *Satyricon* or *Le Neveu de Rameau* than when Pound's 'poem including history' is compared to *The Prelude* or *Song of Myself.* Again, with respect to Pound's contemporaries, the *Cantos* are closer to the poetry of Apollinaire or the Merz pictures of Kurt Schwitters than they are to the poetry of Yeats or Frost or even Eliot. Yeats, we remember, was convinced that Pound had not got 'all the wine into the bowl'.[4]

Read synchronically, against the backdrop of the avant-garde arts of Europe in the period *entre deux guerres*, Pound's structures seem quintessentially modern. Read diachronically, against the paradigm of the Anglo-American lyric from Blake to Emerson to Emily Dickinson, Pound will seem, as he did to Stevens, 'an eccentric person'. A 'Last Romantic' and a 'First Modern' – William Carlos Williams, who was able to appreciate Stevens's 'discipline' even as he admired Pound's experimentation and invention,[5] bridged the gap between the two by finding a third party to vilify. That party was, of course, T. S. Eliot, a bloke whose work both Pound and Stevens had been reading since its inception. But then no one today, whether we look to critics like Bloom or Kenner or Vendler or to poets like John Ashbery or James Merrill or Adrienne Rich or Allen Ginsberg, seems eager to call the first half of the twentieth century the Eliot Era. And thereby hangs another tale – a tale whose telling will help us to work out the puzzle which is Modernism.

Notes

1. Bloom, *Wallace Stevens: The Poems of our Climate*, pp.375–406.
2. Kenner, *The Pound Era*, p.434.
3. Davie, *Ezra Pound: Poet as Sculptor*, p.72.
4. W. B. Yeats, Introduction, *The Oxford Book of Modern Verse, 1892–1935* (1936; Oxford, 1966), p.xxvi.
5. See Williams, 'Wallace Stevens,' *Poetry*, 87, no.4 (Jan. 1956), 234–39.

* * *

In a revised version of the essay in her collection *The Dance of the Intellect*, Perloff offers an answer to the question of why modernism is not known as 'The Eliot Era':

> Perhaps this is the case because Eliot's poetry does not as fully pose the question that came to obsess Modernism: whether poetry should be lyric or collage, meditation or encyclopedia, the still moment or the jagged fragment. It is, as Gregory Ulmer points out, the larger aesthetic dichotomy at the heart of Modernism, the dichotomy between what Kandinsky called the 'two poles' – the expressionist and the constructionist. Not until the sixties did the balance begin to tip in favor of the latter.[26]

It should be noted that the term 'expressionist' here refers to an aesthetics of the expressive, individual lyric voice, and not to the movement that stands in contrast to 'impressionism'. Indeed, Perloff's 'constructionist' seems closer to the other 'expressionism', with its belief that it is 'harder to make than to copy'.

While it is clear from Perloff's concluding paragraph that the poetry of Williams and other post- or late modernists informs her assessment of Pound, the relation of her essay to 'The Rhetoric of Temporality' is harder to gauge. There is a broad resemblance, in that both Perloff and de Man see schools of poetry in tropological terms; moreover, like de Man, she demotes symbol. However, she does not explicitly reference de Man, and, while the literalism of Pound's poetic has some similarities with the 'thinness' of allegory, it is explicitly *not* allegorical. Moreover, in Perloff's account Pound had not abandoned the Romantic quest for the 'translucence of the eternal through and in the temporal'.[27] He had broken with the methods of symbolism without abandoning its aims.

Though the question of modernism's relation to Romanticism begins in a question of literary history, of how much the art of one era owes to the art of the past, it leads to several of the other fundamental problems considered in Part 1. T. E. Hulme's rejection of the expressive element in Romanticism implies an impersonal relation between the art-work and its creator, while his separation of literary and religious forms of knowledge, and of the spilling over of the religious 'infinite' into the literary text, implies that literature cannot seek to justify itself to modernity by affiliating itself with religion. Kermode's approach to the symbol as magical knowledge, on the other hand, implies that modernists were doing just that: in writing symbolist works, they were suggesting that instrumental rationality was insufficient to an understanding of the whole of experience. More recent developments have suggested that, although modernist texts seek to embody a wider knowledge of the world than can be achieved by instrumental reason, they do not seek to do so exclusively through the medium of symbolism. Moreover, if we seek to understand their works with ideas such as 'voice', 'being', and 'imagination', we will fundamentally misunderstand them.

Chapter Notes

1. K. Csengeri, ed., *The Collected Writings of T. E. Hulme* (Oxford: Clarendon, 1994), 59.
2. T. E. Hulme, 'Romanticism and Classicism', in K. Csengeri, ed., *Collected Writings*, 61.
3. Hulme, 'Romanticism and Classicism', 62.
4. Hulme, 'Romanticism and Classicism', 62.
5. Hulme, 'Romanticism and Classicism', 62–63.
6. Hulme, 'Romanticism and Classicism', 62.
7. Hulme 'Romanticism and Classicism', 66.
8. T. S. Eliot, 'The Idea of a Literary Review', *The New Criterion*, 4, no.1 (Jan. 1926), 1–6 (p.5); *For Lancelot Andrewes* (London: Faber and Gwyer, 1928), ix; 'Second

Thoughts about Humanism' [1929], in *Selected Essays*, 3rd edn, (London: Faber and Faber, 1951), 490–1; 'Baudelaire' [1930], *Selected Essays*, 424, 427; *After Strange Gods* (London: Faber and Faber, 1934), 25–9.

9. James Joyce, *A Portrait of the Artist as a Young Man* (1916), ed. Seamus Deane (London: Penguin, 1992), 233.

10. T. S. Eliot, 'Tradition and the Individual Talent' (1919), *Selected Essays*, 21.

11. Ezra Pound, 'A Retrospect' and 'The Hard and Soft in French Poetry', in T. S. Eliot, ed., *Literary Essays of Ezra Pound* (London: Faber and Faber, 1954), 4, 285–9.

12. Edmund Wilson, *Axel's Castle* (New York: Charles Scribner's Sons, 1931), 2.

13. Wilson, *Axel's Castle*, 6.

14. Wilson, *Axel's Castle*, 21.

15. Cleanth Brooks, *Modern Poetry and the Tradition* (1939; London: Editions Poetry London, 1948), 62–8.

16. René Wellek, *A History of Modern Criticism: 1750–1950*, 8 vols. (London: Jonathan Cape, 1955–92), 6, 106-7, 121.

17. Frank Kermode, *Romantic Image* (London: Routledge and Kegan Paul, 1957), 1–2.

18. T. S. Eliot's remarks are anthologized by Christopher Ricks in *Inventions of the March Hare* (London: Faber and Faber, 1996), Appendix D, section vi.

19. Walter Benjamin, 'The Work of Art in the Age of Mechanical Reproduction', in Hannah Arendt, ed., *Illuminations*, tr. Harry Zohn (1970; London: Fontana, 1992), 211–44.

20. Theodor Adorno, *Aesthetic Theory*, tr. Robert Hullot-Kentor (1997; London: Continuum, 2002), 5.

21. Charles Altieri, 'Olson's Poetics and the Tradition', *boundary 2*, 2, no.1–2 (1973), 173–88 (p.179). See also: Robert Kern, 'Composition as Recognition: Robert Creeley and Postmodern Poetics', *boundary 2*, 6, no.3 (1978), 211–32; Joseph N. Riddel, 'Decentering the Image: The "Project" of "American" Poetics?' *boundary 2*, 8, no. 1 (Autumn, 1979), 159–88.

22. David Antin, 'Modernism and Postmodernism: Approaching the Present in American Poetry', *boundary 2*, 1, no.1 (Autumn, 1972), 98–133 (p.122).

23. Paul de Man, 'The Rhetoric of Temporality', in *Blindness and Insight*, 2nd edn (London: Methuen, 1983), 187–228.

24. Jonathan Culler, *The Pursuit of Signs* (London: Routledge, 1981), 64.

25. Arden Reed, 'Introduction', in A. Reed, ed., *Romanticism and Language* (Ithaca: Cornell University Press, 1984), 17.

26. Marjorie Perloff, *The Dance of the Intellect: Studies in the Poetry of the Pound Tradition* (Cambridge: Cambridge University Press, 1985), 23.

27. S. T. Coleridge, qtd by de Man, 'Rhetoric of Temporality', 192.

Further Reading

Imagism and Symbolism

Chadwick, Charles. *Symbolism*, Critical Idiom, 16 (London: Methuen, 1971). A brief and straightforward introduction to the symbolist movement.

Levenson, Michael H. *A Genealogy of Modernism: A Study of English Literary Doctrine, 1908–1922* (Cambridge: Cambridge University Press, 1984). Several chapters examine the contribution of Imagism to high modernism.

Schneidau, Herbert. 'Pound and Yeats: The Question of Symbolism', *ELH*, 32 (1965), 220–37.

Stead, C. K. *The New Poetic* (London: Hutchinson, 1964). Broadly in agreement with Kermode, but wishes to give greater emphasis to the social and public function of poetry in the modern movement; interested in the balance between private and public responsibilities.

——. *Pound, Yeats, Eliot, and the Modernist Movement* (Basingstoke: Macmillan, 1986). Pp.34–56 consider the symbolist inheritance of modernist poetry, while pp.75–7 discuss *Romantic Image*.

Symons, Arthur. *The Symbolist Movement in Literature* (London: Heinemann, 1988). An influential work. Symons lightly revised the text for the 1908 Constable edition, which was the one seen by T. S. Eliot, and revised it extensively for the 1919 edition. The 1958 Dutton edition reprints in the 1908 text, and has an introduction by Richard Ellmann on the books' significance.

Von Hallberg, Robert. 'Libertarian Imagism'. *Modernism / Modernity*, 2, no.2 (1995), 63–79.

Modernism and Romanticism

Abrams, M. H. *The Correspondent Breeze: Essays on English Romanticism* (New York: Norton, 1984). Includes Abrams's essays 'Coleridge, Baudelaire, and Modernist Poetics' and 'Structure and Style in the Greater Romantic Lyric': the latter does not discuss modernism, but has been a key point of reference in later criticism.

Bayley, John. *The Romantic Survival: A Study in Poetic Evolution* (London: Constable, 1957). A study of the romantic legacy in Yeats, Auden, and Dylan Thomas.

Bloom, Harold. *Yeats* (New York: Oxford University Press, 1970). Bloom argues that Yeats was fundamentally Romantic, indebted to the poetic form of the quest. Does not directly engage with Kermode's thesis.

Bornstein, George. *Transformations of Romanticism in Yeats, Eliot, and Stevens* (Chicago: University of Chicago Press, 1976).

—— ed. *Romantic and Modern: Revaluations of Literary Tradition* (Pittsburgh: University of Pittsburgh Press, 1977). The essays tend to deal with poets on a case-by-case basis; the role of theory in revising Romanticism is not made explicit.

De Man, Paul. Blindness and Insight, 2nd edition (Minneapolis: University of Minnesota Press, and London: Methuen, 1983). Includes 'The Rhetoric of Temporality' and 'Literary History and Literary Modernity'. Of the latter, Andreas Huyssen comments that de Man 'projects characteristics and insights of modernism back into the past so that ultimately all literature becomes, in a sense, essentially modernist' (After the Great Divide, 239, n.41).

Gelpi, Albert. *A Coherent Spendor: The American Poetic Renaissance, 1910–1950* (Cambridge: Cambridge University Press, 1989). Traces the development of

American modernist poetry 'out of and against' American Romanticism (i.e. Emerson and Whitman). Sees Imagism and symbolism as distinct and contradictory tendencies.

Jay, Gregory. *T. S. Eliot and the Poetics of Literary History* (1983). Re-examines Eliot's relation to Romanticism in the light of works by Harold Bloom and Paul de Man.

Langbaum, Robert. *The Poetry of Experience: The Dramatic Monologue in Modern Literary Tradition* (London: Chatto and Windus, 1957). Argues that the dramatic monologue form, and particularly the tension between sympathy and judgement that it produces in the reader, connects Romanticism to modernism, through Victorian intermediaries such as Robert Browning.

Perloff, Marjorie. *The Poetics of Indeterminacy: Rimbaud to Cage* (Princeton, NJ: Princeton University Press, 1981). Argues for the existence of an anti-symbolist tradition. 'Modernism was itself a time of tension between rival strains, the Symbolist or 'High Modern' and the 'Other Tradition' [. . .]' (p.33).

Riquelme, J. P. *Harmony of Dissonances: T.S. Eliot, Romanticism, and Imagination* (Baltimore, MD: Johns Hopkins University Press, 1991). In the light of revisionist readings of Romanticism, particularly those inspired by Paul de Man, Riquelme re-evaluates Eliot's relationship to the earlier movement.

Wallace Stevens Journal 26 no. 2 (Fall 2002). A special issue on Pound and Stevens, revisiting Perloff's 'Pound/Stevens' twenty years after its first publication.

2

Realism and Formalism

The insistence of many modernist writers on their difference from their Victorian forebears raises an intriguing question: might the strength of their insistence be due to repression, a wish to conceal hidden debts? The question of what modernist texts, particularly modernist novels, owed to the tradition of Victorian realism has broad similarities to the question of modernism's relation to Romanticism. Modernist writers attempted to put a distance between themselves and their predecessors. As noted in Part I, Virginia Woolf's essays on the 'Edwardian' novelists criticised them for their materialism, but shared an underlying expectation about mimesis.

Woolf's account of modern fiction calls for liberty in the face of confining conventions, but it is not the only contemporary account of modern fiction, and others may seem to contradict it. The works of Joyce and D. H. Lawrence were criticized and prosecuted for amorality. In 1915 *The Rainbow* was seen by several reviewers as diseased and 'morbid'; the result of such reviews was its censorship.[1] Many reviewers and early critics placed Joyce's work up to and including *Ulysses* in the tradition of the French naturalist school of writing; given that naturalist novels had been heavily censored in Britain in the late nineteenth century, this suggested unease about his work.[2] *Ulysses* evoked 'sheer disgust', was seen as a 'sordid' and a 'stupid glorification of mere filth', and as dwelling on 'crude, disgusting and unpalatable facts'.[3]

In the face of such criticism, the earliest defenders of modernist works felt obliged to demonstrate their conscious and careful artistry. Lawrence's defenders (notably F. R. Leavis) emphasised his moral purpose and his advocacy of 'life'. Joyce's emphasised the complex organization of the novel, thus distancing the author from the consciousnesses of his characters. T. S. Eliot's 'Ulysses, Order and Myth' (1923) represents an early instance of this approach. Ezra Pound spoke of the 'sonata form' of the novel; in comparing it to a novel by a contemporary imitator, he took formal verse structures, the canzone and rondeau, as his point of reference.[4] Stuart Gilbert's early study, *James Joyce's Ulysses* (1930), also emphasised the orderliness of the novel, its interlocking rhythms, and its 'discipline'; his schema of correspondences fitted easily into the New Critical model of modernism, and shaped the approach of several generations of critics and students. Harry Blamires, in his influential reader's guide *The Bloomsday Book* (1966), declared himself particularly interested in 'the theological patterns of *Ulysses* created by the numerous implicit correspondences and metaphorical overtones'.[5] Such defenders imply that Joyce was not merely emptying his uncensored daydreams onto the page, but that his novel had a carefully planned architecture. In their accounts, modernism seemed quite distant from naturalism.

Though Woolf sought to distance Joyce's work from the Victorians, others were more critical of the claims of his admirers. In 1928 Rebecca West was scornful of those who recognized parallels between *Ulysses* and *The Odyssey*: the recognition 'plunges Mr Joyce's devotees into profound ecstasies from which they never recover sufficiently to ask what the devil is the purpose that is served by these analogies'.[6] She questioned whether Joyce's method was really new at all. His belief in 'inclusiveness' was 'not a new aesthetic':

> For it is precisely that faith which inspired the well-known artist of the Victorian era, Mr W. P. Frith, to commit his notorious paintings. It was his effort, which was surely crowned with success in a certain sense, to tell the whole story of what happened in an area a hundred yards square on the Derby course which resulted in 'Derby Day' [1856–8; Tate Gallery, London]; and it is true that 'Bronze by gold heard the hoofirons, steely-ringing' [*Ulysses*, p.245], and the ensuing passage vividly convey the effect of a bronze-haired barmaid and her golden-haired colleague standing behind the bar of the 'Ormonde', but consider how well done, how really awfully well done, the cockade on the footman's top-hat in the right-hand foreground of Mr Frith's achievement, and the so veritably pink lobster he is lifting from the luncheon-basket. The brilliantly informative presentation of insufficiently related objects is no novelty in any of the arts. Not only is this method old: it is also logically unsound in both its foundations, since inclusiveness and incoherence can be present in works of art only as a result of interesting and rare special cases. [...] [F]ar from being a way of handling the literary medium, inclusiveness is a condition which may or may not legitimately exist in a work of art owing to factors quite outside the conscious control of the artist [...].[7]

Though West did express her dislike of the 'excrementitious and sexual passages', the passage largely avoids the moralizing of the early reviewers and prosecutors, and arraigns *Ulysses* on aesthetic grounds.

West's criticism of *Ulysses* anticipates Georg Lukács's later and more influential general criticism of modernist aesthetics. Lukács (1885–1971) was a Marxist critic whose views of literature were shaped by the experience of Nazism and the post-1945 influence of Russian Communism. After leaving Germany following the rise of the Nazi Party, he worked for most of his career in Russia and Hungary. His views on modernism took their distinctive form in the 1930s, and were shaped by the European experience of fascism. His essays in the 1930s were focused particularly on the German Expressionist movement. 'Expressionism: Its Significance and Decline' (1934) drew a response in 1938 from Lukács's one-time close friend and philosophical collaborator, Ernst Bloch; Lukács replied in the same year.[8] His criticism of Expressionism was later generalized to include the whole of modernist literature. The cornerstones of Lukács's aesthetics in the 1930s were 'reverence for the classical heritage of the Enlightenment, rejection of any irrationalist contaminations of it, assimilation of modernist trends in literature to irrationalism, identification of irrationalism with fascism'.[9] Irrationalism manifested itself in literature in an underlying philosophy that denied causality, and in the aesthetic formlessness of modernist works.

Lukács's valuation of modernism depends on his theory of realism. Lukács's theory, advanced in *Studies in European Realism* (articles written 1934–44, tr. 1972), *The Historical Novel* (1955, tr. 1969) and elsewhere, is essentially an evaluative one, favouring a realism that is truthful to social structure in its historical moment. The depiction of surface detail is less important than the choice of characters who typify the social trends of their time. Thus Walter Scott's *Waverley*, though a historical fantasy, by having as central characters a rural Tory, an urban Whig, and Waverley himself, represents the main social tensions of the time.[10] The later naturalist writers may have attempted to depict reality with scientific detachment, but without making a good choice of subjects to observe, their work was, for Lukács, worthless. A modernist like James Joyce may have reproduced the modulations of a cat's miaow with great precision (*Ulysses*, pp.53–4), may have boasted that Dublin could be reconstructed from his novel,[11] and may have developed a technique for persuasively portraying the contents of consciousness, but for Lukács his novel would be valuable as realism only if his central characters represented the major social trends of their time. One would have to ask the same question of the central characters in *Mrs Dalloway*. In both cases, one would moreover have to ask whether the single-day time scale of each novel was sufficient to depict real historical change. Lukács saw the longer time periods covered in the nineteenth-century novel as more appropriate to the task.

Evaluative literary theories attract more heated opposition than descriptive ones. Lukács's association with Josef Stalin's imposition of 'socialist realism' on artists in the Soviet Bloc means that he meets with more heated opposition than other evaluative critics, though Fredric Jameson has argued that Lukács's criticism of 'naturalism' was a coded criticism of Stalinist aesthetics; writers in oppressive regimes must criticize obliquely.[12] Nevertheless, the questions that Lukács poses about historical truth are provocative ones, and have proved influential.

The essay from which the present extracts are taken was written after the Second World War, and first published in German in *Wider der mißverstandenen Realismus* (1958); it was translated as *The Meaning of Contemporary Realism* in 1963. The translators rendered Lukács's '*Avantgardeismus*' as 'modernism' rather than the more literal 'avant-gardism'. In view of the important distinction that Peter Bürger and others have drawn between 'modernism' and the 'avant-garde', the translators' decision may seem unfortunate, but one of the few commentators to note the problem has remarked that Lukács probably used the term 'avant-gardism' because there was no better term available in 1958.[13]

Extract from Georg Lukács, 'The Ideology of Modernism' from *The Meaning of Contemporary Realism*, tr. John and Necke Mander (London: Merlin Press, 1963), pp.17–26.

It is in no way surprising that the most influential contemporary school of writing should still be committed to the dogmas of 'modernist' anti-realism. It is here that we must begin our investigation if we are to chart the possibilities of a bourgeois realism. We must compare the two main trends in contemporary bourgeois literature, and look at the answers they give to the major ideological and artistic questions of our time.

We shall concentrate on the underlying ideological basis of these trends (ideological in the above-defined, not in the strictly philosophical, sense). What must be avoided at all costs is the approach generally adopted by bourgeois-modernist critics themselves: that exaggerated concern with formal criteria, with questions of style and literary technique. This approach may appear to distinguish sharply between 'modern' and 'traditional' writing (i.e. contemporary writers who adhere to the styles of the last century). In fact it fails to locate the decisive formal problems and turns a blind eye to their inherent dialectic. We are presented with a false polarization which, by exaggerating the importance of stylistic differences, conceals the opposing principles actually underlying and determining contrasting styles.

To take an example: the *monologue intérieur*. Compare, for instance, Bloom's monologue in the lavatory or Molly's monologue in bed, at the beginning and at the end of *Ulysses*, with Goethe's early-morning monologue as conceived by Thomas Mann in his *Lotte in Weimar*. Plainly, the same stylistic technique is being employed. And certain of Thomas Mann's remarks about Joyce and his methods would appear to confirm this.

Yet it is not easy to think of any two novels more basically dissimilar than *Ulysses* and *Lotte in Weimar*. This is true even of the superficially rather similar scenes I have indicated. I am not referring to the – to my mind – striking difference in intellectual quality. I refer to the fact that with Joyce the stream-of-consciousness technique is no mere stylistic device; it is itself the formative principle governing the narrative pattern and the presentation of character. Technique here is something absolute; it is part and parcel of the aesthetic ambition informing *Ulysses*. With Thomas Mann, on the other hand, the *monologue intérieur* is simply a technical device, allowing the author to explore aspects of Goethe's world which would not have been otherwise available. Goethe's experience is not presented as confined to momentary sense-impressions. The artist reaches down to the core of Goethe's personality, to the complexity of his relations with his own past, present, and even future experience. The stream of association is only apparently free. The monologue is composed with the utmost artistic rigour: it is a carefully plotted sequence gradually piercing to the core of Goethe's personality. Every person or event, emerging momentarily from the stream and vanishing again, is given a specific weight, a definite position, in the pattern of the whole. However unconventional the presentation, the compositional principle is that of the traditional epic; in the way the pace is controlled, and the transitions and climaxes are organized, the ancient rules of epic narration are faithfully observed.

It would be absurd, in view of Joyce's artistic ambitions and his manifest abilities, to qualify the exaggerated attention he gives to the detailed recording of sense-data, and his comparative neglect of ideas and emotions, as artistic failure. All this was in conformity with Joyce's artistic intentions; and, by use of such techniques, he may be said to have achieved them satisfactorily. But between Joyce's intentions and those of Thomas Mann there is a total opposition. The perpetually oscillating patterns of sense- and memory-data, their powerfully charged – but aimless and directionless – fields of force, give rise to an epic structure which is *static*, reflecting a belief in the basically static character of events.

These opposed views of the world – dynamic and developmental on the one hand, static and sensational on the other – are of crucial importance in examining the two schools of literature I have mentioned. I shall return to the opposition later. Here, I want only to point out that an exclusive emphasis on formal matters can lead to serious misunderstanding of the character of an artist's work.

What determines the style of a given work of art? How does the intention determine the form? (We are concerned here, of course, with the intention realized in the work; it need not coincide with the writer's conscious intention). The distinctions that concern us are not those between stylistic 'techniques' in the formalistic sense. It is the view of the world, the ideology or *weltanschauung* underlying a writer's work, that counts. And it is the writer's attempt to reproduce this view of the world which constitutes his 'intention' and is the formative principle underlying the style of a given piece of writing. Looked at in this way, style ceases to be a formalistic category. Rather, it is rooted in content; it is the specific form of a specific content.

Content determines form. But there is no content of which Man himself is not the focal point. However various the *données* of literature (a particular experience, a didactic purpose), the basic question is, and will remain: what is Man?

Here is a point of division: if we put the question in abstract, philosophical terms, leaving aside all formal considerations, we arrive – for the realist school – at the traditional Aristotelian dictum (which was also reached by other than purely aesthetic considerations): Man is *zoon politikon*, a social animal. The Aristotelian dictum is applicable to all great realistic literature. Achilles and Werther, Oedipus and Tom Jones, Antigone and Anna Karenina: their individual existence – their *Sein an sich*, in the Hegelian terminology; their 'ontological being', as a more fashionable terminology has it – cannot be distinguished from their social and historical environment. Their human significance, their specific individuality cannot be separated from the context in which they were created.

The ontological view governing the image of man in the work of leading modernist writers is the exact opposite of this. Man, for these writers, is by nature solitary, asocial, unable to enter into relationships with other human beings. Thomas Wolfe once wrote: 'My view of the world is based on the firm conviction that solitariness is by no means a rare condition, something peculiar to myself or to a few specially solitary human beings, but the inescapable, central fact of human existence.' Man, thus imagined, may establish contact with other individuals, but only in a superficial, accidental manner; only, ontologically speaking, by retrospective reflection. For 'the others', too, are basically solitary, beyond significant human relationship.

This basic solitariness of man must not be confused with that individual solitariness to be found in the literature of traditional realism. In the latter case, we are dealing with a particular situation in which a human being may be placed, due either to his character or to the circumstances of his life. Solitariness may be objectively conditioned, as with Sophocles' Philoctetes, put ashore on the bleak island of Lemnos. Or it may be subjective, the product of inner necessity, as with Tolstoy's Ivan Ilyitsch or Flaubert's Frédéric Moreau in the *Education Sentimentale*. But it is always merely a fragment, a phase, a climax or anti-climax, in the life of the community as a whole. The fate of such individuals is characteristic of certain human types in specific social or historical circumstances. Beside and beyond their solitariness, the common life, the strife and togetherness of other human beings, goes on as before. In a word, their solitariness is a specific social fate, not a universal *condition humaine*.

The latter, of course, is characteristic of the theory and practice of modernism. I would like, in the present study, to spare the reader tedious excursions into philosophy. But I cannot refrain from drawing the reader's attention to Heidegger's description of human existence as a 'thrownness-into-being' (*Geworfenheit ins Dasein*). A more graphic evocation of the ontological solitariness of the individual would be hard to imagine. Man is 'thrown-into-being'. This implies, not merely that man is constitutionally unable to establish relationships with things or persons outside himself; but also that it is impossible to determine theoretically the origin and goal of human existence.

Man, thus conceived, is an ahistorical being. (The fact that Heidegger does admit a form of 'authentic' historicity in his system is not really relevant. I have shown elsewhere that Heidegger tends to belittle historicity as 'vulgar'; and his 'authentic' historicity is not distinguishable from ahistoricity). This negation of history takes two different forms in modernist literature. First, the hero is strictly confined within the limits of his own experience. There is not for him – and apparently not for his creator – any pre-existent reality beyond his own self, acting upon him or being acted upon by him. Secondly, the hero himself is without personal history. He is 'thrown-into-the-world': meaninglessly, unfathomably. He does not develop through contact with the world; he neither forms nor is formed by it. The only 'development' in this literature is the gradual revelation of the human condition. Man is now what he has always been and always will be. The narrator, the examining subject, is in motion; the examined reality is static.

Of course, dogmas of this kind are only really viable in philosophical abstraction, and then only with a measure of sophistry. A gifted writer, however extreme his theoretical modernism, will in practice have to compromise with the demands of historicity and of social environment. Joyce uses Dublin, Kafka and Musil the Hapsburg Monarchy, as the locus of their masterpieces. But the locus they lovingly depict is little more than a backcloth; it is not basic to their artistic intention.

This view of human existence has specific literary consequences. Particularly in one category, of primary theoretical and practical importance, to which we must now give our attention: that of *potentiality*. Philosophy distinguishes between *abstract* and *concrete* (in Hegel, 'real') *potentiality*. These two categories, their interrelation and opposition, are rooted in life itself. *Potentiality* – seen abstractly or subjectively – is richer than actual life. Innumerable possibilities for man's development are imaginable, only a small percentage of which will be realized. Modern subjectivism, taking these imagined possibilities for actual complexity of life, oscillates between melancholy and fascination.

When the world declines to realize these possibilities, this melancholy becomes tinged with contempt. Hofmannsthal's Sobeide expressed the reaction of the generation first exposed to this experience:

> The burden of those endlessly pored-over
> And now forever perished possibilities ...

How far were those possibilities even concrete or 'real'? Plainly, they existed only in the imagination of the subject, as dreams or day-dreams. Faulkner, in whose work this subjective potentiality plays an important part, was evidently aware that reality must thereby be subjectivized and made to appear arbitrary. Consider this comment of his: 'They were all talking simultaneously, getting flushed and excited, quarrelling, making the unreal into a possibility, then into a probability, then into an irrefutable fact, as human beings do when they put their wishes into words.' The possibilities in a man's mind, the particular pattern, intensity and suggestiveness they assume, will of course be characteristic of that individual. In practice, their number will border on the infinite, even with the most unimaginative individual. It is thus a hopeless undertaking to define the contours of individuality, let alone to come to grips with a man's actual fate, by means of potentiality. The *abstract* character of potentiality is clear from the fact that it cannot determine development – subjective mental states, however permanent or profound, cannot here be decisive. Rather, the development of personality is determined by inherited gifts and qualities; by the factors, external or internal, which further or inhibit their growth.

But in life potentiality can, of course, become reality. Situations arise in which a man is confronted with a choice; and in the act of choice a man's character may reveal itself in a light that surprises even himself. In literature – and particularly in dramatic literature – the denouement often consists in the realization of just such a potentiality, which circumstances have kept from coming to the fore. These potentialities are, then, 'real' or concrete potentialities. The fate of the character depends upon the potentiality in question, even if it should condemn him to a tragic end. In advance, while still a subjective potentiality in the character's mind, there is no way of distinguishing it from the innumerable abstract potentialities in his mind. It may even be buried away so completely that, before the moment of decision, it has never entered his mind even as an abstract potentiality. The subject, after taking his decision, may be unconscious of his own motives. Thus Richard Dudgeon, Shaw's Devil's Disciple, having sacrificed himself as Pastor Andersen, confesses: 'I have often asked myself for the motive, but I find no good reason to explain why I acted as I did.'

Yet it is a decision which has altered the direction of his life. Of course, this is an extreme case. But the qualitative leap of the denouement, cancelling and at the same time renewing the continuity of individual consciousness, can never be predicted. The concrete potentiality cannot be isolated from the myriad abstract potentialities. Only actual decision reveals the distinction.

The literature of realism, aiming at a truthful reflection of reality, must demonstrate both the concrete and abstract potentialities of human beings in extreme situations of this kind. A character's concrete potentiality once revealed, his abstract potentialities will appear essentially inauthentic. Moravia, for instance, in his novel *The Indifferent Ones*, describes the young son of a decadent bourgeois family, Michel, who makes up his mind to kill his sister's seducer. While Michel, having made his decision, is planning the murder, a large number of abstract – but highly suggestive – possibilities are laid before us. Unfortunately for Michel the murder is actually carried out; and, from the sordid details of the action, Michel's character emerges as what it is – representative of that background from which, in subjective fantasy, he had imagined he could escape.

Abstract potentiality belongs wholly to the realm of subjectivity; whereas concrete potentiality is concerned with the dialectic between the individual's subjectivity and objective reality. The literary presentation of the latter thus implies a description of actual persons inhabiting a palpable, identifiable world. Only in the interaction of character and environment can the concrete potentiality of a particular individual be singled out from the 'bad infinity' of purely abstract potentialities, and emerge as the determining potentiality of just this individual at just this phase of his development. This principle alone enables the artist to distinguish concrete potentiality from a myriad abstractions.

But the ontology on which the image of man in modernist literature is based invalidates this principle. If the 'human condition' – man as a solitary being, incapable of meaningful relationships – is identified with reality itself, the distinction between abstract and concrete potentiality becomes null and void. The categories tend to merge. Thus Cesare Pavese notes with John Dos Passos, and his German contemporary, Alfred Döblin, a sharp oscillation between 'superficial *verisme*' and 'abstract Expressionist schematism'. Criticizing Dos Passos, Pavese writes that fictional characters 'ought to be created by deliberate selection and description of individual features' – implying that Dos Passos' characterizations are transferable from one individual to another. He describes the artistic consequences: by exalting man's subjectivity, at the expense of the objective reality of his environment, man's subjectivity itself is impoverished.

The problem, once again, is ideological. This is not to say that the ideology underlying modernist writings is identical in all cases. On the contrary: the ideology exists in extremely various, even contradictory forms. The rejection of narrative objectivity, the surrender to subjectivity, may take the form of Joyce's stream of consciousness, or of Musil's 'active passivity', his 'existence without quality', or of Gide's '*action gratuite*', where abstract potentiality achieves pseudo-realization. As individual character manifests itself in life's moments of decision, so too in literature. If the distinction between abstract and concrete potentiality vanishes, if man's inwardness is identified with an abstract subjectivity, human personality must necessarily disintegrate.

T. S. Eliot described this phenomenon, this mode of portraying human personality, as

> Shape without form, shade without colour,
> Paralysed force, gesture without motion.

The disintegration of personality is matched by a disintegration of the outer world. In one sense, this is simply a further consequence of our argument. For the identification of abstract and concrete human potentiality rests on the assumption that the objective world is inherently inexplicable. Certain leading modernist writers, attempting a theoretical apology, have admitted this quite frankly. Often this theoretical impossibility of understanding reality is the point of departure, rather than the exaltation of subjectivity. But in any case the connection between the two is plain. The German poet Gottfried Benn, for instance, informs us that 'there is no outer reality, there is only human consciousness, constantly building, modifying, rebuilding new worlds out of its own creativity'. Musil, as always, gives a moral twist to this line of thought. Ulrich, the hero of his *The Man without Qualities*, when asked what he would do if he were in God's place, replies: 'I should be compelled to abolish reality.' Subjective existence 'without qualities' is the complement of the negation of outward reality.

The negation of outward reality is not always demanded with such theoretical rigour. But it is present in almost all modernist literature. In conversation, Musil once gave as the period of his great novel, 'between 1912 and 1914'. But he was quick to modify this statement by adding: 'I have not, I must insist, written a historical novel. I am not concerned with actual events. ... Events, anyhow, are interchangeable. I am interested in what is typical, in what one might call the ghostly aspect of reality'. The word 'ghostly' is interesting. It points to a major tendency in modernist literature: the attenuation of actuality. In Kafka, the descriptive detail is of an extraordinary immediacy and authenticity. But Kafka's artistic ingenuity is really directed towards substituting his *angst*-ridden vision of the world for objective reality. The realistic detail is the expression of a ghostly un-reality, of a nightmare world, whose function is to evoke *angst*. The same phenomenon can be seen in writers who attempt to combine Kafka's techniques with a critique of society – like the German writer, Wolfgang Koeppen, in his satirical novel about Bonn, *Das Treibhaus*. A similar attenuation of reality underlies Joyce's stream of consciousness. It is, of course, intensified where the stream of consciousness is itself the medium through which reality is presented. And it is carried *ad absurdum* where the stream of consciousness is that of an abnormal subject or of an idiot – consider the first part of Faulkner's *Sound and Fury* or, a still more extreme case, Beckett's *Molloy*.

Attenuation of reality and dissolution of personality are thus interdependent: the stronger the one, the stronger the other. Underlying both is the lack of a consistent view of human nature. Man is reduced to a sequence of unrelated experiential fragments; he is as inexplicable to others as to himself.

* * *

In a middle section, Lukács develops his criticism of the 'image of man' in modern writing, relating it to the existentialist philosophy of Martin Heidegger and others. Such a view of man as consisting of 'unrelated experiential fragments' undoes the complex web of connections between an individual and his or her social environment. Rather than seeking to understand this web, both naturalist and modernist writers have created a false dichotomy between prosaic, conformist members of society and the asocial, 'psychopathological' individual. Lukács's illustration is Robert Musil, but in English literature, a good example would be Woolf's Septimus Warren Smith, whose escape from the normative pressures of society is won at the cost of madness and suicide.

Extract from Georg Lukács, 'The Ideology of Modernism', pp.30–35.

This obsession with the pathological is not only to be found in literature. Freudian psychoanalysis is its most obvious expression. The treatment of the subject is only superficially different from that in modern literature. As everybody knows, Freud's starting point was 'everyday life'. In order to explain 'slips' and day-dreams, however, he had to have recourse to psychopathology. In his lectures, speaking of resistance and repression, he says: 'Our interest in the general psychology of symptom-formation increases as we understand to what extent the study of pathological conditions can shed light on the workings of the normal mind.' Freud believed he had found the key to the understanding of the normal personality in the psychology of the abnormal. This belief is still more evident in the typology of Kretschmer, which also assumes that psychological abnormalities can explain normal psychology. It is only when we compare Freud's psychology with that of Pavlov, who takes the Hippocratic view that mental abnormality is a deviation from a norm, that we see it in its true light.

Clearly, this is not strictly a scientific or literary-critical problem. It is an ideological problem, deriving from the ontological dogma of the solitariness of man. The literature of realism, based on the Aristotelean concept of man as *zoon politikon*, is entitled to develop a new typology for each new phase in the evolution of a society. It displays the contradictions within society and within the individual in the context of a dialectical unity. Here, individuals embodying violent and extraordinary passions are still within the range of a socially normal typology (Shakespeare, Balzac, Stendhal). For, in this literature, the average man is simply a dimmer reflection of the contradictions always existing in man and society; eccentricity is a socially-conditioned distortion. Obviously, the passions of the great heroes must not be confused with 'eccentricity' in the colloquial sense: Christian Buddenbrook is an 'eccentric'; Adrian Leverkühn is not.

The ontology of *Geworfenheit* makes a true typology impossible; it is replaced by an abstract polarity of the eccentric and the socially-average. We have seen why this polarity – which in traditional realism serves to increase our understanding of social normality – leads in modernism to a fascination with morbid eccentricity. Eccentricity becomes the necessary complement of the average; and this polarity is held to exhaust human potentiality. The implications of this ideology are shown in another remark of Musil's: 'If humanity dreamt collectively, it would dream Moosbrugger.' Moosbrugger, you will remember, was a mentally-retarded sexual pervert with homicidal tendencies.

What served, with Musil, as the ideological basis of a new typology – escape into neurosis as a protest against the evils of society – becomes with other modernist writers an immutable *condition humaine*. Musil's statement loses its conditional 'if' and becomes a simple description of reality. Lack of objectivity in the description of the outer world finds its complement in the reduction of reality to a nightmare. Beckett's *Molloy* is perhaps the *ne plus ultra* of this development, although Joyce's vision of reality as an incoherent stream of consciousness had already assumed in Faulkner a nightmare quality. In Beckett's novel we have the same vision twice over. He presents us with an image of the utmost human degradation – an idiot's vegetative existence. Then, as help is imminent from a mysterious unspecified source, the rescuer himself sinks into idiocy. The story is told through the parallel streams of consciousness of the idiot and of his rescuer.

Along with the adoption of perversity and idiocy as types of the *condition humaine*, we find what amounts to frank glorification. Take Montherlant's *Pasiphae*, where sexual perversity – the heroine's infatuation with a bull – is presented as a triumphant return to nature, as the liberation of impulse from the slavery of convention. The chorus – i.e. the author – puts the following question (which, though rhetorical, clearly expects an affirmative reply): 'Si l'absence de pensée et l'absence de morale ne contribuent pas beaucoup à la dignité des bêtes, des plantes et des eaux ... ?' Montherlant expresses as plainly as Musil, though with different moral and emotional emphasis, the hidden – one might say repressed – social character of the protest underlying this obsession with psychopathology, its perverted Rousseauism, its anarchism. There are many illustrations of this in modernist writing. A poem of Benn's will serve to make the point:

> O that we were our primal ancestors,
> Small lumps of plasma in hot, sultry swamps;
> Life, death, conception, parturition
> Emerging from those juices soundlessly.
>
> A frond of seaweed or a dune of sand,
> Formed by the wind and heavy at the base;
> A dragonfly or gull's wing – already, these
> Would signify excessive suffering.

This is not overtly perverse in the manner of Beckett or Montherlant. Yet, in his primitivism, Benn is at one with them. The opposition of man as animal to man as social being (for instance, Heidegger's devaluation of the social as '*das Man*', Klages' assertion of the incompatibility of *Geist* and *Seele*, or Rosenberg's racial mythology) leads straight to a glorification of the abnormal and to an undisguised anti-humanism.

A typology limited in this way to the *homme moyen sensuel* and the idiot also opens the door to 'experimental' stylistic distortion. Distortion becomes as inseparable a part of the portrayal of reality as the recourse to the patho-logical. But literature must have a concept of the normal if it is to 'place' distortion correctly; that is to say, to see it *as* distortion. With such a typo-logy this placing is impossible, since the normal is no longer a proper object of literary interest. Life under capitalism is, often rightly, presented as a distortion (a petrification or paralysis) of the human substance. But to present psycho-pathology as a way of escape from this distortion is itself a distortion. We are invited to measure one type of distortion against another and arrive, neces-sarily, at universal distortion. There is no principle to set against the general pattern, no standard by which the petty-bourgeois and the pathological can be seen in their social context. And these tendencies, far from being relativized with time, become ever more absolute. Distortion becomes the normal condi-tion of human existence; the proper study, the formative principle, of art and literature.

I have demonstrated some of the literary implications of this ideology. Let us now pursue the argument further. It is clear, I think, that modernism must deprive literature of a sense of *perspective*. This would not be surprising; rigorous modernists such as Kafka, Benn, and Musil have always indignantly refused to provide their readers with any such thing. I will return to the ideological implications of the idea of perspective later. Let me say here that, in any work of art, perspective is of overriding importance. It determines the course and content; it draws together the threads of the narration; it enables the artist to choose between the important and the superficial, the crucial and the episodic.

The direction in which characters develop is determined by perspective, only those features being described which are material to their development. The more lucid the perspective – as in Molière or the Greeks – the more economical and striking the selection.

Modernism drops this selective principle. It asserts that it can dispense with it, or can replace it with its dogma of the *condition humaine*. A naturalistic style is bound to be the result. This state of affairs – which to my mind characterizes all modernist art of the past fifty years – is disguised by critics who systematically glorify the modernist movement. By concentrating on formal criteria, by isolating technique from content and exaggerating its importance, these critics refrain from judgment on the social or artistic significance of subject-matter. They are unable, in consequence, to make the aesthetic distinction between *realism* and *naturalism*. This distinction depends on the presence or absence in a work of art of a 'hierarchy of significance' in the situations and characters presented. Compared with this, formal categories are of secondary importance. That is why it is possible to speak of the basically *naturalistic* character of modernist literature – and to see here the literary expression of an ideological continuity. This is not to deny that variations in style reflect changes in society. But the particular form this principle of naturalistic arbitrariness, this lack of hierarchic structure, may take is not decisive. We encounter it in the all-determining 'social conditions' of Naturalism, in Symbolism's impressionist methods and its cultivation of the exotic, in the fragmentation of objective reality in Futurism and Constructivism and the German *Neue Sachlichkeit*, or, again, in Surrealism's stream of consciousness.

These schools have in common a basically static approach to reality. This is closely related to their lack of perspective. Characteristically, Gottfried Benn actually incorporated this in his artistic programme. One of his volumes bears the title, *Static Poems*. The denial of history, of development, and thus of perspective, becomes the mark of true insight into the nature of reality.

> The wise man is ignorant
> of change and development
> his children and children's children
> are no part of his world.

The rejection of any concept of the future is for Benn the criterion of wisdom. But even those modernist writers who are less extreme in their rejection of history tend to present social and historical phenomena as static. It is, then, of small importance whether this condition is 'eternal', or only a transitional stage punctuated by sudden catastrophes (even in early Naturalism the static presentation was often broken up by these catastrophes, without altering its basic character). Musil, for instance, writes in his essay, *The Writer in our Age*: 'One knows just as little about the present. Partly, this is because we are, as always, too close to the present. But it is also because the present into which we were plunged some two decades ago is of a particularly all-embracing and inescapable character.' Whether or not Musil knew of Heidegger's philosophy, the idea of *Geworfenheit* is clearly at work here. And the following reveals plainly how, for Musil, this static state was upset by the catastrophe of 1914: 'All of a sudden, the world was full of violence. ... In European civilization, there was a sudden rift ...'. In short: thus static apprehension of reality in modernist literature is no passing fashion; it is rooted in the ideology of modernism.

* * *

Fredric Jameson, writing of earlier essays by Lukács, has noted the difficulties inherent in the concept of 'decadence', and Astradur Eysteinsson, looking at 'The Ideology of Modernism', has focused on Lukács's concepts of the 'normal'. Eysteinsson's criticism focuses on Lukács's idea that life under capitalism is itself already a distortion of the human substance. This raises problems for Lukács's account of modernist distortion: is it a parallel distortion of the human substance, or a distortion of a distortion? 'If', suggests Eysteinsson

> the reality of the bourgeois-capitalist era is lived as a more or less accepted *order*, as 'the normal', then Lukács's view of the modernist distortion of life calls forth implications radically different from those he seeks to establish, since modernism can only present society as a place of distortion by working against a dominant concept of the normal. This is a dialectics that Lukács will not acknowledge, since his concept of 'the normal' is of a specific ideological order and not the one operative in bourgeois society [...]. Lukács is thus in agreement with a host of other critics in taking modernism to task for distorting reality, for failing to adhere to normal conditions of human life, for creating a sense of chaos in its depiction of the world, and for causing a perceptual crisis in the receiver.[14]

Among the reviewers of the original German text of *The Meaning of Contemporary Realism* was Theodor Adorno. Adorno sees Lukács's career as one of decline: the promising author of *The Theory of the Novel* (1920; tr. 1971) compromised himself through his involvement with Stalinist Communism. In the present work, he criticises Lukács's lack of understanding of the role of 'formal elements' (p.153) in a work of art. 'The core of his theory', writes Adorno, 'remains dogmatic. The whole of modern literature is dismissed except where it can be classified as either critical or socialist realism, and the odium of decadence is heaped on it without a qualm, even though such abuse brings with it all the horrors of persecution and extermination, and not only in Russia. The term decadence belongs to the vocabulary of conservatism'. (pp.154–5).

Extract from Theodor Adorno, 'Reconciliation Under Duress', from *Aesthetics and Politics*, by Ernst Bloch et al. (London: Verso, 1977), pp.157–63.

His efforts to bolster up the naive Soviet verdict on modern art, i.e. on any literature which shocks the naively realistic normal mind, by providing it with a philosophical good conscience, are carried out with a very limited range of tools, all of them Hegelian in origin. In the first place, in order to press home his point that modernist literature is a deviation from reality, he drags in the distinction between 'abstract' and 'real' potentiality: 'These two categories, their affinities, differences and opposition are rooted in life itself. Viewed abstractly, i.e. subjectively, potentiality is always richer than actual life. Countless possibilities seem open to the human mind, of which only a negligibly minute percentage can ever be realized. Modern subjectivism, discerning in this apparent plenitude the authentic abundance of the human soil, contemplates it with a melancholy tinged with admiration and sympathy. However, when reality declines to realize such possibilities, these feelings become transformed into a no less melancholy contempt'. This point cannot simply be shrugged off, despite the percentage. When Brecht, to take an example, devised a kind of childish shorthand to try and crystallize out the essence of Fascism in terms of a sort of gangsterism, he made his 'resistible' dictator, Arturo Ui, the head of an imaginary and apocryphal Cauliflower Trust, instead of the most powerful economic organizations. This unrealistic device proved to be a mixed blessing. By thinking of Fascism as an enterprise belonging to a band of criminals who have no real place in the social system and who can therefore be 'resisted' at will, you strip it of its horror and diminish its social significance. This invalidates the caricature and makes it seem idiotic even in its own terms: the despotic rise of the minor criminal loses its plausibility in the course of the play itself. Satire which fails to stay on the level of its subject lacks spice.

But the demand for pragmatic fidelity to life can only refer to a writer's basic experience of reality and the *membra disjecta* of the subject-matter from which he fashions his work. In Brecht's case, this can only mean the actual bonds connecting politics and the economy as well as the need for the initial situation to fit the facts. It does not apply to what happens to these facts in the course of the work. Proust provides the most striking illustration of the unity of pragmatic fidelity and – in Lukácsian terms – unrealistic manner, for in his work we find the most intimate fusion of an extremely 'realistic' observation of detail with an aesthetic form based on the principle of involuntary recollection. If any of the intimacy of this synthesis is lost, if 'concrete potentiality' is interpreted in terms of an unreflecting overall realism, rigidly partitioned off from the object it observes, while any element of art antithetical to the subject-matter is permitted only as a 'perspective', i.e. in the sense that a meaning is allowed to become visible without reaching the centre of the work, the real objects at its core, then what results is an abuse of Hegel's distinction in the interests of a traditionalism whose aesthetic backwardness provides an index of its historical falsity.

Lukács's central line of attack, however, is the charge of 'ontologism', which, if sustained, would enable him to pin the whole of modernist literature on to the archaic existential notions of Heidegger. Of course, Lukács himself follows the fashion and insists that the question 'What is Man?' has to be put, and that we must not be deterred by the prospect of where it might lead. However, he does at least modify it by reverting to Aristotle's familiar definition of man as a social animal. From this he deduces the scarcely contentious proposition that 'the human significance, the specific individual and typical quality' of the characters in great literature, 'their sensuous, artistic reality, cannot be separated from the context in which they were created'. 'Quite opposed to this', he goes on, is 'the ontological view governing the image of man in the work of leading modernist writers. To put it briefly: in their eyes "man" means the individual who has always existed, who is essentially solitary, asocial and – ontologically – incapable of entering into relationships with other human beings'. This is supported by reference to a somewhat foolish utterance by Thomas Wolfe, which clearly has no relevance to literary works, to the effect that solitariness is the inescapable fact of man's existence. But as someone who claims to think in radically historical terms, Lukács of all people ought to know that in an individualistic society loneliness is socially mediated and so possesses a significant historical content.

All such categories as decadence, formalism and aestheticism can be traced back to Baudelaire, and Baudelaire shows no interest in an unchanging essence of man, his loneliness or his derelict existence [*Geworfenheit*], but rather in the essence of modernity. 'Essence' itself in this poetry is no abstract thing in itself; it is a social phenomenon. The objectively dominant idea in Baudelaire's work is that the new, the products of historical progress, are what has to be conjured up in his verse. To use Benjamin's expression, we find not an archaic, but a 'dialectical' image in his work. Hence the *Tableaux Parisiens*. Even in Joyce's case we do not find the timeless image of man which Lukács would like to foist on to him, but man as the product of history. For all his Irish folklore, Joyce does not invoke a mythology beyond the world he depicts, but instead strives to mythologize it, i.e. to create its essence, whether benign or maleficent, by applying the technique of stylization so despised by the Lukács of today. One is almost tempted to measure the achievements of modernist writing by inquiring whether historical moments are given substance as such within their works, or whether they are diluted into some sort of timelessness.

Lukács would doubtless deprecate as idealistic the use of terms like 'image' and 'essence' in aesthetics. But their application in the realm of art is fundamentally different from what it is in philosophies of essence or of primitive images, especially refurbished versions of the Platonic Ideas. The most fundamental weakness of Lukács's position is probably his inability to maintain this distinction, a failure which leads him to transfer to the realm of art categories which refer to the relationship of consciousness to the actual world, as if there were no difference between them. Art exists in the real world and has a function in it, and the two are connected by a large number of mediating links. Nevertheless, as art it remains the antithesis of that which is the case. Philosophy has acknowledged this situation by defining art as 'aesthetic appearance'. Even Lukács will find it impossible to get away from the fact that the content of works of art is not real in the same sense as social reality. If this distinction is lost, then all attempts to provide a real foundation for aesthetics must be doomed to failure. But artistic appearance, the fact that art has set itself apart in qualitative terms from the immediate actuality in which it magically came into being, is neither its ideological Fall, nor does it make art an arbitrary system of signs, as if it merely reproduced the world without claiming to possess the same immediate reality. Any view as reductive as this would be a sheer mockery of dialectics.

More to the point is the assertion that the difference between art and empirical reality touches on the former's innermost being. It is no idealistic crime for art to provide essences, 'images'; the fact that many artists have inclined towards an idealist philosophy says nothing about the content of their works. The truth of the matter is that except where art goes against its own nature and simply duplicates existence, its task vis-à-vis that which merely exists, is to be its essence and image. This alone constitutes the aesthetic; art does not become knowledge with reference to mere immediate reality, i.e. by doing justice to a reality which veils its own essence and suppresses its truth in favour of a merely classificatory order. Art and reality can only converge if art crystallizes out its own formal laws, not by passively accepting objects as they come. In art knowledge is aesthetically mediated through and through. Even alleged cases of solipsism, which signify for Lukács the regression to an illusory immediacy on the part of the individual, do not imply the denial of the object, as they would in bad theories of knowledge, but instead aim at a dialectical reconciliation of subject and object. In the form of an image the object is absorbed into the subject instead of following the bidding of the alienated world and persisting obdurately in a state of reification. The contradiction between the object reconciled in the subject, i.e. spontaneously absorbed into the subject, and the actual unreconciled object in the outside world, confers on the work of art a vantage-point from which it can criticize actuality. Art is the negative knowledge of the actual world. In analogy to a current philosophical phrase we might speak of the 'aesthetic distance' from existence: only by virtue of this distance, and not by denying its existence, can the work of art become both work of art and valid consciousness. A theory of art which ignores this is at once philistine and ideological.

Lukács contents himself with Schopenhauer's aperçu that the principle of solipsism is 'only really viable with complete consistency in the most abstract form of philosophy' and 'even there only with a measure of sophistry'. But his argument is self-defeating: if solipsism cannot be sustained, if it only succeeds in reproducing what it has begun by 'bracketing out', to use the phenomenological term, then we need have no fear of it as a stylistic principle. Objectively, then, in their works, the modernists have moved beyond the position Lukács ascribes to them. Proust decomposes the unity of the subjective mind by dint of its own introspection: the mind ends by transforming itself into a stage on which objective realities are made visible. His individualistic work becomes the opposite of that for which Lukács derides it: it becomes anti-individualistic. The *monologue intérieur*, the worldlessness of modern art which makes Lukács so indignant, is both the truth and the appearance of a free-floating subjectivity – it is truth, because in the universal atomistic state of the world, alienation rules over men, turning them into mere shadows of themselves – a point we may undoubtedly concede to Lukács. The free-floating subject is appearance, however, inasmuch as, objectively, the social totality has precedence over the individual, a totality which is created and reproduces itself through alienation and through the contradictions of society. The great works of modernist literature shatter this appearance of subjectivity by setting the individual in his frailty into context, and by grasping that totality in him of which the individual is but a moment and of which he must needs remain ignorant. Lukács evidently believes that when the Habsburg monarchy in Kafka and Musil, or Dublin in Joyce make themselves felt as a sort of 'atmospheric backcloth for the action', it somehow goes against the programme but nevertheless remains of secondary importance. But in arguing thus for the sake of his thesis, he clearly reduces something very substantial, a growing epic plenitude with all its negative potential, to the status of a mere accessory. The concept of atmosphere is in any event highly inappropriate as applied to Kafka. It goes back to an Impressionism which Kafka supersedes by his objectivist concern with historical essence. Even in Beckett – and perhaps in him above all – where seemingly all concrete historical components have been eliminated, and only primitive situations and forms of behaviour are tolerated, the unhistorical façade is the provocative opposite of the absolute Being idolized by reactionary philosophies. The primitivism with which his works begin so abruptly represents the final phase of a regression, especially obvious in *Fin de Partie*, in which, as from the far-distant realm of the self-evident, a terrestrial catastrophe is presupposed. His primitive men are the last men. One theme we discover in his works is something which Horkheimer and I have already discussed in *Dialectic of Enlightenment*: the fact that a society wholly in the grip of the Culture Industry displays all the reactions of an amphibian. The substantive content of a work of art can survive in the precise, wordless polemic which depicts the dawn of a nonsensical world; and it can vanish again as soon as it is positively asserted, as soon as existence is claimed for it, a fate similar to the one that befalls the didactic antithesis between a right and a wrong mode of life to be found in Tolstoy after *Anna Karenina*.

Lukács's favourite old idea of an 'immanent meaning' points towards that same dubious faith in the face value of things which his own theory sets out to destroy. Conceptions like Beckett's, however, have an objective, polemical thrust. Lukács twists them into 'the straightforward portrayal of the pathological, of the perverse, of idiocy, all of which are seen as types of the "condition humaine"' – and in this he follows the example of the film censor who regards the content as a defect of the treatment. Above all, Lukács's confusion of Beckett with the cult of Being and even with the inferior version of vitalism to be found in Montherlant exposes his inability to see what is in front of him. This blindness arises from his stubborn refusal to acknowledge the central claims of literary technique. He sticks imperturbably to what is narrated. But in literature the point of the subject matter can only be made effective by the use of techniques – something which Lukács himself hopes for from the more than suspect concept of 'perspective'. One would like to ask what would be left of Greek drama, which Lukács, like Hegel, has duly canonized, if the criterion of its value were the story which could be picked up in the street. The same holds good for the traditional novel and even for writers such as Flaubert who come into Lukács's category of the 'realist' novel: here too composition and style are fundamental.

Today, when empirical veracity has sunk to the level of superficial reportage, the relevance of technique has increased enormously. By structuring his work, the writer can hope to master the arbitrary and the individual against which Lukács so passionately inveighs. He fails to follow the insight contained in his last chapter to its logical conclusion: the purely arbitrary cannot be overcome simply by a determination to look at things in what purports to be a more objective manner. Lukács ought surely to be familiar with the key importance of the technical forces of production in history. No doubt this was more concerned with material than with cultural production. But can he really close his eyes to the fact that the techniques of art also develop in accordance with their own logic? Can he rest content with the abstract assertion that when society changes, completely different aesthetic criteria automatically come into force? Can he really persuade himself that this justifies him in nullifying the technical advance of the forces of production and providing for the canonical restoration of older, outdated forms? Does he not simply don the dictatorial mantle of socialist realism in order to expound an immutable doctrine which differs from the one he rightly repudiates only by its greater insensitivity?

Lukács places himself in the great philosophical tradition that conceives of art as knowledge which has assumed concrete shape, rather than as something irrational to be contrasted with science. This is perfectly legitimate, but he still finds himself ensnared in the same cult of immediacy of which he myopically accuses modernist literature: the fallacy of mere assertion. Art does not provide knowledge of reality by reflecting it photographically or 'from a particular perspective' but by revealing whatever is veiled by the empirical form assumed by reality, and this is possible only by virtue of art's own autonomous status. Even the suggestion that the world is unknowable, which Lukács so indefatigably castigates in writers like Eliot or Joyce, can become a moment of knowledge. This can happen where a gulf opens up between the overwhelming and unassimilable world of things, on the one hand, and a human experience impotently striving to gain a firm hold on it, on the other.

* * *

Adorno's critique of Lukács has itself been criticized in several ways. As the introduction in the collection *Aesthetics and Politics* notes, there is a lack of terminological clarity: 'The fundamental categories of Adorno's aesthetics remain opaque: "autonomous art", the "laws" and "logic" of artistic form, "essences" that are not congeneric with the essences of philosophical idealism – none of these crucial terms is assigned a clearly delimited meaning'.[15] Nevertheless, his work has been influential in allowing one of the most striking aspects of modernist work – its formal experimentation – to be reconciled with an engagement with social issues. Granted, that engagement is far more oblique than anything imagined by Lukács, and more complex than anything available in the dominant realism of contemporary television and film narrative, and in consequence it requires more oblique and complex critical methods; but such approaches to the form of modernist work have been among the most stimulating. Fredric Jameson, writing about Lukács's 1930s essays on expressionism, has argued that rather than criticizing modernist works of art for their 'decadent' evasion of real social issues, we should look for the social and political content buried inside their literary form; this turned out to be the project of Jameson's study of Wyndham Lewis, *Fables of Aggression* (1979), and, more influentially, of *The Political Unconscious* (1981).[16]

Chapter Notes

1. R. P. Draper, ed., *D. H. Lawrence: The Critical Heritage* (London: Routledge and Kegan Paul, 1970), 93–5, 96, 99.
2. Richard Aldington in 1921, in Robert H. Deming, ed., *James Joyce: The Critical Heritage*, 2 vols. (London: Routledge and Kegan Paul, 1970), 187. On naturalism and censorship in Britain, see Peter Keating, *The Haunted Study* (London: Secker and Warburg, 1989), 241–53. Wyndham Lewis later (1927) also situated the novel

in relation to naturalism, though without the moral disquiet: *Time and Western Man* (1927; Santa Rosa: Black Sparrow, 1993), 73–110.

3. Deming, ed., *James Joyce: The Critical Heritage*, 191, 188, 192, 212.
4. Pound in Deming, ed., *James Joyce: The Critical Heritage*, 263, and *Literary Essays of Ezra Pound* (London: Faber and Faber, 1954), 397.
5. Stuart Gilbert, *James Joyce's Ulysses* (1930; London: Faber and Faber, 1952), 41; the schema is reproduced in Jeri Johnson's edition (Oxford: Oxford University Press, 1992), 734–5; Harry Blamires, *The Bloomsday Book* (London: Methuen, 1966), p.x.
6. Rebecca West, *The Strange Necessity* (London: Jonathan Cape, 1928), 28.
7. West, *The Strange Necessity*, 30–1.
8. Georg Lukács, 'Expressionism: Its Significance and Decline' (1934), in R. Livingstone, ed. and intro., *Essays on Realism* (London: Lawrence and Wishart, 1980), 76–113 (also known as 'The Greatness and the Decline of Expressionism'); Ernst Bloch, 'Discussing Expressionism' (1938), in Ernst Bloch, et al., eds., *Aesthetics and Politics* (London: New Left Books, 1977), 16–27; Lukács, 'Realism in the Balance', in *Aesthetics and Politics*, 28–59.
9. 'Presentation I', in *Aesthetics and Politics*, 10. The introductory 'presentations' were prepared by Rodney Livingstone, Perry Anderson, and Francis Mulhern, but are not individually attributed.
10. Lukács, *The Historical Novel* (Harmondsworth: Penguin, 1969), 71.
11. Joyce, quoted in Frank Budgen, *James Joyce and the Making of Ulysses* (1934, Bloomington: Indiana University Press, 1960), 67–8.
12. Fredric Jameson, 'Afterword', in *Aesthetics and Politics*, 202.
13. Astradur Eysteinsson, *The Concept of Modernism* (Ithaca, NY: Cornell University Press, 1990), 2.
14. Eysteinsson, The Concept of Modernism, 23–4.
15. 'Presentation IV', *Aesthetics and Politics*, 146.
16. Fredric Jameson, 'Afterword', 202.

Further Reading

Modernists and the Victorians and Edwardians

Cianci, Giovanni, and Peter Nicholls, eds., *Ruskin and Modernism* (Basingstoke: Palgrave, 2000).
Kaplan, Carola N., and Anne B. Simpson, eds., *Seeing Double: Revisioning Edwardian and Modernist Literature* (Basingstoke: Macmillan, 1996).
Meisel, Perry. *The Absent Father: Virginia Woolf and Walter Pater* (New Haven, CT: Yale University Press, 1980).

Modernism, Realism, and Formalism

Greenberg, Clement. 'Modernist Painting' (1960), in John O'Brian, ed., *The Collected Essays and Criticism* 4 vols. (Chicago: University of Chicago Press, 1986–93), 4.

85–94. Though Greenberg has nothing to say directly about literature, this essay was for many years the central justification for modernist formalism in painting, and so was influential in shaping views of modernism more widely.

Jackson, Tony E. *The Subject of Modernism : Narrative Alterations in the Fiction of Eliot, Conrad, Woolf, and Joyce* (Ann Arbor: University of Michigan Press, 1994). A Lacanian argument that sees modernist fiction as the results of a self-analysis of the realist text's realist urges.

Jameson, Fredric. *Marxism and Form* (Princeton, NJ: Princeton University Press, 1971). Includes 'In Defence of Georg Lukács'.

Lanser, Susan Sniader. *Fictions of Authority: Women Writers and Narrative Voice* (Ithaca, NY: Cornell University Press, 1992). Covers a long time span, and very persuasively notes the survival of the omniscient narrator voice in Virginia Woolf.

Miller, Jane Eldridge. *Rebel Women: Feminism, Modernism and the Edwardian Novel* (London: Virago, 1994). Gives an excellent account of Edwardian plot types.

Sim, Stuart. *Georg Lukács* (New York, London: Harvester Wheatsheaf, 1994). A brief and approachable introduction to Lukács's theories.

Sumner, Rosemary. *A Route to Modernism: Hardy, Lawrence, Woolf* (Basingstoke: Macmillan, 2000). A re-reading of Hardy that highlights his proto-modernist elements and relates them to Lawrence and Woolf.

3

Modernism and the Avant-Garde

The ideas of the artwork becoming mysterious and magical and of the artist as existing 'above, behind, or beyond his work' provide one route into modernism. But a theory of modernism which holds art and artists to be so aloof has difficulty explaining how it was that modernism had such power to disturb and disrupt its audiences. The response that aloofness can be profoundly irritating when one expects engagement is only a partial answer. One solution is to distinguish, as Eysteinsson suggests, between modernism as a cultural force, and modernism as an aesthetic project.[1] Another is to suggest that the literature and art of the early twentieth century were a more complex mixture than can be contained under the single heading 'modernism'. In particular, as Peter Bürger has argued, we should distinguish between modernism, which attempted to retain the idea of the autonomous artwork, and the avant-garde, which attempted to reinstate art as part of everyday life.

Theodor Adorno influentially articulated the conflicts inherent in the idea of the autonomous artwork, as part of a lifetime's work addressing questions of the relation of high art to society and mass culture. Adorno was born in Germany, and in the early 1930s joined the Institute for Social Research in Frankfurt. When the Institute was closed by the Nazi regime in March 1933, he left Germany, first for England and later for the USA, where he began work with Max Horkheimer on *Dialectic of Enlightenment* (1944; tr. 1972). The work responded both to the rise of fascist irrationalism and to the spectacle of American mass culture. Adorno and Horkheimer argue that reason, which in the early modernity of the Enlightenment period was seen as a means by which mankind could be freed from superstition and mythology, has in late modernity become a rigid system, 'incapable of understanding what makes rationality itself possible, the non-rational element which reason depends upon'.[2] Reason tends to become a form of mythology. The idea echoes Georg Lukács's idea of the reification of social institutions and processes: institutions created for the benefit of man take on an existence of their own, and enslave people within and beyond them.[3] It is characteristic of Adorno's style of analysis that it identifies ways in which its objects are transformed into their opposites: leisure time, for example, becomes 'the prolongation of work'.[4]

Of Adorno's various writings on musical and literary aesthetics, the most relevant to modernism is the posthumously published *Aesthetic Theory* (1970, tr. 1984).[5] Though, as Eysteinsson remarks, its validity as a general theory of aesthetics may be called into doubt, it provides a valuable theory of modernism.[6] Adorno's distinctive style makes him quotable in aphorisms, but harder to extract in longer passages. The present account of his view of autonomy is taken from Simon Jarvis' *Adorno: A Critical Introduction* (1998).

Extract from Simon Jarvis, *Adorno: A Critical Introduction* (Cambridge: Polity, 1998), pp.116–23.

Under high capitalism, the characteristic form of ideology was a faith in illusory universals. But in late capitalism the most worrying prospect is that the very idea that our social experience could change will be lost altogether. In these circumstances the attempt to dispel all illusion may merely serve the idea that the real is absolute: that what is cannot, and therefore should not, change. Accordingly, for Adorno, the most pressing task is not so much the dissolution of illusion as a redemptive critique of art's entanglement with social experience.[1] It is important to recognize that this entanglement cannot be regarded as necessarily ideological. It may be an index of art's truth-content as much as of its ideological status, because works of art are not only precipitates of natural-historical experience but are also cognitive, attempts to know and to criticize that experience.

Accordingly, the claim on the part of the artwork to be more than a mere thing, what Adorno calls its illusory character or its 'fetish-character',[2] is not merely an idol in need of shattering. From the perspective of the *Dialectic of Enlightenment*, to take this view would be to perpetuate the process whereby enlightenment against its own best intentions turns into mythology. Instead Adorno emphasizes the distinction between this fetish-character of art and the literal fetishism of a cultic object.[3] Works of art are themselves made possible, for Adorno, by the dialectic of enlightenment. They are a rational refuge for mimesis in a world in which the mimetic impulse of thinking is progressively suppressed in classificatory thinking. Whereas the cultic value of a real fetish is dependent on its heteronomy, its inflexible insertion in a context of magical or ritual function, the fetish-character of art lies in its claim to autonomy – its illusory claim to be a being in and for itself, governed by its own law rather than by a law outside it. Talk about 'the magic of art' sounds crass precisely because it misses this fundamental distinction between literal magical fetishism and the 'fetishism' of the autonomous work of art. 'Ihr Zauber ist Entzauberung': 'the magic of works of art is a disenchantment'.[4]

The progressive deepening of art's claim to autonomy, then, is not to be considered in isolation and then unequivocally celebrated or lamented, because it brings both losses and gains to art. On the one hand, it heightens the illusion of art's independence; yet on the other, it is this illusory being-in-itself which makes possible the thought of real freedom from naked coercion, total dependence. The problem follows from the more general problem of the way in which rationality is entangled with domination. The entanglement is not to be dissolved, say on the grounds that domination would then 'at least be honest'. Rather, only at the price of rationality's partial concealment of domination can freedom from domination be imagined at all. In a similar way, art's claim to autonomy is to be made good rather than got rid of.

The Absolute Commodity

This is the context for Adorno's account of the work of art as a 'fetish against commodity fetishism'.[5] The work of art is an object which makes an illusory claim not merely to be valuable as a for-another but also as something in itself. In the language of Kantian ethics, it claims a dignity rather than merely a price.[6] It is the fact that this claim is illusory which allows Adorno to describe it as art's 'fetish-character'. But this illusory in-itself makes a true criticism of the advancing conversion of everything to a for-another, that is, the advance towards a situation in which things only have substance and value in so far as they can be exchanged with something else. In late capitalism everything, living human activity included, is increasingly so determined by valuation for-another (exchange-value) that its value in and for itself tends to disappear. By persisting with its illusory claim to a non-exchangeable dignity, art resists the notion that the qualitatively incommensurable can be made quantitatively commensurable.

For Adorno this fact is of determining importance in understanding the shift in modern aesthetic practice away from direct reference, representation or communication, whether in the rise of anti-figurative practices in the visual arts, of hermeneutic difficulty in literary texts, or the emancipation of dissonance in twentieth-century music.[7] The more it is insisted that nothing is worth anything in itself but only as it can be valued against something else, the more works of art, in desperate defence of their illusory non-exchangeable character, refuse immediate access to their consumers. They obstruct communication, that is, precisely as a way of communicating a criticism of the idea that all value must be communicable.[8]

Yet the idea of art as a 'fetish against commodity fetishism' is still more paradoxical even than it appears at first sight, because art is only able to claim autonomy as a result of its own commodity character.[9] It is the commodification of culture which frees works of art from serving some immediate function. A work of art which must serve some particular and inflexible political or ritual context has its law given to it from outside; that is, it is 'heteronomous'. Only when artistic labour and artworks themselves become freely alienable does the possibility even arise that the work of art might be autotelic, an end in itself.

The 'fetish against commodity fetishism', then, does not criticize commodity fetishism by being *less* fetishized and accordingly less illusory than the fetishized commodity, but by being *more* fetishized. This is the sense in which Adorno speaks, hyperbolically, of the work of art as 'the absolute commodity'.[10] In commodity fetishism, it will be remembered, relations between people appear as though they were the property of a thing, the commodity. Production which takes place within this relation of production – the commodity form – tends to become, in Adorno's view, the production of exchange value for its own sake. Yet despite this tendency commodities perpetuate the illusion that they exist only to satisfy need, that they are use-values. The 'absolute commodity', on the other hand, would be 'that social product which has utterly thrown off that illusion of being-for-society which commodities otherwise desperately keep alive'.[11] The work of art, as the 'absolute commodity', openly exposes, rather than desperately concealing, its own character as surplus labour, production for no need at all, for its own sake. In consequence it 'would be free of the ideology which inhabits the commodity form, which claims to be a "for-other" whilst it is ironically a mere "for-itself"'.[12]

Yet if the autonomous work of art is free of this particular kind of ideology, it is by no means free of ideology as such. As the 'absolute commodity' the work of art cannot escape the antagonism between the forces and relations of production which governs capitalist production.[13] Accordingly artisanal models of artistic production, in which the work of art is taken to represent a free or unalienated unfolding of productive forces which are alienated in capitalist production, cannot provide a theory of the production of modern art.[14] The artisanal model presents artistic production as production for true need in a world of false needs; but no theory of true needs is yet possible.

Authentic art questions any dogmatic distinction between true and false needs. Instead it implicitly indicts the production of exchange-value for its own sake, by deliberately exposing its own fetish-character. Even the 'absolute commodity', the image of that which would be fetishized to the point of non-exchangeability, has remained saleable in practice. The sale and purchase of works of art is not an external violation of something which should be untouchable but is 'a simple concomitant of their part in the relations of production', of their fetishism. 'It is absolutely impossible for art to be non-ideological through and through',[15] as a consequence, because this fetish-character is constitutive of what art is. Accordingly, this fetish-character itself cannot simply be deleted to provide aesthetics with a remnant which would be its truth-content: 'ideology and truth in art are not like sheep and goats. Art cannot have the one without the other...'[16] Art's truth-content is accessible only by interpreting art's illusory character, not by abruptly deleting or 'demystifying' that illusory character.

Autonomy and Heteronomy in Art

From any perspective informed by a dialectic of enlightenment, of course, the claim of modern art to be autonomous cannot represent unambiguous progress. It is instructive to consider the distinction between autonomous and heteronomous art in the light of the closely related distinction made by Hegel between Greek ('classical') art and post-Greek ('romantic') art. For Hegel the transition from the first to the second can be seen both as an emancipation and as an impoverishment of art. It is an emancipation in the sense that the subject matter and its manner may be autonomously chosen: art acquires an 'infinitely subjective'[17] aspect by this, both in the range of matters it can address and in the reflexive self-consciousness of its treatment of them.[18] Yet Hegel can also refer to this transition as 'the decay and dissolution of art itself'.[19] Just what makes the romantic work of art autonomous – the free alienability of artistic labour and of the work of art – is also what deprives it, in Hegel's view, of the classical artwork's formative cultural and political significance.[20]

Many of the features of Hegel's contrast between the 'classical' and the 'romantic' work of art reappear in Adorno's account of the distinction between heteronomy and autonomy in the work of art. For Adorno the critical transition is less that from classical Greek to Christian and modern art than that from feudalism to capitalism. Adorno too sees losses rather than merely gains in the rise of autonomous art: it is a 'Pyrrhic victory'.[21] The idea of autonomy is not simple, but necessarily internally contradictory. The work of art's claim to autonomy depends upon a heteronomous element: 'the autonomy of the work of art originates in heteronomy, just as the freedom of the subject originates in the sovereignty of the master'.[22] This means that the concepts of heteronomy and autonomy in art cannot be applied as a kind of classificatory schema, with a date setting the border between the two categories. Rather Adorno's focus is on a process of autonomization of the work of art. If this process were completed, it would in fact be the death of art. As Adorno remarks in his essay on Zemlinsky,

'Art which had removed every trace of what is not art, would scarcely continue to be art'.[33]

Art and Political Practice

Much of the reception of Adorno's aesthetic theory has focused on his view of the relationship between works of art and political practice. Unlike some Marxist aestheticians and artists, Adorno does not take an optimistic view of the possibility of deploying artworks as an instrument in the service of social justice. The aim of critical theory is to bring to an end the primacy of instrumental reason — reason used as a tool without regard for the specific qualities of the object. If we regard practice as the first or foundational consideration, then that instrumentality which critical theory wants to bring to an end is actually installed as a transhistorical invariant.

Adorno suggests, instead, that works of art, rather than being instrumental 'interventions', offer a criticism of instrumental reason and action as such. In so far as art is autonomous, it does not criticize some particular good or bad action, as though actions could be weighed outside their increasingly total context, but the whole framework within which practice takes place. Accordingly, works of art cannot simply be pressed into the service of a just practice, because what they criticize is the depracticalization of practice itself. Once works of art are pressed into the service of some higher end, they immediately lose their autonomous character. As sheer instruments they could no longer offer a critique of instrumental reason. Modern works of art are products without an obvious purpose, in a world where everything is presented as existing not for its own sake but for the sake of something else. They thus point to the fact that production is becoming the production of exchange-value for its own sake.

Adorno does not pretend, however, that the work of art can actually stand in some politically disinterested realm outside society. Instead Adorno understands art as 'the social antithesis to society'.[24] All art has a political significance, whether it explicitly thematizes such significance or not. Adorno's critique of the idea of political commitment in art does not attempt to specify art's job description, to insist that art should not dirty its hands with politics. Instead, Adorno's critique of politically committed art is, in part, a political one. The danger for politically committed art is that it will end up as bad art without becoming good politics either.

Adorno illustrates this through a discussion of Brecht's play *The Resistible Rise of Arturo Ui*.[25] In the play Chicago gangsterism is used as an allegory of the rise of the Third Reich. Adorno points out that both terms of the comparison are diminished by this procedure. On the one hand, the world of gangland Chicago becomes an empty cipher for the real political content, an attack on the Third Reich. Still more seriously, however, the use of Chicago gangsterism as a metaphor for Nazism is quite inadequate because it grotesquely under-estimates the systematic power and qualitative novelty of Nazism. The work is as useless towards any just practice as any other piece of weak theory would be. It represents the literary equivalent of arguments that fascism is doomed to collapse because it is against the real interests of the workers.

It is no part of Adorno's argument to insist that work produced with the intention of influencing political practice can never be good art; here as else-where, the producer's intention is by no means the decisive criterion. (Adorno, indeed, on several occasions pays tribute to what he takes to be the aesthetic and critical merits of aspects of Brecht's work.)[26] The decisive fact is not what the author, painter or composer wishes to use the work for, but what happens in the work itself. Adorno is not, then, opposing a purely contemplative notion of the work of art to the instrumental use of art which he wishes to criticize. Indeed, he argues that 'the more thoroughly works of art are deciphered, the less absolute can their opposition to praxis remain'.[27] Works of art, Adorno sug-gests, 'are less than practice, and more'.[28] They are 'less' than practice because, like theory, they put off a practice which 'cannot wait', and are no less com-promised by this than is theory itself. But they are 'more' than practice because they criticize the whole framework within which practice takes place, the abso-lutization of production for its own sake: 'the critique carried out by works of art is a critique of activity as the cryptogram of domination'.[29]

Adorno argues that only works of art which do not cancel out their own autonomous character in the service of some political end can in fact be authen-tically critical. He gives the example of how works of art relate to the experience of monopoly capitalism. The decisive experience of monopoly capitalism is a *loss* of individual experience; the experience of one's own life as utterly contingent, dispensable, and having significance not in itself, but only as it is a means to something else. Naturalist art. Adorno believes, has become inauthentic in late capitalism, because it treats as straightforwardly and unambiguously concrete a social experience which is itself deeply ideologically pre-formed and increas-ingly abstract, emptied of content. The 'reality' which naturalism would imitate is not reality *tout court*, but is entangled in a social context which is a real illusion.

Modern art, by contrast, has become abstract because it senses the need to imitate this loss of experience. 'In Kafka's work monopoly capitalism appears only in the background; yet it codifies in the flotsam of the administered world what human beings have experienced under the total social spell, more faithfully and more powerfully than novels about corrupt industrial trusts'.[30] Authentic modernist art does more justice to the 'loss of experience' under late capitalism by renouncing an attempt to replicate experience. It is still a kind of mimesis, Adorno argues; but it is mimesis of the systematic framework which impover-ishes experience, not a mimesis of individual impoverished experience which misrepresents such experience as though it were immediate and untouched after all.

> Modern art is as abstract as the relations between people have in truth become ... Since the spell of external reality over the subjects and their mode of behaviour has become absolute, the work of art can only oppose it by making itself like that spell. At the point of absolute zero, however, at which Beckett's prose exists, a second world of images is produced, as sad as it is rich, the precipitate of historical experiences which in their immediate form would be unable to impinge on what is decisive, the hollowing out of the subject and of reality. The poverty and damagedness of this world of images is an imprint, a photographic negative of the administered world. To this extent Beckett is a realist.[31]

For Adorno, then, the reproach that modernists are 'formalists', excessively preoccupied with style and technique and uninterested in human experience, misses the point, because it simply posits the richness of 'experience' as a given without considering what has become of such experience. Equally, Adorno argues that 'Kafka's epic style is, in its archaism, mimesis of reification'.[32] Authentic modernist art is not formalism, but a realism of the loss of experience.

This kind of defence of autonomous art as socially critical, then, distinguishes Adorno's approach from any aestheticist appeal to art as inviolably or absolutely autotelic – *l'art pour l'art* (art for art's sake). Adorno does not recommend to works of art that they 'ought' to become autonomous, but interprets the autonomization of the work of art as a historical process which cannot be wished out of existence. Autonomy depends on a heteronomous moment for its very possibility. As soon as art attempts to cut out this heteronomous moment entirely, it also liquidates the conditions for its own autonomous, critical relation to the empirical world. It loses its character as art altogether and shrinks to ornament, to a mere thing. The paradox of the work of art's autonomy is that it can be preserved only in so far as it is not made absolute.[33]

Notes

1. Adorno, *Ästhetische Theorie* (hereafter *AT*), vol. 7 of *Gesammelte Schriften* (hereafter *GS*), 23 vols. (Frankfurt am Main: Suhrkamp, 1970 onwards), p.164; Adorno, *Aesthetic Theory*, tr. Robert Hullot-Kentor (London: Athlone, 1997) (hereafter Hullot-Kentor), p.107.
2. *AT*, pp.334–8; Hullot-Kentor, pp.225–8.
3. *AT*, p.338; Hullot-Kentor, p.228.
4. *AT*, p.337; Hullot-Kentor, p.227.
5. Ibid.
6. Kant, *Groundwork of the Metaphysic of Morals*, tr. H. J. Paton (New York: Harper & Row, 1964), p.102.

7. *AT*, p.335; Hullot-Kentor, p.226.
8. *AT*, p.351; Hullot-Kentor, p.236.
9. 'Zur gesellschaftlichen Lage der Musik' [1932], in *Musikalische Schriften V, GS* 18, p.757.
10. *AT*, p.351; Hullot-Kentor, p.236.
11. Ibid.
12. Ibid.
13. Ibid.
14. *AT*, p.358; Hullot-Kentor, p.241.
15. *AT*, p.351; Hullot-Kentor, p.236.
16. *AT*, p.347; Hullot-Kentor, p.234.
17. G. W. F. Hegel, *Aesthetics*, tr. T. M. Knox, 2 vols. (Oxford: Clarendon Press, 1975), i. 504.
18. Ibid., pp.517–29.
19. Ibid., p.576.
20. Cf. Gillian Rose, *Hegel contra Sociology* (London: Athlone, 1981), pp.121–48.
21. 'Die Kunst und die Künste', *GS* 10, part 1, p.436.
22. *Beethoven*, p.72.
23. 'Zemlinsky', in *Quasi una Fantasia*, tr. Rodney Livingstone (London: Verso, 1992), pp.111–29, p.113.
24. *AT*, p.19; Hullot-Kentor, p.8.
25. 'Engagement', in *GS* 11, pp.409–30, p.417; *Notes to Literature*, tr. Shierry Weber Nicholsen, 2 vols. (New York: Columbia University Press, 1991–2), ii. 83.
26. *AT*, pp.54–5, 123; Hullot-Kentor, pp.32, 79.
27. *AT*, p.358; Hullot-Kentor, p.241.
28. Ibid.
29. *AT*, pp.358–9; Hullot-Kentor, p.241.
30. *AT*, p.342; Hullot-Kentor, p.230.
31. *AT*, p.53; Hullot-Kentor, p.31.
32. *AT*, p.342; Hullot-Kentor, p.230.
33. *AT*, pp.137–8; Hullot-Kentor, p.89.

* * *

One of the most influential criticisms of Adorno came from Peter Bürger in his *Theory of the Avant-Garde* (1974, tr. 1984). Bürger argues that Adorno is too deeply immersed in the institution of art to reflect critically on its categories. In bourgeois society it is not so much the artwork which is autonomous from society as the entire institution of art. While the 'institution of art' is most readily imagined in terms of physical institutions, such as the quasi-sacred spaces of museums, more importantly for Bürger and other cultural critics, the 'institution of art' includes processes of evaluation and fundamental concepts. Bürger criticizes Adorno for employing, in his analysis of modernism, concepts such as 'the new'[7] which gained their current meanings only in the artistic revolutions of the late nineteenth and early twentieth centuries. Similarly, Bürger aims to understand the concept of the autonomy of art in Marxist-historicist terms, as 'a category of bourgeois society'. The detachment of art from 'practical contexts' is neither an ahistorical truth nor even a completed fact, but an historical process; art is only *relatively* dissociated from the praxis of life.[8] The significance of the avant-garde for Bürger is that it attempted to resist this dissociation, and this distinguishes it from the contemporaneous 'modernist' movements. Moreover, the approach of the dadaists and surrealists to art (to take two representative avant-garde movements) was such that it created new categories within aesthetics. Dadaism and surrealism 'raised to a principle the availability of the artistic means of past periods', for example, through painting in a pastiche of past styles. In doing so, they made possible the critical recognition of the categories of 'artistic means' and 'procedures': 'that the various techniques and procedures can be *recognized* as artistic means has been possible only since the historical avant-garde movements'.[9] Before, their seeming inevitability or at least properness had obscured their existence as means and procedures. Bürger's mode of argument opposes the notion that there are ahistorical 'ideas' (such as 'autonomy' or 'procedures') which manifest themselves in given periods. Rather, there are productive practices within art which stimulate the production of new concepts, and which open new critical vistas on earlier art.

Extract from Peter Bürger, *Theory of the Avant-Garde* translated from the German by Michael Shaw (Minneapolis: University of Minnesota Press, 1984), pp.47–53.

The Negation of the Autonomy of Art by the Avant-Garde

In scholarly discussion up to now, the category 'autonomy' has suffered from the imprecision of the various subcategories thought of as constituting a unity in the concept of the autonomous work of art. Since the development of the individual subcategories is not synchronous, it may happen that sometimes courtly art seems already autonomous, while at other times only bourgeois art appears to have that characteristic. To make clear that the contradictions between the various interpretations result from the nature of the case, we will sketch a historical typology that is deliberately reduced to three elements (purpose or function, production, reception), because the point here is to have the nonsynchronism in the development of individual categories emerge with clarity.

A.   Sacral Art (example: the art of the High Middle Ages) serves as cult object. It is wholly integrated into the social institution 'religion'. It is produced collectively, as a craft. The mode of reception also is institutionalized as collective.[1]

B.   Courtly Art (example: the art at the court of Louis XIV) also has a precisely defined function. It is representational and serves the glory of the prince
and the self-portrayal of courtly society. Courtly art is part of the life praxis
of courtly society, just as sacral art is part of the life praxis of the faithful.
Yet the detachment from the sacral tie is a first step in the emancipation of
art. ('Emancipation' is being used here as a descriptive term, as referring to
the process by which art constitutes itself as a distinct social subsystem.) The
difference from sacral art becomes particularly apparent in the realm of production: the artist produces as an individual and develops a consciousness of
the uniqueness of his activity. Reception, on the other hand, remains collective. But the content of the collective performance is no longer sacral, it is
sociability.

C.   Only to the extent that the bourgeoisie adopts concepts of value held by
the aristocracy does bourgeois art have a representational function. When it
is genuinely bourgeois, this art is the objectification of the self-understanding
of the bourgeois class. Production and reception of the self-understanding as
articulated in art are no longer tied to the praxis of life. Habermas calls this the
satisfaction of residual needs, that is, of needs that have become submerged in
the life praxis of bourgeois society. Not only production but reception also are
now individual acts. The solitary absorption in the work is the adequate mode
of appropriation of creations removed from the life praxis of the bourgeois,
even though they still claim to interpret that praxis. In Aestheticism, finally,
where bourgeois art reaches the stage of self-reflection, this claim is no longer
made. Apartness from the praxis of life, which had always been the condition
that characterized the way art functioned in bourgeois society, now becomes
its content. The typology we have sketched here can be represented in the
accompanying tabulation (the vertical lines in boldface refer to a decisive change
in the development, the broken ones to a less decisive one).

	Sacral Art	Courtly Art	Bourgeois Art
Purpose or function	cult object	representational object	portrayal of bourgeois self-understanding
Production	collective craft	individual	individual
Reception	collective (sacral)	collective (sociable)	individual

The tabulation allows one to notice that the development of the categories was not synchronous. Production by the individual that characterizes art in bourgeois society has its origins as far back as courtly patronage. But courtly art still remains integral to the praxis of life, although as compared with the cult function, the representational function constitutes a step toward a mitigation of claims that art play a direct social role. The reception of courtly art also remains collective, although the content of the collective performance has changed. As regards reception, it is only with bourgeois art that a decisive change sets in: its reception is one by isolated individuals. The novel is that literary genre in which the new mode of reception finds the form appropriate to it.[2] The advent of bourgeois art is also the decisive turning point as regards use or function. Although in different ways, both sacral and courtly art are integral to the life praxis of the recipient. As cult and representational objects, works of art are put to a specific use. This requirement no longer applies to the same extent to bourgeois art. In bourgeois art, the portrayal of bourgeois self-understanding occurs in a sphere that lies outside the praxis of life. The citizen who, in everyday life, has been reduced to a partial function (means-ends activity) can be discovered in art as 'human being'. Here, one can unfold the abundance of one's talents, though with the proviso that this sphere remain strictly separate from the praxis of life. Seen in this fashion, the separation of art from the praxis of life becomes the decisive characteristic of the autonomy of bourgeois art (a fact that the tabulation does not bring out adequately). To avoid misunderstandings, it must be emphasized once again that autonomy in this sense defines the status of art in bourgeois society but that no assertions concerning the contents of works are involved. Although art as an institution may be considered fully formed toward the end of the eighteenth century, the development of the contents of works is subject to a historical dynamics, whose terminal point is reached in Aestheticism, where art becomes the content of art.

The European avant-garde movements can be defined as an attack on the status of art in bourgeois society. What is negated is not an earlier form of art (a style) but art as an institution that is unassociated with the life praxis of men. When the avant-gardistes demand that art become practical once again, they do not mean that the contents of works of art should be socially significant. The demand is not raised at the level of the contents of individual works. Rather, it directs itself to the way art functions in society, a process that does as much to determine the effect that works have as does the particular content.

The avant-gardistes view its dissociation from the praxis of life as the dominant characteristic of art in bourgeois society. One of the reasons this dissociation was possible is that Aestheticism had made the element that defines art as an institution the essential content of works. Institution and work contents had to coincide to make it logically possible for the avant-garde to call art into question. The avant-gardistes proposed the sublation of art – sublation in the Hegelian sense of the term: art was not to be simply destroyed, but transferred to the praxis of life where it would be preserved, albeit in a changed form. The avant-gardistes thus adopted an essential element of Aestheticism. Aestheticism had made the distance from the praxis of life the content of works. The praxis of life to which Aestheticism refers and which it negates is the means-ends rationality of the bourgeois everyday. Now, it is not the aim of the avant-gardistes to integrate art into *this* praxis. On the contrary, they assent to the aestheticists' rejection of the world and its means-ends rationality. What distinguishes them from the latter is the attempt to organize a new life praxis from a basis in art. In this respect also, Aestheticism turns out to have been the necessary precondition of the avant-gardiste intent. Only an art the contents of whose individual works is wholly distinct from the (bad) praxis of the existing society can be the center that can be the starting point for the organization of a new life praxis.

With the help of Herbert Marcuse's theoretical formulation concerning the twofold character of art in bourgeois society (sketched in chapter one), the avant-gardiste intent can be understood with particular clarity. All those needs that cannot be satisfied in everyday life, because the principle of competition pervades all spheres, can find a home in art, because art is removed from the praxis of life. Values such as humanity, joy, truth, solidarity are extruded from life as it were, and preserved in art. In bourgeois society, art has a contradictory role: it projects the image of a better order and to that extent protests against the bad order that prevails. But by realizing the image of a better order in fiction, which is semblance *(Schein)* only, it relieves the existing society of the pressure of those forces that make for change. They are assigned to confinement in an ideal sphere. Where art accomplishes this, it is 'affirmative' in Marcuse's sense of the term. If the twofold character of art in bourgeois society consists in the fact that the distance from the social production and reproduction process contains an element of freedom and an element of the noncommittal and an absence of any consequences, it can be seen that the avant-gardistes' attempt to reintegrate art into the life process is itself a profoundly contradictory endeavor. For the (relative) freedom of art vis-à-vis the praxis of life is at the same time the condition that must be fulfilled if there is to be a critical cognition of reality. An art no longer distinct from the praxis of life but wholly absorbed in it will lose the capacity to criticize it, along with its distance. During the time of the historical avant-garde movements, the attempt to do away with the distance between art and life still had all the pathos of historical progressiveness on its side. But in the meantime, the culture industry has brought about the false elimination of the distance between art and life, and this also allows one to recognize the contradictoriness of the avant-gardiste undertaking.[3]

In what follows, we will outline how the intent to eliminate art as an institution found expression in the three areas that we used above to characterize autonomous art: purpose or function, production, reception. Instead of speaking of the avant-gardiste work, we will speak of avant-gardiste manifestation. A dadaist manifestation does not have work character but is nonetheless an authentic manifestation of the artistic avant-garde. This is not to imply that the avant-gardistes produced no works whatever and replaced them by ephemeral events. We will see that whereas they did not destroy it, the avant-gardistes profoundly modified the category of the work of art.

Of the three areas, the *intended purpose or function* of the avant-gardiste manifestation is most difficult to define. In the aestheticist work of art, the disjointure of the work and the praxis of life characteristic of the status of art in bourgeois society has become the work's essential content. It is only as a consequence of this fact that the work of art becomes its own end in the full meaning of the term. In Aestheticism, the social functionlessness of art becomes manifest. The avant-gardiste artists counter such functionlessness not by an art that would have consequences within the existing society, but rather by the principle of the sublation of art in the praxis of life. But such a conception makes it impossible to define the intended purpose of art. For an art that has been reintegrated into the praxis of life, not even the absence of a social purpose can be indicated, as was still possible in Aestheticism. When art and the praxis of life are one, when the praxis is aesthetic and art is practical, art's purpose can no longer be discovered, because the existence of two distinct spheres (art and the praxis of life) that is constitutive of the concept of purpose or intended use has come to an end.

We have seen that the *production* of the autonomous work of art is the act of an individual. The artist produces as individual, individuality not being understood as the expression of something but as radically different. The concept of genius testifies to this. The quasitechnical consciousness of the makeability of works of art that Aestheticism attains seems only to contradict this. Valéry, for example, demystifies artistic genius by reducing it to psychological motivations on the one hand, and the availability to it of artistic means on the other. While pseudoromantic doctrines of inspiration thus come to be seen as the self-deception of producers, the view of art for which the individual is the creative subject is let stand. Indeed, Valéry's theorem concerning the force of pride (*orgueil*) that sets off and propels the creative process renews once again the notion of the individual character of artistic production central to art in bourgeois society.[4] In its most extreme manifestations, the avant-garde's reply to this is not the collective as the subject of production but the radical negation of the category of individual creation. When Duchamp signs mass-produced objects (a urinal, a bottle drier) and sends them to art exhibits, he negates the category of individual production. The signature, whose very purpose it is to mark what is individual in the work, that it owes its existence to this particular artist, is inscribed on an arbitrarily chosen mass product, because all claims to individual creativity are to be mocked. Duchamp's provocation not only unmasks the art market where the signature means more than the quality of the work; it radically questions the very principle of art in bourgeois society according to which the individual is considered the creator of the work of art. Duchamp's Ready-Mades are not works of art but manifestations. Not from the form-content totality of the individual object Duchamp signs can one infer the meaning, but only from the contrast between mass-produced object on the one hand, and signature and art exhibit on the other. It is obvious that this kind of provocation cannot be repeated indefinitely. The provocation depends on what it turns against: here, it is the idea that the individual is the subject of artistic creation. Once the signed bottle drier has been accepted as an object that deserves a place in a museum, the provocation no longer provokes; it turns into its opposite. If an artist today signs a stove pipe and exhibits it, that artist certainly does not denounce the art market but adapts to it. Such adaptation does not eradicate the idea of individual creativity, it affirms it, and the reason is the failure of the avant-gardiste intent to sublate art. Since now the protest of the historical avant-garde against art as institution is accepted as *art*, the gesture of protest of the neo-avant-garde becomes inauthentic. Having been shown to be irredeemable, the claim to be protest can no longer be maintained. This fact accounts for the arts-and-crafts impression that works of the avant-garde not infrequently convey.[5]

The avant-garde not only negates the category of individual production but also that of individual *reception*. The reactions of the public during a dada manifestation where it has been mobilized by provocation, and which can range from shouting to fisticuffs, are certainly collective in nature. True, these remain reactions, responses to a preceding provocation. Producer and recipient remain clearly distinct, however active the public may become. Given the avant-gardiste intention to do away with art as a sphere that is separate from the praxis of life, it is logical to eliminate the antithesis between producer and recipient. It is no accident that both Tzara's instructions for the making of a Dadaist poem and Breton's for the writing of automatic texts have the character of recipes.[6] This represents not only a polemical attack on the individual creativity of the artist; the recipe is to be taken quite literally as suggesting a possible activity on the part of the recipient. The automatic texts also should be read as guides to individual production. But such production is not to be understood as artistic production, but as part of a liberating life praxis. This is what is meant by Breton's demand that poetry be practiced (*pratiquer la poésie*). Beyond the coincidence of producer and recipient that this demand implies, there is the fact that these concepts lose their meaning: producers and recipients no longer exist. All that remains is the individual who uses poetry as an instrument for living one's life as best one can. There is also a danger here to which Surrealism at least partly succumbed, and that is solipsism, the retreat to the problems of the isolated subject. Breton himself saw this danger and envisaged different ways of dealing with it. One of them was the glorification of the spontaneity of the erotic relationship. Perhaps the strict group discipline was also an attempt to exorcise the danger of solipsism that surrealism harbors.[7]

Notes

1. On this, see the recent essay by R. Warning, 'Ritus, Mythos und geistliches Spiel', in *Terror und Spiel. Probleme der Mythenrezeption*, ed. Fuhrmann (München: Wilhelm Fink Verlag, 1971), pp.211–39.
2. Hegel has already referred to the novel as 'the middle-class epic' (*Ästhetik*, ed. F. Bassenge, 2 vols. [Berlin/Weimar, 1965], vol. II, p.452.) [In his translation of the *Aesthetics*, T. M. Knox renders this passage as follows: "But it is quite different with romance, the modern popular epic" (ii. 1092), but this seems wrong. Translator's note.]
3. On the problem of the false sublation of art in the praxis of life, see J. Habermas, *Strukturwandel der Öffentlichkeit* (Neuwied / Berlin, 1968), §18, p.176ff.
4. See P. Bürger, 'Funktion und Bedeutung des *orgeuil* bei Paul Valéry', in *Romantisches Jahrbuch* 16 (1965), pp.149–68.
5. Examples of neo-avant-gardiste paintings and sculptures to be found in the catalog of the exhibit *Sammlung Cremer. Europäische Avantgarde 1950–1970*, ed. G. Adriani (Tübingen, 1973). [...]
6. T. Tzara, 'Pour faire un Poème dadaïste', in Tzara, Lampisteries précédées des sept manifestes dada (n.p., 1963), p.64. A. Breton, 'Manifeste du surréalisme' (1924), in Breton, *Manifestes du surréalisme* (Paris: Coll. Idées 23, 1963), p.42f.
7. On the Surrealists' conception of groups and the collective experiences they sought and partially realized, see Elisabeth Lenk, *Der springende Narziss. André Breton's poetischer Materialismus* (München, 1971), p.57 ff, 73 f.

* * *

In spite of the objections that can be raised to Bürger's approach, his account of the avant-garde has proved influential, not least because in the mid-1980s it helped to answer certain questions about the relation of postmodernism to modernism. Bürger's spotlighting of the avant-garde created a third element in the relationship. Terry Eagleton's 'Capitalism, Modernism and Postmodernism' (1985), though strongly influenced by Adorno in its account of modernism and commodification, takes Bürger's essay as its starting point with regard to postmodernism. Like the avant-garde, postmodernism attempts to 'erase the frontiers between culture and political society and return aesthetic production to its humble, unprivileged place with social practices as a whole', but it does so in a society dominated by commodification.[10] Bürger's account of the revolutionary aspect of the avant-garde allows Eagleton to shape a narrative in which the playfulness of postmodernism, while improving upon an elitist and reactionary modernism, also betrayed a more radical project. The liberal narrative of progress within which many were situating postmodernism became some-thing more complex. Other critics argued that postmodernism needed to be internally differentiated. For Andreas Huyssen, Bürger's account of the early twentieth-century avant-garde also describes the early 'iconoclastic' phase of postmodernism in the 1960s. This movement was in time assimilated by the culture industry into the commodified form described by Eagleton.[11]

The generality of Bürger's account is alien to the Anglo-American critical tra-dition that begins with close reading, and which prizes particularity. In Bürger's defence, one might note that the weakness of that Anglo-American tradition is its inability to see the larger institutional context of literature, right down to the possibility of 'literature' being an institution. However, such a defence does not entirely exonerate Bürger. Several critics have objected that 'the insti-tution of art' is too general a term, and fails to respect the differences between the institutions of the visual arts and the literary, for example.[12] One might even ask whether 'literature' can be considered as a single institution. Bürger would accept its historical variability, but its range and complexity within a given historical moment do not find a place in his theory.

A further argument against Bürger notes his own description of the rein-tegration of art into the 'life process' as 'a profoundly contradictory endeavor' (see extract, p.134). The 'possibility of reconceptualizing social practice' is pre-dicated upon the possibility of achieving a 'critical distance' from the object to be criticized.[13] Though Bürger acknowledges the contradiction, much of his argument seems to overlook the problem. Certainly, later critics have spoken as if the avant-garde project were unproblematic.

More specifically historical objections could be raised to Bürger's insistence that 'representational' art is primarily courtly: it seems to contradict the massive evidence for the rise of the representational novel as the primary bourgeois form in the nineteenth century.[14] Bürger implies that such anachronisms occur because the bourgeoisie adopted concepts of value held by the aristocracy, but one must ask how far the actuality of the bourgeoisie can be allowed to fall out of step with the ideality of Bürger's diagram before the diagram must be rejected. Or, to put it another way, one must ask how 'false consciousness' such as the adoption of courtly values was sustainable in a thoroughly bourgeois world. Bürger's categorization of the reception of bourgeois art as individual also contradicts evidence that, in the nineteenth century, certain kinds of literary art were consumed by the family unit: reading aloud to the family was a common practice; the title of Charles Dickens's periodical *Household Words* identifies an ideal audience which must have been in some cases actual.

Some critics have argued that the division between the avant-garde and modernism is not so clear. Richard Sieburth has suggested that Ezra Pound's 'strategies of quotation and misquotation' in *The Cantos* may have drawn inspir-ation from the Dadaist movement, usually considered avant-garde, and that

Pound's editing of *The Waste Land* may have similarly benefited from his interest in it.[15] Astradur Eysteinsson, drawing on Sieburth, has argued that the movements are interconnected: 'while the avant-garde movements are historical phenomena in their own right, they are also salient motors of modernism'.[16] Such an approach places greater emphasis on the formal techniques employed by the text, and less on the aims of the text; it assumes that we cannot ever know whether the text aimed to provide aesthetic pleasure in a conventional way, or whether it aimed to attack the institution of art.

Bürger's theory of the avant-garde has demonstrated that experimental art in the early twentieth century need not be thought of as autonomous, whether in Kermode's or Adorno's terms. Not all artists wished to be secluded in Axel's castle. It has also produced multiple definitions of modernism, and has freed both modernism and postmodernism from a reductive situation in which each antagonistically defined the other. The multiple definitions are due in part to the difficulty in locating either the avant-garde or modernism in the pure forms that Bürger envisaged. Bürger defines the differences in terms of intentions, but the materials available to literary critics are texts and tentative reconstructions of contexts.

Chapter Notes

1. Astradur Eysteinsson, *The Concept of Modernism* (Ithaca, NY: Cornell University Press, 1990), 16.
2. Simon Jarvis, *Adorn : A Critical Introduction* (Cambridge: Polity, 1998), 14.
3. Jarvis, *Adorno*, 8.
4. Adorno, *The Culture Industry* (London: Routledge, 1991), 187–97.
5. C. Lenhardt's 1984 translation has been superseded by Robert Hullot-Kentor's *Aesthetic Theory* (1997; London: Continuum, 2002).
6. Eysteinsson, *The Concept of Modernism*, 40.
7. Peter Bürger, *Theory of the Avant-Garde*, tr. Michael Shaw (Minneapolis: University of Minnesota Press, 1984), 59–63.
8. Bürger, *Theory of the Avant-Garde*, 46.
9. Bürger, *Theory of the Avant-Garde*, 17–18.
10. Terry Eagleton, 'Capitalism, Modernism and Postmodernism' (1985), in David Lodge, ed., *Modern Criticism and Theory: A Reader* (Harlow: Longman, 1988), 385–98.
11. Andreas Huyssen, 'Mapping the Postmodern', *After the Great Divide: Modernism, Mass Culture and Postmodernism* (1986; Basingstoke: Macmillan, 1988), 191–3.
12. Eysteinsson, *Theory of Modernism*, 164–78.
13. Richard Murphy, *Theorizing the Avant-Garde* (Cambridge: Cambridge University Press, 1998), 27.
14. Eysteinsson, *Theory of Modernism*, 174.

15. Richard Sieburth, 'Dada Pound', *South Atlantic Quarterly*, 83 (1984), 44–68.
16. Eysteinsson,*Theory of Modernism*, 178.

Further Reading

Adorno, Theodor. *Aesthetic Theory*, tr. Robert Hullot-Kentor (1997; London: Continuum, 2002). A dense and intimidating text, but rewarding. The section titled 'Situation' (pp.16–45) is particularly valuable. Hullot-Kentor's translation supersedes that of C. Lenhardt published in 1984.

Calinescu, Matei. 'The Idea of the Avant-Garde', in *Five Faces of Modernity* (Durham, NC: Duke University Press, 1987), 95–148.

Eysteinsson, Astradur. *The Concept of Modernism* (Ithaca, NY: Cornell University Press, 1990), 143–78. Includes extensive discussion of Peter Bürger.

Huyssen, Andreas. *After the Great Divide* (Bloomington: Indiana University Press, 1986). Particularly the essays 'The Search for Tradition' and 'Mapping the Postmodern'.

Murphy, Richard. *Theorizing the Avant-Garde: Modernism, Expressionism, and the Problem of Postmodernity* (Cambridge: Cambridge University Press, 1999). Murphy brings concepts of the avant-garde to bear on German expressionist literature. The first and final chapters contain valuable discussion about the relation of modernism, postmodernism, and the avant-garde.

Perloff, Marjorie. *The Futurist Moment: Avant-garde, Avant guerre, and the Language of Rupture* (Chicago, London: University of Chicago Press: 1986). Examines the sense of optimism in the pre-war avant-garde and its post-war successors, and, like Perloff's *Poetics of Indeterminacy*, is committed to the idea that symbolism was not the only tradition. International in scope, covering Russia, France, Italy, Germany, and Britain, it covers both art and literature.

Poggioli, Renato. *The Theory of the Avant-Garde*, tr. G. Fitzgerald (Cambridge, MA: Belknap Press of Harvard University Press, 1968). Many critics have remarked that Poggioli's 'avant-garde' is everyone else's 'modernism'.

Wolin, Richard. 'Modernism vs. Postmodernism', *Telos*, 62 (1984–5), 9–29. Gives an account and criticism of Bürger's theory on pp.13–16, arguing the need for a third category, de-aestheticized autonomous art, to deal with surrealism.

4

Modernism, the Masses, and the Culture Industry

Modernism came into the world at the same time as many of the mass media familiar to us today: the mass-market newspaper first arrived in Britain with *The Daily Mail* in 1896; the identity of the 'yellow press' in North America emerged at about the same time; wireless telegraphy was invented in the 1890s; in the USA, the Westinghouse radio station KDKA began broadcasting in Pittsburgh in 1920; Britain's first national broadcasting company began broadcasting in modernism's *annus mirabilis*, 1922; moving pictures were another product of the 1890s, with 'talkies' being introduced from the late 1920s onwards.[1] The only significant mass media to postdate modernism are the television and the personal computer: though the BBC made its first television broadcasts in 1936, the medium did not reach a mass audience until after the Second World War. Modernism was also born at the same time as an increasing divide in the literary market between 'highbrow' and 'lowbrow' publications. Modernist artists might have plausibly ignored mass culture altogether, but their response was more complex: many seemed drawn to it, if only to enable gestures of repudiation.

In the English-speaking world, critical approaches to the question of modernism and the mass media have been influenced by three main strands of thought: a native strand which has been primarily concerned with the 'elitism' of modernist writers; another native strand indebted to Raymond Williams's interrogation of the concept of 'culture'; and one indebted to the Frankfurt school, a tradition running from Walter Benjamin and Theodor Adorno through to Peter Bürger and Andreas Huyssen. The socialist criticism of the Williams lineage has been receptive to the work of continental theorists, so the identity of each strand is never pure.

All three are marked by the memory of the rise of Nazism and the holocaust. The concern with the elitism of modernist writers connects – correctly, in many cases – aesthetic elitism and political elitism. Bertrand Russell's remarks in 1956 that D. H. Lawrence's political outlook anticipated fascism, and that his politics 'led straight to Auschwitz', sounded the key note for many critics investigating the politics of other modernists. Russell's thesis was expanded and documented by John Harrison in *The Reactionaries* (1966), and more recently by John Carey in *The Intellectuals and the Masses* (1992).[2] Given that the institution of literary criticism in its modern form began at the same time as modernist literature, it is unsurprising to find the elitism of modernist writers embodied in early and influential critics. Part of Raymond Williams's task in *Culture and Society* (1958) was to disentangle the positive elements of F. R. Leavis's contribution to literary and cultural criticism from an elitist attitude that could state, for example, that '[i]n any period it is upon a very small minority that the discerning appreciation of art and literature depends'.[3] Williams, in response, exposed the complexity of Leavis's apparently simple central concept: 'What, in fact, do we mean by "mass"? Do we mean a democracy dependent on universal suffrage, or a culture dependent on universal education, or a reading-public dependent on universal literacy?' He goes on to ask whether the real 'agents of decay' might be neither suffrage, education, nor literacy, but something closer to the economic base: 'an industrial civilization, dependent on machine-production and the factory system?'[4] Such questions grant greater complexity to the relations of culture and society than do studies like *The Intellectuals and the Masses*.

Carey provides his readers with a reductive version of the Frankfurt School as cultural elitists who shared with writers like George Orwell 'the view that mass culture and mass media, as developed under capitalism, had degraded civilization in the twentieth century'.[5] Carey mistakes the symptom (the quality of mass culture) for the cause, which is capitalism. Andreas Huyssen provides a more nuanced view, beginning with a letter that Adorno wrote to Walter Benjamin, commenting on a draft of his essay 'The Work of Art in the Age of Mechanical Reproduction':

> 'Both [modernist art and mass culture] bear the scars of capitalism, both contain elements of change. Both are torn halves of freedom, to which however they do not add up'.[6] Adorno sees the dichotomy as historically produced, and he clearly interprets modernism as a 'symptom and a result of cultural crisis rather than as a new "solution" in its own right'. Adorno could not agree more with Jameson's claim that the commodity is 'the prior form in terms of which alone modernism can be structurally grasped'. Even though Adorno's dialectical view of the relationship between modernism and mass culture may ultimately not be dialectical enough, it warrants repeating [. . .] that he is miles apart from the evaluative schemes of conservative mass culture critics and does not have much in common with the happy-go-lucky apologists of the triumph of modernism.[7]

'The scars of capitalism': there is no uncertainty in this formulation as to the agent of decay. Adorno as a cultural critic was equally capable of tracing its results in the culture of classical music as in popular culture.[8] Adorno's paradox of the 'torn halves' that do not add up to a whole implies that capitalism has distorted both modernist art and mass culture; it implies that the musical deficiencies of ragtime cannot be compensated for by listening to Ravel, nor vice versa; nor can some simple synthesis of high and popular culture be achieved, because any such synthesis would not escape the distorting effects of the capitalist context.

The present essay, 'Mass Culture as Woman: Modernism's Other', is taken from Huyssen's collection *After the Great Divide* (1986), the title of which alludes to Adorno's 'torn halves', as well as to the divide between modernism and postmodernism. Along with Adorno's accounts of modernism and mass culture, and Bürger's distinction between modernism and the avant-garde, Huyssen's essay also brings a psychoanalytic orientation to bear upon the question: he is concerned with the construction of modern subjectivity, and how it is influenced by questions of gender and mass culture. An important influence in this regard, though one mentioned only briefly in section III, is Klaus Theweleit's *Male Fantasies* (1977–8; tr. 1987). Theweleit's historical study examined letters, memoirs, journals, and literary writing by members of the Freikorps movement, a paramilitary organization in Germany between the wars; in many cases, members of the Freikorps became Nazis. The texts reveal men whose sense of self was threatened by women and femininity, and who constructed an armoured sense of self in response. A feminist critic who has also drawn on Theweleit summarizes the situation thus:

> All that so terrifyingly threatens the fragile, and therefore violently defended, upright armored rigidity of these men is associated with the liberation of desire as embodied by the overtly, genitally erotic woman. It is important that this threatening desire, gendered female, is imaged as a turbulent flood, either of water as a general element or, more specifically, as unleashed red flood of all that dangerous, repressed sexual–political matter; it is crucial for my argument here that this is simultaneously the red flood of socialist revolution and of menstruation and childbirth. The rising flood of the working class, and, historically proximate, of the 'dark' races, is conflated symbolically with that of the repressed maternal feminine, as we will see throughout this study.[9]

The uses to which Theweleit's findings have been put by recent critics of modernism are sometimes questionable: his careful historical researches and findings are sometimes taken to reinforce, justify, or even confirm psychoanalytical theories which themselves informed his interpretations of his material; what was true for the Freikorps in Germany is taken to be true of all men in all parts of Europe and America in the early twentieth century. Huyssen does not employ Theweleit quite so reductively, and, if his essay lacks evidence that the imagery of floods, swamp, and ooze was actually present in the writers under consideration, the metaphoric dualities of hardness / softness are not far to seek in English-language modernists. It should be added that the qualities of Theweleit's work that make him so open to misappropriation are also the qualities that have made him so influential; the same is true for Huyssen's essay. In their focus on metaphor, both offer an approach that allows the personal, in the form of subjectivity, to be combined with the political and the literary; moreover, their approach allows aspects of gender politics to be combined with aspects of class politics, albeit a class politics in which classical Marxist issues such as the means of production have faded into near invisibility.

Extract from Andreas Huyssen, 'Mass Culture as Woman', from *After the Great Divide* (Indiana University Press, 1986; Basingstoke: Macmillan, 1988), pp.44–58.

I

One of the founding texts of modernism, if there ever was one, is Flaubert's *Madame Bovary*. Emma Bovary, whose temperament was, in the narrator's words, 'more sentimental than artistic', loved to read romances.[1] In his detached, ironic style, Flaubert describes Emma's reading matter: 'They [the novels] were full of love and lovers, persecuted damsels swooning in deserted pavilions, postillions slaughtered at every turn, horses ridden to death on every page, gloomy forests, romantic intrigue, vows, sobs, embraces and tears, moonlit crossings, nightingales in woodland groves, noblemen brave as lions, gentle as lambs, impossibly virtuous, always well dressed, and who wept like fountains on all occasions'.[2] Of course, it is well known that Flaubert himself was caught by the craze for romantic novels during his student days in the Collège at Rouen, and Emma Bovary's readings at the convent have to be read against this backdrop of Flaubert's life history – a point which critics rarely fail to make. However, there is ample reason to wonder if the adolescent Flaubert read these novels in the same way Emma Bovary would have, had she actually lived – or, for that matter, as real women at the time read them. Perhaps the answer to such a query will have to remain speculative. What is beyond speculation, however, is the fact that Emma Bovary became known, among other things, as the female reader caught between the delusions of the trivial romantic narrative and the realities of French provincial life during the July monarchy, a woman who tried to live the illusions of aristocratic sensual romance and was shipwrecked on the banality of bourgeois everyday life. Flaubert, on the other hand, came to be known as one of the fathers of modernism, one of the paradigmatic master voices of an aesthetic based on the uncompromising repudiation of what Emma Bovary loved to read.

As to Flaubert's famous claim: 'Madame Bovary, c'est moi', we can assume that he knew what he was saying, and critics have gone to great lengths to show what Flaubert had in common with Emma Bovary – mostly in order to show how he transcended aesthetically the dilemma on which she foundered in 'real life'. In such arguments the question of gender usually remains submerged, thereby asserting itself all the more powerfully. Sartre, however, in his monumental *L'Idiot de la Famille*, has analyzed the social and familial conditions of Flaubert's 'objective neurosis' underlying his fantasy of himself as woman. Sartre has indeed succeeded in showing how Flaubert fetishized his own imaginary femininity while simultaneously sharing his period's hostility toward real women, participating in a pattern of the imagination and of behavior all too common in the history of modernism.[3]

That such masculine identification with woman, such imaginary femininity in the male writer, is itself historically determined is clear enough. Apart from the subjective conditions of neurosis in Flaubert's case, the phenomenon has a lot to do with the increasingly marginal position of literature and the arts in a society in which masculinity is identified with action, enterprise, and progress – with the realms of business, industry, science, and law. At the same time, it has also become clear that the imaginary femininity of male authors, which often grounds their oppositional stance vis-à-vis bourgeois society, can easily go hand in hand with the exclusion of real women from the literary enterprise and with the misogyny of bourgeois patriarchy itself. Against the paradigmatic 'Madame Bovary, c'est moi', we therefore have to insist that there is a difference. Christa Wolf, in her critical and fictional reflections on the question 'who was Cassandra before anyone wrote about her?', put it this way:

> 'We have admired this remark [Flaubert's "Madame Bovary, c'est moi"] for more than a hundred years. We also admire the tears Flaubert shed when he had to let Madame Bovary die, and the crystal-clear calculation of his wonderful novel, which he was able to write despite his tears; and we should not and will not stop admiring him. But Flaubert was *not* Madame Bovary; we cannot completely ignore that fact in the end, despite all our good will and what we know of the secret relationship between an author and a figure created by art'.[4]

One aspect of the difference that is important to my argument about the gender inscriptions in the mass culture debate is that woman (Madame Bovary) is positioned as reader of inferior literature – subjective, emotional and passive – while man (Flaubert) emerges as writer of genuine, authentic literature – objective, ironic, and in control of his aesthetic means. Of course, such positioning of woman as avid consumer of pulp, which I take to be paradigmatic, also affects the woman writer who has the same kind of ambition as the 'great (male) modernist'. Wolf cites Ingeborg Bachmann's tortured novel trilogy *Todesarten* (Ways of Dying) as a counterexample to Flaubert: 'Ingeborg Bachmann *is* that nameless woman in *Malina*, she *is* the woman Franza in the novel fragment *The Franza Case* who simply cannot get a grip on her life, cannot give it a form; who simply cannot manage to make her experience into a presentable story, cannot produce it out of herself as an artistic product'.[5]

In one of her own novels, *The Quest for Christa T*, Wolf herself foregrounded the 'difficulty of saying I' for the woman who writes. The problematic nature of saying 'I' in the literary text – more often than not held to be a lapse into subjectivity or kitsch – is of course one of the central difficulties of the postromantic, modernist writer. Having first created the determining conditions for a certain historically specific type of subjectivity (the Cartesian cogito and the epistemological subject in Kant, as well as the bourgeois entrepreneur and the modern scientist), modernity itself has increasingly hollowed out such subjectivity and rendered its articulation highly problematic. Most modern artists, male or female, know that. But we only need to think of the striking contrast between Flaubert's confident personal confession, 'Madame Bovary, c'est moi', and the famed 'impassibilité' of the novel's style to know that there is a difference. Given the fundamentally differing social and psychological constitution and validation of male and female subjectivity in modern bourgeois society, the difficulty of saying 'I' must of necessity be different for a woman writer, who may not find 'impassibilité' and the concomitant reification of self in the aesthetic product quite as attractive and compelling an ideal as the male writer. The male, after all, can easily deny his own subjectivity for the benefit of a higher aesthetic goal, as long as he can take it for granted on an experiential level in everyday life. Thus Christa Wolf concludes, with some hesitation and yet forcefully enough: 'Aesthetics, I say, like philosophy and science, is invented not so much to enable us to get closer to reality as for the purpose of warding it off, of protecting against it'.[6] Warding something off, protecting against something out there seems indeed to be a basic gesture of the modernist aesthetic, from Flaubert to Roland Barthes and other poststructuralists. What Christa Wolf calls reality would certainly have to include Emma Bovary's romances (the books *and* the love affairs), for the repudiation of *Trivialliteratur* has always been one of the constitutive features of a modernist aesthetic intent on distancing itself and its products from the trivialities and banalities of everyday life. Contrary to the claims of champions of the autonomy of art, contrary also to the ideologists of textuality, the realities of modern life and the ominous expansion of mass culture throughout the social realm are always already inscribed into the articulation of aesthetic modernism. Mass culture has always been the hidden subtext of the modernist project.

II

What especially interests me here is the notion which gained ground during the 19th century that mass culture is somehow associated with woman while real, authentic culture remains the prerogative of men. The tradition of women's exclusion from the realm of 'high art' does not of course originate in the 19th century, but it does take on new connotations in the age of the industrial revolution and cultural modernization. Stuart Hall is perfectly right to point out that the hidden subject of the mass culture debate is precisely 'the masses' – their political and cultural aspirations, their struggles and their pacification via cultural institutions.[7] But when the 19th and early 20th centuries conjured up the threat of the masses 'rattling at the gate', to quote Hall, and lamented the concomitant decline of culture and civilization (which mass culture was invariably accused of causing), there was yet another hidden subject. In the age of nascent socialism *and* the first major women's movement in Europe, the masses knocking at the gate were also women, knocking at the gate of a male-dominated culture. It is indeed striking to observe how the political, psychological, and aesthetic discourse around the turn of the century consistently and obsessively genders mass culture and the masses as feminine, while high culture, whether traditional or modern, clearly remains the privileged realm of male activities.

To be sure, a number of critics have since abandoned the notion of *mass* culture in order to 'exclude from the outset the interpretation agreeable to its advocates: that it is a matter of something like a culture that arises spontaneously from the masses themselves, the contemporary form of popular art'.[8] Thus Adorno and Horkheimer coined the term culture industry; Enzensberger gave it another twist by calling it the consciousness industry; in the United States, Herbert Schiller speaks of mind managers, and Michael Real uses the term mass-mediated culture. The critical intention behind these changes in terminology is clear: they all mean to suggest that modern mass culture is administered and imposed from above and that the threat it represents resides not in the masses but in those who run the industry. While such an interpretation may serve as a welcome corrective to the naive notion that mass culture is identical with traditional forms of popular art, rising spontaneously from the masses, it nevertheless erases a whole web of gender connotations which, as I shall show, the older terminology 'mass culture' carried with it – i.e., connotations of mass culture as essentially feminine which were clearly also 'imposed from above', in a gender-specific sense, and which remain central to understanding the historical and rhetorical determinations of the modernism/mass culture dichotomy.

It might be argued that the terminological shift away from the term 'mass culture' actually reflects changes in critical thinking about 'the masses'. Indeed, mass culture theories since the 1920s – for instance, those of the Frankfurt School – have by and large abandoned the explicit gendering of mass culture as feminine. Instead they emphasize features of mass culture such as streamlining, technological reproduction, administration, and Sachlichkeit – features which popular psychology would ascribe to the realm of masculinity rather than femininity. Yet the older mode of thinking surfaces time and again in the language, if not in the argument. Thus Adorno and Horkheimer argue that mass culture 'cannot renounce the threat of castration',[9] and they feminize it explicitly, as the evil queen of the fairy tale when they claim that 'mass culture, in her mirror, is always the most beautiful in the land'.[10] Similarly, Siegfried Kracauer, in his seminal essay on the mass ornament, begins his discussion by bringing the legs of the Tiller Girls into the reader's view, even though the argument then focuses primarily on aspects of rationalization and standardization.[11] Examples such as these show that the inscription of the feminine on the notion of mass culture, which seems to have its primary place in the late 19th century, did not relinquish its hold, even among those critics who did much to overcome the 19th century mystification of mass culture as woman.

The recovery of such gender stereotypes in the theorizing of mass culture may also have some bearing on the current debate about the alleged femininity of modernist/avant-gardist writing. Thus the observation that, in some basic register, the traditional mass culture/modernism dichotomy has been gendered since the mid-19th century as female/male would seem to make recent attempts by French critics to claim the space of modernist and avant-garde writing as predominantly feminine highly questionable. Of course this approach, which is perhaps best embodied in Kristeva's work, focuses on the Mallarmé-Lautréamont-Joyce axis of modernism rather than, say, on the Flaubert-Thomas Mann-Eliot axis which I emphasize in my argument here. Nevertheless, its claims remain problematic even there. Apart from the fact that such a view would threaten to render invisible a whole tradition of women's writing, its main theoretical assumption – 'that 'the feminine' is what cannot be inscribed in common language'[12] – remains problematically close to that whole history of an imaginary male femininity which has become prominent in literature since the late 18th century.[13] This view becomes possible only if Madame Bovary's 'natural' association with pulp – i.e., the discourse that persistently associated women with mass culture – is simply ignored, and if a paragon of male misogyny like Nietzsche is said to be speaking from the position of woman. Teresa de Lauretis has recently criticized this Derridean appropriation of the feminine by arguing that the position of woman from which Nietzsche and Derrida speak is vacant in the first place, and cannot be claimed by women.[14] Indeed, more than a hundred years after Flaubert and

Nietzsche, we are facing yet another version of an imaginary male femininity, and it is no coincidence that the advocates of such theories (who also include major women theoreticians) take great pains to distance themselves from any form of political feminism. Even though the French readings of modernism's 'feminine' side have opened up fascinating questions about gender and sexuality which can be turned critically against more dominant accounts of modernism, it seems fairly obvious that the wholesale theorization of modernist writing as feminine simply ignores the powerful masculinist and misogynist current within the trajectory of modernism, a current which time and again openly states its contempt for women and for the masses and which had Nietzsche as its most eloquent and influential representative.

Here, then, some remarks about the history of the perception of mass culture as feminine. Time and again documents from the late 19th century ascribe pejorative feminine characteristics to mass culture – and by mass culture here I mean serialized feuilleton novels, popular and family magazines, the stuff of lending libraries, fictional bestsellers and the like – not, however, working-class culture or residual forms of older popular or folk cultures. A few examples will have to suffice. In the preface to their novel *Germinie Lacerteux* (1865), which is usually regarded as the first naturalist manifesto, the Goncourt brothers attack what they call the false novel. They describe it as those 'spicy little works, memoirs of street-walkers, bedroom confessions, erotic smuttiness, scandals that hitch up their skirts in pictures in bookshop windows'. The true novel (*le roman vrai*) by contrast is called 'severe and pure'. It is said to be characterized by its scientificity, and rather than sentiment it offers what the authors call 'a clinical picture of love' (*une clinique de l'amour*).[15] Twenty years later, in the editorial of the first issue of Michael Georg Conrad's journal *Die Gesellschaft* (1885), which marks the beginning of 'die Moderne' in Germany, the editor states his intention to emancipate literature and criticism from the 'tyranny of well-bred debutantes and old wives of both sexes', and from the empty and pompous rhetoric of 'old wives criticism'. And he goes on to polemicize against the then popular literary family magazines: 'The literary and artistic kitchen personnel has achieved absolute mastery in the art of economizing and imitating the famous potato banquet. ...It consists of twelve courses each of which offers the potato in a different guise'.[16] Once the kitchen has been described metaphorically as the site of mass cultural production, we are not surprised to hear Conrad call for the reestablishment of an '*arg gefährdete Mannhaftigkeit*' (seriously threatened manliness) and for the restoration of bravery and courage (*Tapferkeit*) in thought, poetry, and criticism.

It is easy to see how such statements rely on the traditional notion that women's aesthetic and artistic abilities are inferior to those of men. Women as providers of inspiration for the artist, yes, but otherwise *Berufsverbot* for the muses,[17] unless of course they content themselves with the lower genres (painting flowers and animals) and the decorative arts. At any rate, the gendering of an inferior mass culture as feminine goes hand in hand with the emergence of a male mystique in modernism (especially in painting), which has been documented thoroughly by feminist scholarship.[18] What is interesting in the second half of the 19th century, however, is a certain chain effect of signification: from the obsessively argued inferiority of woman as artist (classically argued by Karl Scheffler in *Die Frau und die Kunst*, 1908) to the association of woman with mass culture (witness Hawthorne's 'the damned mob of scribbling women') to the identification of woman with the masses as political threat.

This line of argument invariably leads back to Nietzsche. Significantly, Nietzsche's ascription of feminine characteristics to the masses is always tied to his aesthetic vision of the artist-philosopher-hero, the suffering loner who stands in irreconcilable opposition to modern democracy and its inauthentic culture. Fairly typical examples of this nexus can be found in Nietzsche's polemic against Wagner, who becomes for him the paradigm of the decline of genuine culture in the dawning age of the masses and the feminization of culture: 'The danger for artists, for geniuses ...is woman: adoring women confront them with corruption. Hardly any of them have character enough not to be corrupted – or 'redeemed' – when they find themselves treated like gods: soon they condescend to the level of the women'.[19] Wagner, it is implied, has succumbed to the adoring women by transforming music into mere spectacle, theater, delusion:

'I have explained where Wagner belongs – *not* in the history of music. What does he signify nevertheless in that history? *The emergence of the actor in music.* ...One can grasp it with one's very hands: great success, success with the masses no longer sides with those who are authentic – one has to be an actor to achieve that. Victor Hugo and Richard Wagner – they signify the same thing: in declining cultures, wherever the decision comes to rest with the masses, authenticity becomes superfluous, disadvantageous, a liability. Only the actor still arouses *great* enthusiasm'.[20]

And then Wagner, the theater, the mass, woman – all become a web of signification outside of, and in opposition to, true art: 'No one brings along the finest senses of his art to the theater, least of all the artist who works for the theater – solitude is lacking; whatever is perfect suffers no witnesses. In the theater one becomes people, herd, female, pharisee, voting cattle, patron, idiot – *Wagnerian*'.[21] What Nietzsche articulates here is of course not an attack on the drama or the tragedy, which to him remain some of the highest manifestations of culture. When Nietzsche calls theater a 'revolt of the masses',[22] he anticipates what the situationists would later elaborate as the society of the spectacle, and what Baudrillard chastises as the simulacrum. At the same time, it is no coincidence that the philosopher blames theatricality for the decline of culture. After all, the theater in bourgeois society was one of the few spaces which allowed women a prime place in the arts, precisely because acting was seen as imitative and reproductive, rather than original and productive. Thus, in Nietzsche's attack on what he perceives as Wagner's feminization of music, his 'infinite melody' – 'one walks into the sea, gradually loses one's secure footing, and finally surrenders oneself to the elements without reservation'[23] – an extremely perceptive critique of the mechanisms of bourgeois culture goes hand in hand with an exhibition of that culture's sexist biases and prejudices.

III

The fact that the identification of woman with mass has major political implications is easily recognized. Thus Mallarmé's quip about *'reportage universel'* (i.e., mass culture), with its not so subtle allusion to *'suffrage universel'*, is more than just a clever pun. The problem goes far beyond questions of art and literature. In the late 19th century, a specific traditional male image of woman served as a receptacle for all kinds of projections, displaced fears, and anxieties (both personal and political), which were brought about by modernization and the new social conflicts, as well as by specific historical events such as the 1848 revolution, the 1870 Commune, and the rise of reactionary mass movements which, as in Austria, threatened the liberal order.[24] An examination of the magazines and the newspapers of the period will show that the proletarian and petit-bourgeois masses were persistently described in terms of a feminine threat. Images of the raging mob as hysterical, of the engulfing floods of revolt and revolution, of the swamp of big city life, of the spreading ooze of massification, of the figure of the red whore at the barricades – all of these pervade the writing of the mainstream media, as well as that of right-wing ideologues of the late 19th and early 20th centuries whose social psychology Klaus Theweleit has perceptively analyzed in his study *Male Phantasies*.[25] The fear of the masses in this age of declining liberalism is always also a fear of woman, a fear of nature out of control, a fear of the unconscious, of sexuality, of the loss of identity and stable ego boundaries in the mass.

This kind of thinking is exemplified by Gustave Le Bon's enormously influential *The Crowd* (*La Psychologie des foules*, 1895), which as Freud observed in his own *Mass Psychology and Ego Analysis* (1921) merely summarizes arguments pervasive in Europe at the time. In Le Bon's study, the male fear of woman and the bourgeois fear of the masses become indistinguishable: 'Crowds are everywhere distinguished by feminine characteristics'.[26] And: 'The simplicity and exaggeration of the sentiments of crowds have for result that a throng knows neither doubt nor uncertainty. Like women, it goes at once to extremes. ...A commencement of antipathy or disapprobation, which in the case of an isolated individual would not gain strength, becomes at once furious hatred in the case of an individual in a crowd'.[27] And then he summarizes his fears with a reference to that icon which perhaps more than any other in the 19th century – more even than the Judiths and Salomés so often portrayed on symbolist canvases – stood for the feminine threat to civilization: 'Crowds are somewhat like the sphinx of ancient fable: it is necessary to arrive at a solution of the problems offered by their psychology or to resign ourselves to being devoured by them'.[28] Male fears of an engulfing femininity are here projected onto the metropolitan masses, who did indeed represent a threat to the rational bourgeois order. The haunting specter of a loss of power combines with fear of losing one's fortified and stable ego boundaries, which represent the *sine qua non* of male psychology in that bourgeois order. We may want to relate Le Bon's social psychology of the masses back to modernism's own fears of being sphinxed. Thus the nightmare of being devoured by mass culture through co-option, commodification, and the 'wrong' kind of success is the constant fear of the modernist artist, who tries to stake out his territory by fortifying the boundaries between genuine art and inauthentic mass culture. Again, the problem is not the desire to differentiate between forms of high art and depraved forms of mass culture and its co-options. The problem is rather the persistent gendering as feminine of that which is devalued.

IV

Seen in relation to this kind of paranoid view of mass culture and the masses, the modernist aesthetic itself – at least in one of its basic registers – begins to look more and more like a reaction formation, rather than like the heroic feat steeled in the fires of the modern experience. At the risk of oversimplifying, I would suggest that one can identify something like a core of the modernist aesthetic which has held sway over many decades, which manifests itself (with variations due to respective media) in literature, music, architecture, and the visual arts, and which has had an enormous impact on the history of criticism and cultural ideology. If we were to construct an ideal type notion of what the modernist art work has become as a result of successive canonizations – and I will exclude here the poststructuralist archeology of modernism which has shifted the grounds of the debate – it would probably look somewhat like this:

– The work is autonomous and totally separate from the realms of mass culture and everyday life.
– It is self-referential, self-conscious, frequently ironic, ambiguous, and rigorously experimental.
– It is the expression of a purely individual consciousness rather than of a Zeitgeist or a collective state of mind.

- Its experimental nature makes it analogous to science, and like science it produces and carries knowledge.
- Modernist literature since Flaubert is a persistent exploration of and encounter with language. Modernist painting since Manet is an equally persistent elaboration of the medium itself: the flatness of the canvas, the structuring of notation, paint and brushwork, the problem of the frame.
- The major premise of the modernist art work is the rejection of all classical systems of representation, the effacement of 'content', the erasure of subjectivity and authorial voice, the repudiation of likeness and verisimilitude, the exorcism of any demand for realism of whatever kind.
- Only by fortifying its boundaries, by maintaining its purity and autonomy, and by avoiding any contamination with mass culture and with the signifying systems of everyday life can the art work maintain its adversary stance: adversary to the bourgeois culture of everyday life as well as adversary to mass culture and entertainment which are seen as the primary forms of bourgeois cultural articulation.

One of the first examples of this aesthetic would be Flaubert's famous 'impassibilité' and his desire to write 'a book about nothing, a book without external attachments which would hold together by itself through the internal force of its style'. Flaubert can be said to ground modernism in literature, both for its champions (from Nietzsche to Roland Barthes) and for its detractors (such as Georg Lukács). Other historical forms of this modernist aesthetic would be the clinical, dissecting gaze of the naturalist[29]; the doctrine of art for art's sake in its various classicist or romantic guises since the late 19th century; the insistence on the art-life dichotomy so frequently found at the turn of the century, with its inscription of art on the side of death and masculinity and its evaluation of life as inferior and feminine; and finally the absolutist claims of abstraction, from Kandinsky to the New York School.

But it was only in the 1940s and 1950s that the modernism gospel and the concomitant condemnation of kitsch became something like the equivalent of the one-party state in the realm of aesthetics. And it is still an open question to what extent current poststructuralist notions of language and writing and of sexuality and the unconscious are a postmodern departure toward entirely new cultural horizons; or whether, despite their powerful critique of older notions of modernism, they do not rather represent another mutation of modernism itself.

My point here is not to reduce the complex history of modernism to an abstraction. Obviously, the various layers and components of the ideal modernist work would have to be read in and through specific works in specific historical and cultural constellations. The notion of autonomy, for instance, has quite different historical determinations for Kant, who first articulated it in his *Kritik der Urteilskraft*, than for Flaubert in the 1850s, for Adorno during World War II, or again for Frank Stella today. My point is rather that the champions of modernism themselves were the ones who made that complex history into a schematic paradigm, the main purpose of which often seemed to be the justification of current aesthetic practice, rather than the richest possible reading of the past in relation to the present.

My point is also not to say that there is only one, male, sexual politics to modernism, against which women would have to find their own voices, their own language, their own feminine aesthetic. What I am saying is that the powerful masculinist mystique which is explicit in modernists such as Marinetti, Jünger, Benn, Wyndham Lewis, Céline et al. (not to speak of Marx, Nietzsche, and Freud), and implicit in many others, has to be somehow related to the persistent gendering of mass culture as feminine and inferior – even if, as a result, the heroism of the moderns won't look quite as heroic any more. The autonomy of the modernist art work, after all, is always the result of a resistance, an abstention, and a suppression – resistance to the seductive lure of mass culture, abstention from the pleasure of trying to please a larger audience, suppression of everything that might be threatening to the rigorous demands of being modern and at the edge of time. There seem to be fairly obvious homologies between this modernist insistence on purity and autonomy in art, Freud's privileging of the ego over the id and his insistence on stable, if flexible, ego boundaries, and Marx's privileging of production over consumption. The lure of mass culture, after all, has traditionally been described as the threat of losing oneself in dreams and delusions and of merely consuming rather than producing.[30] Thus, despite its undeniable adversary stance toward bourgeois society, the modernist aesthetic and its rigorous work ethic as described here seem in some fundamental way to be located also on the side of that society's reality principle, rather than on that of the pleasure principle. It is to this fact that we owe some of the greatest works of modernism, but the greatness of these works cannot be separated from the often one-dimensional gender inscriptions inherent in their very constitution as autonomous masterworks of modernity.

V

The deeper problem at stake here pertains to the relationship of modernism to the matrix of modernization which gave birth to it and nurtured it through its various stages. In less suggestive terms, the question is why, despite the obvious heterogeneity of the modernist project, a certain universalizing account of the modern has been able to hold sway for so long in literary and art criticism, and why even today it is far from having been decisively displaced from its position of hegemony in cultural institutions. What has to be put in question is the presumably adversary relationship of the modernist aesthetic to the myth and ideology of modernization and progress, which it ostensibly rejects in its fixation upon the eternal and timeless power of the poetic word. From the vantage point of our postmodern age, which has begun in a variety of discourses to question seriously the belief in unhampered progress and in the blessings of modernity, it becomes clear how modernism, even in its most adversary, anti-bourgeois manifestations, is deeply implicated in the processes and pressures of the same mundane modernization it so ostensibly repudiates. It is especially in light of the ecological and environmental critique of industrial and postindustrial capitalism, and of the different yet concomitant feminist critique of bourgeois patriarchy, that the subterranean collusion of modernism with the myth of modernization becomes visible.

I want to show this briefly for two of the most influential and by now classical accounts of the historical trajectory of modernism – the accounts of Clement Greenberg in painting and of Theodor W. Adorno in music and literature. For both critics, mass culture remains the other of modernism, the specter that haunts it, the threat against which high art has to shore up its terrain. And even though mass culture is no longer imagined as primarily feminine, both critics remain under the sway of the old paradigm in their conceptualization of modernism.

Indeed, both Greenberg and Adorno are often taken to be the last ditch defenders of the purity of the modernist aesthetic, and they have become known since the late 1930s as uncompromising enemies of modern mass culture. (Mass culture had by then of course become an effective tool of totalitarian domination in a number of countries, which all banished modernism as degenerate or decadent.) While there are major differences between the two men, both in temperament and in the scope of their analyses, they both share a notion of the inevitability of the evolution of modern art. To put it bluntly, they believe in progress – if not in society, then certainly in art. The metaphors of linear evolution and of a teleology of art are conspicuous in their work. I quote Greenberg: 'It has been in search of the absolute that the avant-garde has arrived at 'abstract' or 'nonobjective' art – and poetry, too'.[31] It is well known how Greenberg constructs the story of modernist painting as a single-minded trajectory, from the first French modernist avant-garde of the 1860s to the New York School of abstract expressionism – his moment of truth.

Similarly, Adorno sees a historical logic at work in the move from late romantic music to Wagner and ultimately to Schönberg and the second school of Vienna, which represent *his* moment of truth. To be sure, both critics acknowledge retarding elements in these trajectories – Stravinsky in Adorno's account, surrealism in Greenberg's – but the logic of history, or rather the logic of aesthetic evolution, prevails, giving a certain rigidity to Greenberg's and Adorno's theorizing. Obstacles and detours, it seems, only highlight the dramatic and inevitable path of modernism toward its telos, whether this telos is described as triumph as in Greenberg or as pure negativity as in Adorno. In the work of both critics, the theory of modernism appears as a theory of modernization displaced to the aesthetic realm; this is precisely its historical strength, and what makes it different from the mere academic formalism of which it is so often accused. Adorno and Greenberg further share a notion of decline that they see as following on the climax of development in high modernism. Adorno wrote about 'Das Altern der Neuen Musik', and Greenberg unleashed his wrath on the reappearance of representation in painting since the advent of Pop Art.

At the same time, both Adorno and Greenberg were quite aware of the costs of modernization, and they both understood that it was the ever increasing pace of commodification and colonization of cultural space which actually propelled modernism forward, or, better, pushed it toward the outer margins of the cultural terrain. Adorno especially never lost sight of the fact that, ever since their simultaneous emergence in the mid-19th century, modernism and mass culture have been engaged in a compulsive *pas de deux*. To him, autonomy was a relational phenomenon, not a mechanism to justify formalist amnesia. His analysis of the transition in music from Wagner to Schönberg makes it clear that Adorno never saw modernism as anything other than a reaction formation to mass culture and commodification, a reaction formation which operated on the level of form and artistic material. The same awareness that mass culture, on some basic level, determined the shape and course of modernism is pervasive in Clement Greenberg's essays of the late 1930s. To a large extent, it is by the distance we have traveled from this 'great divide' between mass culture and modernism that we can measure our own cultural postmodernity. And yet, I still know of no better aphorism about the imaginary adversaries, modernism and mass culture, than that which Adorno articulated in a letter to Walter Benjamin: 'Both [modernist art and mass culture] bear the scars of capitalism, both contain elements of change. Both are torn halves of freedom to which, however, they do not add up'.[32]

But the discussion cannot end here. The postmodern crisis of high modernism and its classical accounts has to be seen as a crisis both of capitalist modernization itself and of the deeply patriarchal structures that support it. The traditional dichotomy, in which mass culture appears as monolithic, engulfing, totalitarian, and on the side of regression and the feminine ('Totalitarianism appeals to the desire to return to the womb,' said T. S. Eliot[33]) and modernism appears as progressive, dynamic, and indicative of male superiority in culture, has been challenged empirically and theoretically in a variety of ways in the past twenty years or so. New versions of the history of modern culture, the nature of language, and artistic autonomy have been elaborated, and new theoretical questions have been brought to bear on mass culture and modernism; most of us would probably share the sense that the ideology of modernism, as I have sketched it here, is a thing of the past, even if it still occupies major bastions in cultural institutions such as the museum or the academy. The attacks on high modernism, waged in the name of the postmodern since the late 1950s, have left their mark on our culture, and we are still trying to figure out the gains and the losses which this shift has brought about.

Notes

1. Gustave Flaubert, *Madame Bovary*, tr. Merloyd Lawrence (Boston: Houghton Mifflin, 1969), p. 29.
2. Flaubert, p. 30.
3. Cf. Gertrud Koch, 'Zwitter-Schwestern: Weiblichkeitswahn und Frauenhass – Jean-Paul Sartres Thesen von der androgynen Kunst,' in *Sartres Flaubert lesen: Essays zu Der Idiot der Familie*, ed. Traugott König (Rowohlt: Reinbek, 1980), pp. 44–59.
4. Christa Wolf, *Cassandra: A Novel and Four Essays* (New York: Farrar, Straus, Giroux, 1984), p. 300f.
5. Wolf, *Cassandra*, p. 301.
6. Wolf, *Cassandra*, p. 300.
7. Stuart Hall, paper given at the conference on mass culture at the Center for Twentieth Century Studies, Spring 1984.
8. Theodor W. Adorno, 'Culture Industry Reconsidered,' *New German Critique*, 6 (Fall 1975), 12.
9. Max Horkheimer and Theodor W. Adorno, *Dialectic of Enlightenment* (New York: Continuum, 1982), p. 141.
10. Max Horkheimer and Theodor W. Adorno, 'Das Schema der Massenkultur,' in Adorno, *Gesammelte Schriften*, 3 (Frankfurt am Main: Suhrkamp, 1981), p. 305.
11. Siegfried Kracauer, 'The Mass Ornament,' *New German Critique*, 5 (Spring 1975), pp. 67–76.
12. Sandra M. Gilbert and Susan Gubar, 'Sexual Linguistics: Gender, Language, Sexuality,' *New Literary History*, 16, no. 3 (Spring 1985), 516.
13. For an excellent study of male images of femininity since the 18th century see Silvia Bovenschen, *Die imaginierte Weiblichkeit* (Frankfurt am Main: Suhrkamp, 1979).
14. Teresa de Lauretis, 'The Violence of Rhetoric: Considerations on Representation and Gender,' *Semiotica* (Spring 1985), special issue on the Rhetoric of Violence.
15. Edmond and Jules de Goncourt, *Germinie Lacerteux*, tr. Leonard Tancock (Harmondsworth: Penguin, 1984), p. 15.
16. *Die Gesellschaft*, 1, no. 1 (January 1885).
17. Cf. Cäcilia Rentmeister, 'Berufsverbot für Musen,' *Ästhetik und Kommunikation*, 25 (September 1976), 92–113.
18. Cf., for instance, the essays by Carol Duncan and Norma Broude in *Feminism and Art History*, ed. Norma Broude and Mary D. Garrard (New York: Harper & Row, 1982) or the documentation of relevant quotes by Valerie Jaudon and Joyce Kozloff, '"Art Hysterical Notions" of Progress and Culture,' *Heresies*, 1, no. 4 (Winter 1978), 38–42.

19. Friedrich Nietzsche, *The Case of Wagner*, in *The Birth of Tragedy and the Case of Wagner*, trans. Walter Kaufmann (New York: Random House, 1967), p. 161.
20. Nietzsche, *The Case of Wagner*, p. 179.
21. Friedrich Nietzsche, *Nietzsche Contra Wagner*, in *The Portable Nietzsche*, ed. and tr. Walter Kaufmann (Harmondsworth and New York: Penguin, 1976), pp. 665f.
22. Nietzsche, *The Case of Wagner*, p. 183.
23. Nietzsche, *Nietzsche Contra Wagner*, p. 666.
24. For a recent discussion of semantic shifts in the political and sociological discourse of masses, elites, and leaders from the late 19th century to fascism see Helmuth Berking, 'Mythos und Politik: Zur historischen Semantik des Massenbegriffs,' *Ästhetik und Kommunikation*, 56 (November 1984), 35–42.
25. An English translation of the two-volume work will soon be published by the University of Minnesota Press.
26. Gustave Le Bon, *The Crowd* (Harmondsworth and New York: Penguin, 1981), p. 39.
27. Le Bon, p. 50.
28. Le Bon, p. 102.
29. Naturalism is not always included in the history of modernism because of its close relationship to realistic description, but it clearly belongs to this context as Georg Lukács never ceased to point out.
30. On the relationship of the production/consumption paradigm to the mass culture debate see Tania Modleski, 'Femininity as Mas(s)querade: A Feminist Approach to Mass Culture,' forthcoming in Colin MacCabe, ed., *High Theory, Low Culture*, University of Manchester Press.
31. Clement Greenberg, 'Avant-Garde and Kitsch,' in *Art and Culture: Critical Essays* (Boston: Beacon Press, 1961), p. 5f.
32. Letter of March 18, 1936, in Walter Benjamin, *Gesammelte Schriften*, 1, 3 (Frankfurt am Main: Suhrkamp, 1974), p. 1003.
33. T. S. Eliot, *Notes towards the Definition of Culture*, published with *The Idea of a Christian Society* as *Christianity and Culture* (New York: Harcourt, Brace, 1968), p. 142.

* * *

In a final section, not included here, Huyssen turns his attention to the relation of mass culture to postmodernism, and the influence of feminist critiques of patriarchy in shaping postmodern art. More recently, Huyssen has returned to his distinction of high and low, primarily to ask how such concepts might function in the 'expanded field' of globalized economies and globalized cultural studies, but also to correct some misperceptions of *After the Great Divide*. He emphasizes that it is necessary always to historicize the divide, to examine how (and whether) it functioned in particular times and places.

> Much valuable recent work of the editing, marketing, and dissemination of modernism has misconstrued my earlier definition of the Great Divide as a static binary of high modernism vs. the market. My argument was rather that there had been, since the mid-nineteenth century in Europe, a powerful imaginary

insisting on the divide while time and again violating that categorical separation in practice. [...] Thus the recent, detailed documentation of the high modernists' involvement with the marketing of their works, their bickering with publishers, and engagements with small journal enterprises – even with fashion magazines – will not do away with the issue of the divide as a central conceptual trope and energizing norm of the post-World War II period [...].[10]

Huyssen does not specify which recent work he is thinking of, but the involvement of modernist writers in *Vogue* magazine has attracted a great deal of attention, some of it taking 'Mass Culture as Woman' as a starting point; recent work on the marketing of modernism, of which details are given in the 'further reading' section of Chapter 7, has also been informed by Huyssen.[11] The important question for feminist critics has been whether, if mass culture is gendered feminine, women writers bear the same relationship to it as male ones.[12]

Huyssen has provided literary historians and critics with a powerful set of generalizations about modernism and mass culture which can be tested against close readings and archival research into particular authors and texts. David Chinitz has questioned whether Huyssen's distinction of high and low culture holds true in the poetry of T. S. Eliot; he has also questioned whether Peter Bürger's distinction of modernism from the avant-garde is as clear as Bürger implies. In *T. S. Eliot and the Cultural Divide* (2003) Chinitz is less concerned with activities surrounding Eliot's poetry – editing, marketing, and bickering – than with the register and rhythms of the poems themselves. His larger project is to rescue Eliot from his reputation as the embodiment of a culture 'distinguished by high seriousness, traditionalism, and purity or exclusivity'.[13] In an era where popular culture has begun to be taken seriously, such a reputation has become a liability, for Eliot and for the canonical authors of the modernist movement. The Eliot that Chinitz seeks to portray is 'a richer and more engaging figure [...]. He is a multidimensional thinker and artist, whose approach to the modern popular, both as theorized in his critical essays and as practiced in his art, is supple, frequently insightful, and always deeply ambivalent'.[14] Chinitz's project is not entirely new: he cites critics from the 1930s onwards who noted the ways in which Eliot's poetry bore some of the qualities of popular song; Nancy D. Hargrove has also written, more speculatively, about the popular culture that Eliot might have enjoyed in Paris in 1910–11; in the more specific area of modernism's relation to African–American culture, there is a large literature on the Harlem Renaissance, and a smaller one on modernist writers' relationship to it.[15]

The starting point for the first of the three extracts from Chinitz's book is a somewhat cryptic remark in a letter from Eliot to Mary Hutchinson, perhaps in response to a report of a social gathering which he had been unable to attend: 'I am glad to hear that you enjoyed yourself and didn't get tired [...]. But it is a jazz-banjorine that I should bring, not a lute'.[16]

Extract from David E. Chinitz, *T. S. Eliot and the Cultural Divide* (London and Chicago: University of Chicago Press, 2003), pp.28–32.

A 'Black and Grinning Muse'

For a poet to portray himself as playing a 'jazz-banjorine' around 1920 – in fact, for a poet to have any truck with jazz at all – was not only to claim a certain currency but to take sides in an ideological battle over the significance of modernism in the arts and of modernity in general. To unpack fully the meaning of Eliot's self-fashioning we must consider the meaning of jazz itself.

Inevitably, Eliot's conception of jazz would have been more expansive than ours. As Howard Rye asserts, minstrel songs and what we have since isolated as *jazz* and *blues* formed a generic continuum in the 1920s rather than a set of discrete musics (45). The 'symphonic jazz' of the era also belongs to this continuum, as do ragtime and certain strains of 'sheer Tin Pan Alley pop' (Douglas 352). Bernard Gendron has argued sensibly that an 'essentialist construction of "authentic" jazz' was imposed on the Jazz Age by later criticism, creating an insupportable dichotomy between the 'genuine' and the 'counterfeit' (*Between* 90–1). For present purposes, then, it makes sense to imagine jazz in the comprehensive sense it took on in twenties discourse – a sense that includes the 'classic' blues, ragtime, any sufficiently syncopated music of the vaudeville stage, the 'sweet' jazz of orchestras such as Paul Whiteman's, and jazz-inflected popular songs and dance music, as well as the 'hot' New Orleans style to which the term *jazz* is now usually limited.

The popularity of ragtime in the United States dated back to the 1890s, with Britain not far behind, but the smash success of Irving Berlin's 'Alexander's Ragtime Band' initiated a second wave in 1911 that introduced millions of Europeans to African-American musicianship, the 'modern dances' of Nancy Ellicott, and the joys of continual syncopation. At this point a strong sense developed that something permanent had changed in music and in leisure, and that this change heralded or represented in its own right a seismic shift in Western culture. Its way thus prepared by ragtime, jazz was laden with extramusical meanings from the moment the larger public began to hear of it. Despite its subtitle, for example, Edmund Wilson's essay of 1922, 'The Aesthetic Upheaval in France: The Influence of Jazz in Paris and Americanization of French Literature and Art', barely mentions music; the article deals instead with French literary modernism and with the invasion of such phenomena as the skyscraper, the machine, and the motion picture. Jazz, that is, was nearly synonymous with the modern, and the modern with American mass culture. Because of its connection with nightlife, and because of its African-American origins, which allowed it to be figured as a 'primitive' alternative to Western culture, jazz stood not only for skyscrapers but for social informality, for relaxed sexual strictures, for leisure rather than industry, for skepticism rather than faith, and, generally, for moral and aesthetic relativism (Leonard 70). Jazz signified, in short, a rejection of the entire Victorian system of value (North, *Reading* 143–5). Eliot's 'Portrait of a Lady' invokes this symbology when the 'dull tomtom' in the young narrator's brain reflexively hammers out its own rebellion against the lady's romantic worldview.

For a poet to write *jazz* was inevitably to open a window on this discourse, especially since artistic modernism itself was often associated with jazz. As a columnist in the *New York Times* sneered in 1924:

> Jazz is to real music exactly what most of the 'new poetry,' so-called, is to real poetry. Both are without the structure and form essential to music and poetry alike, and both are the products, not of innovators, but of incompetents. ('Topics')

And the American critic Robert Underwood Johnson complained that modern free verse 'disdains the lute, the harp, the oboe, and the 'cello and is content with the tom-tom, the triangle, and the banjo' (265–6) – a comment that further illuminates the context within which Eliot declined the lute for the banjorine. Johnson's first example of 'this so-called modern American poetry' was part I of Eliot's 'Preludes' (268–9).

Despite such criticism, other poets willingly accepted and even pressed the same associations. In 'A High-Toned Old Christian Woman', which dates, like *The Waste Land*, from 1922, Wallace Stevens taunts a member of the ancien régime while specifically linking the 'New Poetry' with jazz. Modernity, which the old woman parses as 'bawdiness', is 'converted' by the poets 'into palms, / Squiggling like saxophones' (*Collected* 59). Stevens's habitual figuration of the imagination as tropical coincides conveniently here with popular representations of 'jungle jazz'. Modern poems (Stevens's 'novelties of the sublime') are verbal analogues to the quintessentially modern music identified with the saxophone and the banjo, whose staccato the poem imitates as 'tink and tank and tunk-a-tunk-tunk'. Stevens's 'Of Modern Poetry' similarly defines the modernist timbre as the 'twanging [of] a wiry string' (240). Jazz is the 'skeptical music' of modern poetry that offers to supplant all preexisting systems of belief (122).

The most vociferous opposition to jazz came from religious, political, and community leaders as well as self-appointed moralists (Stevens's 'high-toned old Christian woman') who read in the enormous popularity of the new music a threat to established values and social structures. Its proponents did not dispute this perception; rather, they treated the disruptive power of jazz as a positive force. Gilbert Seldes's defense is typical in this respect: 'Jazz is roaring and stamping and vulgar, you may say; but you can not say that it is pale and polite and dying' – as opposed, that is, to 'conventional pedantry ...and a society corrupted by false ideas of politeness and gentility in the arts' (qtd. in 'Effort' 29–30). Wilson likewise contrasted American mass culture with the morbidity of a Europe strewn with 'monuments of the dead': American 'films and factories and marimbas [i.e., jazz] are at least of the living world' ('Aesthetic' 100). Jazz, like electric signs, was one of those 'triumphs and atrocities of the barbarous' that the New World offered a new age. By asserting an alliance with jazz – by offering to play his jazz-banjorine at Mary Hutchinson's soirée – Eliot depicts himself as a similarly barbarous invader, confessing his atrocity ('I may simply prove to be a savage') but expecting, like jazz, to triumph.

To an even greater extent than ragtime, jazz was embraced by avant-gardists and progressive intellectuals as a symbol of their onslaught against sterile mores and 'traditional' aesthetics. For these groups, jazz became the cornerstone of a new, more broadminded attitude toward popular culture, often leading to a call for commerce between high culture and the popular. Yet an inability to escape the ideological implications of the high-low binary almost always qualified this position. Jean Cocteau, for example, prided himself on being 'very good at jazz'; playing it, he wrote, gave him 'a score of arms' and made him 'a god of din' (193). Together with the poster, the skyscraper, the circus, and the *café-concert*, jazz represented for him the arrival of a new age. In 1918, Cocteau counseled artists to immerse themselves in popular culture because 'The music-hall, the circus, and American negro-bands' were more full of the 'life force' than all the deliberate 'audacities' of the avant-garde (21). Yet Cocteau values jazz most for what he, as an artist, can make of it. One fills one's imaginary pockets by experiencing the popular – by collecting African sculpture, attending the café-concert, and putting a record on the gramophone – but these things in themselves are 'worthless bric-à-brac'. Cocteau's advice is to absorb these sources and then to 'substitute gradually your own voice for the phonograph and raw metal for the trinkets' (35). In the end, what Cocteau promotes is the aestheticist ideal of an autonomous high art nurtured in an atmosphere of *flânerie* or slumming (Gendron, *Between* 95–7). For all its bravado, his argument leaves the categories of high and low intact, even unquestioned.

Cocteau's approach is manifest in *Parade*, the ballet he created in collaboration with Apollinaire, Picasso, Satie, and Massine and envisioned as 'a kind of renovation of the theater' (Steegmuller 167). Its emblematic characters – acrobat, Chinese magician, lively American girl – dance a 'transposition of the music-hall' to the accompaniment of modernistic mechanical sounds (typewriter, dynamo, train, siren), words spoken through a megaphone, and a musical score with ragtime inflections. 'For the first time,' wrote composer Francis Poulenc, 'the music hall was invading Art with a capital A' (Steegmuller 185). Nevertheless, *Parade* was quite evidently *not* music hall: it appropriated popular culture but was never meant to be popular. On the contrary, Cocteau hoped for – and got – a scandal. Eliot, as we will see, was more complicatedly torn between a similar contempt for public opinion and an intense desire to establish a rapport with a large audience.

Of course there were also a good many intellectuals, even in avant-garde circles, who wanted nothing to do with jazz. Clive Bell of Bloomsbury launched one of the ugliest attacks in a 1921 essay called 'Plus de Jazz'. For Bell, jazz is much less an ethnic music than an artistic movement, a subgenre of modernism, 'a ripple' on a larger wave 'which began at the end of the nineteenth century in a reaction against realism and a scientific paganism' (93). The 'inventors of Jazz,' Bell speculates, considered nineteenth-century art to have been excessively dedicated to 'beauty and intensity'; they founded jazz, therefore, in rebellion against Nobility and Beauty. Their impudence, motivated by a 'childish' hatred of culture and intellect, finds its 'technical equivalent' in syncopation (93). By the 'inventors of Jazz', Bell means European and American avant-gardists, for African-American musicians, in his view, are merely pawns in an aesthetic contest beyond their scope.

When it comes to the work of artists he ascribes to the 'jazz movement', Bell is somewhat more sensitive. Cubism was often identified outright with jazz, and Bell concedes that in their exploration of that generally unprofitable territory Picasso and Braque have 'produced works of the greatest beauty and significance' (95). Stravinsky, too, has been 'influenced much by nigger rhythms and nigger methods' and thus belongs to the jazz movement as much as any great artist can be said to belong to a movement (94).

Jazz in literature, according to Bell, appears in syncopated rhythms and in distorted 'sequences [of] grammar and logic'. Its truest exemplars in poetry are Cocteau and Cendrars, who he says are worth, together, perhaps a half-hour's attention. But Eliot, whom Bell calls 'about the best of our living poets', is also a product of the jazz movement. In a bizarre conceit Bell figures jazz – Eliot's 'black and grinning muse' – as midwife to Eliot's 'agonizing labors' of composition:

> Apparently it is only by adopting a demurely irreverent attitude, by being primly insolent, and by playing the devil with the instrument of Shakespeare and Milton, that Mr. Eliot is able occasionally to deliver himself of one of those complicated and remarkable imaginings of his: apparently it is only in language, of an exquisite purity so far as material goes, but twisted and ragged out of easy recognition that these nurslings can be swathed. (94)

I will be arguing presently that there is something to this. Certainly when Eliot published *The Waste Land* a year later, with its 'Shakespeherian Rag' and its ragging of Shakespeare, Bell must have looked positively prophetic.

More telling than Bell's specific judgments, though, is his assumption that there was such a thing at all as a 'jazz movement' in the arts; that its methods were in some way connected with the musical techniques of jazz; that its aesthetic goals were embodied in the 'meaning' of jazz; that it was socially and culturally revolutionary. Despite his respect for certain 'jazz' artists, Bell is determined to range himself on the side of Beethoven, Beauty, and Nobility against a faction that (he claims) elevates popular culture over Art. It is a grievous mistake, he suggests, for artists to take seriously either waltzes or ragtime: the divide between popular and high art must not be violated (94). This is the sort of argument that is now often taken to characterize modernism's unalloyed horror of mass culture – usually in contrast with postmodernism's embrace. Yet Eliot's position, for one, is considerably more complex and less hysterical; and as Bell realized, Eliot's genius was thoroughly entangled with his 'black and grinning muse'. Indeed, Eliot had accepted his place in the jazz movement a long time before.

* * *

Chinitz goes on to examine the poems from an early notebook published in 1996 as *Inventions of the March Hare*. He notes the long-acknowledged influence of Jules Laforgue, but suggests that it may have been Laforgue's *method* of incorporating popular song into his poetry that was influential, rather than his rhythms as such. Eliot's use of jazz-inflected popular song allowed him to break both from conventional iambic pentameter, and from the 'jagged syntax and concentration of exclamation points' in Laforgue's *Dernier Vers*.[17]

Extract from David E. Chinitz, *T. S. Eliot and the Cultural Divide*, pp.41–49.

Down at Tom's Place

The influence of jazz on *The Waste Land* has been a source of speculation for many years. While later readers have assumed that any relation Eliot might have borne to jazz would have been purely oppositional, Eliot's contemporaries, for whom the existence of a structural correlation between modernism and jazz was a 'commonplace', were inclined to think the opposite (North, *Reading* 146). Thus Louis Untermeyer detected 'jazz-rhythms' among what he considered *The Waste Land*'s poorly orchestrated 'jumble' of ingredients ('Disillusion' 151–2), while John McClure imagined Eliot as 'drowning in a sea of jazz' (170). Even much later, Ralph Ellison paid tribute to the poem that, more than any other text, had launched him into a literary career:

> … *The Waste Land* seized my mind. I was intrigued by its power to move me while
> eluding my understanding. Somehow its rhythms were often closer to those of jazz
> than were those of the Negro poets, and even though I could not understand then,
> its range of allusion was as mixed and as varied as that of Louis Armstrong. (160)

That Ellison, like Untermeyer, made no mistake in tracing Eliot's rhythms to jazz sources we have seen already; that he was right as well about Eliot's use of allusion we shall see presently.

There is more, too, to the subject of jazz in *The Waste Land* than Ellison could have known, for the poem Eliot originally wrote was quite different from the poem that was published. Although Ezra Pound's own use of popular genres has been demonstrated by Michael Coyle, somehow – whether because Pound did not particularly share Eliot's fondness for contemporary popular music or because he mistook Eliot's intent – Pound's editorial work eliminated the majority of Eliot's subliterary allusions from *The Waste Land* and ultimately collapsed its levels of cultural reference while leaving its internationalism and historicism intact. The poem was thus recast, ironically, as the first major counteroffensive in high culture's last stand. Pound is not to be blamed for this turn of events. To be sure, nearly all of his emendations constitute decided improvements to Eliot's draft, and Eliot acceded to the recommendations of 'il miglior fabbro' in almost every instance. Nonetheless, part of Eliot's original impulse in composing *The Waste Land* was lost in this collaborative process. Had he labored to improve the condemned passages instead of agreeing to delete them, he might have given literary modernism a markedly different spin.

Such speculation is inevitably somewhat tenuous. What is certain is that the manuscript of *The Waste Land* shows Eliot drawing on popular song to a greater extent than he uses the Grail myth in the final version. For the long idiomatic passage that was to have opened the poem he considered several popular lyrics. The seventh and eighth lines of the original typescript quote George M. Cohan's 'Harrigan', from the 1907 musical *Fifty Miles from Boston*. Cohan, of course, is best known for his Yankee Doodle persona, his insistent Americanism; but 'Harrigan' has a somewhat different slant, emphasizing rather the defiant self-respect of the Irish-American: 'Proud of all the Irish blood that's in me / Divil a man can say a word agin me'. The sentiment is appropriate to this opening section, which recounts in demotic language the adventures of a rowdy group of Boston Irish out on the town. The association of Irish immigrants with the American popular stage and its music may have been part of the stimulus that produced this episode; Joyce's *Ulysses* was, doubtless, another. For the opening scene of *The Waste Land* was, as Lyndall Gordon has noted, a 'Boston version of the visit to Night-town' (*Eliot's Early Years* 145) – an observation that Peter Barry has extended by pointing out the particularly close parallels of Eliot's scene to the final pages of 'Circe', which Eliot had only just finished reading as he began work on *The Waste Land* (239–40).

By late 1923 and '*Ulysses*, Order, and Myth', Eliot had decided that the 'mythical method' was Joyce's most significant literary contribution in *Ulysses*. There is reason to believe, though, that despite the tendency of critics to account for the poem in the terms of the later essay, Eliot had not formulated this theory by the time he completed *The Waste Land* (Kaufmann 76–80). The canceled opening of the poem suggests that in 1921 Eliot was strongly impressed with Joyce's integration of popular song into his text – for *Ulysses*, which 'revels in the language and forms of popular culture' (Thompson 35), is saturated with song. Apparently Eliot planned to follow Joyce by locating his poem in a similar cultural matrix, conjoining high culture, ancient mythology, and popular allusions in the new American style. His failure to conceptualize such an artistic design without resorting to a Joycean band of inebriated Irish ethnics in an urban red-light district may explain the apparent ease with which Eliot was persuaded to drop the passage. It may even have been the derivative quality of this passage that led Eliot to write to Joyce in May of 1921, apparently speaking of 'Circe', 'I wish, for my own sake, that I had not read it' (*Letters* 455). But he was serious about using this episode to introduce his poem – serious enough to have typed his working title, 'HE DO THE POLICE IN DIFFERENT VOICES: Part I', at the top of the page, and the extant subtitle, 'THE BURIAL OF THE DEAD', beneath it (*WLF* 5).

Next to the lines from 'Harrigan', Eliot has jotted, either as an alternative quotation or as an additional one to be worked into the poem, 'Meet me in the shadow of the / watermelon Vine / Eva Iva Uva Emmaline'. Here he has altered and telescoped lines from two songs: 'By the Watermelon Vine', a 1904 'coon song', and 'My Evaline', first performed in a 1901 vaudeville-minstrel act (North, *Dialect* 85). Eliot probably heard 'My Evaline' at Harvard, where it was often sung as a barbershop quartet. Clearly he had as long a memory for lowbrow as for highbrow materials. Bracketed in the margin just below are the lines 'Tease, Squeeze lovin & wooin / Say Kid what're y' doin'', taken almost verbatim from 'The Cubanola Glide', the very same song Eliot had drawn on a decade earlier in 'The smoke that gathers blue and sinks'. Popularized in 1909 by Sophie Tucker – the model, perhaps, for the zaftig chanteuse in the earlier poem – 'Cubanola' was a ragtime number of some significance as one of the first American tunes to incorporate 'tropical' rhythms (Ewen 173). The composer, Harry von Tilzer, is better known for 'A Bird in a Gilded Cage,' 'Wait 'Til the Sun Shines, Nellie', and 'I Want a Girl Just Like the Girl That Married Dear Old Dad', but 'The Cubanola Glide' contributed directly to the nascent social dance craze and paved the way for such successors as the Grizzly Bear, the Bunny Hug, and the Turkey Trot (Spaeth, *History* 310). Both its 'racial' diction and its eponymous dance, a relative of the cakewalk, added African-American overtones to the Cuban reference of the lyrics. With a light tango rhythm that foreshadows the Latin element in the American popular music of the succeeding decades, 'The Cubanola Glide' was in its day an influential transitional work.

After a disruptive stop in a theater, the raucous crew of Eliot's discarded page drop in to a bar that Eliot himself frequented as a college student after attending the melodrama at Boston's Grand Opera House (*WLF* 125). The coincidence hints at a partial identification between the poet and his characters – an identification anticipated in the very first lines of the poem, in which the young men drink with a friend named 'old Tom'. Tom, as it happens, is 'boiled to the eyes', a description that, as Virginia Woolf and other friends noticed, all too often fit Tom Eliot himself at Jazz-Age parties. Being boiled to the eyes, old Tom is 'blind', and thus an avatar of Tiresias, *The Waste Land*'s central observer and raconteur. Eliot's identification with the crude, boisterous youths of the opening scene is particularly interesting because, as Gregory Jay argues, the passage vividly displays both sides of Eliot's ambivalent relation to mass culture. His 'often affectionate imitation of [working-class] voices', which 'conveys a respect for . . . ordinary lives and feelings', is offset by an 'almost physical disgust for the materiality of existence – for the object world that dominates the lower classes' ('Postmodernism' 236–7). The episode may therefore be said to repeat a pattern that we have found in the earlier Eliot and that will reach its ambiguous zenith later, in *Sweeney Agonistes*. Eliot strains toward a Joycean sympathy in the abandoned opening of *The Waste Land*, but the strain shows.

Eliot and Pound's editorial decision to omit the Boston Irish sequence had important consequences for *The Waste Land* as a whole. With the deletion of this section, the poem's surviving first line places it squarely within the 'Great Tradition' of English poetry, beginning with Chaucer, instead of the contemporary and fundamentally American world of popular culture (Jay, 'Postmodernism' 237). As A. David Moody points out, the long narrative on the wreck of a New England fishing boat, which Pound cut from the 'Death by Water' section, would also have highlighted the poem's American roots. The cancellation of these two major passages, Moody argues,

> meant that the setting of the poem, along with its great range of cultural reference, became exclusively English and European. The only authentically American detail left in the poem is the hermit thrush. ('T. S. Eliot' 81)

Although Moody is forgetting the 'Shakespearian Rag', his observation is otherwise accurate. And likewise, the hints of popular song that survive in the published poem are decisively eclipsed by the more erudite classical and European allusions that predominate. A long poem called *The Waste Land* that begins, 'April is the cruellest month', largely shaped the course of literature and criticism for years to come. One can only imagine the effect of a long poem called *He Do the Police in Different Voices* beginning, 'First we had a couple of feelers down at Tom's place'.

That Shakespeherian Rag

There are other and perhaps deeper senses, too, in which popular culture penetrated *The Waste Land*. Because the song excerpts on the original first page are, as North notes, 'the first examples in the draft of [Eliot's] famous techniques of quotation and juxtaposition', the minstrel or coon-song associations of three of those songs lead him to posit a connection between the minstrel show, an 'art of mélange', and the distinctive form of *The Waste Land* (*Dialect* 85–6). Minstrel shows were in fact full of allusions – to Shakespeare, to melodrama, to opera. All genres, high and low, took on new meaning through their absorption into the minstrel setting, as they do in Eliot's poem:

> But at my back in a cold blast I hear
> The rattle of the bones, and chuckle spread from ear to ear.
> A rat crept softly through the vegetation
> Dragging its slimy belly on the bank
> While I was fishing in the dull canal
> On a winter evening round behind the gashouse
> Musing upon the king my brother's wreck
> And on the king my father's death before him.
> White bodies naked on the low damp ground
> And bones cast in a little low dry garret,
> Rattled by the rat's foot only, year to year.
> But at my back from time to time I hear
> The sound of horns and motors, which shall bring
> Sweeney to Mrs. Porter in the spring.
> O the moon shone bright on Mrs. Porter
> And on her daughter
> They wash their feet in soda water
> *Et O ces voix d'enfants, chantant dans la coupole!*
>
> (CPP 42–3)

This passage, a virtual dramatic performance in its own right, eerily invokes the minstrel context in its second line, where the phrase 'rattle of the bones' conjoins two vastly different frames of reference: the phantasmagoric cityscape of the succeeding lines, with their drowned bodies, and the minstrel stage, where the ear-to-ear grin and the bones, qua percussion instrument, were essential elements of the act. (Eliot may even have known Stephen Foster's 'Ring de Banjo', which proclaims, 'De ladies nebber weary / Wid de rattle ob de bones'.) This minstrel reference follows the first of two allusions to Marvell's 'Coy Mistress' and precedes a transposition of Shakespeare's *Tempest* into the Gothic mode. Similarly, the brilliant closing lines fly from seventeenth-century lyric (Marvell and Day) to a bawdy popular parody of the sentimental song 'Red Wing' – into which Eliot imports his own character, Sweeney – and finally, through the common element of the footbath, to the romance of the Grail Quest by way of a Verlaine sonnet on a Wagner opera. The whole generic crazy quilt that is *The Waste Land* is replicated on a small scale in these eighteen lines, tellingly under the sign of the minstrel show. In a sense, then, it does not matter whether 'My

Evaline' or the 'By the Watermelon Vine' ultimately made it into the published *Waste Land:* the minstrel show leaves its trace in the form of Eliot's profoundest innovations.

At the same time, one need not overemphasize the minstrel show as the inspiration behind Eliot's method, for *The Waste Land*, even on its excised opening page, gestures in other directions as well. Neither 'Harrigan' nor 'The Cubanola Glide' is a minstrel number, and the musical environment in which Eliot sets his Boston scene is fundamentally a ragtime milieu. Nor is the minstrel show the only popular genre that bears analogy to Eliot's practice of 'quotation and juxtaposition'. American vaudeville and English music hall, both of which even incorporated minstrel acts among their 'turns', were similarly miscellaneous, as was, for that matter, the circus. Jazz-Age popular music may offer an even more potent analogy, for jazz musicians engaged so abundantly in quotation, imitation, and parody that such practices were often taken to be the essence of the genre. Its critics frequently denied that jazz had any substance of its own, preferring to characterize it as merely a technique of willful distortion applied to preexisting music. Of course the same charge was leveled by literary critics who considered Eliot's work, and particularly *The Waste Land*, nothing more than a species of plagiarism.

The point is not that Eliot extracted his montage aesthetic from jazz in a direct way, but rather that there is a fundamental convergence between Eliot's poem and the principal popular music of its era, particularly in the areas of structure, rhythm, and allusion. There are other parallels that might be and sometimes have been drawn between the characteristic musical traits of 1920s jazz and the new literary techniques explored in modernist texts like *The Waste Land*. Such synesthetic correlations inevitably seem a bit impressionistic, and I do not want to overreach my evidence. Still, both jazz and *The Waste Land* were read at the time as expressing, through their very form, the conditions of modern life – its instability, its rapid pace, its 'variety and complexity' – as well as the rebellion against it. It should not seem too remarkable, then, if between their structures there is a kind of synergy.

It is thus unfortunate that critics have made so little of Eliot's quotation of the song 'That Shakespearian Rag' in lines 127–30 of *The Waste Land:*

> But
> O O O O that Shakespeherian Rag –
> It's so elegant
> So intelligent

Sigg has speculated interestingly that the allusion may be self-referential. Like a ragtime pianist who has 'spliced together strands of melody and patches of harmony' to generate a new composition, Eliot advertises (or perhaps ironizes) his own poem as 'a kind of rag, a rhythmical weaving of literary and musical scraps from many hands into a single composition' (21). *The Waste Land*, by this reckoning, not only quotes the 'Shakespearian Rag': it is a Shakespearean Rag. Beyond this suggestion, not much else that is cogent has been written about these lines. Taking for granted that *The Waste Land* proposed simply to discredit the barren present by comparison with the fertile past, readers have long assumed that the song represented a degraded (i.e., contemporary and popular) version of Shakespearean high culture – in essence 'what Shakespeare had come down to' in their own and Eliot's time. As one critic has asserted, popular culture in *The Waste Land*, this allusion included, 'exists as an index of the degradation of the modern age' (Thompson 35). Thirty-five years elapsed after the publication of *The Waste Land* before a scholar named B. R. McElderry finally took the trouble to identify the song as a long-forgotten tune from the 1912 Ziegfeld Follies; but even for McElderry, this discovery was material only for a brief scholarly note. Once he had disparaged the lyrics as 'utterly tasteless', there was little more for him to say (185). For McElderry, as for so many others, Eliot used the song merely as a 'symbol of vulgarity', or a 'proper symbol of public taste' in the early twentieth century.

If we overcome the urge to dismiss the song out of hand, we discover that it actually does shed light on *The Waste Land*. For 'That Shakespearian Rag' attempts to undermine exactly the position taken by Eliot's explicators on the value of contemporary popular culture in relation to canonized high culture – the position then blithely attributed to Eliot himself. Shakespeare, the song tells us, is pure caviar, all elegance and intelligence. Ragtime, naturally, is a great deal more fun, and had Shakespeare's characters experienced it, they might have averted their various tragedies:

> 'As you like it' Brutus,
> We'll play a rag today.
> Then old Shylock danced,
> And the Moor, Othello, pranced,
> Feeling gay, he would say, as he started in to sway,
> 'Bring the rag right away'.
>
> (3)

Shakespeare's poetry, the song predictably avers, is exceedingly 'high-browed' and outdated; fortunately, however, ragtime has come along to give 'that old classical drag' new life in a syncopated setting.

At the same time, the song's attempt to sustain an attitude of impudence comes across as rather forced, for the lyrics seem altogether too self-conscious about their own culturally inferior relation to Shakespeare. They protest too much that times have changed and that a rag – 'yes, a rag', the song insists –

can now be 'grand'. In this uneasy self-assurance lies an intriguing analogy to Eliot's own unsettled position as a cultural interloper within the placidly civilized London literary scene – as a crass American 'savage' bursting into the English drawing room declaiming his verse ('War-Paint'). Eliot's personal admixture of cultural anxiety and confidence, his ambivalence toward the modernity he was compelled to choose, is mirrored in 'That Shakespearian Rag', as it is in *The Waste Land* as a whole. Even his readjustment of the established canon is comically figured in the song as the ragging of 'Bill' Shakespeare.

Despite its pretensions to outrageousness, the original 'Shakespearian Rag' was hardly revolutionary; it was rather a latecomer to a fad for similar titles, such as 'That Lovin' Rag' (1908), 'That Beautiful Rag' (1910), and 'That Mysterious Rag' (1911). Its debunking of Shakespeare adopts a formula established on the nineteenth-century American comic stage. And despite the 'Rag' in its title, not to mention its extravagant praise of syncopation, the song is itself rhythmically uninventive and only occasionally syncopated. (Eliot compensates in *The Waste Land* by inserting the extra syllable in 'Shakespe*he*rian', beating composer David Stamper at his own game.) The lyric banks its bid for humor on the shock generated when a culture's most revered texts are treated with an unceremonious familiarity. Perhaps audiences in 1912 found the mere presence of such famous tags as 'Friends, Romans, Countrymen' and 'My kingdom for a horse' in a rag sufficiently funny; at least, there is not much else of the comic to be found in the verses. The application of contemporary slang to what is supposed to be highfalutin 'stuff' has comic possibilities, and the song exploits this technique with deliberate audacity but without real cleverness, as in the chorus:

> *Desdemona was the colored pet,*
> *Romeo loved his Juliet,*
> *And they were some lovers, you can bet, and yet,*
> *I know if they were here today,*
> *They'd Grizzly Bear in a diff'rent way,*
> *And you'd hear old Hamlet say,*
> *'To be or not to be,'*
> *That Shakespearian Rag.*
>
> (4–5)

The rhymes are pedestrian, the assertions trite, and the concluding lines, which create the expectation of a verbal coup de grace as the music rises to a crescendo, anticlimactically fail to deliver the anticipated double meaning. One has only to compare 'That Shakespearian Rag' with Cole Porter's 'Brush Up Your Shakespeare' to see how much more can be done with the same concept. Yet whatever the aesthetic shortcomings of 'That Shakespearian Rag', Eliot clearly understood that the ragging of Shakespeare – his own as well as the song's – had explosive potential to amuse or to offend; to link history and contemporaneity, or to push them apart; and to register the widening gulf between art and popular culture. In connection with the last idea, Shakespeare, who was popular in his own day but elite fare by the time of the 'Shakespearian Rag', would seem to provide the supreme illustration.

Interestingly, the 'Shakespearian Rag' allusion in 'A Game of Chess' seems to emanate from the silent husband in response to the wife's last hysterical attempt to draw him out: 'Are you alive, or not? Is there nothing in your head?' If the 'Shakespearian Rag' is meant as an answer to that question, it may represent the same response – with the same unapportionable degree of irony – that a much younger Eliot had given his similarly abulic speaker in 'The smoke that gathers blue and sinks'. In both cases, a responsiveness to jazz is the one indication of a life within. At the same time, the most obvious, immediate effect of the song quotation in 'A Game of Chess' is to provide an instant of (Shakespearean?) comic relief in the midst of one of the most painful sections of *The Waste Land*. In 'The Fire Sermon', the ballad of Mrs. Porter performs a similar function, breathing momentary life into an otherwise bleak passage on cultural decay.

Its various contexts considered, Eliot's 'O O O O that Shakespeherian Rag' thus gestures in several directions at once. The 'degradation of the modern age' is perhaps one of those directions, though certainly not because popular culture always functioned for Eliot as an 'index' of such degradation. On the contrary, given his other 'lowbrow' interests, one does not doubt that Eliot, in his quizzical, elusively ironic way, enjoyed 'That Shakespearian Rag' for its blend of brash irreverence and outlandish vacuity. Ironically earnest, delectably vulgar, its self-regarding cheek neatly balancing its evident inanity, the 'Shakespeherian Rag' in *The Waste Land* is a sliver of Eliotic camp.

* * *

In the next chapter of *T. S. Eliot and the Cultural Divide*, 'The Dull and the Lively', Chinitz examines Eliot's attitude in his prose writings to the great divide. Eliot questioned the assumption that high art must be dull, and our attitude towards it 'solemn and reverential', and that only the popular arts could be lively. As a point of contrast, we can note John Carey, who argues that modernists sought to exclude mass audiences from their works, and did so by avoiding human interest and by creating a literature too difficult for that audience to understand.[18] Chinitz argues that not only Eliot, but also Yeats, Conrad, Woolf, Lawrence, Joyce and Pound 'at various points in their careers actively sought, and occasionally found, a wide audience'.[19] He identifies a dividing line in Eliot's career in 1920: up to that date, his literary criticism focused on purely literary issues; afterwards, he increasingly places literature in its cultural context, and attempts to write a form of drama which could engage larger audiences than poetry. 'Primitive' art was of particular interest to him because in 'primitive' cultures, art was integrated into life through ritual.

What Eliot envisions, in other words, is a revolution in the relation between art and society along the lines of primitive communities in which art is a central and not a fringe activity – a regular part of the experience of life, closely connected with what people believe, with their community-building, and in short with their relationship to the world and to one another. Such a transformation will also require, and may even have to begin with, a change in the role of the art, whose defensive isolation must yield to an altogether different model of conduct. Eliot's poet is a public figure who 'aspires to the condition of the music-hall comedian' and whose proper medium is drama, envisioned as a public and ritualistic art.[20]

From this view of Eliot's understanding of primitivism, Chinitz moves to more general reflections.

Extract from David E. Chinitz, *T. S. Eliot and the Cultural Divide*, pp.80–84.

An 'Avant-Garde' Program

It will be apparent to readers of Peter Bürger's *Theory of the Avant-Garde* that Eliot's anti-aesthetic cultural program as I have outlined it here bears comparison to the programs of early-twentieth-century European avant-garde movements in Bürger's account. Indeed, if this resemblance seems surprising it is only because Bürger's theory has been used, most influentially by Andreas Huyssen, to argue the existence of a strict separation between 'modernism' and the 'historical avant-garde'. The example of T. S. Eliot, which ought to provide unproblematic evidence for such a generalization (indeed, Huyssen cites it as if it did), actually provides important reasons to question it.

Bürger traces the origins of the avant-garde to a process of self-criticism within the 'social subsystem that is art' (22). 'In bourgeois society,' Bürger writes, art is assigned 'a special sphere of experience', the aesthetic, and becomes detached from the ordinary, daily components of living, which Bürger calls the 'praxis of life' (22–4). For avant-gardists, the dissociation of art from the praxis of life – summed up in the word 'autonomy' and in the slogan 'art for art's sake' – is nothing less than the 'dominant characteristic of art in bourgeois society' (49). The avant-garde arises out of antipathy to this dissociation and to the 'social ineffectuality' that comes as the price of autonomy (27):

> The European avant-garde movements can be defined as an attack on the status of art in bourgeois society. What is negated is not an earlier form of art (a style) but art as an institution that is unassociated with the life praxis of men. When the avant-gardistes demand that art become practical once again, they do not mean that the contents of works of art should be socially significant. The demand is not raised at the level of the contents of individual works. Rather, it directs itself to the way art functions in society, a process that does as much to determine the effect that works have as does the particular content. (49)

And herein, for Huyssen, lies the difference with modernism: 'In modernism art and literature retained their traditional 19th-century autonomy from everyday life' (163). Modernists engaged in technical experimentation that sometimes resembled avant-garde practices, but they did not, according to Huyssen, try to subvert the 'institution of art': 'the traditional way in which art and literature were produced, disseminated, and received, is never challenged by modernism but maintained intact' (163). Avant-garde groups, by contrast, sought 'to undermine, attack and transform the bourgeois institution art and its ideology of autonomy rather than only changing artistic and literary modes of representation' (192).

Yet what Bürger and Huyssen identify as the avant-garde project corresponds in many ways to Eliot's. To be sure, the conservative Eliot hardly shared the activist agendas (whether left wing or right) associated with most avant-garde movements. And though other, relatively apolitical avant-gardes did exist, such as the Parisian group surrounding Jean Cocteau at Le Boeuf sur le Toit, it is quite true that Eliot, unlike Cocteau, studiously avoided avant-garde shock tactics and spectacle in promoting his aesthetic and social programs. 'You let *me* throw the bricks through the front window,' Pound observed to him; 'You go in at the back door and take out the swag' (qtd. in Carpenter 264). Yet the consequences of Eliot's thinking, even when developed in an unobtrusive and fragmentary way in his prose, are often radical – a fact that may help to explain Eliot's acknowledged usefulness to leftist writers of the 1930s as well as his later (and less frequently acknowledged) usefulness to cultural studies. Like the earlier avant-gardes, Eliot is keenly aware that the autonomy of art is a recent and local development, and not an immutable and transcendent reality. No less than they, Eliot opposes the middle-class fetishization of art. And we have seen – not only in Eliot's anthropological reviews but in even so well-known an essay as '*Ulysses*, Order, and Myth' – that Eliot's aim is *not* simply to alter 'artistic and literary modes of representation' but to effect a larger cultural transformation (authorized by Durkheim and Lévy-Bruhl) that would 'reintegrate art into the praxis of life' (Bürger 87). That art, suitably modified, might induce such a change is a notion, perhaps an illusory one, that Eliot and the avant-gardists share. They both seek a 'reorganization of the praxis of life through art' (59).

Huyssen again follows Bürger when he associates modernist aestheticism with its purported rejection of mass culture. Bürger argues that the 'dichotomy between high and low literature' is established by and for the purposes of the 'institution of art' (lii). Because Theodor Adorno, for example, spoke from 'within the institution that is art', he 'almost always viewed serious and pulp literature as radically distinct spheres, thus making the separation that is established in the institution of art/literature his own'. In Adorno's work, Bürger explains, 'the relation between serious and pulp fiction is barely thematized, precisely because both are assigned to distinct spheres from the very beginning' (liii). Huyssen extends this characterization to the whole of modernism. And Eliot, he asserts,

> felt drawn to the constructive sensibility of modernism, which insisted on the dig-
> nity and autonomy of literature, rather than to the iconoclastic and anti-aesthetic
> ethos of the European avantgarde which attempted to break the political bondage
> of high culture through a fusion with popular culture and to integrate art into
> life. (167)

Eliot's criticism before 1920 confirms that he was indeed drawn to the position Huyssen defines as modernist – a position that, as Huyssen neatly explains, attracted American artists because high art in the United States (as opposed to Europe) 'was still struggling hard to gain wider legitimacy and to be taken seriously by the public' (167). But Eliot, having escaped this particular difficulty by emigrating, did not need the reassurances of aestheticism for long, and by the early twenties he was engaged, as we have seen, in interrogating the high/low binary. And this questioning is indeed, as Bürger's theory predicts, linked with a reexamination of the institution of art and a desire to realign the relationship of art with 'the praxis of life'. Eliot's goal is not merely a new and better poetry, but a complete rethinking of the prevailing construction of art.

My objective here is not to abolish all distinctions between modernism and the avant-garde; indeed, a revaluation of Eliot alone would hardly give adequate grounds for doing so. A counterexample of Eliot's magnitude, however, may provide sufficient reason to banish the conviction, from which many invidi-ous conclusions follow, that modernism and the avant-garde are impermeable or mutually exclusive categories. Astradur Eysteinsson identifies some of the 'ensuing value judgments and fruitless distinctions', as, for example, 'seeing the avant-garde as simply a preparatory stage for the masterpieces of modernism or judging the avant-garde as the only significant revolt, while modernism is merely a classicism in disguise' (178). Eysteinsson's rejection of a 'rigid separ-ation' in favor of a more flexible model that recognizes the interpenetration of modernism and the avant-garde is to be commended as both a more 'stimu-lating' and a more accurate representation of early-twentieth-century cultural history.

The efforts of the European avant-garde movements to transform both art and society cannot, evidently, be counted a success. As Bürger bluntly puts it, 'the attack of the historical avant-garde movements on art as an institu-tion has failed, and art has not been integrated into the praxis of life, art as an institution continues to survive as something separate from the praxis of life' (57). In this endeavor Eliot prevailed no more than the avant-garde. His methods, on the other hand, could not have been more different. Pound's bricks-through-the-front-window approach was basically avant-gardist: he wrote polemics, assembled conspirators, orchestrated scandals, published mani-festos, and sought notoriety. Eliot was more level, more calculating, and more ingratiating; his modus operandi was to infiltrate the system and work from the inside – thus the cultivated 'dullness' of the *Criterion* with which we began this chapter. In this way he succeeded, as Pound could not, in dictating artistic principles and canons in a country that was not his own, and ultimately even in capturing the admiration of a significant public.

Aside from the obvious question of whether any modern artist or artists, whatever their aims and whatever their tactics, stood a chance of completely transforming bourgeois culture, two special problems must be acknowledged in Eliot's case. First, Eliot was deeply conservative as well as radical, so that as he insinuated himself into the established 'art institution' he was also to some extent co-opted by it, recoiling from and courting the system all at once (Levenson 217–20). As a result, Eliot the icon and champion of English letters has almost totally obscured Eliot the revolutionist in critical and popular perception since the 1930s. Second, Eliot's desire to alter the 'praxis of life' was quickly and seamlessly absorbed, after his conversion, into advocacy of Christianity and the Church. Though this shift represents a change of focus rather than a reversal of principle, its significance is so obvious that after 1927 Eliot's project quite naturally appears altogether different from, or even antithetical to, the historical avant-garde's. [. . .]

For now it will suffice to observe that although the 'mythical method' is usu-ally discussed in connection with *The Waste Land* – largely because of the light Eliot's analysis of Joyce sheds on his own major work – it is his unfinished play, *Sweeney Agonistes*, that best exemplifies Eliot's attempt to launch his broader program. It was this new project that Eliot had in mind when he wrote '*Ulysses*, Order, and Myth', and not the work he had written almost two years before in a genre on which he had 'definitely given up'. Whereas *The Waste Land* was torn out of Eliot under great psychological pressure, *Sweeney* was a calculated first step toward 'making the modern world possible for art' – for Eliot did not expect to alter modern culture by writing poems. And not coincidentally, it is in *Sweeney Agonistes*, his one pre-Christian play, that Eliot today appears stylistically most avant-garde.

* * *

The identity of modernism emerged in a cultural atmosphere wary of the culture industry, both from a narrow-minded hostility to its products, and a more humane, though patronizing, concern for its consumers. Concerned to justify art in an age that was marginalizing it, modernist writers created a discourse of value in which the qualities which made their works important were sharply differentiated from those characteristic of mass culture: they contrasted the lightness and consumability of mass-cultural works from the density of their own; they contrasted the expressive and sentimental models of the self in mass-cultural works from the impersonality of the modernist.

In the late twentieth century, a reassessment of the value of mass culture and of the means by which it is valued led to an unfavourable reassessment of modernist elitism. Moreover, the modernist wariness of the culture industry was often understood as 'cultural elitism' (a complex and insufficiently analysed phrase), and this 'elitism' in turn was often identified with political authoritarianism. Undoubtedly many modernists had authoritarian sympathies, but the one position is not a necessary concomitant of the other. Indeed, as the culture industry itself can be harnessed by authoritarianism, opposition to it can form part of an anti-authoritarian politics. Since the 1990s, a further reaction has manifested itself, in which critics have reassessed modernist work, looking for signs of receptiveness to popular culture and to the products of the culture industry.

Works Cited by David Chinitz

Barry, Peter. 'The Waste Land Manuscript: Picking up the Pieces—in Order', *Forum for Modern Language Studies*, 15 (1979): 237–47.

Bell, Clive. 'Plus de Jazz,' *New Republic* 21 Sept. 1921: 92–96.

Bürger, Peter. *Theory of the Avant-Garde*, tr. Michael Shaw. Minneapolis: University of Minnesota Press, 1984.

Carpenter, Humphrey. *A Serious Character: The Life of Ezra Pound*. London: Faber and Faber, 1988.

Cocteau, Jean. *A Call to Order*, trans. Rollo H. Myers. New York: Haskell, 1974.

Coyle, Michael. *Ezra Pound, Popular Genres, and the Discourse of Culture*. University Park, PA: Pennsylvania State UP, 1995.

Douglas, Ann. *Terrible Honesty: Mongrel Manhattan in the 1920s*. New York: Farrar, 1995.

'The Effort to Take Jazz Seriously.' *Literary Digest* Apr. 1924: 29–30.

Eliot, T. S. *Complete Poems and Plays, 1909–1950*. New York: Harcourt, 1971. Cited as *CPP*.

—. 'War-Paint and Feathers', *Athenaeum* 17 Oct. 1919: 1036.

—. *The Waste Land: A Facsimile and Transcript of the Original Drafts Including the Annotations of Ezra Pound*, ed. Valerie Eliot. New York: Harcourt, 1971. Cited as *WLF*.

Ellison, Ralph. *Shadow and Act*. 1953. New York: Vintage, 1972.

Ewen, David. *The Death and Birth of Tin Pan Alley*. New York: Funk, 1964.

Eysteinsson, Astradur. The Concept of Modernism. Ithaca: Cornell University Press, 1990.

Gendron, Bernard. *Between Montmartre and the Mudd Club: Popular Music and the Avant-Garde*. Chicago: University of Chicago Press, 2002.

Gordon, Lyndall. *Eliot's Early Years*. Oxford: Oxford University Press, 1977.

Huyssen, Andreas. *After the Great Divide: Modernism, Mass Culture, Postmodernism.* Bloomington: Indiana University Press, 1986.

Jay, Gregory. 'Postmodernism in *The Waste Land*: Women, Mass Culture, and Others', in *Rereading the New: A Backward Glance at Modernism* (Ann Arbor: University of Michigan Press, 1992), 221–46.

Johnson, Robert Underwood. 'The Glory of Words', *Academy Papers: Addresses on Language Problems by Members of the American Academy of Arts and Letters.* New York: Scribner's, 1925.

Kaufmann, Michael Edward. 'T. S. Eliot's New Critical Footnotes to Modernism', in *Rereading the New: A Backward Glance at Modernism* (Ann Arbor: University of Michigan Press, 1992), 73–85.

Leonard, Neil. *Jazz and the White Americans.* Chicago: University of Chicago Press, 1962.

Levenson, Michael H. *A Genealogy of Modernism.* Cambridge: Cambridge University Press, 1984.

McClure, John. Review of *The Waste Land*, by T. S. Eliot, *Double Dealer*, 5 (1923): 173–74.

McElderry, B. R., Jr. 'Eliot's "Shakespeherian Rag"', American Quarterly, 9 (1957): 185–86.

Moody, A. David. 'T. S. Eliot: The American Strain', The Placing of T. S. Eliot, ed. Jewel Spears Brooker (Columbia: University of Missouri Press, 1991), 77–89.

North, Michael. *The Dialect of Modernism: Race, Language, and Twentieth-Century Literature.* New York: Oxford University Press, 1994.

—. *Reading 1922: A Return to the Scene of the Modern.* New York: Oxford University Press, 1999.

Rye, Howard. 'Fearsome Means of Discord: Early Encounters with Black Jazz', *Black Music in Britain*, ed. Paul Oliver (Philadelphia: Open University Press, 1990), 45–57.

Sigg, Eric. 'Eliot as a Product of America', in *The Cambridge Companion to T. S. Eliot*, ed. A. David Moody (Cambridge: Cambridge University Press, 1994), 14–30.

Spaeth, Sigmund. *A History of Popular Music in America.* New York: Random, 1948.

Steegmuller, Francis. *Cocteau: A Biography.* Boston: Little, 1970.

Stevens, Wallace. *The Collected Poems of Wallace Stevens.* New York: Vintage, 1954.

Thompson, Jon. *Fiction, Crime, and Empire.* Urbana: University of Illinois Press, 1993.

'Topics of the Times: Before Long They Will Protest'. *New York Times* 8 Oct. 1924: 18.

Untermeyer, Louis. 'Disillusion vs. Dogma'. *Freeman* 6 (1923): 453. Repr. in *T. S. Eliot: The Critical Heritage*, ed. Michael Grant (London: Routledge, 1982), 151–53.

Wilson, Edmund. 'The Aesthetic Upheaval in France: The Influence of Jazz in Paris and Americanization of French Literature and Art'. *Vanity Fair* Feb. 1922: 49.

Chapter Notes

1. For information on America, see Douglas Tallack, *Twentieth-Century America: The Intellectual and Cultural Context* (London: Longman, 1991), 17–23.

2. Bertrand Russell, *Portraits from Memory* (London: Allen and Unwin, 1956), 105, 107.

3. F. R. Leavis, 1930, quoted Raymond Williams, *Culture and Society* (London: Chatto and Windus, 1958), 253.

4. Williams, Culture and Society, 256–7.

5. John Carey, *The Intellectuals and the Masses* (London: Faber and Faber, 1992), 43.

6. [Huyssen's note:] Printed in Walter Benjamin, *Gesammelte Schriften*, I:3 (Frankfurt am Main: Suhrkamp, 1974), 1003. [Editor's note:] For a translation of Adorno's letter of 18 March 1936, see Ernst Bloch, ed., *Aesthetics and Politics* (London: New Left Books, 1977), 120–6; the quoted phrase appears on p.123.

7. Andreas Huyssen, 'Adorno in Reverse' (1983), in *After the Great Divide* (1986; Basingstoke: Macmillan, 1988), 24–5.

8. E.g., Adorno, 'On the Fetish Character in Music and the Regression in Listening', in J. M. Bernstein, ed., *The Culture Industry*, (London: Routledge, 1991), 29–60.

9. Marianne DeKoven, *Rich and Strange: Gender, History, Modernism* (Princeton, NJ: Princeton University Press, 1991), 34.

10. Andreas Huyssen, 'High/Low in an Expanded Field', *Modernism/Modernity*, 9 (2002), 363–74 (pp.366–7).

11. Nicola Luckhurst, *Bloomsbury in Vogue* (London: Cecil Woolf, 1998); Jane Garrity, 'Selling Culture to the Civilized', *Modernism / Modernity*, 6, no.2 (1999), 29–59; Garrity, 'Virginia Woolf, Intellectual Harlotry, and 1920s British *Vogue*', in Pamela L. Caughie, ed., *Virginia Woolf in the Age of Mechanical Reproduction* (New York: Garland, 2000), 185–218.

12. See Garrity, 'Selling Culture to the Civilized', and Rachel Potter, 'Modernism and Democracy', *Critical Quarterly*, 44, no.2 (Summer 2002), 1–16.

13. David E. Chinitz, *T. S. Eliot and the Cultural Divide* (Chicago: University of Chicago Press, 2003), 3.

14. Chinitz, *T. S. Eliot and the Cultural Divide*, 5.

15. Nancy D. Hargrove, 'Un Présent Parfait': Eliot and La Vie Parisienne, 1910–11', in Marianne Thormählen, ed., *T. S. Eliot at the Turn of the Century*, (Lund: Lund University Press, 1994), 33–58. For further reading on the Harlem Renaissance, see the list at the end of Part Two of the present work.

16. T. S. Eliot, *Letters*, vol. 1, ed. V. Eliot (London: Faber and Faber, 1988), 357.

17. Chinitz, *T. S. Eliot and the Cultural Divide*, 35.

18. Carey, *The Intellectuals and the Masses*, 16–21.

19. Chinitz, *T. S. Eliot and the Cultural Divide*, 62.

20. Chinitz, *T. S. Eliot and the Cultural Divide*, 80.

Further Reading

Carey, John. *The Intellectuals and the Masses: Pride and Prejudice among the Literary Intelligentsia, 1880–1939* (London: Faber and Faber, 1992). Polemical and reductive, but readable and well documented.

Cuddy-Keane, Melba. *Virginia Woolf, the Intellectual, and the Public Sphere* (Cambridge: Cambridge University Press, 1993). In part, a response to accusations of elitism such as John Carey's.

DiBattista, Maria, and Lucy McDiarmid, eds. *High and Low Moderns* (New York: Oxford University Press, 1996). Examines interactions between major and minor modernists, and between moderns and 'Edwardians', including George Bernard Shaw, Rudyard Kipling, and H. G. Wells.

Herr, Cheryl. *Joyce's Anatomy of Culture* (Urbana: University of Illinois Press, 1986). A richly documented account of James Joyce's engagement with popular culture, written before Huyssen's work had made any impact.

Kershner, R. B., ed. *Joyce and Popular Culture* (Gainesville: University Press of Florida, 1996). A collection of essays on different aspects of popular culture, responding to the post-Huyssen debate.

Patterson, Anita. 'Jazz, Realism, and the Modernist Lyric: The Poetry of Langston Hughes', *Modern Language Quarterly*, 61 (2000): 651–82. Like Chinitz, examines Eliot's 'Shakespeherian rag'.

Strychacz, Thomas F. *Modernism, Mass Culture, and Professionalism* (Cambridge: Cambridge University Press, 1993). Examines Henry James, Theodore Dreiser, John Dos Passos, and Nathanael West and their uses of mass culture.

5

Modernity and the City

The modernity towards which modernist writers held such deeply ambivalent attitudes can be defined by reference to many social practices and historical processes, including technology, science, professional specialization, and the sceptical questioning of religious truths; the city, though, has long occupied a central place. The city is the location where the more visible signs of modernity were to be found in the highest concentration: for example, electric light, motorized transport, boulevards, telephone wires, and department stores. In many cases, particularly imperial capitals, it was where the visible signs of empire manifested themselves, in immigrant communities, in the diversity of accents and languages, and in imperial monuments. It was also the place where historical processes such as intellectual and professional specialization were likely to manifest themselves most tangibly, in, for example, specialized institutions of learning and the headquarters of professional bodies. That it was an informing presence in many of the key works of modernism, such as *Ulysses*, *The Waste Land*, and *Mrs Dalloway*, is not surprising, though the process of canon formation which leads to such statements should be borne in mind: the critics who shaped the modernist canon believed that the city was important as subject matter, and so they concentrated on texts that met their criteria; Virginia Woolf's admittance to the modernist canon after several decades of relative neglect was partly due to the respects in which her novels met this criterion.

As was noted in Part I, cultural critics have been trying to understand modernity since the 1820s. The city has been an important part of their inquiries. The work of the sociologist and philosopher Georg Simmel (1858–1918) anticipates the style of investigation that rose to prominence in the later twentieth century. His lecture 'Die Grossstadt und das Geistesleben' (1903, tr. as 'The Metropolis and Mental Life') asks how the external material and social environment shapes the internal psychology of individuals; in this, it anticipates by a few years the possibilities created by internal monologue in novels such as *Ulysses* and

Mrs Dalloway, and anticipates late twentieth-century literary-critical interest in subjectivity. Whereas nineteenth-century British sociologists had operated within a positivist framework, gathering factual data about such things as the incomes and housing of the urban poor, Simmel aimed to reach generalizations by separating the *form* of social interactions from their content. Society was not a reality that existed external to the individual; rather, it existed through 'forms of sociation' which individuals internalized.[1]

Although it anticipates recent work, some aspects of 'The Metropolis and Mental Life' are distinctly late nineteenth-century. Though he refers to the 'unconscious', Simmel's psychology is pre-Freudian; the idea of conscious intellect as a shield protecting the organism from stimuli is one he shares with Henri Bergson and other late nineteenth-century psychologists. Simmel also universalizes 'metropolitan man', without investigating distinctions of class or gender, or of zones within the city such as the inner city and the suburbs; there is no suggestion that the stimuli of metropolitan life might differ according to such variables. Similarly, he universalises 'the metropolis', without differentiating between different types of city. What is true of Dublin is not true of London. 'In the Heart of the Hibernian Metropolis', the first of the headlines in the 'Aeolus' episode of *Ulysses* is ironic, as in 1904 Dublin was the mother-city of a country that was not an independent state (*Ulysses*, p.112).

Simmel's lecture has been enormously suggestive to literary critics, but it offers no more than suggestions: literary readers must develop it in their own directions, treating it sceptically and imaginatively, and recognizing that sociology has no monopoly on truth. The simplest approach is to compare the portrait of 'metropolitan man' in the lecture to characters both male and female in early twentieth-century literature. How do Simmel's insights help us to understand those characters? What insights do particular novelists bring that are not apparent in Simmel's lecture? The problem with such an approach is that it tends to treat the text as a transparent medium. A more literary approach would have to ask how far modernist techniques, such as internal monologue in its various forms, enable modernist writers to create those insights. One might also ask how far the characteristics of Simmel's 'metropolitan man' are characteristics of modernist authors, or, leaving the author in the background, of modernist texts. Can the evolution of modernism's distinctive forms be understood as a result of the same pressures that shape metropolitan man?

Extract from Georg Simmel, 'The Metropolis and Mental Life' (1903), *The Sociology of Georg Simmel*, tr. and ed. Kurt H. Wolff (1950; New York: Free Press of Glencoe, 1964), pp.409–17.

The deepest problems of modern life derive from the claim of the individual to preserve the autonomy and individuality of his existence in the face of overwhelming social forces, of historical heritage, of external culture, and of the technique of life. The fight with nature which primitive man has to wage for his *bodily* existence attains in this modern form its latest transformation. The eighteenth century called upon man to free himself of all the historical bonds in the state and in religion, in morals and in economics. Man's nature, originally good and common to all, should develop unhampered. In addition to more liberty, the nineteenth century demanded the functional specialization of man and his work; this specialization makes one individual incomparable to another, and each of them indispensable to the highest possible extent. However, this specialization makes each man the more directly dependent upon the supplementary activities of all others. Nietzsche sees the full development of the individual conditioned by the most ruthless struggle of individuals; socialism believes in the suppression of all competition for the same reason. Be that as it may, in all these positions the same basic motive is at work: the person resists to being leveled down and worn out by a social-technological mechanism. An inquiry into the inner meaning of specifically modern life and its products, into the soul of the cultural body, so to speak, must seek to solve the equation which structures like the metropolis set up between the individual and the super-individual contents of life. Such an inquiry must answer the question of how the personality accommodates itself in the adjustments to external forces. This will be my task today.

The psychological basis of the metropolitan type of individuality consists in the *intensification of nervous stimulation* which results from the swift and uninterrupted change of outer and inner stimuli. Man is a differentiating creature. His mind is stimulated by the difference between a momentary impression and the one which preceded it. Lasting impressions, impressions which differ only slightly from one another, impressions which take a regular and habitual course and show regular and habitual contrasts – all these use up, so to speak, less consciousness than does the rapid crowding of changing images, the sharp discontinuity in the grasp of a single glance, and the unexpectedness of onrushing impressions. These are the psychological conditions which the metropolis creates. With each crossing of the street, with the tempo and multiplicity of economic, occupational and social life, the city sets up a deep contrast with small town and rural life with reference to the sensory foundations of psychic life. The metropolis exacts from man as a discriminating creature a different amount of consciousness than does rural life. Here the rhythm of life and sensory mental imagery flows more slowly, more habitually, and more evenly. Precisely in this connection the sophisticated character of metropolitan psychic life becomes understandable – as over against small town life which rests more upon deeply felt and emotional relationships. These latter are rooted in the more unconscious layers of the psyche and grow most readily in the steady rhythm of uninterrupted habituations. The intellect, however, has its locus in the transparent, conscious, higher layers of the psyche; it is the most adaptable of our inner forces. In order to accommodate to change and to the contrast of phenomena, the intellect does not require any shocks and inner upheavals; it is only through such upheavals that the more conservative mind could accommodate to the metropolitan rhythm of events. Thus the metropolitan type of man – which, of course, exists in a thousand individual variants – develops an organ protecting him against the threatening currents and discrepancies of his external environment which would uproot him. He reacts with his head instead of his heart. In this an increased awareness assumes the psychic prerogative. Metropolitan life, thus, underlies a heightened awareness and a predominance of intelligence in metropolitan man. The reaction to metropolitan phenomena is shifted to that organ which is least sensitive and quite remote from the depth of the personality. Intellectuality is thus seen to preserve subjective life against the overwhelming power of metropolitan life, and intellectuality branches out in many directions and is integrated with numerous discrete phenomena.

The metropolis has always been the seat of the money economy. Here the multiplicity and concentration of economic exchange gives an importance to the means of exchange which the scantiness of rural commerce would not have allowed. Money economy and the dominance of the intellect are intrinsically connected. They share a matter-of-fact attitude in dealing with men and with things; and, in this attitude, a formal justice is often coupled with an inconsiderate hardness. The intellectually sophisticated person is indifferent to all genuine individuality, because relationships and reactions result from it which cannot be exhausted with logical operations. In the same manner, the individuality of phenomena is not commensurate with the pecuniary principle. Money is concerned only with what is common to all: it asks for the exchange value, it reduces all quality and individuality to the question: How much? All intimate emotional relations between persons are founded in their individuality, whereas in rational relations man is reckoned with like a number, like an element which is in itself indifferent. Only the objective measurable achievement is of interest. Thus metropolitan man reckons with his merchants and customers, his domestic servants and often even with persons with whom he is obliged to have social intercourse. These features of intellectuality contrast with the nature of the small circle in which the inevitable knowledge of individuality as inevitably produces a warmer tone of behavior, a behavior which is beyond a mere objective balancing of service and return. In the sphere of the economic psychology of the small group it is of importance that under primitive conditions production serves the customer who orders the good, so that the producer and the consumer are acquainted. The modern metropolis, however, is supplied almost entirely by production for the market, that is, for entirely unknown purchasers who never personally enter the producer's actual field of vision. Through this anonymity the interests of each party acquire an unmerciful matter-of-factness; and the intellectually calculating economic ego-isms of both parties need not fear any deflection because of the imponderables of personal relationships. The money economy dominates the metropolis; it has displaced the last survivals of domestic production and the direct barter of goods; it minimizes, from day to day, the amount of work ordered by cus-tomers. The matter-of-fact attitude is obviously so intimately interrelated with the money economy, which is dominant in the metropolis, that nobody can say whether the intellectualistic mentality first promoted the money economy or whether the latter determined the former. The metropolitan way of life is certainly the most fertile soil for this reciprocity, a point which I shall docu-ment merely by citing the dictum of the most eminent English constitutional historian: throughout the whole course of English history, London has never acted as England's heart but often as England's intellect and always as her moneybag!

In certain seemingly insignificant traits, which lie upon the surface of life, the same psychic currents characteristically unite. Modern mind has become more and more calculating. The calculative exactness of practical life which the money economy has brought about corresponds to the ideal of natural science: to transform the world into an arithmetic problem, to fix every part of the world by mathematical formulas. Only money economy has filled the days of so many people with weighing, calculating, with numerical determinations, with a reduction of qualitative values to quantitative ones. Through the calculative nature of money a new precision, a certainty in the definition of identities and differences, an unambiguousness in agreements and arrangements has been brought about in the relations of life-elements – just as externally this precision has been effected by the universal diffusion of pocket watches. However, the conditions of metropolitan life are at once cause and effect of this trait. The relationships and affairs of the typical metropolitan usually are so varied and complex that without the strictest punctuality in promises and services the whole structure would break down into an inextricable chaos. Above all, this necessity is brought about by the aggregation of so many people with such differentiated interests, who must integrate their relations and activities into a highly complex organism. If all clocks and watches in Berlin would suddenly go wrong in different ways, even if only by one hour, all economic life and communication of the city would be disrupted for a long time. In addition an apparently mere external factor: long distances, would make all waiting and broken appointments result in an ill-afforded waste of time. Thus, the technique of metropolitan life is unimaginable without the most punctual integration of all activities and mutual relations into a stable and impersonal time schedule. Here again the general conclusions of this entire task of reflection become obvious, namely, that from each point on the surface of existence – however closely attached to the surface alone – one may drop a sounding into the depth of the psyche so that all the most banal externalities of life finally are connected with the ultimate decisions concerning the meaning and style of life. Punctuality, calculability, exactness are forced upon life by the complexity and extension of metropolitan existence and are not only most intimately connected with its money economy and intellectualistic character. These traits must also color the contents of life and favor the exclusion of those irrational, instinctive, sovereign traits and impulses which aim at determining the mode of life from within, instead of receiving the general and precisely schematized form of life from without. Even though sovereign types of personality, characterized by irrational impulses, are by no means impossible in the city, they are, nevertheless, opposed to typical city life. The passionate hatred of men like Ruskin and Nietzsche for the metropolis is understandable in these terms. Their natures discovered the value of life alone in the unschematized existence which cannot be defined with precision for all alike. From the same source of this hatred of the metropolis surged their hatred of money economy and of the intellectualism of modern existence.

The same factors which have thus coalesced into the exactness and minute precision of the form of life have coalesced into a structure of the highest impersonality; on the other hand, they have promoted a highly personal subjectivity. There is perhaps no psychic phenomenon which has been so unconditionally reserved to the metropolis as has the blasé attitude. The blasé attitude results first from the rapidly changing and closely compressed contrasting stimulations of the nerves. From this, the enhancement of metropolitan intellectuality, also, seems originally to stem. Therefore, stupid people who are not intellectually alive in the first place usually are not exactly blasé. A life in boundless pursuit of pleasure makes one blasé because it agitates the nerves to their strongest reactivity for such a long time that they finally cease to react at all. In the same way, through the rapidity and contradictoriness of their changes, more harmless impressions force such violent responses, tearing the nerves so brutally hither and thither that their last reserves of strength are spent; and if one remains in the same milieu they have no time to gather new strength. An incapacity thus emerges to react to new sensations with the appropriate energy. This constitutes that blasé attitude which, in fact, every metropolitan child shows when compared with children of quieter and less changeable milieus.

This physiological source of the metropolitan blasé attitude is joined by another source which flows from the money economy. The essence of the blasé attitude consists in the blunting of discrimination. This does not mean that the objects are not perceived, as is the case with the half-wit, but rather that the meaning and differing values of things, and thereby the things themselves, are experienced as insubstantial. They appear to the blasé person in an evenly flat and gray tone; no one object deserves preference over any other. This mood is the faithful subjective reflection of the completely internalized money economy. By being the equivalent to all the manifold things in one and the same way, money becomes the most frightful leveler. For money expresses all qualitative differences of things in terms of "how much?" Money, with all its colorlessness and indifference, becomes the common denominator of all values; irreparably it hollows out the core of things, their individuality, their specific value, and their incomparability. All things float with equal specific gravity in the constantly moving stream of money. All things lie on the same level and differ from one another only in the size of the area which they cover. In the individual case this coloration, or rather discoloration, of things through their money equivalence may be unnoticeably minute. However, through the relations of the rich to the objects to be had for money, perhaps even through the total character which the mentality of the contemporary public everywhere imparts to these objects, the exclusively pecuniary evaluation of objects has become quite considerable. The large cities, the main seats of the money exchange, bring the purchasability of things to the fore much more impressively than do smaller localities. That is why cities are also the genuine locale of the blasé attitude. In the blasé attitude the concentration of men and things stimulate the nervous system of the individual to its highest achievement so that it attains its peak. Through the mere quantitative intensification of the same conditioning factors this achievement is transformed into its opposite and appears in the peculiar adjustment of the blasé attitude. In this phenomenon the nerves find in the refusal to react to their stimulation the last possibility of accommodating to the contents and forms of metropolitan life. The self-preservation of certain personalities is brought at the price of devaluating the whole objective world, a devaluation which in the end unavoidably drags one's own personality down into a feeling of the same worthlessness.

Whereas the subject of this form of existence has to come to terms with it entirely for himself, his self-preservation in the face of the large city demands from him a no less negative behavior of a social nature. This mental attitude of metropolitans toward one another we may designate, from a formal point of view, as reserve. If so many inner reactions were responses to the continuous external contacts with innumerable people as are those in the small town, where one knows almost everybody one meets and where one has a positive relation to almost everyone, one would be completely atomized internally and come to an unimaginable psychic state. Partly this psychological fact, partly the right to distrust which men have in the face of the touch-and-go elements of metropolitan life, necessitates our reserve. As a result of this reserve we frequently do not even know by sight those who have been our neighbors for years. And it is this reserve which in the eyes of the small-town people makes us appear to be cold and heartless. Indeed, if I do not deceive myself, the inner aspect of this outer reserve is not only indifference but, more often than we are aware, it is a slight aversion, a mutual strangeness and repulsion, which will break into hatred and fight at the moment of a closer contact, however caused. The whole inner organization of such an extensive communicative life rests upon an extremely varied hierarchy of sympathies, indifferences, and aversions of the briefest as well as of the most permanent nature. The sphere of indifference in this hierarchy is not as large as might appear on the surface. Our psychic activity still responds to almost every impression of somebody else with a somewhat distinct feeling. The unconscious, fluid and changing character of this impression seems to result in a state of indifference. Actually this indifference would be just as unnatural as the diffusion of indiscriminate mutual suggestion would be unbearable. From both these typical dangers of the metropolis, indifference and indiscriminate suggestibility, antipathy protects us. A latent antipathy and the preparatory stage of practical antagonism effect the distances and aversions without which this mode of life could not at all be led. The extent and the mixture of this style of life, the rhythm of its emergence and disappearance, the forms in which it is satisfied – all these, with the unifying motives in the narrower sense, form the inseparable whole of the metropolitan style of life. What appears in the metropolitan style of life directly as dissociation is in reality only one of its elemental forms of socialization.

This reserve with its overtone of hidden aversion appears in turn as the form or the cloak of a more general mental phenomenon of the metropolis: it grants to the individual a kind and an amount of personal freedom which has no analogy whatsoever under other conditions. The metropolis goes back to one of the large developmental tendencies of social life as such, to one of the few tendencies for which an approximately universal formula can be discovered. The earliest phase of social formations found in historical as well as in contemporary social structures is this: a relatively small circle firmly closed against neighboring, strange, or in some way antagonistic circles. However, this circle is closely coherent and allows its individual members only a narrow field for the development of unique qualities and free, self-responsible movements. Political and kinship groups, parties and religious associations begin in this way. The self-preservation of very young associations requires the establishment of strict boundaries and a centripetal unity. Therefore they cannot allow the individual freedom and unique inner and outer development. From this stage social development proceeds at once in two different, yet corresponding, directions. To the extent to which the group grows – numerically, spatially, in significance and in content of life – to the same degree the group's direct, inner unity loosens, and the rigidity of the original demarcation against others is softened through mutual relations and connections. At the same time, the individual gains freedom of movement, far beyond the first jealous delimitation. The individual also gains a specific individuality to which the division of labor in the enlarged group gives both occasion and necessity. The state and Christianity, guilds and political parties, and innumerable other groups have developed according to this formula, however much, of course, the special conditions and forces of the respective groups have modified the general scheme. This scheme seems to me distinctly recognizable also in the evolution of individuality within urban life.

* * *

The discourse of sociology is not the only means of reaching an understanding of the city. Literature too is a form of knowledge. The poetry and prose of Charles Baudelaire (1821–67) have been central to the understanding of modernism for many decades. In the English-speaking world, his centrality owed a great deal initially to the importance which T. S. Eliot had granted him, but it has been consolidated by the essays of Walter Benjamin (1892–1940). In the late 1920s and the 1930s, Benjamin was working on a vast cultural study of Paris, the *Passagenarbeit* or *Arcades Project*. Only the essay 'Some Motifs in Baudelaire' appeared in his lifetime; other parts appeared posthumously in German 1955 onwards and later in English; an English edition of the *Arcades Project* itself appeared only in 1999. Although Benjamin was a near-contemporary of modernist writers, his influence on the idea of modernism in the English-speaking world was delayed by several decades. Benjamin approaches Baudelaire's poems with a view to uncovering their hidden relations to the social environment of nineteenth-century Paris. Thus 'A une passante' ('To a passer-by') is, on reflection, a poem whose 'structure of experience' is enabled by the relation of the *flâneur* to the crowd. Benjamin's recovery of the unconscious of a poem anticipates later cultural-materialist practices: 'The masses had become so much a part of Baudelaire that it is rare to find a description of them in his works. His most important subjects are hardly ever encountered in descriptive form'.[2]

Marshall Berman's *All that is Solid Melts into Air* (1982) is an analysis of the experience of modernity which explicitly acknowledges Benjamin's influence.[3] It includes literary criticism, but Berman frames that criticism with an analysis of the key terms of 'modernization' and 'modernism', and reads texts in ways which allow them to open out onto unexpected social contexts. Berman takes two of Baudelaire's late prose poems 'The Eyes of the Poor' and 'Loss of a Halo' to embody 'primal modern scenes'. The phrase 'primal scene' indicates the underlying Freudian influence on both Benjamin and Berman, but, importantly, neither investigates the personal unconscious of the author, but the cultural unconscious of the text. For Berman, the scenes are 'experiences that rise from the concrete everyday life of Bonaparte's and Haussmann's Paris but carry a mythic resonance and depth that propel them beyond their place and time and transform them into archetypes of modern life'.[4] The prose poems show 'how the modernization of the city at once inspires and enforces the modernization of its citizens' souls'.[5] Implicit in Berman's consideration of the desanctification of modern art is 'The Work of Art in the Age of Mechanical Reproduction', in which Benjamin considers the loss of 'aura'.[6]

Extract from Marshall Berman, 'The Mire of the Macadam', *All that is Solid Melts into Air* (1982; London: Verso, 1983), pp.155–64.

Our next archetypal modern scene is found in the prose poem 'Loss of a Halo' (*Paris Spleen* #46), written in 1865 but rejected by the press and not published until after Baudelaire's death. Like 'The Eyes of the Poor', this poem is set on the boulevard; it presents a confrontation that the setting forces on the subject; and it ends (as its title suggests) in a loss of innocence. Here, however, the encounter is not between one person and another, or between people of different social classes, but rather between an isolated individual and social forces that are abstract yet concretely dangerous. Here, the ambience, imagery and emotional tone are puzzling and elusive; the poet seems intent on keeping his readers off balance, and he may be off balance himself.

'Loss of a Halo' develops as a dialogue between a poet and an 'ordinary man' who bump into each other in *un mauvais lieu*, a disreputable or sinister place, probably a brothel, to the embarrassment of both. The ordinary man, who has always cherished an exalted idea of the artist, is aghast to find one here:

> 'What! you here, my friend? you in a place like this? you, the eater of ambrosia, the drinker of quintessences! I'm amazed!'

The poet then proceeds to explain himself:

> 'My friend, you know how terrified I am of horses and vehicles? Well, just now as I was crossing the boulevard in a great hurry, splashing through the mud, in the midst of a moving chaos, with death galloping at me from every side, I made a sudden move [*un mouvement brusque*], and my halo slipped off my head and fell into the mire of the macadam. I was much too scared to pick it up. I thought it was less unpleasant to lose my insignia than to get my bones broken. Besides, I said to myself, every cloud has a silver lining. Now I can walk around incognito, do low things, throw myself into every kind of filth [*me livrer à la crapule*], just like ordinary mortals [*simples mortels*]. So here I am, just as you see me, just like yourself!'

The straight man plays along, a little uneasily:

'But aren't you going to advertise for your halo? or notify the police?'

No: the poet is triumphant in what we recognize as a new self-definition:

'God forbid! I like it here. You're the only one who's recognized me. Besides, dignity bores me. What's more, it's fun to think of some bad poet picking it up and brazenly putting it on. What a pleasure to make somebody happy! especially somebody you can laugh at. Think of X! Think of Z! Don't you see how funny it will be?'

It is a strange poem, and we are apt to feel like the straight man, knowing something's happening here but not knowing what it is.

One of the first mysteries here is that halo itself. What's it doing on a modern poet's head in the first place? It is there to satirize and to criticize one of Baudelaire's own most fervent beliefs: belief in the holiness of art. We can find a quasi-religious devotion to art throughout his poetry and prose. Thus, in 1855: 'The artist stems only from himself. ...He stands security only for himself. ...He dies childless. He has been his own king, his own priest, his own God'.[1] 'Loss of a Halo' is about how Baudelaire's own God fails. But we must understand that this God is worshipped not only by artists but equally by many 'ordinary people' who believe that art and artists exist on a plane far above them. 'Loss of a Halo' takes place at the point at which the world of art and the ordinary world converge. This is not only a spiritual point but a physical one, a point in the landscape of the modern city. It is the point where the history of modernization and the history of modernism fuse into one.

Walter Benjamin seems to have been the first to suggest the deep affinities between Baudelaire and Marx. Although Benjamin does not make this particular connection, readers familiar with Marx will notice the striking similarity of Baudelaire's central image here to one of the primary images of the *Communist Manifesto:* 'The bourgeoisie has stripped of its halo every activity hitherto honored and looked up to with reverent awe. It has transformed the doctor, the lawyer, the priest, the poet, the man of science, into its paid wage-laborers'.[2] For both men, one of the crucial experiences endemic to modern life, and one of the central themes for modern art and thought, is *desanctification.* Marx's theory locates this experience in a world-historical context; Baudelaire's poetry shows how it feels from inside. But the two men respond to this experience with rather different emotions. In the *Manifesto,* the drama of desanctification is terrible and tragic: Marx looks back to, and his vision embraces, heroic figures like Oedipus at Colonnus, Lear on the heath, contending against the elements, stripped and scorned but not subdued, creating a new dignity out of desolation. 'Eyes of the Poor' contains its own drama of desanctification, but there the scale is intimate rather than monumental, the emotions are melancholy and romantic rather than tragic and heroic. Still, 'Eyes of the Poor' and the *Manifesto* belong to the same spiritual world. 'Loss of a Halo' confronts us with a very different spirit: here the drama is essentially comic, the mode of expression is ironic, and the comic irony is so successful that it masks the seriousness of the unmasking that is going on. Baudelaire's denouement, in which the hero's halo slips off his head and rolls through the mud – rather than being torn off with a violent *grand geste*, as it was for Marx (and Burke and Blake and Shakespeare) – evokes vaudeville, slapstick, the metaphysical pratfalls of Chaplin and Keaton. It points forward to a century whose heroes will come dressed as anti-heroes, and whose most solemn moments of truth will be not only described but actually experienced as clown shows, music-hall or nightclub routines – shticks. The setting plays the same sort of decisive role in Baudelaire's black comedy that it will play in Chaplin's and Keaton's later on.

'Loss of a Halo' is set on the same new boulevard as 'Eyes of the Poor'. But although the two poems are separated physically by only a few feet, spiritually they spring from different worlds. The gulf that separates them is the step from the sidewalk into the gutter. On the sidewalk, people of all kinds and all classes know themselves by comparing themselves to each other as they sit or walk. In the gutter, people are forced to forget what they are as they run for their lives. The new force that the boulevards have brought into being, the force that sweeps the hero's halo away and drives him into a new state of mind, is modern *traffic*.

When Haussmann's work on the boulevards began, no one understood why he wanted them so wide: from a hundred feet to a hundred yards across. It was only when the job was done that people began to see that these roads, immensely wide, straight as arrows, running on for miles, would be ideal speedways for heavy traffic. Macadam, the surface with which the boulevards were paved, was remarkably smooth, and provided perfect traction for horses' hooves. For the first time, riders and drivers in the heart of the city could whip their horses up to full speed. Improved road conditions not only speeded up previously existing traffic but – as twentieth-century highways would do on a larger scale – helped to generate a volume of new traffic far greater than anyone, apart from Haussmann and his engineers, had anticipated. Between 1850 and 1870, while the central city population (excluding newly incorporated suburbs) grew by about 25 percent, from about 1.3 million to 1.65 million, inner-city traffic seems to have tripled or quadrupled. This growth exposed a contradiction at the heart of Napoleon's and Haussmann's urbanism. As David Pinkney says in his authoritative study, *Napoleon III and the Rebuilding of Paris*, the arterial boulevards 'were from the start burdened with a dual function: to carry the main streams of traffic across the city and to serve as major shopping and business streets; and as the volume of traffic increased, the two proved to be ill-compatible'. The situation was especially trying and terrifying to the vast majority of Parisians who walked. The macadam pavements, a source of special pride to the Emperor – who never walked – were dusty in the dry months of summer, and muddy in the rain and snow. Haussmann, who clashed with Napoleon over macadam (one of the few things they ever fought about), and who administratively sabotaged imperial plans to cover the whole city with it, said that this surface required Parisians 'either to keep a carriage or to walk on stilts'.[3] Thus the life of the boulevards, more radiant and exciting than urban life had ever been, was also more risky and frightening for the multitudes of men and women who moved on foot.

This, then, is the setting for Baudelaire's primal modern scene: 'I was crossing the boulevard, in a great hurry, in the midst of a moving chaos, with death galloping at me from every side'. The archetypal modern man, as we see him here, is a pedestrian thrown into the maelstrom of modern city traffic, a man alone contending against an agglomeration of mass and energy that is heavy, fast and lethal. The burgeoning street and boulevard traffic knows no spatial or temporal bounds, spills over into every urban space, imposes its tempo on everybody's time, transforms the whole modern environment into a 'moving chaos'. The chaos here lies not in the movers themselves – the individual walkers or drivers, each of whom may be pursuing the most efficient route for himself – but in their interaction, in the totality of their movements in a common space. This makes the boulevard a perfect symbol of capitalism's inner contradictions: rationality in each individual capitalist unit, leading to anarchic irrationality in the social system that brings all these units together.[4]

The man in the modern street, thrown into this maelstrom, is driven back on his own resources – often on resources he never knew he had – and forced to stretch them desperately in order to survive. In order to cross the moving chaos, he must attune and adapt himself to its moves, must learn to not merely keep up with it but to stay at least a step ahead. He must become adept at *soubresauts* and *mouvements brusques*, at sudden, abrupt, jagged twists and shifts – and not only with his legs and his body, but with his mind and his sensibility as well.

Baudelaire shows how modern city life forces these new moves on everyone; but he shows, too, how in doing this it also paradoxically enforces new modes of freedom. A man who knows how to move in and around and through the traffic can go anywhere, down any of the endless urban corridors where traffic itself is free to go. This mobility opens up a great wealth of new experiences and activities for the urban masses.

Moralists and people of culture will condemn these popular urban pursuits as low, vulgar, sordid, empty of social or spiritual value. But when Baudelaire's poet lets his halo go and keeps moving, he makes a great discovery. He finds to his amazement that the aura of artistic purity and sanctity is only incidental, not essential, to art, and that poetry can thrive just as well, and maybe even better, on the other side of the boulevard, in those low, 'unpoetic' places like *un mauvais lieu* where this poem itself is born. One of the paradoxes of modernity, as Baudelaire sees it here, is that its poets will become more deeply and authentically poetic by becoming more like ordinary men. If he throws himself into the moving chaos of everyday life in the modern world – a life of which the new traffic is a primary symbol – he can appropriate this life for art. The 'bad poet' in this world is the poet who hopes to keep his purity intact by keeping off the streets, free from the risks of traffic. Baudelaire wants works of art that will be born in the midst of the traffic, that will spring from its anarchic energy, from the incessant danger and terror of being there, from the precarious pride and exhilaration of the man who has survived so far. Thus 'Loss of a Halo' turns out to be a declaration of something gained, a rededication of the poet's powers to a new kind of art. His *mouvements brusques*, those sudden leaps and swerves so crucial for everyday survival in the city streets, turn out to be sources of creative power as well. In the century to come, these moves will become paradigmatic gestures of modernist art and thought.[5]

Ironies proliferate from this primal modern scene. They unfold in Baudelaire's nuances of language. Consider a phrase like *la fange du macadam*, 'the mire of the macadam'. *La fange* in French is not only a literal word for mud; it is also a figurative word for mire, filth, vileness, corruption, degradation, all that is foul and loathsome. In classical oratorical and poetic diction, it is a 'high' way of describing something 'low'. As such, it entails a whole cosmic hierarchy, a structure of norms and values not only aesthetic but metaphysical, ethical, political. *La fange* might be the nadir of the moral universe whose summit is signified by *l'auréole*. The irony here is that, so long as the poet's halo falls into '*la fange*', it can never be wholly lost, because, so long as such an image still has meaning and power – as it clearly has for Baudelaire – the old hierarchical cosmos is still present on some plane of the modern world. But it is present precariously. The meaning of macadam is as radically destructive to *la fange* as to *l'auréole:* it paves over high and low alike.

We can go deeper into the macadam: we will notice that the word isn't French. In fact, the word is derived from John McAdam of Glasgow, the eighteenth-century inventor of modern paving surface. It may be the first word in that language that twentieth-century Frenchmen have satirically named *Franglais:* it paves the way for *le parking, le shopping, le weekend, le drugstore, le mobile-home,* and far more. This language is so vital and compelling because it is the international language of modernization. Its new words are powerful vehicles of new modes of life and motion. The words may sound dissonant and jarring, but it is as futile to resist them as to resist the momentum of modernization itself. It is true that many nations and ruling classes feel – and have reason to feel – threatened by the flow of new words and things from other shores.[6] There is a wonderful paranoid Soviet word that expresses this fear: *infiltrazya*. We should notice, however, that what nations have normally done, from Baudelaire's time to our own, is, after a wave (or at least a show) of resistance, not only to accept the new thing but to create their own word for it, in the hope of blotting out embarrassing memories of underdevelopment. (Thus the Académie Française, after refusing all through the 1960s to admit *le parking meter* to the French language, coined and quickly canonized *le parcmetre* in the 1970s.)

Baudelaire knew how to write in the purest and most elegant classical French. Here, however, with the 'Loss of a Halo', he projects himself into the new, emerging language, to make art out of the dissonances and incongruities that pervade – and, paradoxically, unite – the whole modern world. 'In place of the old national seclusion and self-sufficiency,' the *Manifesto* says, modern bourgeois society brings us 'intercourse in every direction, universal interdependence of nations. And, as in material, so in intellectual production. The spiritual creations of nations become' – note this image, paradoxical in a bourgeois world – 'common property'. Marx goes on: 'National one-sidedness and narrow-mindedness become more and more impossible, and from the numerous local and national literatures, there arises a world literature'. The mire of the macadam will turn out to be one of the foundations from which this new world literature of the twentieth century will arise.[7]

There are further ironies that arise from this primal scene. The halo that falls into the mire of the macadam is endangered but not destroyed; instead, it is carried along and incorporated into the general flow of traffic. One salient feature of the commodity economy, as Marx explains, is the endless metamorphosis of its market values. In this economy, anything goes if it pays, and no human possibility is ever wiped off the books; culture becomes an enormous warehouse in which everything is kept in stock on the chance that someday, somewhere, it might sell. Thus the halo that the modern poet lets go (or throws off) as obsolete may, by virtue of its very obsolescence, metamorphose into an icon, an object of nostalgic veneration for those who, like the 'bad poets' X and Z, are trying to escape from modernity. But alas, the anti-modern artist – or thinker or politician – finds himself on the same streets, in the same mire, as the modernist one. This modern environment serves as both a physical and a spiritual lifeline – a primary source of material and energy – for both.

The difference between the modernist and the anti-modernist, so far as they are concerned, is that the modernist makes himself at home here, while the anti-modern searches the streets for a way out. So far as the traffic is concerned, however, there is no difference between them at all: both alike are hindrances and hazards to the horses and vehicles whose paths they cross, whose free movement they impede. Then, too, no matter how closely the anti-modernist may cling to his aura of spiritual purity, he is bound to lose it, more likely sooner than later, for the same reason that the modernist lost it: he will be forced to discard balance and measure and decorum and to learn the grace of brusque moves in order to survive. Once again, however opposed the modernist and the anti-modernist may think they are, in the mire of the macadam, from the viewpoint of the endlessly moving traffic, the two are one.

Ironies beget more ironies. Baudelaire's poet hurls himself into a confrontation with the 'moving chaos' of the traffic, and strives not only to survive but to assert his dignity in its midst. But his mode of action seems self-defeating, because it adds yet another unpredictable variable to an already unstable totality. The horses and their riders, the vehicles and their drivers, are trying at once to outpace each other and to avoid crashing into each other. If, in the midst of all this, they are also forced to dodge pedestrians who may at any instant dart out into the road, their movements will become even more uncertain, and hence more dangerous than ever. Thus, by contending against the moving chaos, the individual only aggravates the chaos.

But this very formulation suggests a way that might lead beyond Baudelaire's irony and out of the moving chaos itself. What if the multitudes of men and women who are terrorized by modern traffic could learn to confront it *together*? This will happen just six years after 'Loss of a Halo' (and three years after Baudelaire's death), in the days of the Commune in Paris in 1871, and again in Petersburg in 1905 and 1917, in Berlin in 1918, in Barcelona in 1936, in Budapest in 1956, in Paris again in 1968, and in dozens of cities all over the world, from Baudelaire's time to our own – the boulevard will be abruptly transformed into the stage for a new primal modern scene. This will not be the sort of scene that Napoleon or Haussmann would like to see, but nonetheless one that their mode of urbanism will have helped to make.

As we reread the old histories, memoirs and novels, or regard the old photos or newsreels, or stir our own fugitive memories of 1968, we will see whole classes and masses move into the street together. We will be able to discern two phases in their activity. At first the people stop and overturn the vehicles in their path, and set the horses free: here they are avenging themselves on the traffic by decomposing it into its inert original elements. Next they incorporate the wreckage they have created into their rising barricades: they are recombining the isolated, inanimate elements into vital new artistic and political forms. For one luminous moment, the multitude of solitudes that make up the modern city come together in a new kind of encounter, to make a *people*. 'The streets belong to the people': they seize control of the city's elemental matter and make it their own. For a little while the chaotic modernism of solitary brusque moves gives way to an ordered modernism of mass movement. The 'heroism of modern life' that Baudelaire longed to see will be born from his primal scene in the street. Baudelaire does not expect this (or any other) new life to last. But it will be born again and again out of the street's inner contradictions. It may burst into life at any moment, often when it is least expected. This possibility is a vital flash of hope in the mind of the man in the mire of the macadam, in the moving chaos, on the run.

Notes

1. Charles Baudelaire, *Art in Paris 1845–1862*, tr. Jonathan Mayne (Oxford: Phaidon, 1965), 127.
2. This connection is explicated, in very different terms from the ones here, by Irving Wohlfarth, '*Perte d'Auréole* and the Emergence of the Dandy,' *Modern Language Notes*, 85 (1970), 530–71.
3. David Pinkney, *Napoleon III* (1958; Princeton, 1972), on census figures, 151–4; on traffic counts and estimates, and conflict between Napoleon and Haussmann over macadam, 70–2; on dual function of boulevards, 214–15.
4. Street traffic was not, of course, the only mode of organized motion known to the nineteenth century. The railroad had been around on a large scale since the 1830s, and a vital presence in European literature since Dickens' *Dombey and Son* (1846–48). But the railroad ran on a fixed schedule along a prescribed route, and so, for all its demonic potentialities, became a nineteenth-century paradigm of order. We should note that Baudelaire's experience of 'moving chaos' antedates the traffic light, an innovation developed in America around 1905, and a wonderful symbol of early state attempts to regulate and rationalize the chaos of capitalism.
5. Forty years later, with the coming (or rather the naming) of the Brooklyn Dodgers, popular culture will produce its own ironic version of this modernist faith. The name expresses the way in which urban survival skills – specifically, skill at dodging traffic (they were at first called the *Trolley* Dodgers) – can transcend utility and take on new modes of meaning and value, in sport as in art. Baudelaire would have loved this symbolism, as many of his twentieth-century successors (e.e. cummings, Marianne Moore) did.
6. In the nineteenth century the main transmitter of modernization was England, in the twentieth century it has been the USA. Power maps have changed, but the primacy of the English language – the least pure, the most elastic and adaptable of modern languages – is greater than ever. It might well survive the decline of the American empire.
7. On the distinctively international quality of twentieth-century modernist language and literature, see Delmore Schwartz, 'T. S. Eliot as International Hero,' in Howe, *Literary Modernism*, 277–85. This is also one of Edmund Wilson's central themes in *Axel's Castle* and *To the Finland Station*.

* * *

Berman's book has established itself as a classic, but the fundamentals of his argument have not passed without criticism. One of the earliest criticisms, Perry Anderson's 'Modernity and Revolution', has itself become an influential account of modernism. Anderson criticises Berman's argument on four counts. First, his 'perennialism': his account of modernization assumes a process of continuous, smooth development, a 'homogeneous' form of time unlike Karl Marx's idea of 'a complex and *differential* temporality'. Marx's idea of time allows for distinct epochs, and for the possibility of revolutionary change. Secondly, and most pertinently to the passage above, Anderson notes that all the literary texts examined by Berman predate 'modernism' as it is normally understood. Moreover, he notes that modernism was not equally vigorous in all Western countries: we need an account of modernism that allows for a differential *space*. In relation to the passage above, we might ask how far Baudelaire's experience of the modernity of Paris was true for the English-language modernists of Dublin and London. Thirdly, Berman tends to homogenize modernism, giving no account of the sharply conflicting movements within it, such as expressionism, impressionism, and futurism. Finally, Berman apparently feels that there has been a cultural decline since modernism, yet such a narrative is incompatible with his account of modernization as a continuous process.[7]

Anderson set out his own account of modernism 'as a cultural field of force triangulated by three decisive coordinates'. The first was 'the codification of a highly formalized academicism in the visual and other arts, which itself was institutionalized within official regimes of states and society still massively pervaded, often dominated, by aristocratic or landowning classes'. The second coordinate stands in contrast to the first: it is the relative *novelty* of 'the key technologies or inventions of the second industrial revolution: telephone, radio, automobile, aircraft and so on. Mass consumption industries based on the new technologies had not yet been implanted anywhere in Europe, where clothing, food and furniture remained overwhelmingly the largest final-goods sectors in employment and turnover down to 1914'. Thirdly, the era of modernism was marked by the 'hope or apprehension' of social revolution.[8] Crucially, in Anderson's account, modernity is represented not by the city, but by two distinct coordinates, one an emergent sector of production and consumption, the other a widespread feeling about social revolution. Though the new technologies and inventions were more prominent in the cities than the provinces, Anderson's approach to modernity is fundamentally different from Berman's, and questions the centrality of the city to many account of modernism. Its great methodological attraction is that the space mapped by these 'coordinates' allows for internal differentiation: for different relations to the academicism of the old regime, for attraction and repulsion towards the new inventions, and for divergent attitudes to the possibility of revolution. It allows for a plurality of modernisms.

Considerations of the city and modernism have increasingly been framed by the idea that space does not have an independent existence, but is socially constructed. This is not simply a matter of the spaces constructed by architecture, but of the spaces constructed through communications technology, and the spaces constructed through social practices such as commuting, solitary walking, and communal marching. The city is a different place when a telephone call can cut through physical space, but it can also be transformed by less miraculous services such as messenger boys and underground railways. Importantly, because social practices affect social groups differentially, the space of the city will be experienced differently according to, for example, gender, class, age, sexuality, and race. Important influences on these developments include the work of the geographers Henri Lefebvre and Edward Soja, and particularly David Harvey's *The Condition of Postmodernity* (1989), a book which, belying its title, contains many important insights into modernity and modernism.

The new focus on the construction of space has tended to demote some aspects of the modern city that had traditionally been of critical interest – the city is less directly identified with the 'machine age', for example – and introduce new ones, such as department stores; but others, such as the *flâneur*, have survived. However, in what Andrew Thacker has called 'the great *flâneur* debate', critics have scrutinized the idea of the *flâneur* from the standpoint of gender, questioning the universality of this figure, and asking how the exclusion of women from city space in the nineteenth-century should cause us to revise our attitudes to it.[9] Such debates have also stimulated interest in literary representations by women of the city and of women's relation to urban space: Woolf's *Mrs Dalloway* and her essay 'Street Haunting' have been particularly fruitful.[10]

If any one essay was responsible for initiating the debate, it was Janet Wolff's 'The Invisible Flâneuse' (1985). Though Wolff has a background in sociology, and worked from 1973 to 1987 in the Department of Sociology at the University of Leeds, her research has primarily concerned the social context and history of the arts; she later formally moved disciplines, becoming Director of the Program in Cultural and Visual Studies at the University of Rochester, USA. The article first appeared in *Theory, Culture, and Society*, a journal focused on the interest in culture within the social sciences. For these reasons, like Berman's book, it is a work that engages with 'literature' in the broadest sense, but which does not follow the conventional processes of interpretative literary criticism; nevertheless, it has large implications for the study of modernist literature.

Extract from Janet Wolff, 'The Invisible Flâneuse: Women and the Literature of Modernity' (1985). Text taken from *The Problems of Modernity: Adorno and Benjamin*, ed. Andrew Benjamin (London 1988), pp.141–56.

The Experience of Modernity

The literature of modernity describes the experience of men. It is essentially a literature about transformations in the public world and in its associated consciousness. The actual date of the advent of 'the modern' varies in different accounts, and so do the characteristics of 'modernity' identified by different writers. But what nearly all the accounts have in common is their concern with the public world of work, politics and city life. And these are areas from which women were excluded, or in which they were practically invisible. For example, if the chief characteristic of modernity is the Weberian idea of increasing rationalization, then the major institutions affected by this process were the factory, the office, the government department. There have, of course, always been women working in factories; the growth of bureaucracies was also to some extent dependent on the development of a new female work force of clerks and secretaries. Nevertheless, it is appropriate to talk of this world as a 'male' world, for two reasons. First, the institutions were run by men, for men (owners, industrialists, managers, financiers), and they were dominated by men in their operation and hierarchical structure. Second, the development of the factory and, later, the bureaucracy coincides with that process, by now well documented, of the 'separation of spheres', and the increasing restriction of women to the 'private' sphere of the home and the suburb.[1] Although lower middle-class and working-class women continued to go out to work throughout the nineteenth century, the ideology of women's place in the domestic realm permeated the whole of society, at least in England, as evidenced by the working-class demand for a 'family wage' for men.[2] The public sphere, then, despite the presence of some women in certain contained areas of it, was a masculine domain. And in so far as the experience of 'the modern' occurred mainly in the public sphere, it was primarily men's experience.

In this essay, however, I shall not pursue the more orthodox sociological analyses of modernity, which discuss the phenomenon in terms of the rationalization process (or perhaps the 'civilizing process' – this, of course, places the event at a much earlier date). I want to consider the more impressionistic and essayistic contributions of those writers who locate the specially 'modern' in city life: in the fleeting, ephemeral, impersonal nature of encounters in the urban environment, and in the particular world-view which the city-dweller develops. This focus is not foreign to sociology; the essays of Georg Simmel immediately come to mind as studies in the social psychology of city life,[3] and the more recent sociology of Richard Sennett has revived interest in the diagnosis of the modern urban personality.[4] But a particular concern for the experience of modernity has also run through literary criticism; here its early prophet was Charles Baudelaire, the poet of mid-nineteenth-century Paris.[5] Walter Benjamin's essays on Baudelaire, written in the 1930s, provide a fascinating (though typically cryptic and fragmentary) series of reflections of Baudelaire's views on 'the modern'.[6] As a starting-point for the investigation of this particular literature of modernity, I take Baudelaire's statement, in the essay written in 1859–60, *The Painter of Modern Life*: 'By "modernity" I mean the ephemeral, the fugitive, the contingent, the half of art whose other half is the eternal and the immutable'.[7] This is echoed in Marshall Berman's recent book on the experience of modernity, which describes the 'paradoxical unity' of modernity:

> A unity of disunity: it pours us all into a maelstrom of perpetual disintegration and renewal, of struggle and contradiction, of ambiguity and anguish. To be modern is to be part of a universe in which, as Marx said, 'all that is solid melts into air'.[8]

It also recalls Simmel's account of the metropolitan personality: 'The psychological basis of the metropolitan type of individuality consists in the *intensification of nervous stimulation* which results from the swift and uninterrupted change of outer and inner stimuli,'[9] (italics in original).

For Simmel, this is closely related to the money economy, dominant by the late nineteenth century. It is worth stressing that, although cities were not new in the nineteenth century, the critics (and defenders) of modernity believed that urban existence took on an entirely different character around the middle of the nineteenth century. Though any such dating is, to some extent, arbitrary (and will vary, anyway, from Paris to London to Berlin),[10] I think it is useful to take this period of accelerated urbanization, coupled with the transformations in work, housing and social relations brought about by the rise of industrial capitalism, as the crucial years of the birth of 'modernity'. Berman gives modernity a prehistory, in those elements of the modern which began to appear in the period before the French Revolution and which found their expression in Goethe's *Faust*.[11] Bradbury and McFarlane, who focus on the later period of 1890 to 1930, credit Baudelaire as an 'initiator' of modernism.[12] But they are writing about the rather different phenomenon of modern*ism* in the arts; although 'modernism' and 'modernity' are often conflated, I do not think anyone has claimed that Baudelaire was a modernist poet, in the sense of revolutionizing poetic language and form.[13] There is no contradiction in locating the early experience of 'modernity' in the mid-nineteenth century, and its later expression in the arts at the end of the century.

The peculiar characteristics of modernity, then, consist in the transient and 'fugitive' nature of encounters and impressions made in the city. A sociology of modernity must, ultimately, be able to identify the origins of these new patterns of behaviour and experience, in the social and material aspects of the contemporary society. Simmel, as I have said, relates the metropolitan personality and what he calls the 'blasé attitude' to the money economy. Marshall Berman, beginning from Marx's account of the 'melting vision',[14] seems to take over at the same time Marx's analysis of the basis of this vision in the radical changes wrought in society by the bourgeoisie and the capitalist mode of production. Baudelaire, on the other hand, considers the phenomenon itself, and not its causes. It is not my task here to provide a sociology of modernity, and so I shall not assess competing accounts of the social or economic base of the modern experience, nor even examine very closely the adequacy of the conceptions of 'modernity' I discuss. What I do want to do is to take those accounts which do describe, more or less sociologically, the modern urban experience, and consider them from the point of view of gender divisions in nineteenth-century society. To that extent, it does not really matter whether a particular account is adequately grounded in a social-historical understanding of the period, or even whether an account is internally consistent. (As Berman shows, Baudelaire employs several different conceptions of 'modernity', as well as changing evaluations of the phenomenon.)[15]

Baudelaire's comments on modernity are most explicit in his writings on art criticism, though the same themes can be found in his poetry and in his prose poems. An early reference appears at the end of his review of *The Salon of 1845*, appended almost as an afterthought in the final paragraph. Here he commends contemporary painting, but laments its lack of interest in the present.

> No one is cocking his ear to tomorrow's wind; and yet the heroism of *modern life* surrounds and presses upon us. We are quite sufficiently choked by our true feelings for us to be able to recognize them. There is no lack of subjects, nor of colours, to make epics. The painter, the true painter for whom we are looking, will be he who can snatch its epic quality from the life of today and can make us see and understand, with brush or with pencil, how great and poetic we are in our cravats and our patent-leather boots. Next year let us hope that the true seekers may grant us the extraordinary delight of celebrating the advent of the *new*.[16]

But the following year was no better, and again Baudelaire bemoans the absence of any really contemporary art, concerned with modern themes and characters in the way that Balzac's novels are. This time he devotes several pages – the final section of the review of *The Salon of 1846* – to the theme of 'the heroism of modern life'. Modern life here begins to acquire some identifiable features: the uniform drabness of the colours of people's dress, the modern phenomenon of the 'dandy' who reacts against this, the 'private subjects' which Baudelaire extols as far more 'heroic' than the public and official subjects of painting:

> The pageant of fashionable life and the thousands of floating existences – criminals and kept women – which drift about in the underworld of a great city; the *Gazette des Tribunaux* and the *Moniteur* all prove to us that we have only to open our eyes to recognize our heroism. ...The life of our city is rich in poetic and marvellous subjects.[17]

These subjects are itemized in more detail in 'The Painter of Modern Life' of 1859–60. By this time, Baudelaire has found a painter he considers equal to the task of depicting the modern: Constantin Guys, the subject of the essay. Guys' watercolours and drawings are generally considered to be talented but superficial works, of little importance in the history of art – though judgments like these do, of course, beg all sorts of questions about critical assessment. Berman dismisses Guys's 'slick renderings of the 'beautiful people' and their world', and wonders that Baudelaire should think so highly of an art which 'resembles nothing so much as Bonwit's or Bloomingdale's ads'.[18] Nevertheless, the essay is interesting for its expansion of the notion of 'modernity'. Guys, the 'painter of modern life', goes out into the crowd and records the myriad impressions of day and night.

> He goes and watches the river of life flow past him in all its splendour and majesty. …He gazes upon the landscapes of the great city – landscapes of stone, caressed by the mist or buffeted by the sun. He delights in fine carriages and proud horses, the dazzling smartness of the grooms, the expertness of the footmen, the sinuous gait of the women, the beauty of the children. …If a fashion or the cut of a garment has been slightly modified, if bows and curls have been supplanted by cockades, if *bavolets* have been enlarged and *chignons* have dropped a fraction towards the nape of the neck, if waists have been raised and skirts have become fuller, be very sure that his eagle eye will already have spotted it from however great a distance.[19]

This is the passage Berman dismisses as 'advertising copy'. But if it is an inventory of the superficial and the merely fashionable, then that is the point – the modern consciousness consists in the parade of impressions, the particular beauty appropriate to the modern age. And, more importantly, it is in this essay that Baudelaire suggests the formal features of the modern mind, which grasps 'the ephemeral, the fugitive, the contingent'. The dandy appears again, to be compared and also contrasted with Guys, similar in their concern for appearance and for personal originality, divided by the blasé and insensitive attitude of the former which Guys (according to Baudelaire)[20] abhors. Guys is the *flâneur*, in his element in the crowd – at the centre of the world and at the same time hidden from the world.[21]

The *flâneur* – the stroller – is a central figure in Benjamin's essays on Baudelaire and nineteenth-century Paris. The streets and arcades of the city are the home of the *flâneur*, who, in Benjamin's phrase, 'goes botanizing on the asphalt'.[22] The anonymity of the crowd provides an asylum for the person on the margins of society; here Benjamin includes both Baudelaire himself as a *flâneur*, and the victims and murderers of Poe's detective stories (which Baudelaire translated into French).[23] For Benjamin, however, the city of the *flâneur* is historically more limited than for Baudelaire. Neither London nor Berlin offers precisely the conditions of involvement/non-involvement in which the Parisian *flâneur* flourishes; nor does the Paris of a slightly later period, when a 'network of controls' has made escape into anonymity impossible.[24] (Baudelaire, and Berman, on the contrary, argue that the Paris increasingly opened up by Haussmann's boulevards, which broke down the social and geographical divisions between the classes, is even more the site of the modern gaze, the ambit of the *flâneur*.)[25]

The *flâneur* is the modern hero; his experience, like that of Guys, is that of a freedom to move about in the city, observing and being observed, but never interacting with others. A related figure in the literature of modernity is the stranger. One of Baudelaire's prose poems is entitled *L'Étranger*.[26] It is a short dialogue, in which an 'enigmatic man' is asked what or whom he loves – his father, mother, sister, brother? his friends, his country, beauty, gold? To all of these he answers in the negative, affirming that he simply loves the passing clouds. For Simmel, the stranger is not a man without attachments and involvements, however. He is characterized by a particular kind of 'inorganic' membership of the group, not having been a member from its beginning, but having settled down in a new place. He is 'the person who comes today and stays tomorrow';[27] in this he differs from both the *flâneur* and Baudelaire's *étranger*, neither of whom will settle down or even make contact with those around him. But Simmel's stranger is always a 'potential wanderer': 'Although he has not moved on, he has not quite overcome the freedom of coming and going'.[28] These heroes of modernity thus share the possibility and the prospect of lone travel, of voluntary up-rooting, of anonymous arrival at a new place. They are, of course, all men.

Women and Public Life

It is no accident, and no fault of a careless patriarchal use of language, that Richard Sennett's book on modernity is called *The Fall of Public Man*. The 'public' person of the eighteenth century and earlier, whose demise is charted, and who passed the time in coffee-houses, paraded in the streets and at the theatre, and addressed strangers freely in public places, was clearly male. (Although Sennett says that it was quite proper to address strange women in the parks or the street, as long as men did not thereby assume that a reply meant they might call on the woman at home, there is no suggestion that *women* might address strangers.)[29] In the nineteenth-century city, no longer the arena of that public life, the *flâneur* makes his appearance – to be watched, but not addressed.[30] Men and women may have shared the privatization of personality, the careful anonymity and withdrawal in public life; but the line drawn increasingly sharply between the public and private was also one which confined women to the private, while men retained the freedom to move in the crowd or to frequent cafés and pubs. The men's clubs replaced the coffee-houses of earlier years.

None of the authors I have discussed is unaware of the different experience of women in the modern city. Sennett, for example, recognizes that the 'right to escape to public privacy was unequally enjoyed by the sexes', since even by the late nineteenth century women could not go alone to a café in Paris or a restaurant in London.[31] As he says, '"The lonely crowd" was a realm of privatized freedom, and the male, whether simply out of domination or greater need, was more likely to escape in it'. He notes, too, that in the earlier period of 'public life' women had to take a good deal more care about the 'signs' of their dress, which would be scrutinized for an indication of their social rank; in the nineteenth century, the scrutiny would be in order to differentiate 'respectable' from 'loose' women.[32] Simmel, whose essayistic sociology I have used very selectively, also paid much attention elsewhere to the condition of women. He wrote essays on the position of women, the psychology of women, female culture, and the women's movement and social democracy.[33] He was one of the first to permit women in his private seminars, long before they were admitted as full students at the University of Berlin.[34] Berman, too, considers women, acknowledging somewhat belatedly (on page 322 of his book) that they have a totally different experience of the city from that of men. He suggests that Jane Jacobs' *The Death and Life of Great American Cities* gives a 'fully articulated woman's view of the city'.[35] Published in 1961, Jacobs' book describes her own daily life in the city – a life of neighbours, shopkeepers, and young children, as well as work. The importance of the book, says Berman, is that it reveals that 'women had something to tell us about the city and the life we shared, and that we had impoverished our own lives as well as theirs by not listening to them till now'.[36]

The problem is, though, that it is also the literature of modernity which has been impoverished by ignoring the lives of women. The dandy, the *flâneur*, the hero, the stranger – all figures invoked to epitomize the experience of modern life – are invariably male figures. In 1831, when George Sand wanted to experience Paris life and to learn about the ideas and arts of her time, she dressed as a boy, to give herself the freedom she knew women could not share.

> So I had made for myself a *redingote-guérite* in heavy gray cloth, pants and vest to match. With a gray hat and large woollen cravat, I was a perfect first-year student. I can't express the pleasure my boots gave me: I would gladly have slept with them, as my brother did in his young age when he got his first pair. With those little iron-shod heels, I was solid on the pavement. I flew from one end of Paris to the other. It seemed to me that I could go round the world. And then, my clothes feared nothing. I ran out in every kind of weather, I came home at every sort of hour, I sat in the pit at the theatre. No one paid attention to me, and no one guessed at my disguise. ...No one knew me, no one looked at me, no one found fault with me; I was an atom lost in that immense crowd.[37]

The disguise made the life of the *flâneur* available to her; as she knew very well, she could not adopt the non-existent role of a *flâneuse*. Women could not stroll alone in the city.

In Baudelaire's essays and poems, women appear very often. Modernity breeds, or makes visible, a number of categories of female city-dwellers. Among those most prominent in these texts are: the prostitute, the widow, the old lady, the lesbian, the murder victim, and the passing unknown woman. Indeed, according to Benjamin, the lesbian was for Baudelaire the heroine of modernism; certainly it is known that he originally intended to give the title *Les Lesbiennes* to the poems which became *Les Fleurs du mal*.[38] (Yet, as Benjamin also points out, in the major poem about lesbians of the series, 'Delphine et Hippolyte', Baudelaire concludes by condemning the women as 'lamentable victims', bound for hell.)[39] The prostitute, the subject of the poem 'Crépuscule du soir' and also discussed in a section of 'The Painter of Modern Life'[40] elicits a similarly ambivalent attitude of admiration and disgust (the poem comparing prostitution to an anthill, and to a worm stealing a man's food). More unequivocal is Baudelaire's sympathy for those other marginal women, the old woman and the widow; the former he 'watches tenderly from afar' like a father, the latter he observes with a sensitivity to her pride, pain and poverty.[41] But none of these women meet the poet as his equal. They are subjects of his gaze, objects of his 'botanizing'. The nearest he comes to a direct encounter, with a woman who is not either marginal or debased, is in the poem, 'A une passante'.[42] (Even here, it is worth noting that the woman in question is in mourning – *en grand deuil*.) The tall, majestic woman passes him in the busy street; their eyes meet for a moment before she continues her journey, and the poet remains to ask whether they will only meet again in eternity. Her return of his gaze is confirmed in the last line: 'Ô toi que j'eusse aimée, ô toi qui le savais'. Benjamin's interpretation of this poem is that it is the very elusiveness of the passing encounter which fascinates Baudelaire: 'The delight of the city-dweller is not so much love at first sight as love at last sight'.[43] The meeting is characterized by the peculiarly modern feature of 'shock'.[44] (But if this is the rare exception of a woman sharing the urban experience, we may also ask whether a 'respectable' woman, in the 1850s, would have met the gaze of a strange man.)

There is, in any case, an apparently common assumption that women who do participate in 'the public' on anything like the same terms as men somehow manifest masculine traits. One of the widows observed by Baudelaire is described as having mannerisms of a masculine character.[45] His mixed admiration for the lesbian has much to do with her (supposed) 'mannishness', according to Benjamin.[46] Benjamin himself explains that, as women in the nineteenth century had to go out to work in factories, 'in the course of time masculine traits were bound to manifest themselves in these women'.[47] Even Richard Sennett (without much evidence, and despite the benefit of contemporary perspectives on the construction of gender) claims that women at the end of the nineteenth century who were 'ideologically committed to emancipation' dressed like men and developed bodily gestures which were 'mannish'.[48] But perhaps this perception of the 'masculine' in women who were visible in a man's world is only the displaced recognition of women's overall exclusion from that world. Baudelaire's general views on women, in his letters and his prose, are illuminating as a context for his poetic expressions of fascination with 'women of the city'. This is his own admission, in a letter to one of the women he idolized and idealized: 'I have hateful prejudices about women. In fact, *I have no faith*; you have a final soul, but, when all is said, it is the soul of a woman'.[49] Woman as a non-person is extolled in 'The Painter of Modern Life':

> Woman, in a word, for the artist in general, and Monsieur G. in particular, is far more than just the female of Man. Rather she is a divinity, a star, which presides at all the conceptions of the brain of man; a glittering conglomeration of all the graces of Nature, condensed into a single being; the object of the keenest admiration and curiosity that the picture of life can offer its contemplator. She is a kind of idol, stupid perhaps, but dazzling and bewitching, who holds wills and destinies suspended on her glance. ...Everything that adorns woman, everything that serves to show off her beauty, is part of herself; and those artists who have made a particular study of this enigmatic being dote no less on all the details of the *mundus muliebris* than on Woman herself. ...What poet, in sitting down to paint the pleasure caused by the sight of a beautiful woman, would venture to separate her from her costume?[50]

The classic misogynist duality, of woman as idealized-but-vapid/real-and-sensual-but-detested, which Baudelaire displays (and to which his biographers attest) is clearly related to the particular parade of women we observe in this literature of modernity.

But the other authors I have discussed were not misogynists; they were or are, on the contrary, sympathetic to women's condition and to the case of women's emancipation and equality with men. We need to look deeper than particular prejudices to explain the invisibility of women in the literature of modernity. The explanation is threefold, and lies in 1) the nature of sociological investigation, 2) the consequently partial conception of 'modernity', and 3) the reality of women's place in society. Much of this has been discussed in the recent work of feminist sociologists and historians, but it is worth rehearsing here in the specific context of the problem of modernity.

The Invisibility of Women in the Literature of Modernity

The rise and development of sociology in the nineteenth century was closely related to the growth and increasing separation of 'public' and 'private' spheres of activity in western industrial societies. The condition for this was the separation of work from home, with the development of factories and offices. By the mid-nineteenth century, this had made possible the move to the suburbs in some major cities (for example, the industrial cities of England, such as

Manchester and Birmingham).[51] Although women had never been engaged on equal terms (financial, legal or otherwise) with men, this physical separation put an end to their close and important involvement in what had often been a family concern – whether in trade, production, or even professional work. Their gradual confinement to the domestic world of the home and the suburb was strongly reinforced by an ideology of separate spheres.[52] At the same time, a new public world was in process of formation, of business organizations, political and financial establishments, and social and cultural institutions. These were almost invariably male institutions, though women might occasionally be granted some sort of honorary membership or allowed minimal participation as guests on particular occasions. In the second half of the century, the rise of the professions excluded women from the other expanding areas of activity, some of which they had traditionally been engaged in (like medicine), some of which had already excluded them (like the law and academic occupations), and some of which were new (the education of artists, for example). The two major implications for sociology as a new discipline were, first, that it was dominated by men, and second, that it was primarily concerned with the 'public' spheres of work, politics and the market place.[53] Indeed, women appear in the classic texts of sociology only in so far as they relate to men, in the family, or in minor roles in the public sphere. As David Morgan has said about Weber's *The Protestant Ethic and the Spirit of Capitalism*:

> It cannot have escaped many people's attention, at least in recent years, that women are very much hidden from this particular history; the lead parts – Franklin, Luther, Calvin, Baxter and Wesley – are all played by men and women only appear on the stage fleetingly in the guise of German factory workers with rather traditional orientations to work.[54]

And, to the extent that 'the separation of spheres' was a very incomplete process, many women still having to go to work to earn a living (though a very high proportion of these did so in domestic service), even these women, in their factories, mills, schools and offices, have been invisible in traditional sociological texts. The public institutions in which they did participate were rarely those accorded most importance by analysts of contemporary society.

This also meant that the particular experience of 'modernity' was, for the most part, equated with experience *in* the public arena. The accelerated growth of the city, the shock of the proximity of the very rich and the destitute poor (documented by Engels – and in some cities avoided and alleviated by the creation of suburbs), and the novelty of the fleeting and impersonal contacts in public life, provided the concern and the fascination for the authors of 'the modern', sociologists and other social commentators who documented their observations in academic essays, literary prose or poetry. To some extent, of course, these transformations of social life affected everyone, regardless of sex and class, though they did so differently for different groups. But the literature of modernity ignores the private sphere and to that extent is silent on the subject of women's primary domain. This silence is not only detrimental to any understanding of the lives of the female sex; it obscures a crucial part of the lives of men, too, by abstracting one part of their experience and failing to explore the interrelation of public and private spheres. For men inhabited both of these. Moreover, the public could only be constituted as a particular set of institutions and practices on the basis of the removal of other areas of social life to the invisible arena of the private.[55] The literature of modernity, like most sociology of its period, suffers from what has recently been called 'the oversocialisation of the public sphere'.[56] The skewed vision of its authors explains why women only appear in this literature through their relationships with men in the public sphere, and via their illegitimate or eccentric routes into this male arena – that is, in the role of whore, widow or murder victim.[57]

The real situation of women in the second half of the nineteenth century was more complex than one of straightforward confinement to the home. It varied from one social class to another, and even from one geographical region to another, depending on the local industry, the degree of industrialization, and numerous other factors. And, although the solitary and independent life of the *flâneur* was not open to women, women clearly were active and visible in other ways in the public arena. Sennett, as I have already mentioned, refers to the importance of careful attention to dress which women must maintain, a point made much earlier by Thorstein Veblen:

> It has in the course of economic development become the office of the woman to consume vicariously for the head of the household; and her apparel is contrived with this object in view. It has come about that obviously productive labor is in a peculiar degree derogatory to respectable women, and therefore special pains should be taken in the construction of women's dress, to impress upon the beholder the fact (often indeed a fiction) that the wearer does not and cannot habitually engage in useful work.[58]

Here, the particular visibility of women is that of sign of their husbands' position. Their important role in consumption is stressed:

> At the stage of economic development at which the women were still in the full sense the property of the men, the performance of conspicuous leisure and consumption came to be part of the services required of them. The women being not their own masters, obvious expenditure and leisure on their part would redound to the credit of their master rather than to their own credit; and therefore the more expensive and the more obviously unproductive the women of the household are, the more creditable and more effective for the purpose of reputability of the household or its head will their life be.[59]

The establishment of the department store in the 1850s and 1860s provided an important new arena for the legitimate public appearance of middle-class women.[60] However, although consumerism is a central aspect of modernity, and moreover mediated the public/private division, the peculiar characteristics of 'the modern' which I have been considering – the fleeting, anonymous encounter and the purposeless strolling – do not apply to shopping, or to women's activities either as public signs of their husband's wealth or as consumers.

We are beginning to find out more about the lives of women who were limited to the domestic existence of the suburbs;[61] about women who went into domestic service in large numbers;[62] and about the lives of working-class women.[63] The advent of the modern era affected all these women, transforming their experience of home and work. The recovery of women's experience is part of the project of retrieving what has been hidden, and attempting to fill the gaps in the classic accounts. The feminist revision of sociology and social history means the gradual opening up of areas of social life and experience which to date have been obscured by the partial perspective and particular bias of mainstream sociology.

It is not at all clear what a feminist sociology of modernity would look like. There is no question of inventing the *flâneuse*: the essential point is that such a character was rendered impossible by the sexual divisions of the nineteenth century. Nor is it appropriate to reject totally the existing literature on modernity, for the experiences it describes certainly defined a good deal of the lives of men, and were also (but far less centrally) a part of the experience of women. What is missing in this literature is any account of life outside the public realm, of the experience of 'the modern' in its private manifestations, and also of the very different nature of the experience of those women who *did* appear in the public arena; a poem written by 'la femme passante' about her encounter with Baudelaire, perhaps?

Notes

1. Catherine Hall, 'Gender Divisions and Class Formation in the Birmingham Middle Class, 1780–1850', in *People's History and Socialist Theory*, ed. Raphael Samuel, Routledge & Kegan Paul, London 1981; Leonore Davidoff and Catherine Hall, 'The Architecture of Public and Private Life: English Middle-class Society in a Provincial Town 1780–1850', in *The Pursuit of Urban History*, ed. D. Fraser and A. Sutcliffe, Edward Arnold, London 1983.
2. Hilary Land, 'The Family Wage', *Feminist Review* 6, 1980; Michèle Barrett and Mary McIntosh, 'The "Family Wage": Some Problems for Socialists and Feminists', *Capital & Class* 11, 1980. The ideology of separate spheres, and even of the equation of male/public/rational, has persisted to the present day, its recent sociological expression being found in Parsonian theories of the family. Talcott Parsons, 'Family Structure and the Socialization of the Child', in *Family, Socialization and Interaction*

Process, Talcott Parsons and Robert F. Bales, Routledge & Kegan Paul, London 1956.

3. Georg Simmel, 'The Stranger' and 'The Metropolis and Mental Life', in *The Sociology of Georg Simmel*, ed. Kurt H. Wolff, The Free Press, New York 1950.
4. Richard Sennett, *The Fall of Public Man*, Cambridge University Press, Cambridge 1974.
5. Charles Baudelaire, 'The Painter of Modern Life', in *The Painter of Modern Life and Other Essays*, tr. and ed. Jonathan Mayne, Phaidon Press, Oxford 1964 (first published 1863). For Baudelaire's other writings on modernity, see below.
6. Walter Benjamin, *Charles Baudelaire: A Lyric Poet in the Era of High Capitalism*, New Left Books, London 1973.
7. Baudelaire, op. cit., p. 13.
8. Marshall Berman, *All That is Solid Melts into Air*, Verso, London 1983, p. 15.
9. Simmel, op. cit., pp. 409–10.
10. Benjamin, for example, argues that conditions in the three cities were significantly different. Benjamin, op. cit., pp. 128–31.
11. Berman, op. cit., pp. 16–17 and chapter 1.
12. Malcolm Bradbury and James McFarlane, 'The Name and Nature of Modernism', in their (ed.) *Modernism 1890–1930*, Penguin, Harmondsworth 1976, p. 36.
13. For example, Joanna Richardson, translator of Baudelaire's poems, says in her introduction to *Baudelaire: Selected Poems* (Penguin, Harmondsworth 1975, p. 20): '*Les fleurs du mal*, may not be technically original. The only poem in which Baudelaire really seems to have invented his rhythm is 'L'invitation au voyage'. His one revolutionary innovation is in the versification, it is the complete suppression of the auditive caesura in a certain number of lines'.
14. The title of his book, *All That is Solid Melts into Air*, is a quotation from the *Communist Manifesto*.
15. Berman, op. cit., pp. 133–42.
16. Charles Baudelaire, 'The Salon of 1845', in *Art in Paris 1845–1862*, Phaidon Press, Oxford 1965, pp. 31–2. Italics in original.
17. Charles Baudelaire, 'The Salon of 1846', op. cit., pp. 118–19.
18. Berman, op. cit., p. 136.
19. Baudelaire, 1964, op. cit., p. 11.
20. Baudelaire, 1964, op. cit., pp. 26–9.
21. Baudelaire, 1964, op. cit., p. 9.
22. Benjamin, op. cit., p. 36.
23. Benjamin, op. cit., pp. 40 and 170. However, elsewhere Benjamin argues that Baudelaire is *not* the archetypical *flâneur*. Benjamin, op. cit., p. 69.
24. Benjamin, op. cit., pp. 49, 128, 47.
25. Berman, op. cit., pp. 150–5.
26. Charles Baudelaire, *Petits Poèmes en Prose (Le Spleen de Paris)*, Garnier-Flammarion, Paris 1967, p. 33.
27. Simmel, op. cit., p. 402.
28. Simmel, op. cit., p. 402.

29. Sennett, op. cit., p. 86.
30. Sennett, op. cit., pp. 125, 213.
31. Sennett, op. cit., p. 217. However, there were exceptions to this. See Robert Thorne, 'Places of Refreshment in the Nineteenth-Century City', in *Buildings and Society*, ed. Anthony D. King, Routledge & Kegan Paul, London 1980.
32. Sennett, op. cit., pp. 68 and 166. In these references to Sennett's book, I am again considering fairly uncritically (from any other point of view) a text on modernity. For a critical review of his use of evidence, his historical method, and his sociological explanation for the changes in manners, see Sheldon Wolin, 'The Rise of Private Man', *New York Review of Books*, 14 April 1977.
33. David Frisby, *Sociological Impressionism. A Reassessment of Georg Simmel's Social Theory*, Heinemann, London 1981, pp. 15, 17, 27, 139.
34. Frisby, op. cit., p. 28.
35. Berman, op. cit., p. 322.
36. Berman, op. cit., p. 323.
37. Quoted in Ellen Moers, *Literary Women*, Anchor Press, New York 1977, p. 12.
38. Benjamin, op. cit., p. 90; Richardson, op. cit., p. 12.
39. Benjamin, op. cit., pp. 92–3; Charles Baudelaire, *Selected Poems*, Penguin, Harmondsworth 1975, p. 224.
40. Baudelaire, 1967, op. cit., p. 185; 1964, op. cit., pp. 34–40.
41. Baudelaire, 1975, op. cit., p. 166; 1967, op. cit., pp. 63–5.
42. Baudelaire, 1975, op. cit., p. 170.
43. Benjamin, op. cit., p. 45.
44. Benjamin, op. cit., p. 125; also pp. 118 and 134.
45. Baudelaire, 1967, op. cit., p. 64.
46. Benjamin, op. cit., p. 90.
47. Benjamin, op. cit., p. 93.
48. Sennett, op. cit., p. 190.
49. Letter to Apollonie Sabatier, quoted in Richardson, op. cit., p. 14. Italics in original.
50. Baudelaire, 1964, op. cit., pp. 30–1.
51. Maurice Spiers, *Victoria Park Manchester*, Manchester University Press, Manchester 1976; Davidoff and Hall, op. cit.
52. Catherine Hall, 'The Early Formation of Victorian Domestic Ideology', in *Fit Work for Women*, ed. Sandra Burman, Croom Helm, London 1979.
53. Margaret Stacey, 'The Division of Labour Revisited or Overcoming the Two Adams', in *Practice and Progress: British Sociology 1950–1980*, ed. Philip Abrams et al., Allen & Unwin, London 1981; Sara Delamont, *The Sociology of Women*, Allen & Unwin, London 1980, chapter 1.
54. David Morgan, 'Men, Masculinity and the Process of Sociological Enquiry', in *Doing Feminist Research*, ed. Helen Roberts, Routledge & Kegan Paul, London 1981, p. 93.
55. Sennett does discuss, in passing, some changes in the home – for example, the development of a 'private' form of dress – but his central focus is on the public sphere, and he does not present a systematic account of the private or of the relationship between the two spheres. Sennett, op. cit., pp. 66–7.

56. Eva Gamarnikow and June Purvis, Introduction to *The Public and the Private*, ed. Eva Gamarnikow et al., Heinemann, London 1983, p. 2.

57. References to the murder victim, whom I have not discussed, originate in Poe's detective stories, which greatly influenced Baudelaire. Benjamin, op. cit., pp. 42–4.

58. Thorstein Veblen, *The Theory of the Leisure Class*, Unwin Books, London 1970, p. 126. First published in 1899.

59. Veblen, op. cit., pp. 126–7.

60. Thorne, op. cit., p. 236.

61. Davidoff and Hall, op. cit.; Catherine Hall, 'The Butcher, the Baker, the Candlestick-Maker: The Shop and the Family in the Industrial Revolution', in *The Changing Experience of Women*, ed. Elizabeth Whitelegg et al., Martin Robertson, Oxford 1982.

62. Leonore Davidoff, 'Mastered for Life: Servant and Wife in Victorian and Edwardian England', *Journal of Social History*, vol. 7, no. 4, 1974.

63. Ivy Pinchbeck, *Women Workers and the Industrial Revolution 1750–1850*, Frank Cass, London 1977. First published in 1930. Sally Alexander, 'Women's Work in Nineteenth-Century London. A Study of the Years 1820–1850', in *The Rights and Wrongs of Women*, ed. Juliet Mitchell and Ann Oakley, Penguin, Harmondsworth 1976: also in Whitelegg et al. (eds.) op. cit.

* * *

In another important essay, Wolff remarks that by the late nineteenth-century, 'middle-class women had been more or less consigned (in ideology, if not in reality) to the private sphere'.[11] The question of how ideological exclusion relates to real exclusion is an important one, and this point of uncertainty has prompted Elizabeth Wilson to ask whether Wolff understands the *flâneur* to be 'a gendered concept', 'a descriptive account', or both.[12] Wilson's essay, rather than identifying the *flâneur* figure with the dominating patriarchal gaze, valuably draws attention to his melancholy and insecurity, and concludes that he never really existed. Rather, he was 'an embodiment of the special blend of excitement, tedium and horror aroused by many in the new metropolis, and the disintegrative effect of this on the masculine identity'; he is 'a shifting projection of angst rather than a solid embodiment of male bourgeois power'.[13] If this is so, then the interesting questions for literary critics concerned with modernism and the city do not immediately concern the *flâneur*, but, rather, the excitement, tedium and horror of the city, to which the *flâneur* is one of many possible responses. Similarly, though the detached subject position of the *flâneur* is an important response to modernity, it is not the only one possible. If this is recognized then, rather than employing the detached position normatively, the critic can situate it among other possible responses.

More recently, critics have tried to engage with the particularity of individual cities: Deborah Parsons has argued that the theorization of 'the city' from Baudelaire to Benjamin has led to the relative neglect of specific histories of individual cities. It seems likely that future studies will continue to draw on Simmel in examining the penetration of urban forms of socialization into individual consciousness, on Berman in examining the ways that urban forms of life enter the unconscious of the text, and Wolff and Wilson in considering the different cities produced by variables such as gender, but that they will also attempt to inflect these general theories in relation to the local details of particular cities at particular times.

Chapter Notes

1. Alan Swingewood, *A Short History of Sociological Thought*, 3rd edition (Basingstoke: Macmillan, 2000), 84–85.
2. Walter Benajmin, *Charles Baudelaire: A Lyric Poet in the Era of High Capitalism*, tr. Harry Zohn (1973; London: Verso, 1997), 122.
3. Marshall Berman, *All that is Solid Melts into Air* (1982; London: Verso, 1983), p.146.
4. Berman, *All that is Solid Melts into Air*, 148.
5. Berman, *All that is Solid Melts into Air*, 147.
6. Walter Benjamin, 'The Work of Art in the Age of Mechanical Reproduction', in *Illuminations*, tr. Harry Zohn (1970; London: Fontana, 1972), 211–44.
7. Perry Anderson, 'Modernity and Revolution', *New Left Review*, no.144 (Mar.–Apr. 1984), 96–113 (pp.100–3)
8. Anderson, 'Modernity and Revolution', 104.
9. Andrew Thacker, *Moving through Modernity* (Manchester: Manchester University Press, 2003), 82.
10. Rachel Bowlby, 'Walking, Women and Writing: Virginia Woolf as *flâneuse*', in Isobel Armstrong, ed., *New Feminist Discourses* (London: Routledge, 1992), 26–47; Tracey Seeley, 'Virginia Woolf's Poetics of Space', *Woolf Studies Annual*, 2 (1996), 89–116.
11. Wolff, 'Feminism and Modernism', qtd. Elizabeth Wilson, 'The Invisible *Flâneur*', *New Left Review*, 191 (Jan.–Feb. 1992), 90–110 (p.99).
12. Wilson, 'The Invisible *Flâneur*,' 99.
13. Wilson, 'The Invisible *Flâneur*,' 109.

Further Reading

Benjamin, Walter. *Charles Baudelaire: A Lyric Poet in the Era of High Capitalism*, tr. Harry Zohn (London: New Left Books, 1973). Essays written in the 1930s, but not available in English until the late 1960s. Highly influential, particularly on discussions of the *flâneur* in relation to the city.

Buck-Morss, Susan. 'The *Flâneur*, the Sandwichman and the Whore: the Politics of Loitering', *New German Critique*, no.39 (Fall 1986), 99–140.

Lehan, Richard. *The City in Literature: An Intellectual and Cultural History* (Berkeley: University of California Press, 1998). A traditionalist intellectual history of the ways the city has been conceptualized, from the Enlightenment to the present. Includes discussions of Conrad, Joyce, and Eliot.

Harvey, David. *The Condition of Postmodernity* (Oxford: Blackwell, 1990). Though he has little to say about modernist literature, Harvey provides a comprehensive account of modernity and postmodernity. Section three, 'The Experience of Space and Time', is particularly relevant to the themes examined in the present chapter.

Parsons, Deborah L. 'Paris is not Rome, or Madrid: Locating the City of Modernity', *Critical Quarterly*, 44, no.2 (Summer 2002), 17–29.

—. *Streetwalking the Metropolis: Women, the City, and Modernity* (Oxford: Oxford University Press, 2000). Responds to the work of Janet Wolff and others on the *flâneuse*; covers many female writers, including Richardson, Woolf, Rhys, and Barnes.

Rignall, John. 'Benjamin's *Flâneur* and the Problem of Realism', in Andrew Benjamin, ed., *The Problems of Modernity: Adorno and Benjamin* (London 1988), 112–40.

Thacker, Andrew. *Moving through Modernity: Space and Geography in Modernism* (Manchester: Manchester University Press, 2003). An approach informed by theorizations of space by geographical theorists such as Henri Lefebvre and Michel de Certeau.

Williams, Raymond. 'Metropolitan Perceptions and the Emergence of Modernism' in Edward Timms and David Kelley, eds., *Unreal City: Urban Experience in Modern European Literature* (Manchester: Manchester University Press, 1985); reprinted in Williams, *The Politics of Modernism*, ed. Tony Pinkney (London: Verso, 1989), 37–48.

Wilson, Elizabeth, 'The Invisible *Flâneur*', *New Left Review*, 191 (Jan.–Feb. 1992), 90–110.

6

Regendering Modernism

In principle, any of the topics identified in this guide could be approached from the perspective of feminism and gender studies. In practice, some have been more attractive than others. As is apparent from other essays in the guide, the question of 'the masses' can be a question as much of gender as of class, and old certainties concerning the *flâneur* have been brought into question by feminist critics. Questions that originated in literary history, such as modernism's relation to Romanticism, have attracted less interest from feminist critics, perhaps because women writers have less investment in a tradition from which they have long been excluded. However, the shaping of tradition through the shaping of modernist canon has been a significant issue for feminist critics of modernism. So too has the publication and non-publication of texts by women.

The earliest gender criticisms of modernist works were contemporary with modernism itself: Virginia Woolf's description of Dorothy Richardson as having evolved 'the psychological sentence of the feminine gender' has often been quoted.[1] Wyndham Lewis' criticism of Woolf for adopting a timid attitude to reality, 'peeping' in an 'old-maidish' manner, is also a form of gender criticism, though a provocatively misogynistic one.[2] In Britain at least, modernism was forged in the middle of a raging debate about the roles of the sexes and their places in the nation-state, focused above all on the suffrage campaign. The First World War, which led to the effective suspension of the suffrage campaign, raised new questions about masculinity and manliness, and opened new areas of employment to women.

The period in which the modernist canon was shaped, after the Second World War, was dominated by forms of criticism which were notionally apolitical, and often in effect conservative in their unwillingness to question the boundaries of their own activity. The feminist reappraisal of modernism can be said to begin, tentatively, with Kate Millett's *Sexual Politics* (1969). Millett's work, enormously influential on feminist literary criticism, is well known for its criticisms of two modernist writers, D. H. Lawrence and Henry Miller. However, it is important to distinguish the criticism of modernists from the criticism of modernism. Millett does not discuss the more fundamental qualities of modernism and their relation to gender; there is nothing to indicate that Lawrence and Miller would not have been equally patriarchal had they chosen a classic realist mode of representation. It is notable too, that Millett mentions Joyce only in passing, and does not discuss the two leading poets and theorists of English-language literary modernism, Eliot and Pound. These limitations are not Millett's alone. The so-called 'images of women' criticism[3] in the 1970s treated the text as a transparent medium. This mode yielded valuable works, such as *Women in Joyce*, edited by Suzette Henke and Elaine Unkeless (1982), but was not best suited to deal with the distinctive qualities of modernist literature. In the case of Eliot, biographical studies such as Lyndall Gordon's *Eliot's Early Years* and James E. Miller's *T. S. Eliot's Personal Waste Land* (both in 1977) noted his misogyny, but the biographical framework did not allow for a larger investigation of modernism as such.

As structuralist and post-structuralist theory became more influential in the mid- to late 1980s, and as the achievements of post-war women writers in non-realist modes of fiction became recognized, feminist criticism became more open to dealing with issues more fundamental to modernism. The shift in modes may be measured by the difference between Bonnie Kime Scott's *Joyce and Feminism* (1984), which approaches the subject biographically and historically, and her later *James Joyce* (1987) in the Harvester Feminist Readings series, in which the works of Hélène Cixous and Julia Kristeva are more prominent. Though the title of Tony Pinkney's *Women in the Poetry of T. S. Eliot* (1984) suggests an 'images of women' study, Pinkney's psychoanalytic methods give it greater depth, and, in its readings of key prose texts by Hulme and Pound, it points the way to a feminist theory of modernism.

At least as important as the reappraisal of male writers was the rediscovery of neglected women writers, a process that implicitly questioned the established canon. Hugh Kenner's *The Pound Era* (1971), which implied a modernist canon centred on the 'men of 1914', was a provocation to many feminist scholars. Some of the most important feminist works of the 1980s sought to recover not only individual writers, but networks of writers, patrons, and publishers. This method echoed Kenner, even as it challenged his assumptions. Gillian Hanscombe and Virginia Smyers contrasted the network they had investigated in *Writing for their Lives* (1987) with the better known Bloomsbury Group: 'Unlike Virginia Woolf's set, these women, who knew each other, or each other's work, or both, were often expatriate; many were poor; all were more bohemian than bourgeois; and they were more linked by shared choices and interests than by the tighter ties of traditional background and common blood. Nor were all the women poets or novelists; some were editors and publishers,others ran bookshops, yet others provided patronage of both spiritual and material kinds'.[4] Shari Benstock's *Women of the Left Bank* (1987) undertook a very similar project. The collaborative enterprise that scholars recovered reflected the ideals of feminism at that time: many collections of essays on modernist women are the products of seminars and conferences. *The Gender of Modernism* (1990), an anthology edited by Bonnie Kime Scott, gathers together important and, in some cases, previously unpublished materials relating to gender and women writers.

Studies of networks are, by their nature, difficult to anthologize; the effect of works such as *Women of the Left Bank* is cumulative, as figures glimpsed in one chapter reappear in other contexts. Bonnie Kime Scott's diagram from *The Gender of Modernism* is not without its limitations, as Aaron Jaffe has argued,[5] but in the present context may usefully stand as an emblem of an important area of feminist scholarship.

Bonnie Kime Scott, diagram, 'A Tangled Mesh of Modernists', in Bonnie Kime Scott, ed., *The Gender of Modernism* (Bloomington: Indiana University Press, 1990), p.10.

* * *

Alongside the investigation of networks, there was much important scholarly activity in the editing, republication, and assessment of women writers. Editions of Virginia Woolf's letters (published 1975–80) and diaries (1977–84) led the way. Selections of Rebecca West's early essays appeared in 1982, edited by Jane Marcus. Reflecting the interest in networks, *Time and Tide Wait for No Man* (1984), ed. Dale Spender, reprinted selections from an important feminist political journal of the 1920s. Crucially, from 1978 onwards, in its Modern Classics series, Virago Press reprinted fiction by women writers of the early twentieth century, including Dorothy Richardson, Djuna Barnes, Gertrude Stein, Rebecca West, Vita Sackville-West, and Rosamond Lehmann. The aim of the series was

> to demonstrate the existence of a female tradition in fiction which is both enriching and enjoyable. The Leavisite notion of the 'Great Tradition', and the narrow, academic definition of a 'classic', has meant the neglect of a large number of interesting secondary works of fiction. In calling the series 'Modern Classics' we do not necessarily mean 'great' – although this is often the case. Published with new critical and biographical introductions, books are chosen for many reasons: sometimes for their importance in literary history; sometimes because they illuminate particular aspects of women's lives, both personal and public. They may be classics of comedy or storytelling; their interest can be historical, feminist, political or literary.[6]

The practical value for readers and scholars was immense. It is important to note that relatively few of the titles reprinted could be described as 'modernist' by the traditional criteria of New Criticism; many were traditionally realist in their mode. Some critics working in the early twentieth century have begun to produce definitions of modernism which are inclusive enough to admit such texts; others have argued that there is a lost tradition of realist writing which has been obscured by modernism, and that to stretch 'modernism' is to capitulate to its hegemonic power.[7] The texts examined by Alison Light in *Forever England* (1991), though dating from 1918 to 1939, are formally and politically conservative. The rediscovery of realist writing has been of interest to scholars beyond the feminist community, as may be seen by Rosa Maria Bracco's *Merchants of Hope* (1993), on British 'middlebrow' writers and the First World War, and the collections *High and Low Moderns* (1996), ed. Maria DiBattista and Lucy McDiarmid, *Seeing Double* (1996), ed. Carola M. Kaplan and Anne B. Simpson, and *Outside Modernism* (2000), ed. Lynne Hapgood and Nancy L. Paxton. *Edwardian Fiction: An Oxford Companion*, by Sandra Kemp, Charlotte Mitchell, and David Trotter (1997) provides a valuable overview of fiction, predominantly realist in mode, before the First World War. While realist works lie beyond the scope of the present collection, they are a valuable reminder that modernism is not the only possible literary response to modernity.

In the 1980s and early 1990s many scholars, including feminists, perceived modernism as authoritarian, exclusive of female traditions, and, in deconstructive terminology, logocentric. Postmodernism appeared to offer an alternative tradition in which the self was fragmentary and decentred.

During this period, modernism and postmodernism were evaluative, not simply descriptive terms; they appeared mutually exclusive, and identifying with one or the other carried a political overtone. The plurality of modernisms had not been fully recognized; nor had postmodernism's problematic relationship to late capitalism. Though some recognized that male-centred modernism was a critical construct, it was more attractive to identify with postmodernism than to reconstruct its predecessor. The small but significant exception lay in French feminism's reception of James Joyce (particularly the Joyce of *Finnegans Wake*): his use of language was taken as an example of *écriture feminine*.[8]

Shari Benstock's introduction (1984) to the collection *Feminist Issues in Literary Scholarship* is, in respect of the relationship it assumes between modernism and postmodernism, of its time: it assumes, for example, that we must choose between seeing Gertrude Stein as 'a marginal modernist' or a 'thorough-going post-modernist', with the implication that the latter is preferable. A later critic might have used 'avant-gardist' as an alternative to 'modernist'. Nevertheless, Benstock's overview marks a significant adjustment in thinking about the cultural crisis that, in earlier accounts, was understood to have precipitated modernism. The account she quotes from Friedman of disorder and despair could have come from any one of many accounts of modernism from the period 1955 to 1980. In the often conservative atmosphere of post-1945 cultural criticism, it was assumed that the loss of certainties – above all, of Christian belief – was regrettable, and that modernism was driven by such feelings of regret. Feminist criticism questions the universality of such responses: 'would it have been the same for women?' it asks, or, avoiding the universalisation of 'woman', 'would it have been the same for this particular group of women writers, or this individual woman?' A similar tactic can be seen in feminist responses to Andreas Huyssen, and feminist accounts of the *flâneur*.

Benstock begins her introductory 'letter' by reflecting on the place of French literary theory in Anglophone feminist criticism, and the ambivalent relationship of feminism to 'the great men of France whose theories of psychoanalysis and philosophy structure current critical practice'. The inscription on the western facade of the Panthéon, '*Aux Grands Hommes La Patrie Reconnaissante*', signifies 'a monolithic culture in which egalitarianism extends only to men'. She suspects that even those male theorists who align themselves with marginal groups do so to secure 'a firmer grip on the center of theoretical discourse'.[9]

Extract from Shari Benstock, 'Beyond the Reaches of Feminist Criticism: A Letter from Paris', in S. Benstock, ed., *Feminist Issues in Literary Scholarship* (Bloomington and Indianapolis: Indiana University Press, 1987), pp.9–15.

Perhaps, then, the western facade of the Panthéon is not as smooth as it appears. It situates itself on the original burial place of Saint Geneviève, patron saint of Paris. The building was used first as a church, now as a burial place for distinguished men. If we were to dig deep enough among the ruins that support the present building – the Roman ruins that the architect Soufflot feared might cause the collapse of his building design – would we find the female culture that supports this monument to male culture? When we found Saint Geneviève among the ruins, what could she tell us? And how – that is, in what language – would we speak to her? My search for her will begin against the facade of another seemingly monolithic institution of contemporary culture – modernism – precisely because it seems to me that modernism found more than mere setting in the Paris of the 1920s. It also discovered a subtle affinity between its literary goals and the French cultural imperative. As well, the critical method that elucidated the modernist project, that explained the works of James Joyce, T. S. Eliot, and Ezra Pound, has duplicated both the aesthetic and cultural values imbedded in the work of these men. In order to present this smooth facade of patriarchal values, modernism found it necessary – as have many literary movements before it – to hide all that was antithetical to its undertaking, all that was marginal in the culture it examined. And we know precisely who is to be found buried among the foundations of this gigantic edifice, whose works – diverse and rich – support the very columns on which modernism is constructed. We will find, among others, women. And not just the Virginia Woolfs and Gertrude Steins, acknowledged in their own time as exemplary writers. We will find all the others – Nancy Cunard, Caresse Crosby, Mina Loy, and Winifred Ellerman among them – who cooperated in this endeavor. What is frightening about such a critical venture is the very proximity of these women to us: women whose actions were well known to every major male modernist sixty years ago are almost beyond recall now. If it is difficult to rediscover women of our own century, how overwhelming the task of finding Geneviève, born in 422 AD.

The project I suggest is related to, but importantly different from, the one outlined several years ago by Elaine Showalter, and subtly different too from the one initially undertaken by *Tulsa Studies in Women's Literature*:

> Before we can even begin to ask how the literature of women would be different and special, we need to reconstruct its past, to rediscover the scores of women novelists, poets and dramatists whose work has been obscured by time, and to establish the continuity of the female tradition from decade to decade, rather than from Great Woman to Great Woman. As we recreate the chain of writers in this tradition, the patterns of influence and response from one generation to the next, we can also begin to challenge the periodicity of orthodox literary history, and its enshrined canons of achievement.[1]

An 'enshrined canon of achievement', modernism has already come under the critical scrutiny of postmodernist literary theory, one of whose founding claims is the 'putting into question' of founding claims. The postmodernist worm has turned – against the very institution that gave it birth – to undermine the orthodoxy and institutionalization of modernism as a literary enterprise. To resurrect those lost women writers, publishers, booksellers, memoirists, and *salonières* is the first move in a critical project that might very well bring down the temple in which modernism has been enshrined. The question left unanswered, however, is how we go about resurrecting those buried behind the modernist facade, for surely the techniques we use to rediscover these women will influence the nature of our findings. And once we have rediscovered these women, what will we do with them – how will we treat their lives and works? Will we argue that their works be added to the canon, their names included on the list of authors graduate students preparing for doctoral examinations must memorize? Or will we set up an alternative canon, a hierarchy of women authors, placing Virginia Woolf (perhaps) at the top, Gertrude Stein in second place, Edith Sitwell in third? Will we find other ways of assessing the value of these individual contributions, avoiding the rank ordering of writers that itself seems one of the most unfortunate aspects of the patriarchal literary critical enterprise? Can we define a modernist aesthetic and poetic exclusive to women writers of the twentieth century? Will we divide the modernist canon between those works signed by males and those by females? Will we discover that women modernists suffered from an 'anxiety of authorship' of the kind described by Sandra M. Gilbert and Susan Gubar for nineteenth-century women writers? Were those women writers embarked on creating a 'literature of their own'? Can the theoretical models already established for discussing American and English women writers of the nineteenth century be applied to these twentieth-century women writers? And how do we assess, then, the contributions of those women and men who did not themselves write, but who contributed in other important ways to modernism?

Gertrude Stein, of course, would be furious at being grouped with these women writers – or any other set of women writers. Thoroughly aware of the risks of womanhood – its powerlessness and enforced isolation – Stein took on the powers of manhood by doing what no other female modernist dared do: she claimed the center for herself, toppling James Joyce from his elegant, but precarious, perch on the throne. What gall such an action required! And how galling that critical acclaim and book sales continued to suggest that Joyce, not Stein, held court among the expatriates. Not having successfully convinced the locals that she was the center of modernist activity, Stein next redefined the literary project that was hers, claiming that her methods had nothing in common with the outmoded literary forms practiced by others. For her, Joyce was old-fashioned and Hemingway 'smelled of the nineteenth century'. Stein was at one with the twentieth century, her work was 'where the twentieth century was'. Ironically, the isolation Stein feared as a woman writer found a correlative of sorts in the very *gloire* she sought: to be alone at the top, the one and only, the center of an activity that she herself defined. Nor did her daring claims for the centrality in the literary canon spare her the painful isolation of her Paris life: it is one of many pernicious expatriate myths that Gertrude Stein controlled a powerful Left Bank salon from which she dictated literary aesthetics. Gertrude Stein's Paris existence was, mostly, a separate one: like the James Joyce who so troubled her thoughts, she spent her time alone, writing. She was quite correct in redefining modernism in her own terms, however, and in separating her practice from that of others (notably Joyce). Her writing project differed from modernist 'experimentalism' in every conceivable way. The discovery of Gertrude Stein and her work has been a recent one, but one predicted by Stein herself, who always argued that really original artists are so in advance of their time that they cannot be understood by their contemporaries: to be so would mean they inhabited the past. And it is post-modernist literary theory that has provided the tools for the discovery of Stein's work. By maintaining her separatism, she created the myth that she was at the center of a literary period whose borders were, in reality, sealed against her. Perhaps this separatism allowed her to create a literature very much of her own. This literature required, however, a methodology of its own – and it is precisely that methodology that is at issue: where to place Gertrude Stein and her work.

Obviously, our feminist project is not to recreate the orthodox forms that have traditionally excluded women, that divided a Gertrude Stein from her own womanhood, that forced her to deny for many years the wellspring of her creativity (what Adrienne Rich would call 'the Lesbian in her'[2]). But in discovering our pantheon are we building a Panthéon? Are we duplicating the implicit patriarchal values that have insured our own burial in the march of literary history, as Gertrude Stein duplicated a heterosexual power structure in her relationship with Alice Toklas? Do we want the women writers we discover to join the canon of male writers or do we want a separate canon, and if we want a separate literary canon and a separate critical practice – *our own* – how will these differ from the 'enshrined canons of achievement' around which course descriptions, dissertations, scholarly journals, and academic careers construct themselves? Do we claim the center for ourselves (taking up the modernist project) or do we redefine the limits of authority by which the center constitutes itself (taking up the post-modernist project)? Or do we, like Gertrude Stein, try to do both? Certainly the reconstruction of women's literary past implies that such questions be asked at the moment of rediscovery, that they not be deferred until a later moment in our feminist history. And such questions poise themselves – and in so doing poise us – on that awkward border between modernism and post-modernism, between practice and theory. As feminist critics we participate in a *modernity* that is discomforting. We both welcome and fear the literary discoveries we invite because these discoveries inevitably unsettle the very foundations of our feminism.

Having just rediscovered Gertrude Stein, for instance, where do we put her? (The more important question, where does Gertrude Stein put *us*, is the ultimate concern of this essay.) Do we make her a marginal modernist or a thoroughgoing post-modernist, a woman whose genius was well in advance of her male compatriots? We might begin by reviewing the characteristics that mark modernism as a literary movement. The following description of the cultural condition that produced modernism is taken from Susan Stanford Friedman's work on H. D.:

> The starting point of modernism is the crisis of belief that pervades twentieth-century western culture: loss of faith, experience of fragmentation and disintegration, and shattering of cultural symbols and norms. At the center of this crisis were the new technologies and methodologies of science, the epistemology of logical positivism, and the relativism of functionalist thought – in short, major aspects of the philosophical perspectives that Freud embodied. The rationalism of science and philosophy attacked the validity of traditional religious and artistic symbols while the growing technology of the industrialized world produced the catastrophes of war on the one hand and the atomization of human beings on the other. Art produced after the First World War recorded the emotional aspect of this crisis; despair, hopelessness, paralysis, angst, and a sense of meaninglessness, chaos, and fragmentation of material reality. In a variety of ways suited to their own religious, literary, mythological, occult, political, or existentialist perspectives, they emerged from the paralysis of absolute despair to an active search for meaning. The search for order and pattern began in its own negation, in the overwhelming sense of disorder and fragmentation caused by the modern materialist world. The artist as seer would attempt to create what the culture could no longer produce: symbol and meaning in the dimension of art, brought into being through the agency of language, the Word or Logos of the twentieth century.[3]

This description situates modernism historically as a post-World War I phenomenon, grounds its psychology in reaction to despair, and describes its pursuit as 'an active search for meaning ... through the agency of language, the Word or Logos'. Fixing the modernist 'moment' as post-war, this description renders troublesome discussions of modernist texts that preceded the First World War (the early work of H. D., Joyce, Eliot, and Pound), and eliminates from discussion those who did not survive the war years (Guillaume Apollinaire, for instance). What this analysis of modernism's defining features does not mention – but which is evident in all of Friedman's work on H. D. – is the set of masculine claims and heterosexual values embedded in the work of modernism. (Thus Marcel Proust is excluded because his artistic subject was homosexuality, and several writers, women and men alike, are overlooked because their work in no way demonstrates the despair and crisis of faith that the war presumably produced. Notable in this group is Gertrude

Stein.) Nonetheless, there are several modernist practitioners who clearly fit Friedman's working definition: T. S. Eliot (*The Waste Land*), Ezra Pound (*Hugh Selwyn Mauberley*), Franz Kafka (*The Castle*), Wyndham Lewis (*Tarr*); included as well would be the various literary movements incorporated under the modernist logo: vorticism, futurism, Dadaism, surrealism. Such a definition pitches the tent of modernism on the ashes of burned-out rationalism and positivism.

Nothing is mentioned here of the ironic tone that marks this literary method, but irony has often been seen as the hallmark of modernist writing, the tool used to recast the impotence of despair into aggressive literary production. The 'despair, hopelessness, paralysis, angst, sense of meaninglessness, chaos, and fragmentation of material reality produced by the collapse of traditional values' cited by Friedman became grist for the ironic mode. Irony, like various other literary techniques and experimental narrative modes, served as a mask to disguise the very traditional values – a belief in order and meaning – against which this writing set itself. A description of modernism that fixes its origins in a crisis of belief and despair at the 'shattering of cultural symbols and norms' also eliminates, by definition, the acknowledged father of modernism, James Joyce, and, among others such as Wallace Stevens and e. e. cummings, at least six important women modernists: Edith Sitwell, H. D., Virginia Woolf, Djuna Barnes, Marianne Moore, and Mina Loy. The work of these writers does not situate itself in *reaction to* a collapse in cultural values, taking as its defense the ironic mode, but rather exposes the continuing hegemony of traditional material and patriarchal values. Unfortunately, the First World War had not made the world safe for democracy, but neither had it blown sky high the values that had supported western culture. When the air cleared from the smoke bombs, the old order quickly re-established itself. Alienated by this world, unwilling (and unable) to share its values, some of these writers turned away from the modern world, creating an interior landscape in which language recorded the psyche. In place of traditional material values, literature turned its attention to the ways in which the mind perceived the external world and recorded its impressions. Various modernists were interested in cultural symbols and norms as subjects under analysis, writing a literature that exposed the operations of these cultural norms as they were present *in* language. The ironic defense mechanism, the need for which exposed an attachment to the very culture whose loss it announced, was replaced by the mask of objectivity: the writer did not react, but rather perceived.

Of course, such descriptions of modernist operations are deceptive, if not actually deceiving. It would be virtually impossible to derive a definition of modernism – or any other literary movement – that included all whose work shared some of the defining characteristics without exposing important differences among those listed. Some definitions of modernism emphasize the role the war played in creating a new literary sensibility (Paul Fussell, *The Great War and Modern Memory*), another emphasizes the work of psychoanalysis (Leon Edel, *The Psychological Novel*), another the influence of individual writers (Hugh Kenner, *The Pound Era*). A complex literary phenomenon, modernism resists an all-inclusive description that either catalogues component phenomena or stamps the movement by a single, recognizable characteristic. Or does it? Gertrude Stein's work puts into relief the single shared assumption that would seem to support the modernist project: the commitment to the Logos, the Word.

Modernist writing focused on the 'agency of language' as a vehicle of meaning. To whatever degree other defining characteristics of modernism operated in juxtaposition to each other, in contradiction to each other, in uneasy alignment with each other, the determined emphasis on the Word or Logos overshadowed all other divergences among these writers. The one sacred belief common to them all seemed to be the indestructibility of the bond between the word and its meanings, between symbol and substance, between signifier and signified. Multiple linguistic experiments – juxtaposition of unlike words, typographical experimentation, translations of language into the dreamworld of the night or the idiolect of the mad – only reinforced the linguistic claims on meaning. The word was the one thing in this modern world that remained sacred: it survived wars, resisted the claims of materialist culture, masked despair and exposed cultural hypocrisy. The word held within it the possibilities of restructuring and rewriting the world. The writer would succeed where God had failed. Indeed, 'the artist as seer would attempt to create what the culture could no longer produce: symbol and meaning in the dimension of art, brought into being through the agency of language' (Friedman, 97–8). The discovery, however, that language could join symbol and meaning, that the artist could forge again the bond between sign and substance that the modern world threatened to dislodge, that despair could never be total as long as language held the power to create meanings, was discovered well before the catastrophe of World War I. It was the founding premise of Imagism, where form and substance were intimately and irrevocably joined through the image, through language. All the various experiments in the working of language, from Imagism through Surrealism, could only confirm what the modernists already knew in their secret hearts: that the power of language was a transformative one, one that could remake the perception of the world and against which the world – despite its wars and crises of belief, despite radical changes in cultural norms, and redefinitions of physical and psychic occurrences – would remain stable. Experiments in language only revealed surprising new ways that language could 'mean', by which language ordered itself, through which language could invest an otherwise bankrupt modern society with sense. James Joyce discovered, early in the writing of *Finnegans Wake*, that he could do anything he wanted with language. He had learned the principles by which language worked, he had broken its 'code', he had mastered its secret, he had harnessed its energy for his own creative vision.[4] He had realized his early dream of becoming an Author, a 'God of creation', the absent center of a linguistic universe.

Notes

1. Elaine Showalter, 'Towards a Feminist Poetics', in *Women Writing and Writing about Women*, ed. Mary Jacobus (New York: Barnes and Noble, 1979), 35.
2. Adrienne Rich, 'It is the Lesbian in Us ...' in "On Lies, Secrets and Silence" *Selected Prose, 1966–1978* (New York: Norton, 1978).
3. Susan Stanford Friedman, *Psyche Reborn: The Emergence of H.D.* (Bloomington: Indiana University Press, 1981), 97-98.
4. Richard Ellmann, *James Joyce* (New York: Oxford University Press, 1982), 702.

* * *

In a later essay, 'Expatriate Modernism', Benstock developed several of these themes. The idea that 'the crisis in faith in social values' was 'a primary effect of World War I' is one she challenged more pointedly: 'It assumes Modernism to a be a war-related phenomenon, so that early Modernist texts anticipate the war and later Modernist texts live in its wake. The roots of Modernism in the nineteenth century and its extension into post-World War II literary practices are overlooked, even denied'.[10] The First World War had a significant effect on American writers, as the devaluation of European currencies after 1918 made Europe, and particularly Paris, an attractive destination; in consequence, the War occupies a different place in American-oriented histories of modernism from that in British accounts. Benstock's 'Expatriate Modernism' also investigates the relation between expatriation and women's sense of exclusion from patriarchal society: 'expatriate' is etymologically rooted in the Latin *pater*, 'father'. A woman's experience of leaving a society from which she is already excluded is very different from a man leaving his native patriarchy. Virginia Woolf's remark in *Three Guineas* (1938) is relevant here: 'as a woman, I have no country'.[11]

Feminism and Modernity

One of the ways that a monolithic modernism has been transformed into a plurality of modernisms is through reflection on modernism's relation to modernity. Perry Anderson's three 'coordinates', summarized in the previous chapter, offer one particularly flexible means of remapping the terrain.

However, one must ask '*whose* modernity'? Not only has modernity developed unevenly across the Western world, but even in a particular place and time it is likely to be experienced differentially. Rita Felski's 'Modernism and Modernity: Engendering Literary History' (1994) engages with exactly this question. Like several of the pieces on modernism and the city, her essay draws on sociology and cultural history. In this it marks a partial break with critics of the previous decade, for whom French literary theory was a more dominant presence. Felski's rejection of the 'comforting notion of "women's time"', a reference to Julia Kristeva's influential essay, is significant in this regard.

Extract from Rita Felski, 'Modernism and Modernity: Engendering Literary History', in Lisa Rado, ed., *Rereading Modernism* (New York: Garland, 1994), pp.191–208.

If I happen to mention to someone that I'm currently writing about gender and modernity, I'm likely to be asked at some later date how my work on modernism is progressing. This symptomatic confusion of a historical period (modernity) with an artistic movement (modernism) is not unduly surprising, given the circular logic that frequently frames the discussion of these two terms. The modernist artwork is seen to offer exemplary insights into the modern condition, crystallizing the contradictory impulses of an epoch through its use of radical and experimental form. For the literary critic, it seems as if the very idea of the modern is synonymous with modernist innovation. On the other hand, our own view of what modernity *is* has itself been influenced by the cultural power, prestige and visibility of particular modernist icons: the fractured figures of Picasso, the parodic gestures of Brecht, the verbal fireworks of Joyce. We typically derive our view of the modern not only from the metanarratives of historical and sociological thought, but also from the primacy of certain exemplary works of high art in received histories of Western culture. The modernist canon, paradoxically, is seen to provide a heightened perception of a historical reality that it has itself helped to construct.

In recent years, the proliferation of writing on the postmodern condition has given way to a renewed interest in this question of the modern itself. The dethroning of the white bourgeois male as privileged subject of history reopens and leaves unresolved the question of what modernity might mean for women and other subaltern groups. If recent feminist criticism is said to involve a return to history, what might history signify in the aftermath of the poststructuralist challenge to epochal unity and unilinear narrative? How can we rethink the temporality of texts in such a way as to do justice to the complexities of gender politics? Here a once-established feminist view of the modern as exemplifying a uniform logic of rationalization, repression and masculine domination no longer appears quite so compelling. Clearly, this is only one possible narrative of modernity, and one that appears signally impoverished in its denial of the conflictual logics of historical processes and the significance of women's agency in those processes. Such an account of historical development assumes the necessary identity of modernity and masculinity, thereby erasing the distinctive and varied dimensions of women's engagements with the discourses and institutions of the modern. By contrast, a number of writers such as Nancy Armstrong, Rachel Bowlby and Elizabeth Wilson are beginning to address the complex and shifting intersections between woman and modernity, the mutual imbrication as well as tension between these two categories. In such analyses, aspects of culture that were previously neglected or else defined as retrogressive rather than authentically modern – romantic love, consumerism, motherhood, fashion, popular fiction – gain dramatically in importance, whereas themes once considered central to the sociocultural analysis of modernity fade into the background. As a result, our sense of what counts as meaningful history is subtly, yet profoundly, altered as the landscape of the modern acquires a different, less familiar set of contours.

In this paper, I can begin to address only one facet of this far-reaching project: that of the relationship between women's modernity and female modernists. The last few years have seen a dramatic upsurge of interest in such writers as H. D., Virginia Woolf, Dorothy Richardson, Djuna Barnes and Gertrude Stein, as feminist critics begin to rediscover and reinterpret a half-effaced lineage of women's experimental art practice. This rediscovery of female modernists in turn poses significant questions for feminist accounts of the relationship between literature and history. Do the works of such writers, as some critics suggest, provide us with an exemplary key to women's distinctive experiences of the modern age? Or should we rather concur with Meaghan Morris's more skeptical response to Kristeva's focus on the literary avant-garde: 'I prefer to study ... the everyday, the so-called banal, the supposedly un- or non-experimental, asking not 'why does it fall short of modernism?' but 'how do classical theories of modernism fall short of women's modernity?' (Morris 202). In other words, how might feminism begin to conceptualize the relationship between historical modernity and aesthetic modernism?

Gender and Modernism

The high point of European and American modernist production is usually seen to encompass the period between about 1890 and 1940. While comprising a broad and heterogeneous range of styles rather than a unified school, modernism is usually associated with such features as decentered subjectivity, aesthetic self-consciousness, subversion of narrative continuity and an emphasis on paradox, contradiction and ambiguity (Lunn 33–7). These formal features of modernist experimentation are explained with reference to the cataclysmic transformations marking the birth of the twentieth century: the rapidity of social and technological change, the crisis of linguistic meaning and scientific knowledge, the death of God, the discovery of the unconscious, the horror of the Great War. To quote one representative view, modernism is 'the art consequent on the dis-establishing of communal reality and conventional notions of causality, on the destruction of traditional notions of the wholeness of individual character, on the linguistic chaos that ensues when public notions of language have been discredited and when all realities have become subjective fictions' (Bradbury and McFarlane 27).[1]

Until recently, however, most writers on modernism have depicted it as a purely masculine affair, drawing on the rhetoric of Oedipal struggle and fraternal rivalry, on close readings of the works of great men and on the history of male avant-garde sub-cultures in order to convey the distinctive qualities of modernist consciousness. With the inevitable exception of Virginia Woolf, women's key contribution to the development of modernist art has been largely ignored. By contrast, emerging theories, histories and readings of modernism by feminist critics are helping to reconstitute the map of literary history, not only by offering gendered readings of the existing modernist canon, but by rediscovering a largely forgotten history of women's experimental art. Such rereadings are serving to complicate already shaky generalizations about the aesthetics and politics of modernist art. The impersonal and abstract formalism of a writer such as Pound, for example, is of little relevance to understanding those female modernists such as H. D. who sought to evoke in their writing the intimate and fragmentary fluctuations of the psyche. The frequent juxtaposition of radical form with traditional gender images among male authors differs markedly from the struggles of many women to think literary and social, linguistic and erotic change together. Indeed, as Sandra Gilbert and Susan Gubar have argued, frequent descriptions of the modern period as a period of deepening despair, paralysis and anxiety fail to address the visions of many female modernists, for whom the idea of the modern was to embody exhilarating possibilities and the potential of new and previously unimaginable sexual and political freedoms.

These feminist revisions of modernism are beginning to uncover women's significant historical contribution to the formation of modernist poetics and practice, while simultaneously developing theoretical accounts of the gender politics of modernist form. In a recent book, for example, Marianne DeKoven posits a profound connection between the historical emergence of late-nineteenth century feminist and socialist movements and the development of modernist literature. 'Modernist writing *is* "rich and strange,"' DeKoven argues, 'its greatness lies in its density and its estranging dislocations' (DeKoven 3). The unresolved contradictions, unsynthesized dialectic and self-cancelling statements of modernist writing are read as expressions of the crises of gender relations which characterized the fin de siècle. The modernist text is thus seen to offer superior insight into the truth of modernity, crystallizing in its very structure the underlying fissures that the realist text glosses over. The 'irresolvable ambivalence' which DeKoven perceives in the works of such modernist authors as Conrad and Woolf serves as a prism through which the radical social upheavals of the period can be more adequately grasped.

Whereas DeKoven directs our attention to the sociopolitical reality behind modernist form, other critics such as Susan Stanford Friedman and Rachel Blau DuPlessis have been more centrally concerned with the links between art and psychic interiority. Here the fascination of modernist artists with Freudian theory and the discovery of the unconscious coincides with the renewed impact of psychoanalysis in recent feminist and literary theory. The experimental text is seen to be less bound by the logic of repression and the demands of the reality principle, providing a conduit for the anarchic impulses of desire. Psycholinguistic theories of meaning are invoked in order to interpret the fissures and contradictions with modernist texts as eruptions of libidinality that threaten and destabilize fixed patterns of gender identity. Modernism's disruption of hierarchical syntax and of linear time and plot, its decentering of the knowing and rational subject, and its fascination with the aural and rhythmic qualities of language thus provide the basis for a subversive aesthetic connected to the maternal and the pre-Oedipal.

These new feminist readings of modernism are distinguished by a careful attentiveness to the formal specificity and complexity of modernist texts by both women and men. Distancing themselves from the more reductive, content-based analyses of early feminist criticism, they explore the tropes, metaphors, wordplays and rhythms of modernist writing as a means of demonstrating its radical questioning of textual and sexual norms. With some notable exceptions, such as Shari Benstock's exemplary study *Women of the Left Bank*, these accounts have, however, been less interested in examining the sociohistorical conditions shaping the production, circulation and reception of modernist texts. Rather, the close reading of the modernist artwork magnifies its exemplary importance as a site of resistive impulses and radical indeterminacy. Through its revelation of a repressed political or psychic unconscious, the fractured text is seen to challenge the authority of dominant social and symbolic structures. In this context, modernism is elevated over realism paradoxically because it is a 'truer' realism; going beyond the superficial stability of surface literary conventions, it reveals that reality *is* fluidity, fragmentation, indeterminacy (Marcus 14).

The writings of modernists such as Woolf or Stein, however, may reveal much more about the artistic subcultures of Bloomsbury and the Left Bank in the 1920s than about some repressed and exemplary Ur-femininity. Such writings offer us elegant and ironic explorations of the fragility of linguistic and sexual norms, embodying the view that human nature is 'elusive, indeterminate, multiple, often implausible, infinitely various and essentially irreducible'

(McFarlane 400). They thereby invoke a particular consciousness of modernity prevalent among the cosmopolitan, bohemian, white, middle- and upper-class female artists of the period, a consciousness shaped by the impact of Freudianism and feminism, of linguistic philosophies and artistic manifestos. However, they tell us much less about those aspects of modernity that shaped the lives of other kinds of women: the modernity of department stores and factories, of popular romances and women's magazines, of mass political movements and bureaucratic constructions of femininity. Such concerns are not of course completely absent from modernism, but they are mediated and refracted through an aesthetic lens of irony, defamiliarization and montage specific to an artistic and intellectual – if not necessarily political – elite of the period. The connection of such an aesthetic to the discourses, images and representations shaping the lives of other classes and groups of women is by no means self-evident. As one critic notes, 'Any adequate reading of the modern period ... must take account of the fact that the debates over women's public freedom, over fashion and femininity, cosmetics and house-cleaning were as essential to the fabrication of modernity as cubism, Dada or futurism, as symbolism, fragmented form or the stream-of-consciousness narrative' (Pumphrey 181). In other words, the version of modernity generated by debates over modernism provides only a partial and limited account of women's multiple and diverse relations to modern discourses and institutions.

If epistemological claims for the truth of modernist writing may be in need of some modification, so, surely, are political ones. Thus, writers such as Gertrude Stein are often singled out by feminist critics for their defiance of linguistic and social conventions and their transgressive rewriting of femininity. Such a reclamation of a female avant-garde tradition can be seen as a necessary part of the feminist rewriting of literary history, allowing for the construction of a counter-canon of radical, inspiratory, female artists. On the other hand, however, it tends to perpetuate a standard dichotomy of literary and political value that identifies formal experimentation as the most authentically resistive practice, with a consequent stigma attached to both representational art forms and to the regressive, sentimental texts of mass culture. Such a future-oriented, progressivist rhetoric, I would suggest, may provide an insufficiently nuanced way of approaching the gender politics of cultural texts within the uneven histories of the modern.

Nonsynchronicity and Modernity

At this point it becomes necessary to unpack the various meanings of modernity in greater detail. While an exhaustive genealogy of the term is beyond the scope of this paper, it should be noted that such meanings differ significantly across national cultural traditions and specific disciplinary frameworks. This ambiguity relates not just to conflicting estimations of the nature and the value of the modern, but also to its location in historical time: The birth of modernity can and has been situated anywhere between the sixteenth and the nineteenth centuries. Rather than a precise historical periodization, in other words, modernity comprises a shifting set of temporal coordinates, a collection of interlocking economic, institutional, cultural and aesthetic strands that emerge and develop at different moments and are often only defined as modern retrospectively.

Here one can usefully distinguish amongst the 'family of terms' associated with the idea of the modern (I am indebted at this point to Mike Featherstone's helpful gloss). *Modernization* typically refers to a pattern of socioeconomic development that originated in Western societies but has since manifested itself in various forms around the globe: scientific and technological innovation, the industrialization of production, rapid urbanization, an ever-expanding capitalist market, the development of the nation state, and so on. *Modernism*, by contrast, defines the specific aesthetic phenomenon to which I have already referred: the emergence of a self-consciously adversarial art practice in late nineteenth-century Europe and America. The French term *modernité*, while also concerned with a distinctively modern experience of dislocation and ambiguity, locates it in the more general experience of everyday life, as exemplified in the ephemeral and transitory qualities of an urban culture shaped by the imperatives of fashion, consumerism and constant innovation. Finally, *modernity* is often used as an overarching label to designate the worldview of an entire historical period, subsuming diverse elements of that period within an epochal vision that defines itself in explicit opposition to the authority of tradition and the past.

It is this epochal and philosophical sense of the term that can cause the most difficulties for feminist theory. These difficulties are twofold: As it is often deployed, the category of modernity is both homogenizing and normative. It is homogenizing in that a complex and uneven array of power hierarchies and social processes is subsumed within a singular logic of historical development that serves to render women invisible. It is precisely this problem that has inspired some feminists to reject the notion of modernity outright. Here, however, the periodizing category is often confused with the events that it claims to describe. After all, it is not the eighteenth or nineteenth century itself that should be seen as totalizing or monologic, but rather the conceptual prisms that have sought to reduce such periods to exemplary realizations of a single idea of reason, history or progress. At the same time, however, the category of the modern also has a normative dimension. Even as it seeks to encompass all aspects of the social within a single historical path, some of these aspects are invariably deemed to be more modern and more advanced than others. In the context of mainstream philosophical and sociological thought, for example, modernity has become identified with large-scale processes of rationalization, alienation and differentiation that are seen as distinctively masculine. By contrast, femininity is equated with either a primitive condition of underdevelopment or an edenic state of nonalienated plenitude, depending on the writer's particular standpoint. In either case, however, femininity is typically positioned outside of the trajectory of historical development; the project of modernity is, it seems, the project of masculinity.[2]

One can, however, begin to imagine the modern differently, as exemplifying an intersection of multiple and nonsynchronous temporalities that cannot be readily subsumed within a uniform logic and seamless narrative of development. Here I have found Homi Bhabha's discussion of the interconnection of race and modernity directly pertinent to my own interest in the historicity of gender – not surprisingly, given the simultaneous positioning of the woman and the native outside of historical time. Querying the elevation of a radical new postmodernity over an outmoded modernity, a theoretically naive maneuver in its unwitting duplication of the very progress narrative it seeks to contest, Bhabha argues instead for an attentiveness to the politics of nonsynchronicity within the modern itself. Such a notion of the nonsynchronous recognizes that the histories of different social groups do not necessarily conform to the same temporal logic, while seeking to disinvest such disjunctures from automatic classification as either progressive or outdated. Rather, it becomes clear that what appear to be similar discourses may in fact have quite diverse meanings and effects; a set of ideologies or narratives which may appear discredited and outmoded for one social group may acquire a new and significantly different function for another. Thus, the dethroning of the white bourgeois male as subject of history brings with it a fracturing or splitting of a previously unified historical narrative, a recognition of the ambivalent temporalities within the modern itself. 'Each repetition of the sign of modernity is different, specific to its historical and cultural conditions of enunciation' (Bhabha, 'Race', 207).

Such a critique of universal history should not, however, be confused with a mere celebration of plural identities or a fragmentation of the social into dispersed and isolated sites. Rather, as Bhabha emphasizes, global simultaneities coexist with particular disjunctures, and particularities are themselves shaped by broader developmental logics. Hence the continuing relevance of the category of the modern as a means of coming to grips with long-term processes of structural change, as well as the equally crucial task of assessing the differing and uneven impact of such processes on given social groups. For feminists, a double stratagem thus comes into play: reconceiving the modern in terms of gender specificity as well as using theories of modernity to explain historically changing forms of femininity. Here a frequent distinction between a masculine time that is evolutionary, historical and linear, and a women's time that is cyclical, monumental and spatial reveals its evident insufficiency. Such a splitting of multiple and complex temporalities into a gendered dualism oversimplifies the nature of women's relationship to modernity, reiterating the familiar gesture of expulsion which projects feminine otherness into an archaic timeless condition.[3]

Feminist theory, in other words, is not adequately served by either totalizing or singular models of history. It is clearly opposed to progress-oriented narratives that position women as lacking or backward in relation to a male-centered path of development. Neither, however, can it take refuge in some comforting notion of a 'women's time', a counter-sphere of nonlinear mythic temporality. Clearly, women's lives have been radically transformed by such quintessentially modern phenomena as industrialization, urbanization, the advent of the nuclear family, new forms of time-space regulation and the development of the mass media, all of which have shaped women's perceptions of self and world at the most intimate and personal level. In this sense, there can be no separate sphere of women's history outside the prevailing structures and logics of modernity. At the same time, however, women have experienced these changes in gender-specific ways that have been further fractured by their various and overlapping identities as worker, consumer, mother, artist, lover, activist, reader and so on. It is these distinctively feminine encounters with the various facets of the modern that have been largely ignored by cultural and social metatheories that remain oblivious to the gendering of historical processes.

Such an understanding of history as *enactment*, as an uneven reproduction of discursive and social relations across different fields, in turn affords a particular understanding of the formation of gender identity. Women's experience cannot be seen as a pre-given ontology that precedes its expression, but fractures into a number of often contradictory, albeit connected, strands, which are not simply reflected but constructed through the 'technologies of gender' of particular cultures and periods (De Lauretis). Rather than inhabiting a quasi-metaphysical field of ineffable plenitude or otherworldly negativity, femininity thus resides in the actuality of its multiple, diverse but determinate articulations, which are themselves crisscrossed by other cultural logics and hierarchies of power. Gender is continually in process, an identity that is performed, enacted and actualized within given historical constraints.

Revisioning Literary History

A theory which links the temporal and spatial particularity of enunciation to broader structural hierarchies in this way has significant consequences for a feminist account of the relationship between literature and history. It allows us to imagine the relationship between modern history and modernist art in terms other than a dichotomous distinction between a repressive patriarchal social totality and a transgressive feminine avant-gardism. As Catherine Gallagher points out, internal disputes within literary studies obscure a remarkable degree of consensus among liberal humanists, Marxists, deconstructionists, and one might add, many feminists, that the literary text is the exemplary site of ambiguity, irony, subversion and self-referentiality (Gallagher 45). By contrast, Gallagher seeks to redistribute some of these standard value judgments of critical theory. The social is itself redefined in terms of a multiplicity of competing discourses, thus taking on some of the heteroglossic energies previously seen as the exclusive property of the aesthetic. At the same time, the transgressive alterity of the literary text is itself reinscribed into power relations through its circulation and exchange as a symbol of cultural capital and prestige. Thus, the parodistic and self-interrogating gesture of modern art may in certain instances be completely complicit with oppressive social relations. In other instances, of course, it may not. The crucial point, however, is that forms of textuality cannot be defined as either intrinsically liberatory or oppressive. Difference is located not in the text itself, but in the temporal and spatial particularity of its enunciation, in the *translation* of the various discourses of modernity into the contingent histories and localities of particular social groups. As Bhabha argues, 'the disruptive temporality of enunciation displaces the narrative of ... homogeneous, serial time ... the meaning and symbols of culture have no primordial unity or fixity ... even the same signs can be appropriated, translated, rehistoricised, and read anew' (Bhabha, 'Commitment', 130).

Such a recognition of the varying temporal logics shaping the politics of cultural and artistic production clearly calls into question the teleological narratives of conventional literary and art history. Within such narratives, artistic styles – romanticism, realism, modernism, postmodernism – are deemed to replace each other in a seamless sequence of development, as each style in turn expresses the underlying truth of a particular epoch or zeitgeist. In the context of modernism, as Griselda Pollock notes, this encourages a classification of certain twentieth-century artworks as advanced, avant-garde and authentically of their time, while others are deemed residual, reactionary or historically irrelevant and hence unworthy of study (Pollock 103). By exploring the gender politics of nonsynchronicity, feminist critics can relativize such oppositions between the old-fashioned and the absolutely new in order to grasp the shifting valences of particular techniques of representation in the history of women's art. The assumption that only one aesthetic is adequate to the truth of the modern – that of avant-garde innovation – gives way to a wider analytical focus upon differing artistic practices which do not simply reflect, but help to construct, the various facets of modernity. As a result, the question of what counts as innovative or radical art cannot simply be read off from a formal analysis of the text in question, but requires a careful account of the particular contextual locations and systems of value within which meanings are produced and circulated.

An excellent example of such an approach can be found in a recent article by Bridget Elliot and Jo-Anne Wallace. The authors ask why it is that the works of writer Natalie Barney and artist Romaine Brooks, both active in the 1920s and 1930s, have been seen as outmoded and second-rate by many feminist as well as mainstream critics. The fetish of formal experimentation in modern art history, they argue, has led to a blindness to other forms of potentially radical practice. Thus Brooks's reliance on the conventions of portraiture has been dismissed as derivative and old-fashioned, reinforcing the stigma often attached to representational art. Within the tradition of *female* portraiture, however, Brooks's paintings offered distinctively different representations of the female self that helped shape the contours of an emergent and newly visible lesbian counter-discourse. Such representations were not oppositional in any absolute way in that a radical critique of sexual orientation coexisted with a largely conservative view of class privilege. Nevertheless, both Brooks and Barney were involved in reproducing and recycling existing images and conventions for new ends in ways that cannot be accounted for by existing art-historical definitions of originality and radicalism. Here Elliot and Wallace's conclusion coincides with my own view that a strategy of representation that may seem old-fashioned from the perspective of the dominant group may acquire quite different meanings and functions when used by a marginal group to challenge previous exclusion.[4]

The implications of such an argument, furthermore, clearly go well beyond the specific domain of the aesthetic as traditionally defined to encompass a wide array of different texts. The isolation of literature as a privileged realm of representation gives way to a recognition of the mutual interactions and contaminations across the diverse fictional and factual, popular and avant-garde texts that have shaped the articulation of modern forms of femininity. Here my claim that the contradictory energies within the modern cannot be restricted to the modernist artwork is obviously indebted to those feminist rereadings of popular culture that have challenged entrenched divisions between an authentically progressive modernist art and a retrogressive, sentimental, mass culture. I have also found Peter Brooks's account of the fundamental modernity of melodrama a compelling one in its engagement with some of the distinctive features of women's popular culture of the late nineteenth and early twentieth centuries. By enlarging our critical vision beyond the standard dichotomy of realist and modernist aesthetics, the work of Brooks, and more recently of feminist critics such as Suzanne Clarke, allows us to come to grips with the sentimental and the melodramatic, not as anachronistic and conservative remnants of the past, but as central and complex dimensions of a feminine modernity.

In conclusion, I would like to return to the question with which I began, that of theorizing the relationship between modernism and modernity. I have suggested that the conflation of cultural radicalism with modernist artwork frequently rests on the prior, and highly problematic, assumption that modern history enacts an inexorable logic of masculine rationalization. By insisting on the multiple temporalities within the modern itself, however, feminism can develop a model of agency that is not restricted to the canonization of female modernism but can address diverse cultural and institutional locations of resistance and critique. For example, feminists who have fought against women's subordination in the public domain have invariably drawn upon the discourses of science and reason as well as those of poetry, on the language game of truth as well as the language game of parody. To argue that their use of such discourses merely reinserts women into the trap of phallocentrism is surely to oversimplify the politics of reiteration. Repetition does not necessarily imply a simple reproduction of a patriarchal logic of identity, insofar as difference is produced in the historical and spatial contingency of particular acts of enunciation. The social positioning and material embodiment of speakers fundamentally affect the political meanings accruing to what might otherwise seem to be similar sets of discourses and ideas, so that women's engagement with the modern leaves neither the categories of femininity nor of modernity unchanged. In this light I would suggest that the various philosophical and political – as well as aesthetic – discourses of modernity are more flexible and heterogeneous in their effects than either their defenders or their critics have allowed. By refusing to ontologize particular spheres of culture and language as either patriarchal or feminine, rational or irrational, conservative or transgressive, we can move towards a more nuanced understanding of the many and changing meanings of the modern for women.

In presenting such an argument, I have not sought to negate the significance of female modernists. On the contrary, paying careful attention to the history of women's experimental art surely forms a crucial part of a feminist politics of culture. By affirming women's historical presence within spheres often seen as the province of men, such as the avant-garde, feminist critics continue to challenge all attempts to confine women to a circumscribed and devalued sphere of activity. My own current work on the modern, for example, includes a reading of the French writer Rachilde, whose parodistic and highly self-conscious representations of vampirism, female sadism, fetishism, necrophilia and the erotics of cross-dressing made her a scandalous yet celebrated figure among the literary intelligentsia of the fin de siècle. Yet this kind of intervention within the sphere of avant-garde art is only one of a continuum of cultural practices, which can by definition only have a limited applicability within a particular sphere. Feminists thus need to pay tribute to women's important contribution to modernist art, while resisting the isolation of the modernist text as an exemplary locus of women's modernity. To use quintessentially avant-gardist notions of parody, performance and experimentation as the basis for a general theory of feminist transgression is to impoverish and to simplify the projects of both modernity and feminism.

Notes

1. For a recent comprehensive survey of modernism as a category within literary theory, see Astradur Eysteinsson, *The Concept of Modernism*.
2. This account is itself a somewhat schematic and totalizing one. For a more detailed investigation of some differing nineteenth-century views of the relationship between 'femininity' and 'modernity', see Felski, 'The Gender of Modernity'.
3. Such a dualism remains evident in Julia Kristeva's otherwise suggestive 'Women's Time'.
4. This argument has also been recently made by Brooke Thomas.

* * *

Felski's *Gender of Modernity* (1995), which presents a fuller version of the above argument, has been an important inspiration to later work. The collection of essays, *Women's Experience of Modernity* (2003), took as its starting point the questions posed by Felski of how 'our understanding of modernity' might look different if, 'instead of taking male experience as paradigmatic', we were to look at female-authored texts.[12]

Sociologically inspired criticism employs a method and a discourse far removed from the tradition of close-reading. The consequences for critical practice are many. With a revised sense of what 'modernity' was, it is possible to revise definitions of 'modernism' in a more inclusive way. (It should be noted, however, that Felski's own preference is to retain 'modernism' in its traditional meaning, and to leave other responses to modernity without a definitive label). As we have seen in the case of Friedman, until the mid-1980s, many critics saw modernism as troubled reaction to the decline of ideological certainties, and such definitions had an inhibiting effect on the understanding of women writers. Critics defining modernism in relation to the city have often constructed urban experience in relation to an unsexed universal human subject for whom the city is simultaneously invigorating and bewildering. The category of 'experience' is problematic. A feminist reassessment of 'modernity' would ask what was distinctive about female urban experience, as well as what was shared.

A dominant concern of feminist critics, difficult to represent in the present anthology, has been the recovery of lost women writers, assessing them, in so far as it is possible, on their own merits. A related exercise has been the recovery of those women writers who were noticed – Woolf and Stein – from the sometimes patronizing praise of traditional critics. Again, criticism focused exclusively on individual writers is not always illuminating with regard to modernism in general, and so has not been represented here. Beyond these projects, however, feminist critics have attempted to reconstruct the conditions which enabled and inhibited women writers in the early twentieth century. 'Modernism' in its traditional definition cannot be taken for granted in such investigations, as it may have incorporated definitions of literary value which tend to marginalize women. For this reason, and for reasons of its intrinsic interest, one of the most recent phases of feminist reassessment has involved the reassessment of 'modernity' seen in writers like Felski.

Chapter Notes

1. Virginia Woolf, 'Romance and the Heart' (1923), in Andrew McNeillie, ed., *Essays of Virginia Woolf*, to be 6 vols. (London: Hogarth Press, 1986 onwards), 3. 367.
2. Wyndham Lewis, *Men without Art* (1934), ed. Seamus Cooney (Santa Rosa: Black Sparrow Press, 1987), 139.
3. Toril Moi, *Sexual/Textual Politics* (London: Methuen, 1985), 42–9.
4. Gillian Hanscombe, and Virginia L. Smyers, *Writing for their Lives: The Modernist Women, 1900–1940* (London: Women's Press, 1987), 2.
5. Aaron Jaffe, *Modernism and the Culture of Celebrity* (Cambridge: Cambridge University Press, 2005), 164–8.
6. Note included in Virago Modern Classics c. 1986–9.
7. Nancy L. Paxton, 'Eclipsed by Modernism', in Lynne Hapgood and Nancy L. Paxton, eds., *Outside Modernism: In Pursuit of the English Novel, 1900–30* (Basingstoke: Macmillan, 2000), 10.
8. Toril Moi, *Sexual/Textual Politics*, 170. See also Bonnie Kime Scott, *James Joyce* (Brighton: Harvester, 1987) and Suzette Henke, *James Joyce and the Politics of Desire* (London: Routledge, 1990).
9. Shari Benstock, 'Beyond the Reaches of Feminist Criticism: A Letter from Paris', in S. Benstock, ed., *Feminist Issues in Literary Scholarship* (Bloomington: Indiana University Press, 1987), 7–29 (p.9). Benstock's essay was first published in 1984 as part of a special issue of *Tulsa Studies in Women's Literature*.
10. Shari Benstock, 'Expatriate Modernism: Writing on the Cultural Rim', in Mary Lynn Broe and Angela Ingram, eds., *Women's Writing in Exile* (Chapel Hill: University of North Carolina Press, 1989), 19–40 (pp.20–1, 21–2).
11. Virginia Woolf, *Three Guineas* (1938), *A Room of One's Own and Three Guineas*, ed. M. Shiach (Oxford: Oxford University Press, 1992), 313.
12. Rita Felski, qtd in A. L. Ardis and L. W. Lewis, 'Introduction', *Women's Experience of Modernity, 1875–1945* (Baltimore, MD: Johns Hopkins University Press, 2003), 1.

Further Reading

Ardis, Ann L., and Leslie W. Lewis, eds., *Women's Experience of Modernity, 1875–1945* (Baltimore, MD: Johns Hopkins University Press, 2003). A collection of essays broadly following the lead of Rita Felski's *The Gender of Modernity* (1995).

Benstock, Shari. *Women of the Left Bank* (Austin: University of Texas Press, 1986; London: Virago, 1987). A biographical approach to female modernist communities.

———. 'Expatriate Sapphic Modernism', in Lisa Rado, ed., *Rereading Modernism* (New York: Garland, 1994), 97–121. An expansion of ideas in *Women of the Left Bank* and 'Expatriate Modernism'.

Broe, Mary Lynn, and Angela Ingram, eds. *Women's Writing in Exile* (Chapel Hill: University of North Carolina Press, 1989). Includes Benstock's 'Expatriate Modernism', Celeste M. Schenk's 'Exiled by Genre', and other valuable essays.

DeKoven, Marianne. *Rich and Strange: Gender, History, Modernism* (Princeton, NJ: Princeton University Press, 1991). Brings psychoanalytic theory and Theweleit's theories to bear on modernism and gender. Joseph Conrad is prominent, along with Gertrude Stein, Henry James, Virginia Woolf, Charlotte Perkins Gilman, and Kate Chopin.

Felski, Rita. *The Gender of Modernity* (Cambridge, MA and London: Harvard University Press, 1995). As noted above, a development of her 1994 essay, and an influential text.

Gilbert, Sandra M., and Susan Gubar. *No Man's Land: The Place of the Woman Writer in the Twentieth Century*, 3 vols. (New Haven, CT: Yale University Press, 1988–94). Somewhat diffuse; essentially a collection of provocative essays exploring key themes. Tends to draw more on feminist scholarship than on modernist.

Hackett, Robin. *Sapphic Primitivism: Productions of Race, Class, and Sexuality in Key Works of Modern Fiction* (2004). On the overlap of markers of race, class and sexuality, and the possibility of using one to code for another. Woolf's *The Waves* is the only high modernist text examined in detail, but there are chapters on figures marginal to canonical modernism, e.g. Olive Schreiner and Sylvia Townsend Warner.

Hanscombe, Gillian, and Virginia L. Smyers, *Writing for their Lives: The Modernist Women, 1900–1940* (London: Women's Press, 1987). A study of feminist publishing networks.

Heilbrun, Carolyn. 'Virginia Woolf and James Joyce', *Hamlet's Mother and Other Women* (New York: Columbia University Press, 1990), 58–88. An essay written in 1982, but first published in this collection, on the history of the belittling of Woolf.

Koestenbaum, Wayne. *Double Talk: The Erotics of Male Literary Collaboration* (New York, London: Routledge, 1989), pp.112–39, examines Pound and Eliot, through a close reading of letters and literary texts.

Lamos, Colleen. *Deviant Modernism* (Cambridge: Cambridge University Press, 1998). Examines the displacement of gender anxieties in the works of Joyce, Eliot, and Proust.

Miller, Jane E. *Rebel Women: Feminism, Modernism and the Edwardian Novel* (London: Virago, 1994). Argues that modernism owes something to neglected Edwardian novels about women and feminism. Contains many insights into obscure sub-genres of the period.

Rado, Lisa, ed. *Rereading Modernism: New Directions in Feminist Criticism* (New York: Garland, 1994). Seventeen essays, some on particular authors, including Dorothy Richardson, Rebecca West, Woolf, Wyndham Lewis, and Hemingway, others on themes such as biography and science.

Rado, Lisa, ed. *Modernism, Gender, and Culture: A Cultural Studies Approach* (New York: Garland, 1997).

Scott, Bonnie Kime. *Refiguring Modernism*, 2 vols. (Bloomington: Indiana University Press, 1995). Concentrates on Virginia Woolf, Rebecca West, and Djuna Barnes.

——, ed. *The Gender of Modernism: A Critical Anthology* (Bloomington: Indiana University Press, 1990). The source of the 'tangled web' diagram above, and a valuable collection of primary texts, some of them previously unpublished.

Stevens, Hugh, and Caroline Howlett, eds. *Modernist Sexualities* (Manchester: Manchester University Press, 2000). 'Sexualities' is somewhat misleading, as the collection contains essays on many aspects of gender roles.

Wolff, Janet. *Feminine Sentences: Essays on Women and Culture* (Oxford: Polity, 1990). In particular, includes her 'Feminism and Modernism', a useful overview of the task that faced feminist critics in the late 1980s.

Works Cited

Armstrong, Nancy. *Desire and Domestic Fiction: A Political History of the Novel*. Oxford: Oxford University Press, 1987.

Benstock, Shari. *Women of the Left Bank: Paris, 1900–1940*. Austin: University of Texas Press, 1986.

Bhabha, Homi K. "The Commitment to Theory." In *Questions of Third Cinema*, eds., Jim Pines and Paul Willemen. London: BFI, 1989.

——. " 'Race', Time and the Revision of Modernity." *Oxford Literary Review*, 13 (1991): 193–219.

Bowlby, Rachel. *Just Looking: Consumer Culture in Dreiser, Gissing and Zola*. New York: Methuen, 1985.

Bradbury, Malcolm, and James McFarlane. "The Name and Nature of Modernism." In *Modernism 1890–1930*, ed. Malcolm Bradbury and James McFarlane. Harmondsworth: Penguin, 1976.

Brooks, Peter. *The Melodramatic Imagination: Balzac, Henry James and the Mode of Excess*. New York: Columbia University Press, 1984.

Clarke, Suzanne. *Sentimental Modernism: Women Writers and the Revolution of the Word*. Bloomington: Indiana University Press, 1991.

DeKoven, Marianne. *Rich and Strange: Gender, History, Modernism*. Princeton, NJ: Princeton University Press, 1991.

De Lauretis, Teresa. *Technologies of Gender*. Bloomington: Indiana University Press, 1987.

DuPlessis, Rachel Blau. *The Pink Guitar*. New York: Routledge, 1990.

Elliot, Bridget, and Jo-Ann Wallace, "Fleurs Du Mal or Second-Hand Roses? Natalie Barney, Romaine Brooks, and the 'Originality of the Avant-Garde.'" *Feminist Review*, 40 (1992): 6–30.

Eysteinsson, Astradur. *The Concept of Modernism*. Ithaca, NY: Cornell University Press, 1990.

Featherstone, Mike. "In Pursuit of the Postmodern." *Theory, Culture and Society*, 5, 2/3 (1988): 195–215.

Felski, Rita. "The Gender of Modernity." In *Political Gender: Texts and Contexts*, ed. Sally Ledger, Josephine McDonagh and Jane Spencer. Brighton, England: Harvester, 1994. 144–55.

Friedman, Susan Stanford. *Ariadne's Web: Gender, Modernity, H.D.'s Fiction*. Cambridge, England: Cambridge University Press, 1991.

Gallagher, Catherine. "Marxism and the New Historicism." In *The New Historicism*, ed. H. Aram Veeser. New York: Routledge, 1989.

Gilbert, Sandra M., and Susan Gubar. *No Man's Land: The Place of the Woman Writer in the Twentieth Century*. Vol. 1, *The War of the Worlds*. New Haven, CT: Yale University Press, 1988. Vol. 2, *Sexchanges*. New Haven, CT: Yale University Press, 1989.

Kristeva, Julia. "Women's Time." In *The Kristeva Reader*, ed. Toril Moi. Oxford: Basil Blackwell, 1986.

Lunn, Eugene. *Marxism and Modernism*. Berkeley: University of California Press, 1982.

Marcus, Laura. "Feminist Aesthetics and the New Realism." In *New Feminist Discourses*, ed. Isobel Armstrong. London: Routledge, 1992.

McFarlane, James. "The Mind of Modernism." In *Modernism 1890–1930*, ed. Malcolm Bradbury and James McFarlane. Harmondsworth: Penguin, 1976.

Morris, Meaghan. "Things to do with Shopping Centres." In *Grafts: Feminist Cultural Criticism*, ed. Susan Sheridan. London: Verso, 1988.

Pollock, Griselda. "Feminism and Modernism." In *Framing Feminism* eds., Roszika Parker and Griselda Pollock. London: Pandora, 1987.

Pumphrey, Martin. "The Flapper, the Housewife and the Making of Modernity." *Cultural Studies*, 1, 2 (1987): 179–194.

Thomas, Brooke. *The New Historicism and other Old-Fashioned Topics*. Princeton, NJ: Princeton University Press, 1991.

Wilson, Elizabeth. *Adorned in Dreams: Fashion and Modernity*. Berkeley: Universtiy of California Press, 1987.

——. *The Sphinx in the City: Urban Life, the Control of Disorder and Women*. London: Virago, 1991.

7

Publishing Modernism

Above the quiet dock in mid night,
Tangled in the tall mast's corded height
Hangs the moon. What seemed so far away
Is but a child's balloon, forgotten after play.
(T. E. Hulme, 'Above the Dock')

In Frank Kermode's account, the symbolists and the imagists held the poem to have quasi-magical powers, lying beyond the realm of rational discourse. It is perhaps ironic, given their imagist technique, that several of T. E. Hulme's poems are concerned with effects of bathos, of the unreachable moon or stars being brought down to a human scale. 'Above the Dock' is a suitable emblem for this chapter. Much recent criticism of modernism has been directed towards understanding how poetry can seem to possess magical powers, and yet how, at the same time, it can be entangled with social experience and ordinary human communication. There are abstract theoretical approaches to such questions, and these have stimulated more text-orientated ways of reading modernist works. It is also possible to approach the entanglement of art in ordinary human experience by considering the materiality of texts, the practical means by which they travelled from authors to readers. Such investigations borrow from longer-established scholarly pursuits such as textual editing and descriptive bibliography, but emphasise the socially produced nature of the text and the pages that embody it. They ask what the text cost to produce, and what financial rewards the author and other agents received. They ask what the printed text looked like, and how the typeface, paper quality, and binding would have signified to a contemporary readership. They ask whether and how the publication was promoted and distributed: what advertisements were placed, and where. They ask which bookshops sold it, and to whom. They use evidence from reception history about reviewers and reviewing. The text is not a commodity, but it is dependent for its life on the book, which is.

One stimulus to such approaches came through a critique of traditional editorial theory. Traditionally, editors of scholarly editions had sought to establish the ideal version of the author's text, without the amendments introduced by editors and the errors introduced in the typesetting process. Such a theory depended on a concept of creativity in which the text sprang fully formed and pristine from the author's brain, only to undergo gradual degradation *en route* to the reader. The textual scholar G. Thomas Tanselle has written that every artefact displays 'the effort of a human being to transcend the human'.[1] It is clear, however, that many authors expected their publishers to correct and punctuate their manuscripts before publication, and that many others engaged in a creative dialogue with sensitive and intelligent editors. A model of communication which sees it as transcendent of the human may lose sight of the ways in which communication is inescapably rooted in the human. The search for a single correct text may be mistaken: it might be better to see each version of a given work as the correct text for its particular social context and historical moment. One of the pioneers of this approach, Jerome J. McGann, has argued that we need to understand the 'textual condition' as irreducibly material and historical.[2]

D. F. McKenzie, another influential thinker and teacher in this area, approached the question with a greater emphasis on bibliography and publishing history. Bibliography, as he defined it, was 'the discipline that studies texts as recorded forms, and the processes of their transmission, including their production and reception'. He argued that this definition, unremarkable as it may seem, had the potential to develop into a 'sociology of texts', if it were recognized that the discipline should include the social as well as the technical aspects of transmission, and if it were recognized that 'texts' might include all manner of recorded information. Bibliography needed to adopt a broad definition of itself: 'any history of the book which excluded study of the social, economic, and political motivations of publishing, the reasons why texts were written and read as they were, why they were rewritten and redesigned, or allowed to die, would degenerate into a feebly degressive book list and never rise to a readable history'.[3]

From the point of view of the literary historian, to investigate the circumstances of production is to expose the processes by which literary canons are produced. Such questions have been important for feminist criticism, and, while works such as Hanscombe and Smyers's *Writing for their Lives* and Benstock's *Women of the Left Bank* are not publishing histories in the usual sense, feminist reassessments of modernist literary history have been one spur to a renewal of interest in the sociology of texts. From the point of view of literary interpreters, to investigate the circumstances of production is also to remove some of the mystique that has come to surround the canonical texts of modernism; it opens the way for fresh interpretation. Most readers of *The Waste Land* are likely to encounter it in a selected or collected edition of Eliot's works, published by Faber and Faber in London, or in an anthology aimed at students. Both forms presuppose the importance of the text. While, in an anthology, an editorial introduction may inform the reader that the text first appeared in the journals *The Criterion* and *The Dial*, and that it was not at that time supplemented by Eliot's notes, such an introduction can never reproduce the quality of the text in its original situation, surrounded by other matter. Readers of 'Tradition and the Individual Talent' may have noticed a strangely redundant recapitulation of the first section at the beginning of the second. For the original readers in 1919, the gap between the two sections would have been experienced as the gap between the September and the December issues of *The Egoist*. Readers of Joyce's *Ulysses* may feel themselves to be in a better situation, as the Oxford World's Classics edition of the novel (1992) provides an affordable facsimile of the first edition. However, the very ease with which it can be obtained contrasts with the difficulty of obtaining a banned book from Paris in 1922. Moreover, although the 1922 Shakespeare and Co. edition was the first edition in book form, the 1922 publication of *Ulysses* did not have the same potential to shock as the publication of *The Waste Land*: chapters had already appeared in *The Little Review* and *The Egoist*, and many who bought the complete book would have been familiar with them already.

The circumstances that surround the production of any given text are usually peculiar to it, and, even when they are to some extent generic, require careful documentation. In consequence, there has been no high-level theorisation of modernist publishing, nor is such a theorisation imaginable; critics continue to engage with the particular circumstances of actual texts, offering more general remarks by way of introduction or conclusion. Nevertheless, one can identify certain parameters or questions that recur. Was the text first published in a periodical, and what processes were involved in its transmission from periodical to book? What relations of payment and patronage were involved in its production? What was the material appearance of the book or periodical in which the text appeared? What does the appearance tell us about the text's intended readership? How far, in producing and marketing the work, were the author and publishers conscious of the existence of a 'modern movement' or of 'modernism'? How far did they aim to make the book or periodical a collectable artefact? Do any of these factors support or modify the idea of a 'great divide' between elite and mass-market literary culture? Do they support or modify the idea of a divide between modernism and the *avant-garde*? What do they tell us about the way that the author or the publishers shaped the modernist canon? Some of these questions apply to all investigations of publishing history; others are more specific to the conditions that prevailed in the late nineteenth and early twentieth centuries.

Lawrence Rainey's *Institutions of Modernism* (1998) has been described as 'one of the most ambitious, stylish and richly researched studies of modernism and publishing' to arise from the renewal of the field in the 1980s.[4] Although the author of these words has also noted flaws in Rainey's arguments, it is a book that is likely to stimulate further research in this area. Its title implicitly questions Peter Bürger's idea of there being a singular 'institution of art', and Rainey is more explicit in his criticism of Bürger within the book. As Astradur Eysteinsson has asked, in the same connection, 'Are we really talking of a unified sphere of social activity, and where do we draw its limits?'[5]

Rainey's research involves some very traditional textual detective work, such as a consideration of the typewriters T. S. Eliot used in the early 1920s, and the different papers on which he wrote his letters. He has located many letters by Eliot not included in the first volume of Valerie Eliot's edition, and he draws upon them as evidence in the essay 'The Price of Modernism'.[6] An early version of the essay appeared in 1989, and an augmented version in *Institutions of Modernism*. The following extract omits a central section in which Rainey considers the three journals in which Eliot considered publishing *The Waste Land*, *The Little Review*, *The Dial*, and *Vanity Fair*. For reasons of space, many of Rainey's endnotes have been reduced in length or omitted.

Extracts from Lawrence Rainey, 'The Price of Modernism', *Institutions of Modernism* (New Haven, CT: Yale University Press, 1998), pp.77–91, 98–106.

The Waste Land

'History is a nightmare,' wrote James Joyce. 'History has cunning passages, contrived corridors / And issues,' murmured T. S. Eliot. It characterizes the epic, declared Ezra Pound, in a transparent reference to his own life's work, *The Cantos*.[1] The modernists were obsessed with history. They mourned it and damned it, contested it as tenaciously as Jacob wrestling with the image of God: 'I will not let thee go, except thou bless me'. Yet if the deity of history had ever deigned to reply to them, it might have said: 'Behold, I set before you this day a blessing and a curse'. Modernism, scholars announced in 1965, had 'passed into history'. The comment appeared in the preface to a textbook; it was in part a historical description and in part a speech act enacting what it appeared to describe, a key moment in modernism's passage to academic respectability.[2] Today, of course, we confess that we live on the hither side of that moment. We take for granted modernism's place in the canon or even equate its progress among the professors with its trajectory through history. Yet in doing so, we forget that modernism flourished long before 1965, that it had erupted into the public consciousness at least forty years earlier, and that its status as a cultural resource had been secured by an array of institutions quite removed from the tepid confines of the academy. The event that epitomized this process was the publication of *The Waste Land* in late 1922, which announced modernism's unprecedented triumph. It generated an avalanche of publicity that marked a crucial moment in its critical fortunes, establishing the poem as a reference point for the assessment of modernism by a wider public. Long before textbooks about it were written, popular and critical understanding of modernism had already been configured by the specific dynamics of transmission that characterized modernism's productive processes and grounded its extraordinary success. The complex events that culminated in the publication of *The Waste Land* articulated both its essential features and its contradictions. It behooves us to reconsider that earlier, more fractured moment, to reconnoiter the problematic terrain suggested by the preposition *into* in the phrase *into history*. For *into* evokes transition, a liminal moment attended by the possibility of failure, a risk that modernism's passage through the 'contrived corridors' might have miscarried.

A core of basic facts about the publication of *The Waste Land* has long been known. In October 1922 it was simultaneously published in two journals: the *Criterion* in England, on 16 October, and the *Dial* in the United States, around 20 October (though in the November issue). In December it appeared in a third form as an independent volume that for the first time included Eliot's explanatory notes, published by the American firm of Boni and Liveright. Together these constituted an event that has become a staple in the legend of modernism's emergence and triumph. Yet a reconsideration of that event might begin by exploring not where the poem was ultimately published but where it was *not* published: in the witty, sophisticated pages of *Vanity Fair*, or the intransigent leaves of the *Little Review*. Though neither has been discussed in connection with the release of *The Waste Land*, both were considered as potential publishers at various points in 1922 as negotiations for the poem followed their unpredictable course. And together these possibilities, with the untold stories that lie behind them, hint at the variety of possibilities of modernist publishing – how modernism negotiated its way among the 'contrived corridors' of its own production.

One might begin by examining an unnoticed occasion in early August 1922, when John Peale Bishop visited the Paris studio of Ezra Pound. Two weeks earlier Bishop had resigned his post as managing editor of *Vanity Fair*, and ostensibly he was traveling on an extended honeymoon after his recent marriage. Unofficially, however, Bishop had come to visit the savage god of modern experimentalism – and to talk business. The topic was the publication of *The Waste Land*, a work that Bishop had never read but whose vicissitudes he had been following for five months. In early March, while still in New York and laboring for *Vanity Fair*, he had received an article for publication from Aldous Huxley that reported the poem's composition and announced – mistakenly, it would turn out – its imminent publication in the *Dial*. An astute and conscientious editor, Bishop had phoned to confirm the report with his colleague and counterpart at the *Dial*, Gilbert Seldes. Seldes was puzzled, having heard nothing about the poem; on 6 March he cabled *Dial* co-owner and chief editor Scofield Thayer, who was then residing in Vienna: CABLE WHETHER ELIOT POETRY COMING SELDES. Three days later Thayer replied: ELIOT REFUSA THAYER. Seldes immediately contacted Bishop and urged him to alter Huxley's article to indicate that the poem's appearance in the *Dial* was, as Seldes expressed it, 'problematical but probable'.[3] More important, Bishop had now glimpsed the growing rift between Eliot and the *Dial*.

By late April 1922, in fact, relations between Eliot and Thayer had completely broken down, and in the wake of their collapse Pound had begun to intervene actively in the search for a publisher. On 6 May 1922 he wrote to Jeanne Foster, beloved companion of New York lawyer and patron John Quinn, occasional contributor to *Vanity Fair*, and friend of Bishop.[4] Pound was soliciting an offer of publication for the poem in the bluntest possible terms: 'What wd. Vanity Fair pay Eliot for "Waste Land." Cd. yr. friend there [Bishop] get in touch with T. S. E., address 12 Wigmore St., London W.1'. By August, when he visited Pound, Bishop was clearly apprised of the situation – indeed, was responding to a suggestion advanced by Pound himself. The two met on 3 August, and two days later Bishop reported their conversation to Edmund Wilson, his closest friend and his successor as managing editor at *Vanity Fair*:

> Pound I met the other afternoon. I found him extended on a bright green couch, swathed in a hieratic bathrobe made of a maiden aunt's shit-brown blanket. His head is quite fine, but his voice is offensively soft, almost effeminate and [illegible word], and his body is rather disagreeably soft. However, he was quite gracious, and the twinkle of his eyes whenever he makes a point is worth something. He held forth for two hours on the intellectual moribundity of England – the old stuff. Here's the thing however – Eliot is starting a quarterly review: he is to run 'Waste Land,' the new series of lyrics in the first number: he and Thayer have split and the *Dial* will not publish it. Perhaps you might want to arrange for the American publication. Pound says they are as fine as anything written in English since 1900. I'm lunching with EP tomorrow [6 August] and will report further.

Whether Bishop wrote again to Wilson as he promised is unknown. On 7 August he left for Vienna, and by the time his letter could have reached Wilson in New York (around 16 August) and Wilson could have replied, his proposal had already been overtaken by events previously set in motion.[5] Yet the seriousness with which it was advanced by both Bishop and Pound should indicate that *Vanity Fair* was considered a serious contender to publish the poem. How serious, indeed, we shall see later.

Bishop's meeting in August also indicates the centrality of Pound's role in prompting and facilitating this abortive plan, recapitulating a story that grows increasingly familiar: Pound was the cultural impresario and entrepreneur who, precisely by virtue of these roles, occupied a critical position at the heart of modernism. It is this position, in fact, that informs the rhetoric in which he articulated his advocacy of *The Waste Land*'s publication: 'Pound says they are as fine as anything written in English since 1900,' wrote Bishop, evidently quoting him verbatim. A month earlier Pound had written to Felix Schelling, his former professor at the University of Pennsylvania: 'Eliot's *Waste Land* is I think the justification of the "movement," of our modern experiment, since 1900'.[6] Bishop had clearly been subjected to a variant of the same argument: the poem was important precisely for its representative quality, and publishing it was not necessarily a matter of appreciating its literary quality or sympathizing with its substantive components – whatever those were – but of one's eagerness to position oneself as the spokesperson for a field of cultural production, the voice of an array of institutions ('the justification of the "movement," of our modern experiment, since 1900'). How much this animated Bishop's interest in the poem is underscored by a curious anomaly in the nature of his enthusiasm, for Bishop was praising a poem that he had yet to read – indeed, whose exact title was still a bit obscure to him ('"Waste Land," the new series of lyrics').

Bishop's imperfect knowledge was not unique. Indeed, insofar as he knew the title of the poem at all, he knew more than Horace Liveright had known when he first advanced his own offer of publication for the poem on 3 January 1922 – the date being notable because it was before the poem had been completed, before it had even acquired its present title. Liveright's interest, like Bishop's, was the consequence not of an aesthetic encounter with a work he had read and admired but of an eagerness to buy a product that promised to meet a series of minimum conditions. Yet what were these conditions?

Liveright's access to Eliot's poem, like Bishop's, had been mediated by Pound. It was he who assumed the function of stage director cuing the characters in their parts: the shy, reserved poet played by T. S. Eliot, the brash young publisher acted by Horace Liveright. Eliot had arrived in Paris on 2 January 1922 and would stay for two weeks, until 16 January. He had come from Lausanne, bearing the disorderly sheaf of manuscripts that he and Pound began to edit and revise, producing a quasi-final version of *The Waste Land*. His arrival coincided with the visit of Liveright, the partner who was guiding editorial policy at Boni and Liveright. Liveright was touring Europe to acquire new works of literature, and his visit to Pound was designed to set their relations on firmer ground. In 1919 he had published Pound's *Instigations*, in 1920 he had undertaken *Poems, 1918–1921*, a volume released only three weeks before his arrival in

Paris, and in the summer of 1921 he had paid Pound for a translation of Remy de Gourmont's *Physique de l'amour*, an engagement that had helped Pound avert financial disaster. Now Liveright hoped to establish more stable relations; he trusted Pound's capacity to recognize new talent, saw him as a valuable link to other authors whose work interested him, and even entertained the idea that Pound's work might prove commercially viable at some point in the future. In turn, Pound thought that he might make Liveright into the principal publisher of modernism and hoped to secure a long-term agreement guaranteeing financial security and time for work.

Poet and publisher courted one another actively. During the six days of Liveright's stay in Paris (30 December 1921–4 January 1922), they saw each other daily. Pound treated Liveright to visits with Paul Morand and Constantin Brancusi, and the young publisher left 'a good impression' on Pound, who felt that he was 'going toward the light[,] not from it'. He was 'much more of a man than publishers usually are', and indeed 'perhaps the only man in the business'.[7] He was 'a pearl among publishers'.[8] The masculine publisher had arrived at an opportune moment. Joyce was seeking an American publisher for *Ulysses*, and Eliot would need a publisher for his unfinished poem. On 3 January 1922, Liveright had an extraordinary dinner with Joyce, Eliot, and Pound to discuss a milestone publishing program. The encounter was productive. With Joyce he agreed to publish *Ulysses* and to give $1,000 against royalties. To Pound he offered a contract guaranteeing $500 annually for two years in addition to translator's fees for any work from French agreed upon by both parties. To Eliot he offered $150 advance against 15 percent royalties and promised publication in the fall list. Liveright was nervous only about length; in a brief note dated 11 January, a week before Eliot had even left Paris, he worried that the poem might not be long enough. 'I'm disappointed that Eliot's material is as short. Can't he add anything?' he pleaded with Pound.[9]

Pound, it is clear, was eager to gather under one roof the principal authors and works of modernism, including Yeats, whom he encouraged to abandon a long-standing contract with Macmillan in favor of Liveright.[10] At stake in these efforts was an attempt to present modernist writings as the articulation of an idiom, a serviceable language that was shared (and in this sense collective in character) yet amenable to a high degree of individuation: the voice of a '"movement," of our modern experiment since 1900'. In short, his activity was characterized by programmatic ambitions and a coherent sense of their interaction with market conditions.

The same traits surface in his dealings with Scofield Thayer, the editor of the *Dial* who was eventually to purchase *The Waste Land*. Pound lobbied forcefully for the poem's publication from the outset, invoking a rhetoric by now familiar. On 18 February 1922, when Thayer and Eliot were still at a preliminary stage of discussion, Pound wrote to Thayer: 'Eliot's poem is very important, almost enough to make everyone else shut up shop'. When Thayer replied (5 March) that he could not comment on the poem's merits, since Eliot had not yet sent him the text, Pound persisted: 'His poem is as good in its way as *Ulysses* in its way, and there is so DAMN little genius, so DAMN little work that one can take hold of and say, "This at any rate stands, makes a definite part of literature"'. *The Waste Land* was represented as a verse equivalent of *Ulysses*, a work that epitomized not just the experiences of an individual, whether author or protagonist, but the modernist claim to a hegemonic position in the institution of 'literature', an ambiguous entity that was distinct yet inseparable from the commercial production of reading matter and discourse. Its merits resided not in a specific set of words or text but in its capacity to articulate this collective aspiration of an elite.

Pound's letter of 9–10 March also outlined practical suggestions that would prove pivotal both for *The Waste Land* and for subsequent literature: 'I wish to Christ he had had the December award,' he hinted. But other solutions were also available. Eliot might be granted 'a professorship', as Robert Frost had recently been. Or he might be given a job on the *Century* or the *Atlantic*, since 'he is not an alarming revolutionary, and he don't, as I at moments, get mistaken for a labour-leader or bolshy bomb-thrower'.[11] Yet it was the hint of 'the December award', the Dial Award for services in the cause of letters (granted for the first time four months earlier), that would bear fruit both for Eliot and for modernism.

Pound's suggestions were advanced just when communications between Eliot and Thayer were breaking down. On 8 March Eliot had telegraphed Thayer that he could not accept less than £50 ($250). Unfortunately, the message was distorted in transmission, and Thayer had received a shocking request for an unprecedented sum: 'cannot accept under !8!56 pounds = eliot + [*sic*]'. In reply, on 12 March Thayer reiterated his offer of $150 for the poem, a figure that was advanced without sight of the manuscript and was 25 percent higher than the $110 to $120 he would normally have paid. (One should recall that income per capita in the United States at this time was about $750 per annum; by contrast, the 1986 income per capita was $14,166. Viewed as a percentage of these figures, Thayer's offer was the equivalent of roughly $2,850 in 1986 dollars.)[12] Not unreasonably, Thayer also asked to receive a copy of the manuscript. In addition, he pointed out the staggering deficits the *Dial* was incurring and argued that it could not alter its policy of 'pay[ing] all contributors famous and unknown at the same rates'. In reply Eliot was curt and frankly insulting, and he proceeded to withdraw the poem entirely:

> Please excuse my not replying sooner to your letter, except by my wire; but I have had a good deal of trouble over letting my flat furnished and moving here, where I shall be till the 20th June. In addition, there have been engrossing personal affairs, and I have been prevented from dealing with any correspondence.
>
> I also took some days to think about your offer, during which time I happened to hear on good authority that you paid £.100 to George Moore for a short story,

and I must confess that this influenced me in declining $150 [£30] for a poem which has taken me a year to write and which is my biggest work. To have it published in a journal was not in any case the way I should choose for bringing it out; and certainly if I am to be offered only 30 to 35 pounds for such a publication it is out of the question.

I have written to Ezra Pound to explain my reasons for refusing to dispose of the poem to the Dial at that price and he concurs with me. ...

You have asked me several times to give you the right of first refusal of any new work of mine, and I gave you the first refusal of this poem.

Opposite Eliot's charge about George Moore, Thayer noted in pencil: 'novellette length/serially'. At the bottom of the letter he also noted: 'Seen Moore work[,] exception for him[;] and because review had offended[,] Moore had already sacrificed several hundred dollars'. True, the *Dial* had paid Moore a higher than usual fee, but in part this was because of the work's length, in part because the *Dial* had been remiss in fulfilling earlier obligations to Moore ('had offended'), thereby forcing him to sacrifice 'several hundred dollars', for which the larger payment had been a form of compensation. But more important was Thayer's remark opposite Eliot's last sentence withdrawing the offer to publish. Thayer vented his tart indignation: 'Not submitted'.[13]

Eliot's allegations about Moore appeared to invoke a principle of equal pay for all contributors. In fact, it was precisely the opposite principle that interested him, as he had explained a few days earlier to Pound: 'I think these people should learn to recognize Merit instead of Senility, and I think it is an outrage that we should be paid less merely because Thayer thinks we will take less and be thankful for it, and I thought that somebody ought to take steps to point this out'.[14] At first sight Eliot's argument may strike us as sympathetic, if only because it seems so familiar. But the issues were rather more complicated: in an important sense the question of aesthetic value is inseparable from commercial success in a market economy, a difficulty that beset every argument for the intrinsic merit of literary modernism. By 1922 literary modernism desperately required a financial-critical success that would seem comparable to the stunning achievement of modernist painting, yet every step in this direction was hampered by market constraints less amenable to the kinds of pressure from elite patronage and investment that had secured the fortunes of Cubism and modern painting. The legal definition of intellectual property – which continued to belong to the author after its purchase by the consumer, in contrast to a painting or a statue, which became the property of the purchaser – posed a series of intractable dilemmas. Patronage could nurture literary modernism only to the threshold of its confrontation with a wider public; beyond that point it would require commercial success to ratify its viability as a significant idiom. That was the question that permeated discussion about publication of *The Waste*

Land: assuming that the poem epitomized the investment of twenty years in the creation of a collective idiom – 'our modern experiment, since 1900' – the protagonists were obliged to find a return on their investment in modernity.

Thayer was shocked and insulted by Eliot's letter of 16 March and refused to engage in further communications with him. Instead he turned to Pound, who was more vulnerable to the threat of losing his job with the *Dial* and might be reproached for having encouraged Eliot's intransigence. On 10 April Thayer demanded that he explain himself: 'Perhaps you will be able to enlighten me as to why you concur with Eliot in his refusal to let The Dial have his poem'. In reply Pound rehearsed the same charge (which Eliot had communicated to him), that George Moore was 'getting special rates from *The Dial* (also Sherwood Anderson),' and he concluded: 'That being the case I can hardly reprove Eliot – if you have put the thing on a commercial basis, for holding out for as high a price as he can get. [Added in autograph in margin:] (i.e. if The Dial is a business house, it gets business treatment. If The Dial is a patron of literature T. contends it should not pay extra rates for 'mere senility', all of which is extreme theory-ism, perhaps, on his part.)' But in passing, Pound added another point. He could hardly attest to the veracity of Eliot's or Thayer's claims, but in general he preferred that the poem be published in the *Dial:* 'I shd. perhaps prefer one good review to several less good ones. I have, as I think you know, always wanted to see a concentration of the authors I believe in, in one review. The Dial perhaps looks better to me than it does to Eliot. (Life in general does.)' As always, Pound displayed a keen understanding of the nexus between cultural ambitions and their institutional actualization.[15] Implicit in his remarks to Thayer was his view that literary modernism could best present itself as a shared language through a centralization suggesting the coherence of its ambitions – the same project that animated his endeavor to unite the works of Joyce, Eliot, Yeats, and himself under the umbrella of a single publisher. Such a project would facilitate the perception of modernism as an idiom both collective and capable of individuation: an identifiable, distinctive, and serviceable language. Yet with equal acuteness Pound also articulated a central dilemma that characterized the *Dial* and the role it might play in any such project. Was the *Dial* a form of patronage, or was it a commercial venture? Unlike the traditional journals that were organs of publishing houses, the *Dial* could shun the increasing diversity and heterogeneity that typified the ordinary journals, presenting itself as a benign and 'disinterested' patron. Its owners, by contrast, were actively engaged in purchasing works of modern painting and sculpture and in this sense were investors in a market commodity whose value was rapidly rising, in part through the efforts of the publicity apparatus that they themselves owned and controlled. Literary modernism, by analogy, was now courting the risk of becoming 'smart art', an investment that would pay and pay big if successful in an expanding market. But pay whom?

The contradictions were irreconcilable. Driven by conflicting imperatives, the participants muddled through the summer of 1922. On 30 April Thayer summarized the state of his relations with Eliot: 'We now correspond only through Pound with whom my relations are also strained, but who seems to desire to keep his job'. Pound himself was more cavalier. On 6 May, while travelling through Italy, he paused to send Thayer a postcard: 'My present impression of the case is "Oh you two Bostonians"'.[16] The surface gaiety, however, was a pose. The same day he also posted his letter inquiring about the price that might be offered by *Vanity Fair*.

Discussions remained stalled throughout the rest of May and June as the participants reconsidered their strategies. On 2 June Pound and Eliot met in Verona, a meeting recorded a few weeks later by Pound in a series of drafts and draft fragments suggesting the substance of their conversations. One of these (later incorporated into *The Cantos*) makes clear that they considered the editorial program of Eliot's new review (still untitled, but soon to be named the *Criterion*), a topic that probably led to another: where to publish *The Waste Land*.[17] From the outset of his undertaking the *Criterion*, Eliot had entertained the idea that it might collaborate with American reviews in simultaneous publication; his first letter announcing the new journal to Pound, written on 12 March, had proposed exactly this: 'I also see no reason why some things should not appear in this and in the Little Review concurrently'.[18] The timing of this suggestion should be noted: it was four days after Eliot had sent his provocative telegram to Thayer and four days before he withdrew his offer of publication to the *Dial*. It was a curious proposal: Eliot had not published in the *Little Review* since 1918 and had never evinced particular interest in its fortunes. Yet if Eliot was already assuming that *The Waste Land* would be published by his own journal in England, then his 12 March reference to the *Little Review* – addressed to Pound, a primary force behind its editorial activity – was probably an effort to suggest a replacement for the *Dial*. The same idea, we may suppose, arose in their discussions at Verona. And quite naturally so, since the editors of the *Little Review* were now in Paris and often in touch with Pound, who had recently assembled a special Brancusi issue for them. Like *Vanity Fair*, the *Little Review* was also a possible candidate for what had now become a project of simultaneous publication.

In the wake of the Verona meeting, the decisive episodes in the story unfolded quickly. Pound returned to Paris on 2 July 1922 and two weeks later received a personal visit from James Sibley Watson, Jr., the co-owner and co-editor of the *Dial* and the partner of Thayer. Two days later Pound reported the meeting to his wife, Dorothy, who was away in London: 'Usual flood [of people visiting]: Lunch with Watson of Dial, on Wed. [19 July], amiable ...wants T's poem for Dial, etc'. The report leaves no doubt about the purpose of Watson's visit: he had come to purchase *The Waste Land*.[19] No doubt he was treated to a variant of

Pound's argument that the poem was 'as good in its way as Ulysses in its way' – resonant, even haunting terms to Watson now that he was in Paris. When he had gone to Beach's bookstore to pick up his own copy (number 33, at 350 francs) of *Ulysses*, he had learned that the last of the 150-franc copies had already soared to 500 francs. Watson and Thayer, after all, had ordered nine copies of the first edition for themselves, the *Dial*, and various staff members (Thayer purchased copy number 73). And Thayer understood the kind of publicity such a work could generate: he had been called as a witness at the *Little Review* trial and seen at first hand its sensational newspaper coverage. Influenced by these events and the assumption that the poem vindicated the project of modern experimentalism, Watson was seized with anxiety that the *Dial* would suffer an ignominious defeat in its effort to position itself as *the* representative of advanced cultural life. What if the poem were published in the *Little Review* or even *Vanity Fair*? The day after his meeting with Pound, Watson flew to Berlin and met with Thayer.[20]

The chief subject of discussion in Berlin was *The Waste Land* and the *Dial*'s prospects for publishing it. Increasingly fearful and excited, the two editors reached an unprecedented decision: they would offer Eliot the second annual Dial Award with its $2,000 prize as payment for the poem, in confidence, but officially they would pay only the $150 that had been their original offer.[21] Literary history records few spectacles so curious or so touching as two editors of a major review offering a figure nearly three times the national income per capita – in 1986 terms, the payment would exceed $40,000 – for a poem neither of them had seen or read. What they had decided to purchase was less a specific poem, more a bid for discursive hegemony. Moreover, their strategy for reaching their goal was exquisitely self-fulfilling: since news of the Dial Award would attract media attention, it would augment the sales of the work and further redound to the credit of the *Dial*.

Seven days after his encounter with Thayer, Watson returned to Paris and met with Pound a second time. Two accounts of the meeting survive, one by Pound addressed to his wife, Dorothy: 'Watson in Thursday [27 July] with Cummings …Wat. troubled at not having T. S.'s poem for Dial'.[22] More revealing is Watson's account, addressed to Thayer:

> Pound has written a [autograph addition:] *very* veiled hint to Eliot. He took me to see Brancusi, who [illegible word] appears very anxious not to be reproduced anymore. I gather this is mostly a pose. Such chittering and apologizing and kowtowing as Pound indulged in I have never before seen. It was disgusting. I pointed out several things I thought you would like, but no, I must take what the master will give. 'You win the victory,' says Brancusi, as though I had been beseeching him for a week. A dam' Pyrrhic victory, by me! …He will, of course, be furious if we don't take any; and Pound will say that we have destroyed his only remaining Parisian friendship. I hope you will write Brancusi rather than

have me go to see him again; if I go, I shan't take Pound, that's sure....Pound looks pretty unhealthy. He handed me two lemons which he recommends very highly and which I send to you on the [canceled: hope] chance you may like one of them.[23]

Pound's letter to Eliot, which has not survived, was written immediately after Watson's visit on 27 July. And though his 'hint' had been '*very* veiled' when issued from Paris, a certain rending evidently took place as it crossed the channel. Eliot understood fully the implications of his request for a typescript: 'I will let you have a copy of the Waste Land for confidential use as soon as I can make one. ...I infer from your remarks that Watson is at present in Paris. I have no objection to either his or Thayer's seeing the manuscript'.[24] Evidently it took Eliot some two weeks to arrange (or type himself) a copy of the typescript, and it was not until 12 or 13 August that he sent it to Watson in Paris. When it arrived, Watson hastily read it and reported the news to Thayer in Vienna:

In response to Pound's letter Eliot has assumed a more conciliatory attitude and has sent on a copy of Wasteland for our perusal. I am forwarding it to you....Anyway I wrote him more plainly about the prize and await his answer. I found the poem disappointing on first reading but after a third shot I think it up to his usual – all the styles are there, somewhat toned down in language [autograph addition:] *adjectives!* and theatricalized in sentiment – at least I thought.[25]

Here again, one is struck by the discrepancy between Watson's initial assessment of the poem and views of it enshrined in later criticism. 'On first reading' Watson found the poem 'disappointing', and after perusing it three times he considered it merely 'up to [Eliot's] usual'. Indeed, in some respects it was below his usual: the diction seemed flat ('somewhat toned down'), the tone 'theatricalized'. Yet all this makes only more remarkable Watson's decision to advance a publication proposal that entailed an unprecedented scale of payment, which he presented to Eliot in a letter of 13 or 14 August.

Eliot responded on 15 August: 'Subject to Mr. Liveright's consent, I would let the *Dial* publish the poem for $150, not before November 1st. In this event I would forego the $150 advance from Mr. Liveright, and he would delay publication as a book until the new year. Possibly he would be glad to do this, on the possibility of the book's getting the prize, which might increase the sales'.[26] His proposal reached Watson late in the afternoon of 16 August. The next day, however, he was seized with panic at the audacity of his proposal and sent a telegram reporting that he could not make up his mind. On 19 August Watson reported both events to Thayer:

Got a letter from Eliot [received 16 August] regretting his haste in thinking we were trying to rob him, and offering us the right of publishing his poem

simultaneously in Dial with its pub. in the Criterion. I find from Pound that Bel
Esprit hasn't enough yet for one year, that it goes to Eliot only when he leaves his
bank and engages in writing exclusively. He gets only a nominal salary from Lady
Rothermere. In other words I don't see why we shouldn't be doing something
moderately popular in giving him the award. But the next day [17 August] I
got a [canceled: cable] telegram saying 'don't act till you receive a second letter'.
Haven't received it yet, though it may come on board tonight when we touch
at Plymouth. So the matter is still in the air. Please don't do anything definitive
without letting me know first. I reach New York probably August 26, and there
is also the telegraphie sans fil.[27]

Pound, clearly, had informed him about the difficult state of Eliot's personal
finances. Watson, in turn, hoped that this might be exploited to the advantage
of the *Dial*, that it might be viewed as 'doing something moderately popular
in giving him the award'. Eliot's actual services to letters (the ostensible justification for the award) and the merits of *The Waste Land* were issues that
never appeared in his discussion of the Dial Award. Instead, Watson cheerily
admitted his view that the proposal was a device intended to garner goodwill
for the *Dial*, a tactic in its struggle to consolidate its position as the dominant
journal of advanced culture.

Meanwhile, on 21 August Eliot sent his own letter to Quinn, apprising him
of the recent developments and leaving open the possibility for action: 'A few
days ago I had an attractive proposal from Mr. Watson of the *Dial* who are
very anxious to publish the poem....They suggested getting Liveright to say
postpone the date of publication as a book, but I have written to them to say
that it seemed to me too late to be proper to make any change now and that I
should not care to trouble either Mr. Liveright or yourself with any questions of
alterations in the contract'.[28] Nine days later Eliot wrote to Pound and reported
his letters to Watson and Quinn:

I received a letter from your friend Watson most amiable in tone ...offering
$150 for the 'Waste Land' (not 'Waste Land,' please, but '*The* Waste Land,' and
(in the strictest confidence) the award for virtue also. Unfortunately, it seemed
considerably too late, as I had the preceding day [14 August] got contract, signed
by Liveright and Quinn, book to be out by Nov. 1st, etc.) I can't bother Quinn
any more about it, I don't see why Liveright should find it to his advantage to
postpone publication in order to let the Dial kill the sale by printing it first, and
there has been so much fluster and business about this contract that I don't want
to start the whole thing up again, so I see nothing but to hope that the Dial
will be more businesslike with other people. Watson's manner was charming, if
Thayer had behaved in the same way the Dial might have published it long ago,
instead of pretending that I had given him the lie as if he was *ehrenfähig* anyhow.
Anyway, it's my loss, I suppose; if Watson wants to try to fix it up with Liveright
I suppose he can, that's his affair. I suppose the move was entirely due to your

beneficent and pacific efforts, which are appreciated. Dam but [why] don't they give the prize to you? More presently.[29]

Notwithstanding the disingenuous demurral by Eliot, the issue was already all but settled. The suggestion he had advanced – that the *Dial* undertake to arrange terms with Liveright – was rapidly realized through the agency of Watson. On 29 August his ship arrived in New York; the next day he received Eliot's letter of 21 August broaching the new arrangement. He set to work immediately, as Gilbert Seldes duly reported to Thayer: 'Watson has just come back and the Eliot affair is taking up much of our time'.[30] A week later he and Seldes met with Liveright in the New York office of the lawyer John Quinn, and there the deal was concluded. Liveright required that the *Dial* purchase 350 copies of the volume at standard discounts, assuring himself an advance sale and adding $315 to the *Dial*'s costs for procuring the poem. But the *Dial* had achieved its victory, and the outcome was a remarkable success.

Liveright reported on the later events in a letter to Pound written on 5 February 1923, eleven weeks after the poem's publication in the *Dial*, seven weeks after his own release of the book-cum-notes: 'God bless you and Cantos IX to XII. If we can get as much publicity from them as The Waste Land has received, you will be a millionaire. The Waste Land has sold 1000 copies to date and who knows, it may go up to 2000 or 3000 copies. Just think, Eliot may make almost $500 on the book rights of this poem. And Gene Stratton Porter makes $40,000.00 to $60,000 a year out of her books. Well, it's all in a life time, so who cares'.[31]

Liveright's sales estimate was remarkably accurate. Yet more important was the tenor of his comments, insofar as it tended to echo Watson's rationale in urging Thayer to take on the poem: the argument that the *Dial* would 'be doing something moderately popular in giving him the award'. Liveright's stress on how much publicity the award-and-publication package received is telling. For by now it should be clear that the publication of *The Waste Land* marked the crucial moment in the transition of modernism from a minority culture to one supported by an important institutional and financial apparatus.

The contours of this transition can best be understood by a rapid survey of the three journals that were considered for simultaneous publication in the United States – the *Little Review*, the *Dial*, and *Vanity Fair*. Each represented a moment in the growth and triumph of modernism. When Eliot suggested in March 1922 that the *Criterion* engage in simultaneous publication with the *Little Review*, his proposal looked back to the world of modernism's past, to its origins in a *littérature de cénacle*, to the heady days of 1917–18 when his own poems and articles had appeared in the rebellious journal. When Pound suggested in May and August that the poem be published by *Vanity Fair*, his proposal looked forward to modernism's future, to the ease and speed with which a market economy could purchase, assimilate, commodify, and reclaim as its own the works of a literature whose ideological premises were bitterly inimical toward its ethos and cultural operations. These distinct moments were mediated by what, in the early 1920s, was modernism's present: the sensibility epitomized by the *Dial*, a form of production supported by massive and unprecedented patronage that facilitated modernism's transition from a literature of an exiguous elite to a position of prestigious dominance. [. . .]

Much can be learned from the interaction among the three journals and their common role as potential publishers of *The Waste Land*. For these journals, it is clear, are best viewed not as antagonists who represented alien or incompatible ideologies but as protagonists who shared a common terrain, whose fields of activity overlapped and converged at crucial points within a shared spectrum of marketing and consumption. Their activity suggests that there was no single or essential feature that distinguished the avant-garde from modernism. These were not irreconcilable poles of a dichotomy, as has been argued by scholars such as Peter Bürger, Andreas Huyssen, or Marjorie Perloff, who have urged that a set of formal devices (montage, for example) constituted a vague yet potent ideology that challenged dominant cultural norms, assaulted the bourgeois concept of art, or anticipated the concerns of postmodernism.[32] Such arguments are sustained only by confining one's attention to formal values viewed in isolation from their social actualization. When seen in institutional terms, the avant-garde was neither more nor less than a structural feature in the institutional configuration of modernism. It played no special role by virtue solely of its form, and it possessed no ideological privilege; instead it was constituted by a specific array of marketing and publicity structures that were integrated in varying degrees with the larger economic apparatus of its time. Its typical endeavor was to develop an idiom, and that, indeed, is how the editors who purchased *The Waste Land* perceived it: they were buying 'the justification of the "movement," of our modern experiment, since 1900'. They were purchasing a work whose scope and pretensions could vindicate an emerging idiom – vindication that could, in a market economy, be ratified only in the conspicuous expenditure of money: whence the Dial Award with its lavish expenditure for a single poem; whence Liveright's decision to double his normal per copy expenditure on advertising for *The Waste Land*;[33] whence Thayer's concern to register every reference to the *Dial*'s announcement of the award and publication of the poem. They were organizing an event that might be 'moderately popular' (Watson), an occasion to generate 'much publicity' (Liveright) – itself the surest commodity of the modernist economy.

The three journals that were considered as candidates for *The Waste Land* formed a tripartite structure within the productive apparatus of modernism. But a similar structure, with analogous kinds of relations, also informed modernism's larger productive economy. In particular, a modernist work was typically published in three forms: first, in a little review or journal; second, in a limited edition of recently collected poems (or as an individual volume if the work was large enough); and third, in a more frankly commercial or public edition issued by a mainstream publisher and addressed to a wider audience. Especially important were the two forms of book publication, the limited and the public editions. These were part of a protocol that had become normative in the course of a complex fusion of heterogeneous and to some degree conflicting traditions of publishing. On one hand, there was the program of multiple publication itself, with its origins in practices that had been developed by Alfred, Lord Tennyson as part of his effort to be a truly national poet: in 1878, to cite only one instance, Tennyson had issued his collected works in both a thirteen-volume Shilling Edition and a single-volume Crown Edition printed in three bindings (plain, gilt, and Roxburgh), a program that effectively addressed a diverse and heterogeneous audience (first-year sales of roughly thirty thousand and sixty thousand, respectively).[34] On the other hand, there was the limited edition, with its origins in the publishing practices of William Morris and the Kelmscott Press. Originally the limited edition had realized a programmatic rejection of the capitalist production of texts. In its production, for example, the role of the publisher was minimized and authorial control was maximized, the standardized design and formatting that had become publishing norms were replaced with special typography and layout, and the altered author-publisher relations were embodied in differing contractual arrangements: instead of a small advance against 15 percent royalties, the author usually received a guaranteed advance against 50 percent profits and a right to republish in another (more commercial) form within a specified amount of time. But the rebellious impulses of the Morris enterprise were Janus-faced: Though Morris had at first intended to produce books solely for his own interest, the sheer cost of his experiments had obliged him to issue them as limited editions that might recoup at least a share of the expenses. The limited editions, in turn, had been rapidly assimilated by the rare and antiquarian book markets that had matured in the nineteenth century, turning them into commodities and potential investments. Thus, while the book increasingly resembled the work of art, as indeed its producers hoped, the work of art itself had already become subject to a commodity economy. Inevitably the limited edition was rapidly appropriated by other constituencies that were not merely indifferent but even hostile to the socialist impulses that had animated Morris.

One constituency was represented by William Butler Yeats, whose sisters founded the Dun Emer (later the Cuala) Press in 1902 with advice and help in typographical design from Emery Walker, a close associate of Morris at the Kelmscott Press.[35] Beginning with *In the Seven Woods* in 1903, all of Yeats's works were published first in a limited edition at the Dun Emer/Cuala, then in a public-commercial edition with Macmillan. In turn, through Yeats's influence on his young admirer Ezra Pound, the practice of publishing books in two forms was adopted by the emerging English avant-garde, for which it became an indispensable instrument. The limited edition established a kind of special productive space insulated from the harsh exigencies of the larger marketplace. It bypassed a broad public receptive to standardized products (such as the six-shilling novel) and suspicious of novelty, and instead addressed a prosperous minority with a luxury good that emphasized innovation and was produced in small quantities (though with high profit margins per sale). It enacted, in other words, a return to an essentially precapitalist economic structure, an artisanal economy producing luxury goods in limited quantities for aristocratic consumption. By the early 1920s it had become a routine step in a tripartite publishing program – journal, limited edition, and public or commercial edition – that was now normative for the avant-garde.

Yeats did not represent the only constituency that appropriated and adapted the ways of Morris. In the United States, similar forms of book production were soon adopted by the ensemble of figures and institutions often labeled the genteel tradition and associated with Boston and Harvard University. The entire process is epitomized in the career of the typographer Bruce Rogers.[36] After working briefly in Indianapolis for a journal called *Modern Art*, Rogers moved to Boston in 1895, where he was soon frequenting circles that evinced a growing interest in fine books and the experiments of Morris. Among them were the Grolier Club, a society founded in 1884 to promote the collecting of fine books, *The Knight Errant*, a review that devoted extensive discussion to William Morris, established in 1892, and the Tavern Club, founded the same year, headed by Professor Charles Eliot Norton, and devoted to fine books. From 1895 to 1912 Rogers worked for the Riverside Press, which acted as Harvard's printer, during which time he assimilated Morris's interest in the well-made book to his anachronistic and classicizing style of typography. After several other jobs, Rogers settled down. Between 1920 and 1928 he was serving as typographical adviser to Cambridge University Press and working for the printing firm of William Edwin Rudge, for which he issued a series of limited editions published by Maurice Firuski, owner of the Cambridge, Massachusetts, bookstore known as Dunster House. Which, strangely, brings us back to T. S. Eliot.

The Waste Land, as is well known, was not published in book form solely by Horace Liveright; nearly ten months later (12 September 1923) it appeared a second time, issued by Virginia Woolf's Hogarth Press in a limited edition of about 460 copies. The date suggests it was an afterthought, as if Eliot had been seeking to retrace a missed step in the normal process of avant-garde publishing. Yet the idea of a limited edition was anything but tardy. Eliot had begun to worry about the precarious implications of his agreement with

Liveright almost immediately after their encounter in January 1922. It was a precipitous move that bypassed the normal rhythms of avant-garde production, in which a work was transmitted from a small elite to an ever wider yet presumably less discriminating audience, and therefore a move that threatened the status of his work. Like anyone who works within a specific institution, Eliot had internalized an array of unwritten protocols considered normal and appropriate. No soone had he completed the poem in its final version (probably in the first week of February 1922) than he began to seek a publisher who would issue a limited edition. On 14 February he lunched with Conrad Aiken and discussed his dilemma. Aiken, the next day, reported their conversation to Maurice Firuski, the Cambridge bookseller and publisher who was issuing Aiken's own book of poetry *The Pool of Priapus:*

> Brief is this note, and chiefly occasioned by a talk with Tom Eliot at lunch yesterday. He has a poem, 450 lines long, wh. I haven't seen. He seeks a publisher who will produce it nicely, and in America, and in a small edition. Firuski! cried I, and there you are. When I elucidated, mentioning [Bruce] Rogers and 450 copies and two years exclusive right and a possible hundred dollars and a beautifully produced book, his eyes glowed with a tawny golden light like fierce doubloons, his hands took on singularly the aspect of claws, his nails tore the table-cloth, and he took your address. ... As I say, I have not seen the poem. It may or may not be good, or intelligible. But, reflect: Eliot has a real reputation; a poem of that length by him will be a real curiosity, even perhaps an event; and he assumes that you will have of course, the English as well as the American market. He may have to get Knopf's permission, as I did, to make the arrangement: he doesn't remember how his contract stands. But that, I fancy, will present no difficulty, for the book is too small for Knopf, and besides Knopf doesn't regard Eliot as a golconda ...Address: 9 Clarence Gate Gardens, London, W. W. 1.[37]

Eleven days later, on 26 February, Eliot himself also wrote to Firuski, pursuing the same question more fully in a letter that has not previously been published.

> Your name has been given me by Mr. Conrad Aiken, who has also shown me a volume of poems by Mr. John Freeman, recently published by you, with the appearance of which I was very much pleased.
>
> I have now ready a poem for which that form of publication seems to me the most suitable. I understand that you issue these books in limited editions, and that for the volumes you take in this series you give a sum down in advance royalty.
>
> My poem is of 435 lines; with certain spacings essential to the sense, 475 book lines; furthermore, it consists of five parts, which would increase the space necessary; and with title pages, some notes that I intend to add, etc., I guess that it would run to from 28 to 32 pages.
>
> I have had a good offer for the publication of it in a periodical. But it is, I think, much the best poem I have ever written, and I think it would make a much more distinct impression and attract much more attention if published as a book.

> If you are interested in this, I should be glad to hear from you what terms you
> would be prepared to offer for it, at your earliest convenience, as the other offers
> for it cannot be held in suspence very long.

Eliot's letter, of course, is fascinating.[38] Among other things, it affects the long-standing debate about the poem's notes, suggesting that they were not merely a late and arbitrary addition imposed by the publishing exigencies of Horace Liveright, as often argued, but an integral part of the work as Eliot himself wished to have it published – a nod to the eighteenth-century tradition of poetry (Alexander Pope's notes to *The Dunciad*, for instance) that had so informed some of the poem's earliest drafts. But more important for our purpose, the letter demonstrates how fully Eliot understood the protocols of avant-garde publishing, as well as how easily those procedures could be assimilated to features already long established in a genteel tradition of private and limited editions. The book of poems by John Freeman (1880–1929) that Eliot had admired was *The Red Path, a Narrative, and the Wounded Bird*, a slender volume of poems issued in 425 copies that were printed for Firuski's Dunster House at the press of William Edwin Rudge, its design executed by Bruce Rogers. The volume was handsome and, like all of Rogers's work, inspired by classical models of typography and design; it suggested a tone of genteel decorum, a distinctly Harvardian note, and yet it sounded that tone with even greater subtlety, as if to hint at an elite within the elite, a more reflective minority with discriminating taste opposed to that of a broader elite that unreflectively assumed its privileges solely on the basis of class, money, and inherited status.

Despite having already received 'a good offer' of $150 for the poem from Thayer and the *Dial*, and despite his preliminary agreement with Liveright in Paris, Eliot preferred to see the work issued in a limited edition: 'I think it would make a much more distinct impression and attract much more attention if published as a book'. To be sure, Liveright had also offered to publish the poem as a book, but a different kind of book: a public and more commercial edition that would directly address a wider audience and not be preceded by the limited edition typical of the avant-garde. That proposal violated the institutional logic of avant-garde production, so much so that Eliot instinctively sought a form of publication that would set matters right. Firuski, however, was slow to respond. Moreover, by 12 March (only two weeks after his letter to Firuski), Eliot had received another note from Liveright reaffirming his interest in publishing the poem. As Eliot promptly informed Pound: 'Liveright wrote to say he wanted it, and I have written asking what he wants to give and telling him the exact length,' adding cryptically, 'and I have other plans also if Thayer doesn't cough out'.[39] The other plans, of course, were those with Firuski, plans presented as an acceptable alternative to publication in the *Dial*. The plans underscore a common procedure of publication: just as the *Dial* occupied the middle position in the tripartite structure of journal publication (between the *Little Review* and *Vanity Fair*), so the limited edition occupied the middle position within the larger tripartite structure of avant-garde and modernist publishing (between journal and commercial edition). Indeed, it was the violation of this logic that distinguished the actual publication of *The Waste Land*, its first appearance in book form being the commercial edition by Liveright, and it was a late and retrospective effort to 'correct' this anomaly that prompted Eliot to issue a limited edition with the Hogarth Press in 1923.

Eliot, it is clear, wanted his poem to be successful, yet not too successful. For the prospect of immediate publication by a commercial firm raised prospects that were largely unimaginable within the logic of modernism. And similar considerations must also have influenced the discussions concerning *Vanity Fair* as a possible venue for the poem. Pound, after first raising the issue on 6 May 1922, presumably reported his action to Eliot during their meeting in Verona a month later, though how they viewed this prospect cannot be stated with any degree of certainty. Still, it is clear enough not only that Pound and Eliot considered *Vanity Fair* a potential publisher but also that *Vanity Fair* considered itself a serious candidate. The journal not only sent John Peale Bishop to discuss the project with Pound in Paris, it even advanced an explicit offer of publication. The proposal appeared in a letter written by Edmund Wilson to Eliot on 1 August 1922. Eliot, in another letter that has not been previously published, replied on 14 August: 'Thank you for your letter of the 1st inst., I should be very glad to do for you such an article as you suggest. For the next two months I shall be far too busy to attempt such a thing, but I think that I should be able to provide one during October or November if that is satisfactory to you. As for a poem, I am afraid that is quite impossible at present as I have only one for which I have already contracted'.[40] Eliot, plainly, was not being straightforward; as yet he had not 'contracted' for *The Waste Land* in a journal at all. Only a day or two before his letter to Wilson, in fact, Eliot had sent off the typescript of *The Waste Land* to Pound and James Sibley Watson, Jr., in Paris, and only the day *after* his letter to Wilson did he write to Watson announcing his terms for the poem: the Dial Award plus $150, provided he publish the poem not much before the book issued by Liveright. Eliot, it is clear, rejected the offer from *Vanity Fair* not because he had 'already contracted' for its serial publication but because *Vanity Fair* represented a degree of commercial success and popular acceptance that would have undermined the status that he was trying to establish for the work. That status, however, was not simply intrinsic or implanted in the poem's text, it was a function of the institutional structures that had informed its production at every step in the poem's life.

In retrospect, we can see that the proposal for a limited edition by Firuski looked not only back to the Cambridge and Harvard environment of Eliot's college days but also forward to modernism's future, to the moment when Eliot would make his triumphant return to Harvard in 1932 and seal the fateful association between modernism and the academy. Yet that association, which has been so much commented on, did not occur naturally or without relations to other changes in the wider culture. By the early 1930s, in fact, all the magazines that Eliot had once considered for *The Waste Land* were dead or dying. The *Little Review* and the *Dial* had both closed in 1929, and *Vanity Fair* would expire in 1936. The Great Depression effectively eliminated the structures of private patronage that had sustained modernism's growth and its emergence as a significant idiom within the languages of the twentieth century. Thereafter, modernism would be slowly but inexorably absorbed into the university, as it had also been appropriated by the marketing and publicity apparatus of *Vanity Fair*.

The price of modernism, in this sense, was a double one. In part, it was a specific and concrete figure epitomized in the sums paid to Eliot for publication of *The Waste Land:* $150 as the price of the poem proper, $2,000 for the Dial Award, a subsequent $580 in royalties on the sales of the Liveright edition, and perhaps another $100 from the Hogarth Press edition – altogether about $2,800, a figure that in modern terms would surely be somewhere between $45,000 and $55,000. (It was two and a half times the $1,150 earned annually by the executive secretary to the editor of *Vanity Fair*).[41] But hidden among such figures was another, more important price: an obscuring of a determinate productive space, the elision of boundaries between specific institutions and wider zones of cultural activity, the illusion that 'art' or 'the poem' or 'the text' had been the central concern of participants whose decisions were consistently made when as yet they had not read a word of the work in question. And not without reason, for the text was largely irrelevant. *The Waste Land* was transmitted not through a conduit that received and reproduced a neutral image of its original but through a multiplicity of social structures driven by conflicting imperatives: it became part of a social event in a discontinuous yet coherent process, an unprecedented effort to affirm the output of a specific marketing-publicity apparatus through the enactment of a triumphal and triumphant occasion. It was not simply the institutions that were the vehicle of the poem; the poem also became the vehicle of the institutions. Like any cultural work, it was more than a sum of meanings implanted or intended by its author; it was inseparable, finally, from the contradictory network of uses in which it was historically constituted.

If nothing else, reconsidering the publication history of *The Waste Land* might prompt us to question the dominant methodology of modern literary studies since roughly the end of World War II. Generations of students have been exhorted to look closely at the poem, to examine only the text, to indulge in a scholastic scrutiny of linguistic minutiae. Yet if we consider more fully the experience of those who actually engaged in modern textual production, assuming that the case of *The Waste Land* tells us anything, we might elect a rather different procedure. Indeed, if we named it in their honor, we could call it the modernist principle of reading and formulate it thus: The best reading of a work may, on some occasions, be one that does not read it at all. Such an extreme formulation would doubtless be misleading. Yet it might remind us that close reading is itself a historical form of activity that appears at a precise moment in the development of professional literary studies and that other kinds of reading are and have been practiced – not least among them the not-reading that was practiced by the editors of the *Dial*, itself a trenchant 'reading' of *The Waste Land*'s place in the structural logic and development of literary modernism. We might learn from them. Reading as we do, instead of as they did, we leave the ambiguous heritage of modernism in history just as desocialized and unexplored as it was before. History may be a nightmare, as the modernists often claimed, but when they entered what Eliot called the 'contrived corridors' of its making, at least they never failed to 'protract the profit of their chilled delirium'.

Notes

1. The quotations are from Joyce's *Ulysses*, Eliot's 'Gerontion,' and Pound's *Guide to Kulchur*.
2. Richard Ellmann and Charles Feidelson, Jr., eds., *The Modern Tradition: Backgrounds of Modern Literature* (New York: Oxford University Press, 1965), vi.
3. Seldes to Scofield Thayer, cable of 6 March 1922 (NHYB, New Haven, Yale University, Beinecke Rare Book and Manuscript Library, *DP*, Box 40, Folder 1138). Thayer to Seldes, cable of 9 March 1922, and Seldes to Thayer, letter of 11 March 1922 (NHYB, *DP*, Box 40, 1139).
4. Ezra Pound to Jeanne Foster, 6 May 1922 (Harvard University, Houghton Library, bMS Am 1635).
5. John Peale Bishop to Edmund Wilson, 5 August 1922 (NHYB, Edmund Wilson Papers, Series 2). The letter is reported by Spindler, *John Peale Bishop*, 68–9, though with numerous errors.
6. Pound to Felix Schelling, 8–9 July 1922, in Ezra Pound, *Selected Letters, 1907–1941*, D. D. Paige, ed. (New York: New Directions, 1971), 180.
7. Pound to Jeanne Foster, 5 April 1922 (Harvard University, Houghton Library, bMS Am 1635).
8. Pound to Quinn, 20 June 1920 (NYPL, New York Public Library *QP*, Box 34, Folder 4).
9. Liveright to Pound, 11 January 1922, NHYB, *BP*, Folder 23.
10. See Liveright to Pound, 12 October 1922, NHYB, *BP*, Folder 23.
11. Pound to Thayer, 18 February 1922, NHYB, *DP*, Box 38, Folder 1070; Thayer to Pound, 5 March 1922, and Pound to Thayer, 9–10 March 1922, NHYB, *DP*, Box 38, Folder 1071.
12. It must be stressed that there is no straightforward procedure that would enable us to establish an exact value in current dollars for a specific income from 1922.

13. Eliot to Thayer, 16 March 1922, NHYB, *DP*, Box 31, Folder 810.
14. Eliot to Pound, 12 March 1922, *Letters of T. S. Eliot*, ed. Valerie Eliot (London: Raber, 1988), 1. 507. Hereafter cited as *LOTSE*.
15. Pound to Thayer, 23 April 1922, NHYB, *DP*, Box 38, Folder 1072.
16. Pound to Thayer, 6 May 1922, NHYB, *DP*, Box 38, Folder 1073.
17. The visit is mentioned in Eliot to Sidney Schiff, attributed to 'early June 1922' by Valerie Eliot in *LOTSE 1*, 528: 'I also went to Verona and saw Pound'.
18. Eliot to Pound, 12 March 1922, *LOTSE 1*, 508.
19. Pound to Dorothy Shakespear Pound, 21 July 1922 (BIUL, Bloomington, Indiana University, Lilly Library *PM.3*, 1922).
20. Thayer to Seldes, 20 July 1922, NHYB, *DP*, Box 40, Folder 1148.
21. Thayer to Eliot, 5 October 1922, NHYB, *DP*, Box 31, Folder 810.
22. Pound to Dorothy Shakespear Pound, 29 July 1922, BIUL, *PM.3*.
23. Watson to Thayer, 29 July 1922, NHYB, *DP*, Box 44, Folder 1260.
24. Eliot to Pound, 28 July 1922, *LOTSE 1*, 552.
25. Watson to Thayer, 16 August 1922, NHYB, *DP*, Box 44, Folder 1260.
26. Eliot to Watson, 15 August 1922, *LOTSE 1*, 560.
27. Watson to Thayer, 19 August 1922, NHYB, *DP*, Box 44, Folder 1260.
28. Eliot to Quinn, 21 August 1922, *LOTSE 1*, 564.
29. Eliot to Pound, 30 August 1922, *LOTSE 1*, 567; punctuation here reproduces the original.
30. Eliot to Watson, 21 August 1922, *LOTSE 1*, 564–5; Seldes to Thayer, 31 August 1922, NHYB, *DP*, Box 40, Folder 1151.
31. Liveright to Pound, 5 February 1922, BIUL, *PM.1*, Liveright.
32. See Peter Bürger, *Theory of the Avant-Garde*, trans. Michael Shaw (Minneapolis: University of Minnesota Press, 1984); Andreas Huyssen, *After the Great Divide* (Bloomington: Indiana University Press, 1986); and Marjorie Perloff, *The Poetics of Indeterminacy* (Princeton: Princeton University Press, 1981; reprint, Evanston: Northwestern University Press, 1983). See also Charles Russell: *Poets, Prophets, and Revolutionaries: The Literary Avant-Garde from Rimbaud Through Postmodernism* (Oxford: Oxford University Press, 1985).
33. See Walker Gilmore, *Horace Liveright: Publisher of the Twenties* (New York: David Lewis, 1970), 38.
34. On the multiple collected editions of Tennyson, see June Steffensen Hagen, *Tennyson and His Publishers* (University Park: Pennsylvania State University Press, 1979), 149–50.
35. See Liam Miller, *The Dun Emer Press, Later the Cuala Press* (Dublin: Dolmen Press, 1973).
36. See John Dreyfus, *Bruce Rogers and American Typography* (Cambridge: Cambridge University Press, 1959).
37. Conrad Aiken to Maurice Firuski, 15 February 1922, Chapin Library, Williams College, T. S. Eliot Collection. I wish to thank Robert L. Volz, Rare Book Custodian, for his kindness in drawing this letter to my attention.
38. T. S. Eliot to Maurice Firuski, 26 February 1922, Chapin Library, Williams College, T. S. Eliot Collection. Mention of this letter is made by Valerie Eliot in

LOTSE 1, 515n.1. I am grateful to Mrs. Eliot for permission to quote this letter in its entirety, and for her kindness in responding to my inquiries. The letter from T. S. Eliot to Edmund Wilson quoted below is also printed by permission of Mrs. Eliot, and both are copyrighted by her.

39. T. S. Eliot to Ezra Pound, 12 March 1922, *LOTSE 1*, 507.
40. T. S. Eliot to Edmund Wilson, 14 August 1922, Beinecke Library, Yale University, Edmund Wilson Papers.
41. For the wages of Crowninshield's executive secretary, Jeanne Ballot, who earned $22 per week, or $1,144 per year, see Cohn Cooper, 'Frank Crowninshield and *Vanity Fair*,' 48. The $2,000 paid to Eliot in the form of the Dial Award was a remarkable figure: the highest sum *Vanity Fair* ever paid was $100, to F. Scott Fitzgerald in 1925 for a short story.

* * *

Peter D. McDonald has criticized the arguments of the *Institutions of Modernism*. McDonald argues that Rainey's presentation of the cultural conditions of modernism rests too exclusively on a sketch of the years 1902 to 1906, and that, had Rainey taken a longer view stretching from 1870 onwards, he might have found that some of the developments he deems unprecedented had been seen in the late nineteenth century.[7] A further point that is of more immediate relevance to 'The Price of Modernism' is the problem of arguing a general case from the specific and peculiar circumstances of individual texts. For example, Rainey uses the instant collectability of the first edition of *Ulysses* as evidence of the retreat of modernists from public culture. One might as well, responds McDonald, argue that the serialization of Conrad's *Nostromo* in a mass-market weekly 'is evidence of modernism's consummate populism'.[8] The discipline of publishing history produces a multiplicity of histories, and, in the case of modernism at least, we have not yet created a meta-historical discourse or 'grand narrative' that can make them cohere.

Chapter Notes

1. G. Thomas Tanselle, qtd. Jerome J. McGann, *The Textual Condition* (Princeton, NJ: Princeton University Press, 1991), 7.
2. Jerome McGann, *The Textual Condition*, 9.
3. D. G. McKenzie, *Bibliography and the Sociology of Texts* (1986; Cambridge: Cambridge University Press, 1999), 12, 13.
4. Peter D. McDonald, 'Modernist Publishing: "Nomads and Mapmakers", in David Bradshaw, ed., *A Concise Companion to Modernism* (Oxford: Blackwell, 2003), 221–42 (p.223).
5. Astradur Eysteinsson, *The Concept of Modernism* (Ithaca, NY: Cornell University Press, 1990), 164.

6. Rainey provides a full list in *Revisiting The Waste Land* (New Haven, CT: Yale University Press, 2005).
7. McDonald, 'Modernist Publishing', 224–7.
8. McDonald, 'Modernist Publishing', 228.

Further Reading

Beja, Morris. *James Joyce: A Literary Life* (Basingstoke: Macmillan, 1992). A biography in the 'Literary Lives' series. The series promised to 'follow the outline of writers' working lives, not in the spirit of traditional biography, but aiming to trace the professional, publishing and social contexts which shaped their writing'. The traditional biographical emphasis on interiority is replaced by a detailed account of the social matrix and the writer's interaction with it. See also Mepham, Nadel, and Worthen, below.

Bornstein, George, —— ed. *Representing Modernist Texts: Editing as Interpretation* (Ann Arbor: University of Michigan Press, 1991). As the title suggests, orientated towards editing rather than the history of publication and reception.

—— *Material Modernism: The Politics of the Page* (Cambridge: Cambridge University Press, 2001). A collection of essays on Yeats, Moore, Joyce, and the Harlem Renaissance, informed by McGann and other editorial theorists and historians of the book.

Dettmar, Kevin J. H., and Stephen Watt, eds., *Marketing Modernisms: Self-promotion, Canonization, Rereading* (Ann Arbor: University of Michigan Press, 1996). Areas covered include Pound, Eliot, Woolf, Joyce, Williams, and authors of the Harlem Renaissance.

Hoffman, Frederick J., Charles Allen, and Carolyn F. Ulrich. *The Little Magazine; A History and a Bibliography* (Princeton, NJ: Princeton University Press, 1946). A pioneering account of a key modernist form.

Jaffe, Aaron. *Modernism and the Culture of Celebrity* (Cambridge: Cambridge University Press, 2005). A study of the relation of literary modernism and modern celebrity culture, focusing on the 'Men of 1914'.

Kaufmann, Michael. *Textual Bodies: Modernism, Postmodernism, and Print* (Lewisburg, PA: Bucknell University Press, 1994). Outside the mainstream, in that it does not explicitly draw on the work of McGann or McKenzie. Includes chapters on Faulkner, Stein, and Joyce.

Lyon, Janet. *Manifestoes: Provocations of the Modern* (Ithaca, NY: Cornell University Press, 1999). Provides a history and a theory of the manifesto as a form from the seventeenth century to the present, with two chapters on modernist and avant-garde manifestos.

McGann, Jerome. *The Textual Condition* (Princeton, NJ: Princeton University Press, 1991). Argues that the embodiment of text in print need not be seen as a process of corruption, and that the ideal of a perfect textual state (prior to corruption) is false. Three chapters examine Ezra Pound and the printed page.

—— *Black Riders: The Visible Language of Modernism* (Princeton, NJ: Princeton University Press, 1993). Examines the debt of modernist poetry to the various 'fine press' styles of printing that were revived in the late nineteenth century. Particular focus on William Morris, Yeats, Pound, Stein, and Riding.

McKenzie, D. F. *Bibliography and the Sociology of Texts* (1986; Cambridge: Cambridge University Press, 1999). Apart from a few remarks on Ulysses, McKenzie has little to say about modernist texts, but his concept of the sociology of texts has been highly influential on the study of books, including modernist ones.

Marek, Jayne E. *Women Editing Modernism: "Little" Magazines and Literary History* (Lexington: University Press of Kentucky, 1995). Considers the roles of seven women in the editing of little magazines (*Poetry, Little Review, The Dial*) and other works, and their interactions with male modernists.

Mepham, John. *Virginia Woolf: A Literary Life* (Basingstoke: Macmillan, 1991). See note for Beja, above.

Morrisson, Mark S. *The Public Face of Modernism: Little Magazines, Audiences, and Reception, 1905–1920* (Madison: University of Wisconsin Press, 2001). Looks at the *English Review, Poetry and Drama, The Egoist, BLAST, Little Review*, and *Masses*.

Nadel, Ira Bruce. *Ezra Pound: A Literary Life* (Basingstoke: Palgrave Macmillan, 2004). See note for Beja, above.

Parkes, Adam. *Modernism and the Theater of Censorship* (New York: Oxford University Press, 1996). Parkes is concerned with censored novels – *The Rainbow, Ulysses, Lady Chatterley's Lover*, and *The Well of Loneliness* – and emphasises issues of gender and sexuality.

Pease, Allison. *Modernism, Mass Culture, and the Aesthetics of Obscenity* (Cambridge: Cambridge University Press, 2000). Pease examines the appropriation of pornography by a late-Victorian poet (Swinburne) and artist (Beardsley) and two modernists (Joyce and Lawrence). In so far as pornography is 'mass culture', her study also responds to post-Huyssen debates.

Peters Corbett, David, and Andrew Thacker. 'Cultural Formations in Modernism: Movements and Magazines, 1890–1920', Prose Studies, 16, no.2 (Aug. 1993), 84–106.

Turner, Catherine. *Marketing Modernism Between the Two World Wars* (Amherst: University of Massachusetts Press, 2003). A detailed study of the advertising policy of five American publishers: B. W. Huebsch, Alfred A. Knopf, Harcourt Brace, Charles Scribner's Sons, and Random House.

Wexler, Joyce. *Who Paid for Modernism? Art, Money, and the Fiction of Conrad, Joyce, and Lawrence* (Fayetville: University of Arkansas Press, 1997). A study of three key modernist novelists as professional authors.

Willison, Ian, Warwick Gould, and Warren Chernaik, eds. *Modernist Writers and the Marketplace*. Basingstoke: Macmillan, 1996. Contains few general reflections on modernism, but is nevertheless a valuable collection of essays on canonical modernists from a variety of angles within the publishing history/sociology of texts framework.

Worthen, John. *D. H. Lawrence: A Literary Life* (London: Macmillan, 1989). See note for Beja, above.

8

Late Modernism

The academic study of modernism began to flourish once its subject appeared to be dead: it is far easier to dissect a corpse when it has stopped moving. What, though, if modernism had not died on the date stated on its gravestone, but had continued to live for some time afterwards? What if a coffin-load of books had been buried in its place? What if it were still alive today, eking out an obscure existence? 'Late modernism' is one possible term for modernism's contemporary phase, though it is a term without an agreed meaning: some critics use it to denote a late phase of modernism within the accepted academic boundaries, others for a still-vital tradition.

If the starting date for modernism has been difficult to pin down, the terminal date has been, on the face of it, easier: 1945. One might say the start of the Second World War, but the end of the war allows not only for the deaths of W. B. Yeats and Sigmund Freud in 1939, but also those of James Joyce and Virginia Woolf in 1941. However, more detailed examination of academic writing and literary reviews reveals a wider range of opinion. For some, the stock market crash of October 1929 was the crucial date, because of the economic depression it ushered in: 'The Great Depression effectively eliminated the structures of private patronage that had sustained modernism's growth and its emergence as a significant idiom within the languages of the twentieth century'.[1] Those who identify the Second World War as the crucial event do so for widely differing reasons. For Perry Anderson, the war was the event that removed the three 'coordinates' of modernism (see above, p.198). Some writers at the time turned on modernist writers for their failure to oppose Nazism or for their elitism: Archibald Macleish's *The Irresponsibles* (1940) was the best known version of the former, while a leading article in the London *Times* on 25 March 1941 marked the latter.[2] Bertrand Russell's remark about D. H. Lawrence's worldview leading 'straight to Auschwitz' suggests that the liberation of the concentration camps was the crucial date; Randall Stevenson has remarked on the extent to which post-war literature is shaped by the knowledge of the Holocaust.[3]

However important 1939 and 1945 were, it seems that their full cultural significance was not understood until some years later. A large number of critics, at the time and later, have identified the mid-1950s as the point of closure. In 1957, Richard Chase declared that, although the avant-garde was not dead, 'its recent phase of "modernism" and experimentalism in the arts is, after forty years of struggle, finally exhausted'.[4] A number of critics, including Graham Hough, Robert Graves, and Karl Shapiro, identified 1957 as the year in which modernism died, to be succeeded by neo-Romanticism. It was the year in which Robert Lowell began to pioneer the confessional mode of writing poetry, and the year in which Ted Hughes' first volume, *The Hawk in the Rain*, appeared.[5] To place the moment of death slightly later, we might note Lionel Trilling's 'On the Modern Element in Modern Literature' (1960), in which he laments the domestication of modern literature through academic study, or, in the same year, Harry Levin's 'What was Modernism?' and Graham Hough's 'Reflections on a Literary Revolution'.[6] Against these regretful but appreciative accounts we must place Karl Shapiro's *In Defense of Ignorance* (1960), in which he lashed out at '[t]he dictatorship of intellectual "modernism"' and 'the sanctimonious ministry of "the Tradition"'.[7]

One might also trace the death of modernism through the growing use of the term 'postmodernism' (with or without a hyphen.) Again, Robert Lowell's poetry marked an important break. For Randall Jarrell, reviewing *Lord Weary's Castle* in 1947, Lowell's poetry was 'a unique fusion of modernist and traditional poetry, and there exist side by side in it certain effects that one would have thought mutually exclusive; but it is essentially a post-or anti-modernist poetry, and as such is certain to be influential'.[8] Charles Olson's use of 'postmodern' in the 1950s has drawn more critical attention,[9] but is more problematic, given Olson's close affinity with Ezra Pound, and the respects in which his major project, *The Maximus Poems*, drew on the documentary, referential quality of *The Cantos*.

Although the emergence of postmodernism threatened to kill modernism, the codification of postmodernism stimulated some critics to reassess the earlier movement. In the early 1980s Ihab Hassan produced several versions of a schematic list of differences between the two movements, excerpted here:

Modernism	Postmodernism
Romanticism / Symbolism	'Pataphysics / Dadaism
Form (conjunctive, closed)	Antiform (disjunctive / open)
Purpose	Play

Design	Chance
Hierarchy	Anarchy
Mastery / Logos	Exhaustion / Silence
Art Object / Finished Work	Process / Performance / Happening
Distance	Participation
Creation / Totalization	Decreation / Deconstruction
[...]	[...]
Hypotaxis	Parataxis
Metaphor	Metonymy
Selection	Combination

Hassan cautioned that the list was schematic and reductive: he cautioned that there was not an impermeable barrier between the two movements, and that differences can shift or collapse.[10] Nevertheless, the list was more striking than the cautionary note. To some critics, it may have reinforced the sense of a rigid divide, but to others it was a provocation. Marjorie Perloff noted in 1992 how difficult it was to see, for example, *The Cantos* as 'closed', adding 'it is the variety of modernisms that strikes us'.[11] Her remark suggests that the pluralisation of modernism that began in the early 1990s was a direct response to the reductive treatment of modernism by proponents of the postmodern.

The term 'high modernism' crept into critical discourse at some point in the mid-1970s, and, as its history is entwined with that of 'postmodernism' and 'late modernism', its emergence needs to be traced. It is used to denote both the core period of modernism, and also a mode of writing. The 'high modernist mode' is usually characterised in terms compatible with the New Critical concept of modernism. Charles Altieri used the term in 1976, distinguishing contemporary American poetry from 'the earlier high modernism of Yeats, Eliot, and Pound'.[12] For Altieri, high modernism was an essentially symbolist aesthetic. The term reached a wider audience in the same year through David Perkins' *A History of Modern Poetry* (1976), a literary-historical survey, the first part of which is titled 'From the 1890s to the High Modernist Mode'. However, Perkins's definition of the high modernist mode as 'a synthesis of different types of poetry' tells us less about the pressures which led to the formation of this particular concept in 1970s criticism.[13] In Altieri's account, it is clear that the term helps to differentiate the poetry of Yeats, Eliot, and Pound from a later poetry which is nevertheless modernistic.

Though 'high modernism' is not used in Bradbury and McFarlane's influential collection *Modernism*, they refer to both the 'high season' of modernism and its period of 'highest intensity'.[14] In architectural criticism, it has been used in a way that implies analogy with the 'high renaissance' and the 'high baroque'.[15] In such uses, the concept of 'high modernism' served to bring shape to a modernist canon that was increasingly diverse in terms of temporal and geographical range. The shape it brings implies a set of aesthetic values, in which the mode of *Ulysses* and *The Waste Land* stands at the peak.

Fredric Jameson has also done much to make the term current. In some of his writings on postmodernism, 'high modernism' is placed in contrast with the later movement, though somewhat ambiguously: in 'The Politics of Theory' (1984), Jameson implies that the need to distinguish 'high or classical modernism' arose only with the advent of postmodernism.[16] This could imply that modernism has now altogether passed, but it could also mean that postmodernism is simply its latest phase, one that has brought the nature of high modernism into relief. Jameson's earliest reference to 'high modernism' came in 1977,[17] but his more significant contribution to the concept appears in *The Political Unconscious* (1981). The section on modernism concentrates on Conrad's early, impressionist mode of modernism. At its conclusion, Jameson writes that:

> After the peculiar heterogeneity of the moment of Conrad, a high modernism is set in place which it is not the object of this book to consider. The perfected poetic apparatus of high modernism represses History just as successfully as the perfected narrative apparatuses of high realism did the random heterogeneity of the as yet uncentered subject. At that point, however, the political, no longer visible in the high modernist texts, any more than in the everyday world of appearance of bourgeois life, and relentlessly driven underground by accumulated reification, has at last become a genuine Unconscious.[18]

Jameson's definition suggests that the aesthetic success of high modernism goes hand in hand with a politically unwelcome ideological success, a retraining of citizens for life in the market economy.[19] Rather than restricting the canon, Jameson's use of 'high modernism' suggests that the broader range of modernisms might be of greater critical and political interest.

'Late modernism' emerges at about the same time, and it would appear that it and 'high modernism' produced each other: the two phrases define each other oppositionally. 'Late modernism' has been used to denote both a transitional period between high modernism and postmodernism, and the continuation of a distinct modernist tradition alongside postmodernism. It first emerges in 1975, very tentatively, though its scope is clearer in 1978 when Robert Kern uses it to discuss similarities between the poetics of William Carlos Williams and Charles Olson. The similarities between the supposedly modernist Williams and the supposedly postmodern Olson suggest that there was no total 'rupture of continuity' between the two movements: 'Is Williams a late modernist, or an early postmodernist?' asks Kern.[20] In the meantime, 'late modernist' had entered into architectural criticism: Charles Jencks in *The Language of Postmodern Architecture* (1977) made a distinction between those architects who treated architecture 'as language', and who were therefore postmodern, and those who did not, the 'Late Modernists'.[21] Jencks used a related term more prominently in the title of his *Late Modern Architecture* (1980). For Jencks architectural late modernism is something more than a transitional period: its distinct stylistic qualities are not a midpoint between high modernism and postmodernism.

In literary criticism, Alan Wilde used the term in 1979, and then in *Horizons of Assent* (1981) in the 'transitionalist' sense.[22] For Wilde, 'late modernism' is roughly equivalent to the 1930s, but also marks an aesthetic that, with its increasing emphasis on surface and flatness, begins to resemble postmodernism.[23] For Fredric Jameson, in his influential *Postmodernism* (1991), late modernism is also transitional; however, periods overlap, so that 'late moderns' can also be 'those who persist into postmodernism'.[24] The term has appeared in recent criticism on W. H. Auden and on women writers of the 1930s: for Michael Murphy, it is a transitional category; for Jean Radford, it is something more complex, as it allows her to escape the reductive equation of the 1920s with high modernist formalism and the 1930s with realism; nevertheless, she does not see modernism as a movement surviving the Second World War.[25]

The first extract is taken from Alan Wilde's *Horizons of Assent*, a study of the function of irony in high modernist, 'late' modernist, and postmodernist fiction. Wilde distinguishes three main modes of irony. The first, pre-modernist phase, he calls *mediate irony* as it serves to mediate 'a fundamentally satiric vision'. Man may exist in a fallen state, but 'harmony, integration, and coherence' can still be reclaimed, and satire can assist. E. M. Forster represents for Wilde the last phase of mediate irony before modernism. In the second mode, *disjunctive irony*, the world appears 'inherently disconnected and fragmented'. At its furthest point of development, disjunctive irony 'both recognizes the disconnections and seeks to control them'. It cannot help us regain paradise, but by shaping the fragments into 'an equal poise of opposites' it substitutes aesthetic wholeness for the lost harmony in life. The idea is derived from New Critical theories of poetry. The third mode, suspensive irony, which Wilde connects with postmodernism, 'abandons the quest for paradise altogether', and simply accepts 'multiplicity, randomness, contingency, and even absurdity'.[26]

Extract from Alan Wilde, 'The Epistemology of Late Modernism', *Horizons of Assent* (Baltimore and London: Johns Hopkins University Press, 1981), pp.106–9.

"I daresay many people are not what they are thought to be."
"Most of them are what they are known to be," said Naomi.
– Ivy Compton-Burnett, *A Heritage and Its History*

Writing to Isherwood after he had twice read *Mr Norris Changes Trains*, Forster expressed, along with 'much admiration and enjoyment', a slight hesitancy, a hint of polite discomfort. It was not, he suggested, 'altogether [his] sort of book', because, as he went on to explain, it 'dwells on the contradictions rather than the complexities of character, and seems to reveal people facet by facet whereas The Memorial if my memory serves tackled strata'.[1] The reservation illuminates a fundamental difference between the practice and conceptions of Forster's generation and Isherwood's – or, to adopt now somewhat broader, more flexible categories, between those of modernism (early modernism, as it will henceforth be convenient to call it in this chapter) and late modernism. And it does something besides. Read today, the comment seems prescient of a still more radical change: the replacement of 'well-made-characters who carry with them a fixed identity, a stable set of social and psychological attributes – a name, a situation, a profession, a condition, etc.' (characters like Forster's, presumably) by what Raymond Federman, speaking for one group of postmodern writers, calls 'word-beings', fictional creatures who 'will be as changeable, as unstable, as illusory, as nameless, as unnamable, as fraudulent, as unpredictable as the discourse that makes them'.[2]

The postmodern attitude, along with the full force of its disintegrations, may be left until later. Forster's own position is clarified in *Aspects of the Novel*, where, in the discussion of flat and round characters, he reveals his preference for those who, growing and changing, are 'capable of surprising in a convincing way' (p.54) and who, because of their roundness or complexity, their comprehensible depth, make more vivid what Forster sees as the major consolation of fiction, its ability to provide us with 'a reality of a kind we can never get in daily life' (p.44). The contrast between the unsatisfactoriness of life, in which 'we never understand each other' (p.32), and the power of art to create a structured space of belief, or desire, and thus to 'solace us' (p.44) runs throughout *Aspects* (and through most of modernism): a gloomy leitmotif which, by way of its insistence on the integrity of the fictional self at least, simultaneously expresses Forster's rearguard action against the instabilities of his world and reveals the nostalgia that underlies his aesthetic theories.

How legitimate it is to generalize from those theories is another matter, however, since in the treatment of character in his own fiction Forster is probably the least innovative of the early modernists. Virginia Woolf's celebrated announcement of a change in human character 'in or about December, 1910'[3] sounds a bolder, if chronologically debatable, note. And the boldness is, of course, justified by her indefatigable experimentation. There is no need here to dwell on her various techniques of interiorization, on the ways in which the recesses of consciousness are made, ever more obliquely, available to the reader's inspection in order to demonstrate how significantly she alters the presentation of character. The question is whether in her work – or Joyce's or Conrad's or Ford's – the consequences of that change manifest themselves in a conception of character that is substantively different from Forster's.

Consider *Jacob's Room*. 'It is no use trying to sum people up', her narrator writes. 'One must follow hints, not exactly what is said, nor yet entirely what is done'.[4] And later: 'It seems that a profound, impartial, and absolutely just opinion of our fellow-creatures is utterly unknown' (p.70). But we will misread the book badly if we assume that Woolf – or her narrator – simply throws up her hands in despair at the mystery of Jacob. Undoubtedly character has become a good deal more fluid and shifting, more elusive than Forster suggests, but what is at issue is the same epistemology of the hidden. For Woolf, and other early modernists, the tracking down of a character's (or for that matter, the world's) unity or truth, its essence, proceeds through more covert levels of being and demands from the reader more strenuous efforts at comprehension. But however speculative and inferential knowledge has become, the center – Jacob, 'a young man alone in his room' (p.94) – holds; and we are enjoined 'to penetrate' (p.92) the reality behind phenomena: 'the skeleton [that] is wrapped in flesh' (p.162). Character has not been dissolved, nor has the self been lost; though both have become manifestly more problematic. Indeed, the faith in some central core of being not only persists, as in Forster's theory, it is deepened by the mystery of that core's recessive presence; and the passion of the quest for dozens of Jacobs in the early decades of the century, translated into an almost obsessive concern with depth, is validated by just that underlying belief that, at some level, character remains intact.

With the thirties, as I've already argued, there is a noticeable, if somewhat ambiguous, shift to surface and along with it, inevitably perhaps, a change in attitudes toward character and characterization. If for no other purpose than to avoid a too tidy mapping of developments and movements, it should be recalled that there are proponents of surface throughout the century – Pound, Hulme, the imagists, Wyndham Lewis, Isherwood, Orwell, Waugh, to choose names almost at random and to stop for the moment with its fourth decade – but it is only toward the end of the twenties that one can begin to identify the rise of something like a new sensibility. The qualification of 'something like' is deliberate: we are dealing with a reaction against modernism by writers who retain a good many modernist presuppositions and strategies and who, in a variety of ways, differ from one another as much as they do from the early modernists. The common thread, I suggested a moment ago as well as in chapter 3, is a new attention to surface, and that concern implies something still more interesting: a reversal – dramatic even when incomplete or unintended – in epistemological assumptions, which (rather than the attractions of political commitment, say, or the attempt to escape the confinements of the ivory tower) defines in the most basic way both the moral program of late modernism and the aesthetic retrenchments of its writers.

The reversal is fundamental. The early modernist tendency to connect truth with depth, and at times to sacrifice the phenomenal for the reality that is presumed to underlie it, gives way to a counterassertion that truth inheres in the visible. Thus the repeated announcements that things *are* what they seem – provided, of course, that the seeing eye is clear, unclouded by the mists of convention and tradition, free from the deliberate evasions and sentimentalities of the past and from the still more insidious deceptions of the self. The trick, then, is to see not more deeply but differently. The interrelated problems of knowing and evaluating present themselves less as inherent than accidental: matters not of necessarily limited but of correctably faulty perception. Auden's prewar poems, with their repeated injunctions to look, see, consider, and watch are relevant here: a repeated summons to attention or, more accurately, to attentiveness. And so too, to press into service again Auden's and Isherwood's usefully revealing play, is *The Dog Beneath the Skin*, that brash, mordant contribution to the ideology of the thirties, in which Alan Norman undertakes a circular journey that describes a movement not toward complexity (Alan is in all essentials unchanged) but toward 'disenchantment'. He learns, in other words, to recognize what was always there, obvious and unconcealed: the genteel corruption of his native village, which only a fatuously naive reading of appearances keeps him from recognizing at the start.

Reading appearances correctly is, in fact, the project of late modernism, its enemy not a failure to penetrate to some more authentic reality but a sort of cultural or psychological dyslexia, which blurs vision itself. Sifting appearances rather than plumbing depths: that is the nature of the enterprise and the central clue to its redefinition of character in terms of the 'facets' and 'contradictions' Forster found in *Mr Norris*. But to limit oneself to Isherwood, even to take into account other members of the Auden circle, is to construct too narrow a base for the change I've been describing. And there is, I think, no need to. Taking as central an epistemology of surfaces brings into the fold of late modernism other writers, some of the thirties, some not, whose relation to Auden and his friends is tangential at best and in some cases nonexistent, but whose inclusion actually establishes the validity of the category.

Notes

1. Forster's letter, in which this remark appears, is quoted by Isherwood, in *Christopher and His Kind, 1929–1939* (New York: Farrar, Straus & Giroux, 1976), pp. 203–4. It can also be found in P. N. Furbank's *E. M. Forster: A Life*, 2 vols. (London: Secker & Warburg, 1977–8), 2:209, where an additional sentence is included.

2. Raymond Federman, "Surfiction – Four Propositions in Form of an Introduction," in *Surfiction: Fiction Now … and Tomorrow*, ed. Raymond Federman (Chicago: Swallow Press, 1975), pp. 12–13.
3. Virginia Woolf, "Mr Bennett and Mrs Brown," in *Collected Essays*, ed. Leonard Woolf, 4 vols. (New York: Harcourt, Brace & World, 1967), 1:320.
4. Virginia Woolf, *Jacob's Room*, new ed. (London: Hogarth Press, 1954), p. 29.

* * *

Wilde goes on to consider irony in Ivy Compton-Burnett's novel *Manservant and Maidservant* (1947), finding her characters to be, '[n]otwithstanding their participation in still recognizable plots', 'creatures of language, caught reflexively in a web of words'.[27] By beginning with irony, and the reader's experience of it, Wilde creates a literary history that is closely tied to the text, yet which is capable of generating large generalizations, at least with regard to fiction. In this, his work is more subtle and flexible than that of some more theory-inspired literary historians. Nevertheless, its 'transitionalist' assumption that modernism was replaced by postmodernism is open to question.

Critics who believe that modernism died in 1939 will have been surprised to see the jacket of J. H. Prynne's *Poems* (1999) describe him as 'Britain's leading late Modernist poet'; the statement was retained on the 2005 edition. Moreover, for such critics, one of the more surprising publications of 2004 will have been the anthology *Vanishing Points* with its subtitle 'New Modernist Poems'. With a few exceptions (John Ashbery, Roy Fisher, and Prynne), the poets it collects were born after 1939, and most of the poems date from the 1990s or the first decade of the twenty-first century. In his introduction, Rod Mengham insists that 'they are not postmodernist, but late modernist writers'. The statements that immediately follow this sentence provide some pointers to a definition of late modernism.

> Each writer has a definable project, her or his work refers to a body of concepts even if the literary method employed appears to be non-referential; each has maintained a significant degree of contact with the speaking voice, even when the manner in which the speaking voice has dominated the history of literature in English is challenged and complicated; all are concerned with working in or against the grain of the literary forms and genres that have evolved in the course of that same history.[28]

The 'definable project' implies that, even when impersonal in their poetics, the poets acknowledge a concept of authorial identity. Their 'contact with the speaking voice' certainly does not imply that they are expressive or confessional, or that they subscribe to a Wordsworthian ideal of poetry as 'a man speaking to men', but it distances them from postmodernist 'language' poetics. Their connection to a tradition also distinguishes them from the avant-garde, though this should not be taken to imply that (in Peter Bürger's terms), they do not question the institution of art. The tradition they connect to is often defined as being the modernism not of Pound and Eliot but of Pound and Williams.[29] They are also, Mengham goes on to say, committed to examining 'the political scope of poetry' and to critiquing 'the discourses of power'.[30] While to a New Critic, such a definition may seem to have separated them from the high modernist writers (producers of autonomous art-works), at the present moment the political urge of high modernism is clear enough. Late modernism, however, takes cognisance of high modernism's disastrous flirtation with authoritarianism; it continues high modernism with the benefit of Adorno's critiques.

Although the poets in *Vanishing Points* have sometimes been described as 'neo-modernist,' or as 'the Cambridge School,' 'late modernism' is the most widely used label.[31] In using the term in his *Late Modernist Poetics: From Pound to Prynne* (2005) Anthony Mellors finds it necessary to distinguish his concept of 'late modernism' from that of critics who see it as a transitional category. Prominent among the 'transitionalists' is Tyrus Miller, whose *Late Modernism* (1999) concentrates on work dating from the late 1920 and the 1930s, and examines Wyndham Lewis, Djuna Barnes, Samuel Beckett, and Mina Loy as 'exemplary late modernist figures'.[32]

Extract from Anthony Mellors, *Late Modernist Poetics* (Manchester: Manchester University Press, 2005), pp.19–24.

In a basic sense, albeit one that has been consistently overlooked by literary historians, late modernism can be said to refer to the continuation of modernist writing into the war years and until at least the end of the 1970s. This was a period of consolidation, when substantial parts of long poems begun before 1939 were composed and published, and new ones were written: *The Cantos, Four Quartets*, Louis Zukofsky's *A*, David Jones's *The Anathemata*, William Carlos Williams's *Paterson*, Charles Olson's *The Maximus Poems*, Basil Bunting's *Briggflatts*, Charles Reznikoff's *Testimony: The United States*. Many poets whose modernist aesthetic was formed earlier in the century developed it beyond the 1930s; some, like Marianne Moore, found a wide audience in later years; others, such as Lorine Niedecker, Nelly Sachs and Bunting, did not publish major work until long afterwards. More significantly, new conceptual, concrete and performance-based poetries inspired by the avant-garde gained international recognition, and younger poets working within modernist traditions appeared, among them Olson, Jack Spicer, Edmond Jabes, Robert Duncan, Anne-Marie Albiach, Paul Celan, Andrea Zanzotto, Charles Tomlinson, Rosemary Tonks and J. H. Prynne. A curiosity of periodisation is the general acceptance almost to the point of hegemony of post-1945 modernism in the plastic arts, music, and architecture. Paintings by, say, Roger Hilton and Gillian Ayres, or compositions by Pierre Boulez and Iannis Xenakis, are seen as unquestionably modernist even though they were made in the 1950s and 1960s. This does not apply to poetry, where late modernist writing is commonly regarded by academic critics and metropolitan reviewers alike as anachronistic. Arguing the case in 1959 for Charles Tomlinson as the 'most profound and original of all our postwar poets', Donald Davie noted that 'he refuses to join the silent conspiracy which now unites all the English poets from Robert Graves down to Philip Larkin, and all the critics, editors, and publishers too, the conspiracy to pretend that Eliot and Pound never happened'.[1]

Identifying the lineage in this general way is fine as far as it goes, since the newer poets and poetics mentioned here are clearly not antimodernist. But why not simply call them 'postmodernist'? Confining late modernism to the tail-end of the 1920s and the 1930s, Tyrus Miller argues that

> At first glance, late modernist writing appears a distinctly self-conscious manifestation of the ageing and decline of modernism, in both its institutional and ideological dimensions. More surprising, however, such writing also strongly anticipates future developments, so that without forcing, it might easily fit into a narrative of emergent postmodernism ... It is as if the phosphorescence of decay had illumined the passageway to a reemergence of innovative writing after modernism ... the double life of this significant body of writing – its linkage forward into postmodernism and backward into modernism – has not, by and large, been accounted for by critics of this period.[2]

According to this version of events, modernism – Miller means Anglo-American modernism – was moribund shortly after peaking in 1922, rallied for a brief time in parodic form, then expired with the onset of World War Two; its reemergence as innovative writing is therefore best described as postmodern. While there are precedents for this account in the work of postwar poets – Charles Olson, for example, saw himself as a 'post-modernist' reclaiming the negative landscape of *The Waste Land* for a positive mythos[3] – the thesis begs serious questions. First, Miller's sophisticated analysis of the cultural factors contributing to the 'end' of modernism shows that World War One was a crucial turning-point in the development of high modernist aesthetics, but it says next to nothing about its imputed demise by 1939. According to Miller, the modernists' emphasis on autonomy and formal originality was compromised by the arrival of the political avant-gardes, which threw into crisis any belief in the separation of art from its political context, and was made archaic by the highly technologised dissemination of mass culture, so that 'By the immediate postwar years, the movement had already begun to show signs of drift, neoclassical reaction, and nationalist or provincialist obstacles to new ideas. A cunning dialectic had seized the process of stylistic innovation, confronting the writer with historical limits and threatening to exhaust modernism's dynamic from within'.[4] What Miller reductively terms *the movement* appears to have been over almost before it had begun. His contention that modernism's already fragile self-image was eroded by the forces of modernity (history, trauma, technocracy, metropolitanism, commodification, the 'loss of a stable, authentic social ground'[5]) inverts the relationship of modernism to modernity. While it is fair to say that the onward march of modernity put increasing ideological pressure on an aesthetic dedicated to preserving cultural aristocracy, it can hardly account for the decline of modernism since modernism is nothing if not a response *to* modernity and is therefore an effect *of* modernity. Furthermore, Anglo-American modernism was not simply reactionary; as Lawrence Rainey argues, writers colluded with the commodification process by turning their works into

> a commodity of a special sort, one that is temporarily exempted from the exigencies of immediate consumption prevalent within the larger cultural economy, and instead is integrated into a different economic circuit of patronage, collecting, speculation, and investment – activities that precisely in this period begin to encroach upon and merge into one another in unexpected ways. Modernism marks neither a straightforward resistance nor an outright capitulation to commodification but a momentary equivocation that incorporates elements of both in a brief, necessarily unstable synthesis.[6]

The circuit of patronage, subscriptions, private presses and limited editions which floated many of the early modernists show these writers negotiating with capitalist society in a 'creative' fashion. A world in which the literary work escapes mechanical reproduction only by becoming that economically ambiguous entity the 'priceless' artefact is already the world of modernity, and the modernists' hostility to exchange value did not prevent them from trading themselves and their products as elite goods. While such niche marketing was a way of maintaining the value of traditional art in an increasingly popularised cultural marketplace, the modernists were painting themselves into a corner, and Miller argues that the period *entre deux guerres* left them struggling with a 'lack of credible options' for self-justification.[7] This explains the turn to bitter caricature, parody and satire in the fiction of Wyndham Lewis, Mina Loy, and Djuna Barnes, which Miller sees as definitively late modernist, but by making these baroque tirades stand for the decline of modernism in general he ignores the fact that key figures like Pound and Eliot were carried beyond the 1930s by the success of imprints such as James Laughlin's New Directions and Faber & Faber, and a new phase of modernist writing came into being after 1945 with the transformation of elite support for the arts into the more liberal circuit of universities and colleges, public endowments, and the rise of influential 'little' magazines and presses (now published by artists themselves instead of wealthy benefactors). Modernism carved out a vital, if still marginal, space within mass culture, a space that was to coincide for a brief period with popular counterculture.

Secondly, limiting late modernism to the inter-war period means that Miller has to use the term postmodernism to define all 'innovative writing after modernism'. For all his caveats about assigning periods and commonalities, he is sure that modernism 'peaked much earlier' in literature than in the other arts, and that its 'undeniable historical "decline"' (the scare quotes are not applied to this word elsewhere) led to a variety of aesthetic positions united only by their abandonment of any belief in the transcendent power of art.[8] The modern world finally rushed in, leaving a heap of broken images that could not be restored by a higher symbolism. Late modernism toyed with the fragments for a while before giving way to postmodernism, which registers 'the disenchantment of modernism's redemptive myth', deconstructing its desire for unity and totality.[9] However, Miller concurs with Fredric Jameson and Alan Wilde in seeing the need for late modernism as an intermediate concept that would finesse the period of transition between modernism and postmodernism. According to Jameson, it is exemplified by Nabokov, Beckett, Olson and Zukofsky, who prolonged 'unseasonable forms' through an exilic period spanning the 'two eras'; Wilde argues that it is a weakened form of modernist irony that fails to offer any 'embracing vision' or 'symbolic compensation for the chaos and impoverishment of modern life'.[10] Rather than complicating the relationship between modernism and postmodernism, late modernism reifies Jameson's assumption that there are indeed two separate eras, and Wilde seems convinced that modern life is chaotic and impoverished without pausing to consider that this narrative of disorder and decline may itself be a modernist fiction. These difficulties apart, the fixing of a 'transitional' moment remains problematic. Miller has already taken issue with Charles Jencks's periodisation of late modernism (an architectural style, in coexistence with postmodernism, emerging in the 1960s) by arguing that its literary form occurs between 1926 and 1939; but Miller ought not to subscribe to Jameson's literary periodisation either, since it includes Charles Olson, a poet of the 1950s and 1960s. (And Samuel Beckett, included by Jameson and also one of Miller's examples, wrote his major work after 1945, though because his formative years were the 1930s he can be safely included in Miller's late modernist canon.) The point, however, is not that Miller should not be able to revise the time-line, but that periodisation becomes increasingly difficult to contain. If late modernism presages the end of modernism, why does it seem so interminable? And if postmodernism is the condition of art after modernism, how is it that poets such as Olson can be seen as belonging to both the late modernist and postmodernist camps? The simple answer is that Miller's periodisation is more flexible than it appears; as he states, late modernist writing 'might easily fit into a narrative of emergent postmodernism'. But then why bother with the between-the-wars apparatus and the death of modernism thesis in the first place? My own view is that Miller is right to see the emergence of a troubled, belated version of Anglo-American modernism, but wrong to confine it to the period before World War Two, and wrong to define it as essentially negative in character:

> Late modernist writers were divested, by political and economic forces, of the cultural 'cosmos' – the modernist 'myth' in its most encompassing sense – in which the singular works of high modernism seemed components of an aesthetically transfigured world. In the empty spaces left by modernism's dissolution, late modernists reassembled fragments into disfigured likenesses of modernist masterpieces: the unlovely allegories of a world's end.[11]

If modernism dissolved, its solution was more modernism. If it died, it had an afterlife, not an empty space. Its survival is still a powerful force in aesthetic practice and cultural ideals today. I argue that although late modernists were disenchanted by the political consequences of high modernist culture, they continued to uphold its mythic values against perceived threats to selfhood and community. Late modernism is therefore antithetical to postmodernism, which discloses myth as ideology and treats the 'self' as a construct, not as an organic unity. A complicating factor here is that, when presented in the context of mid-century American poetics, postmodernism is sometimes defined as an organic theory of culture based on the rejection of modernist values. Charles Altieri has argued that the turn to postmodernism in American poetry – under which heading he includes poets as diverse as Robert Lowell, Denise Levertov, Gary Snyder, Robert Bly, Richard Wilbur, Theodore Roethke and John Ashbery, but which coalesces in the 'immanent' poetics of Charles Olson and Robert Duncan – is a fundamental rejection of modernism's humanist drive to order and commprehend experience through the aesthetic appropriation of myth.[12] By contrast with modernism, the postmodernists use myth as a way of intensifying experience, with or without order. Mythic consciousness attests to cosmic powers that allow 'man' to recover and participate in natural processes rather than symbolising the division between human significance and a chaotic universe. The shift is towards an ecological theory of artistic enactment: man is created by his environment, therefore he must learn to express himself through it, to permit himself to be expressed by it, instead of trying to beat it into shape. Hence the value placed on 'primitive' ways of seeing by Olson, Duncan, Snyder, Jerome Rothenberg and other key figures in the development of ethnopoetics; while these poets take it as read that native peoples are more in touch with the rhythms of the natural world than modern man, they insist that their interest in the primitive is not 'directed backward toward a past viewed with feelings of decontextualized nostalgia' but reflects

> a concern over the last two centuries with new communalistic and anti-authoritarian forms of social life and with alternatives to the environmental disasters accompanying an increasingly abstract relation to what was once a living universe. Our belief in this regard is that a re-viewing of 'primitive' ideas of the 'sacred' represents an attempt – by poets and others – to preserve and enhance

primary human values against a mindless mechanization that has run past any uses it may once have had.[13]

The scare-quotes around the words 'primitive' and 'sacred' evince a cautious approach to subject-matter swamped in romantic and modernist cliché. The new 'totality' of which Robert Duncan speaks (again in inverted commas) runs counter to modernism in seeking to include 'all the old excluded orders ... the female, the proletariat, the foreign; the animal and vegetative; the unconscious and the unknown; the criminal and failure – all that has been outcast and vagabond must return to be admitted in the creation of what we are'.[14] Even so, the enterprise is belatedly modernist and somewhat disingenuous, since it is firmly attached to atavistic beliefs about the decline of an organic, whole, concrete, centred, religious mode of being into the fragmented, alienated, abstract and mechanised culture of modernity. Far from being 'antihumanist', as Altieri claims, this postmodernism continues to set denatured consciousness against 'primary human values' which approximate religious experience (and which are essentially masculine: it is always modern man who is in search of a soul, even when soul is placed under the sign of woman). In order to distance this divine ecology from modernism, Altieri talks up the latter's subjective investment in the poetic act, eliding its classicist, antihumanist strain. The real difference is political: an inclusive, liberal humanist and/or revolutionary project versus an exclusive, conservative and/or fascistic one; yet both orientations are problematically ordered by the ideological figure of 'totality'.[15] This retention of the totality and its sublimation into the religious is what I would call the condition of late modernism. Postmodernism, for better or worse, destroys immanence. Altieri's definition, for all its sophistication and its reservations concerning the plausibility of a sacramental poetic in an age that no longer believes in ritual absolution, is inadequate because symptomatic of the very condition it claims to analyse. If it is the case that 'While incarnation for the moderns exemplified the union of form and significant value on an otherwise empty and chaotic natural world, God for the contemporaries manifests himself as energy, as the intense expression of immanent power', Altieri's postmoderns remain adepts of the Hermetic order that Surette identifies as a key element in the birth of modernism.[16]

Notes

1. Donald Davie, *The Poet in the Imaginary Museum: Essays of Two Decades*, ed. Barry Alpert (Manchester: Carcanet, 1977), 66–7. The situation can't have been quite that bad, otherwise Tomlinson, Bunting and Roy Fisher would never have been published by Oxford University Press. Until *very* recently, however, J. H. Prynne's poetry was

regularly invoked by reviewers in *The Times Literary Supplement* wishing to dismiss what they saw as the crazy and irrelevant world of British modernism.

2. Miller, *Late Modernism*, 7.
3. See George Butterick, *A Guide to* The Maximus Poems of *Charles Olson* (Berkeley: University of California Press, 1980), xxii–v.
4. Miller, *Late Modernism*, 29.
5. Miller, *Late Modernism*, 43.
6. Lawrence Rainey, *Institutions of Modernism: Literary Elites and Public Culture* (New Haven: Yale University Press, 1998), 3.
7. Miller, *Late Modernism*, 32.
8. Miller, *Late Modernism*, 9; 24.
9. Miller, *Late Modernism*, 125.
10. Quoted in Miller, *Late Modernism*, 10–11. The texts referred to are Jameson's *Post-modernism, or, The Cultural Logic of Late Capitalism* (Durham: University of North Carolina Press, 1991) and Wilde's *Horizons of Assent: Modernism, Postmodernism, and the Ironic Imagination* (Baltimore: Johns Hopkins University Press, 1981).
11. Miller, *Late Modernism*, 14.
12. Charles Altieri, 'From Symbolist Thought to Immanence: The Ground of Post-modern American Poetics', in Paul A. Bové, ed., *Early Postmodernism: Foundational Essays* (Durham, N. C.: Duke University Press, 1995). 'Early Postmodernism' is yet another variation on the theme. In submitting a revisionary theory of late modernism, I hope I am providing a critique of conceptual and periodic vagueness rather than merely adding to the proliferation of jargon. On a recent BBC Radio 4 programme, John Cage was described as 'a pre-post-modern ironist'.
13. Jerome Rothenberg and Diane Rothenberg, *Symposium of the Whole: A Range of Discourse Towards an Ethnopoetics* (Berkeley: University of California Press, 1983), vii.
14. Quoted in Rothenberg and Rothenberg, *Symposium of the Whole*, xii.
15. In a later survey of poetry from after World War Two, Rothenberg writes that 'There was a breakdown, first, of the more tyrannical aspects of the earlier literary and art movements, and a turning away with that from totalizing/authoritarian ideo-logies and individuals', which led to 'an alliance for some with previously suppressed religions and cultural forms: shamanism, tantrism, sufism, kabbala, peyotism, etc.'. Introduction to Jerome Rothenberg and Pierre Joris, *Poems for the Millennium: The University of California Book of Modern and Postmodern Poetry. Vol. 2: From Postwar to Millennium* (Berkeley: University of California Press, 1998), 5; 7. 'Totality' is now linked with modernist authoritarianism instead of being a synonym for 'holism'. Late modernists struggle constantly to redefine terminology, either to prise them-selves free of reactionary language or to make their own atavism more acceptable to public scepticism.
16. Altieri, 'From Symbolist Thought to Immanence', 106.

* * *

Charles Olson in 'Projective Verse' rejected Eliot's 'symbology' in favour of Pound's use of documentary fact. Mellors considers Olson's approach to metaphor and to the construction of the poem as an 'embodied enigma' (p.30), before returning to the issue of late modernism.

Extract from Anthony Mellors, *Late Modernist Poetics*, pp.41–5.

Late modernism, then, identifies a specific, belated appropriation of high modernist culture which distinguishes it from neo avant-grade tendencies and postmodernism. Postmodern facture is based on the assumption that art is always already enmeshed in ideology, 'its deconstructive thrust ... aimed not only against the contemporary myths that furnish its subject matter, but also against the symbolic, totalizing impulse which characterizes modernist art'.[1] Responding to this account, Tyrus Miller argues that postmodernism's radical cultural scepticism 'may be more melancholy than liberating', in that to 'lose faith in the modernist myth was to recognize that art no longer had an essential function; that it could offer no comprehensive answers to spiritual, sexual, or social problems. It was to realize that the arcadia of the text or painting was not significantly different from anywhere else. Art offered no secure position from which to oppose oneself to the rest of the social world'.[2] While Miller's jeremiad may be prone to the belated modernist thinking it seeks to explain, it does highlight a very real crisis in the arts today, and nowhere more so than in the world of poetry, which offsets its often debilitating sense of irrelevance by retreating into identity politics and tribal warfare. The cultic nature of aesthetic mysticism arguably causes rather than transcends sectarian conflict, and the turn to postmodernism represents a general movement away from the belief in art as religion by other means. For many poets and critics, however, the identification of art with one form of redemptive power or another is so complete that any attempt to think otherwise negates the very essence of poetry. The late modernist poets whose work forms the basis of this study write on the brink of the postmodern abyss. Distinct, if not entirely separate, from mid- to late twentieth-century poetries which are indebted to modernism but which return to highly individualised, bardic modes of expression, such as the neo-romantics of the 1940s, the Beats of the 1950s, and the countercultural visionaries of the 1960s, they continue to affirm a redemptive aesthetic that links *poesis* with occult power while disowning the reactionary politics of high modernists such as Yeats, Eliot and Pound. Art remains the alternative order to rationalising and inevitably compromised political systems. But precisely by being posited as alternative to the political, art becomes the political alternative, albeit in the guise of 'culture'. Upholding culture, the province of the organic community, over the institutionalised collectivity, late modernism misrecognises its own temporal investment in the political. As with high modernism, its aesthetic ideology is its equation of culture with nature. Late Modernism is belated because it maintains this ideology while dissociating it from Anglo-American modernism's complicity with authoritarian regimes.

Not surprisingly, the experience of World War Two testified to the political consequences of literature that regularly attacked women, Jews and the poor, and represented dictators as cultural saviours; after this, few poets of any political tendency were about to fly the modernist flag as if nothing had muddied the pitch.

The chastening effect of the war years did not, however, bring an end to aesthetic practice predicated on the belief that modernism remains in essence a vital force which bespeaks cultural redemption. Sara Blair points out that understanding the commitment to modernism 'as necessarily linked with conservative, fascist, or right-wing political ideals is to miss the contestatory nature of Modernism's investment in form, technique, and literary value. If the landscape of modernity reads to Eliot and company as a symbolic wasteland, it appears for other writers to be a Mecca, a metropolis of multivalent possibilities'.[3] Significantly, this plea for the heterogeneity of international modernism finds its retort to the reactionary 'men of 1914' (Hulme, Eliot, Pound, Lewis) in the progressive *mêlée* of literary life in contemporary New York, with its preference for the 'American now' over the nostalgic quest for pre-modern values in the Cradle of Civilisation. The division is a little simplistic; it would be complicated by, for example, the more wide-ranging approach taken by Peter Nicholls's *Modernisms*.[4] Even so, Blair is right to see in the United States a positive reception of modernity disinclined to equate formal innovation with aesthetic autonomy.[5] Late modernism owes much of its impetus to the American scene, which maintained an avant-garde trajectory long after the taste for experimentation in Britain had soured. Charles Olson and the poets associated with Black Mountain College tended towards liberalism and the left, as did the San Franciscan coterie of Robert Duncan, Jack Spicer and Robin Blaser, and therefore appear less in tune with the Anglo-Americans Eliot and Pound than with Williams, Zukofsky, Niedecker and Oppen, who all rejected Pound's Eurocentrism, had no truck with his fascist politics, and produced work devoid of any occult or mythic investment. And when British poetry rediscovered modernism in the 1960s, notably through J. H. Prynne and what is erroneously known as the 'Cambridge School', its primary inspiration was the United States, with its seemingly unbroken tradition of artistic experimentation. Contributors to the fugitive journal *The English Intelligencer* looked forward to a time when the British Isles would no longer be separated from America, symbolically reinstating their 'union' before continental drift fragmented the great land mass of Pangaea. Yet Pound remains the crucial influence on these poets, ostensibly because his work remained the galvanising force it was for the early modernists; the *Cantos* were an ongoing project, demanding endless exegesis in the tradition of great occult texts, and the disturbing relationship between his luminous teachings on poetic form and his postwar status as a deluded Nazi propagandist represented a huge challenge to reconcile aesthetic mysticism with contemporary ethics and politics. Until recent (postmodern?) times, liberal and left-wing poets were reluctant to equate the mythic sources of modernist tradition with the rise of fascism, even though such links were latent in the mystery cults – such as that of the *Georgekreis* – rampant in Central Europe in the late nineteenth and early twentieth centuries.[6] As Robert Casillo argues,

> Many Poundian values which critics do not consider fascistic – among them his anti-monotheism, his agrarian paganism, his solar worship, his phallocentrism, his anti-feminism, his attacks on abstraction, his anti-usury, his longing for mythical rather than historical time, his demand for a ritualized and hierarchical society – are characteristics of many versions of fascist ideology.[7]

Olson, a regular visitor to St Elizabeth's, the mental hospital where Pound was held from 1946 to 1958, deplored the ravings of 'this filthy apologist and mouther of slogans which serve men of power', whose belief in the degenerateness of Semitic cultures was 'the same god damned kind of medical nonsense Hitler and the gang used with the same seriousness, the same sick conviction'.[8] Yet he kept faith with Poundian tradition, embracing the occult, archetypal, and diffusionist cultural theories of such figures as Spengler and Jung and their mentor Frobenius, described by Janheinz Jahn as 'a pace-setter of fascism'.[9] Pound's preferred word for 'culture' is Frobenius's term *Paideuma*, used throughout his writings after 1930 to distinguish between sick and healthy racial, linguistic, aesthetic and economic 'symptoms'.[10] Olson's distinction between the moribund West and the potential resurgence of archaic consciousness is similarly indebted to Frobenius's *Kultursymptome*. An entire (late modernist) tradition of poetry and scholarship has dissociated aetiological theories of history and anthropology from their racist origins, seeing them as benignly pluralist and relativist alternatives to rational thought. That the two academic journals devoted to Pound studies are called respectively *Paideuma* and *Sagetrieb* ('myth-drive') testifies to the esteem in which these key concepts are held.

Eva Hesse's remark that although 'Pound is known to have expressed … some of the most purblind and even vicious notions of his generation, it is no less true that his fundamental instincts and sympathies have generally been sound' is both revealing and symptomatic of wider trends in the interpretation of modernism.[11] Hesse's assumption that humanist 'instincts and sympathies' outlast superficial political 'notions' fails to address Pound's identification of moral goodness, aesthetic beauty, and intellectual clarity with masculine power and blind faith in charismatic leadership. Neither does it comprehend the extent to which Pound's phallic, racist and authoritarian beliefs follow from his theories of instinct, nature and secret wisdom. The separation of Pound's fascist ideas from his 'fundamental instincts' has long been recognised as an inadequate response to the complex relationship between modernist aesthetics and ideology. However, the persistence of his aesthetic mysticism into later modernist poetry has never been fully acknowledged. In order to approach this issue, we need to understand how an apparently retrograde mysticism was seized as a progressive creative device in the twentieth century.

Notes

1. Craig Owens, 'The Allegorical Impulse: Towards a Theory of Postmodernism', in Brian Wallis, ed., *Art After Modernism: Rethinking Representation* (New York: New Museum of Contemporary Art, 1984), 235.
2. Miller, *Late Modernism*, 125.
3. Sara Blair, 'Modernism and the Politics of Culture', in Michael Levenson, ed., *The Cambridge Companion to Modernism* (Cambridge: Cambridge University Press, 1999), 166. Blair's essay shows the difficulty of containing the modernist 'period'. One of her key texts is William Carlos Williams's epic poem *Paterson* (1946–58); like most academic surveys of modernism, the *Cambridge Companion* makes 1939 its cut-off point.
4. Peter Nicholls, *Modernisms: A Literary Guide* (London: Macmillan, 1995). Nicholls's history of literary international relations complements Bradbury and McFarlane's *Modernism* in emphasising the plurality of artistic responses to the condition of modernity. Even so, the 'men of 1914' are seen as standing for the 'hegemonic' definition of modernism as a critique of modernity, in contrast to the expressionistic and revolutionary tendencies of the European avant-gardes. The 'tangential' writings of women modernists such as H. D., Stein and Loy 'seem to stand outside "modernism"' because they disrupt both the phallic classicism of the Anglo-American tradition and 'the gendered aesthetics of the various avant-gardes' (222). The modernism in scare quotes continues to act as what, in her paean to H. D.'s marginalism, Susan Stanford Friedman calls 'the reactionary center' from which revised definitions of modernism radiate, even if the tag is a contradiction in terms. (Friedman, 'Modernism of the "Scattered Remnant": Race and Politics in the Development of H. D.'s Modernist Fiction', quoted in Rainey, *Institutions of Modernism*, 148.) H. D. may be described as marginal for current critical purposes, yet it is hard not to recall her centrality to early modernist polemics. (Rainey derides her aesthetic as a thin assimilation of mainstream modernism: 'a mix of bland notions from popular occultism and generalizations that denounce contemporary humanity in the abstract and yet promise everyone that he or she is assured of becoming a god.' *Institutions*, 164.)
5. By contrast, Vorticism and Imagism, often described as the British avant-garde, asserted autonomy. Again, see Rainey, *Institutions*, 30: 'Imagism, in short, was a movement to end all movements: informal, antitheoretical, absorbed in matters of writerly technique, and averse to more global programs that linked poetry

to contemporary social transformations or posed questions about the status and functions of art. Though Imagism is commonly treated as the first avant-garde in Anglo-American literature, it was really something quite different – the first anti-avant-garde'.

6. Hindsight is, of course, all too easy. Many adepts of vitalist cults did not know where their cultural experiments were leading. Stefan George himself was horrified by the emergence of Nazism and anti-Semitism, and fled from Germany in 1933. Another member of the *Kreis*, Ernst Kantorowicz, was a Jew and Polish aristocrat who emigrated to California, where he became a professor of medieval history. At Berkeley, where his pupils included Spicer and Blaser, Kantorowicz was a flamboyant and somewhat anti-authoritarian figure who nevertheless (like Olson) 'discouraged women from attending his classes; his male students thought of him as a god'. (Lewis Ellingham and Kevin Killian, *Poet Be Like God: Jack Spicer and the San Francisco Renaissance* (Hanover: Wesleyan University Press/University Press of New England, 1998), 20–1.) The influence of Central European scholars with a background in 'secret wisdom' on the intellectual and artistic life of the United States cannot be overestimated, the pervasive presence being that of C. G. Jung.

7. Casillo, *The Genealogy of Demons*, 22.

8. Olson, quoted in E. Fuller Torrey, *The Roots of Treason: Ezra Pound and the Secrets of St Elizabeth's* (London: Sidgwick and Jackson, 1984), 226–7. Pound is the only US poet to be convicted of treason. His incarceration in St Elizabeth's was the result of a successful campaign by members of the American literary establishment (including Archibald MacLeish, Dudley Fitts, James Laughlin, T. S. Eliot, H. D., and Robert Frost) to save him from trial and execution by pleading insanity. According to Torrey, Dr Winfred Overholser, the presiding government psychiatrist in the case, 'had exaggerated Pound's symptoms and disabilities; when exaggeration under oath crosses an indefinable line it can be perjury. Some of Dr Overholser's colleagues think he may have crossed the line but say such perjury was carried out with the best of intentions. As one of them succinctly summarized it: "Of course Dr Overholser committed perjury. Pound was a great artist, a national treasure. If necessary I would have committed perjury too – gladly" ' (218).

9. Janheinz Jahn, *Leo Frobenius: The Demonic Child* (Austin: University of Texas African and Afro-American Studies and Research Center, 1974), 13–17. On Frobenius and diffusionist theories of history see Surette, *The Birth of Modernism*, 60–73.

10. In a letter to T. S. Eliot of 1 February 1940, Pound writes 'I know you jib at China and Frobenius cause they ain't pie church, and neither of us likes sabages, black habits, etc. ... I shd. claim to get on from where Frobenius left off, in that his Morphology was applied to savages and my interest is in civilizations at their *most. (The Selected Letters of Ezra Pound 1907–1941.* ed., D. D. Paige (London: Faber & Faber, 1950), 336.) See Casillo, *The Genealogy of Demons*, 76: 'Pound uses the term Paideuma in a racial sense, as when he tells the supposedly pro-Semitic English that they are at the end of their "paideuma", that is their "race conviction", their "race consciousness" '. See also Jean-Michel Rabaté's discussion of 'organic symptoms'

in *Language, Sexuality and Ideology*, in Ezra Pound's *Cantos* (London: Macmillan, 1986), 47–51.

11. Eva Hesse, Introduction to *New Approaches to Ezra Pound*, 49.

* * *

'Late modernism' is still an emerging label, the meaning of which is still under debate. It is not without its problems. As Derek Attridge has noted, it implies a literary historical narrative 'in which contemporary uses of modernist methods are merely survivors, soon to be eliminated altogether'.[64] Nevertheless, as a way of understanding modernism, it has much to commend it. It connects contemporary writers with a modernist tradition of critiquing modernity, without suggesting that their work is merely a repetition of high modernism; later writers have learned from the mistakes of the earlier ones, above all, from their disastrous association with fascism. The concept of late modernism suggests that modernism was not some temporary aberration, but a serious attempt to forge new ways of understanding the world and to embody them in literature.

Chapter Notes

1. Lawrence Rainey, *Institutions of Modernism* (New Haven, CT: Yale University Press, 1998), 105.

2. Archibald Macleish, *The Irresponsibles* (New York: Duell, Sloan and Pearce, 1940); 'Eclipse of the Highbrow', *The Times* (25 Mar. 1941) 5. See also various writers, 'On the "Brooks-Macleish Thesis"', *Partisan Review*, 9, no.1 (Jan.–Feb. 1942), 38–47, and T. S. Eliot, 'A Letter to the Editors', *Partisan Review*, 9, no.2 (Mar.–Apr. 1942), 115–16.

3. Bertrand Russell, *Portraits from Memory* (London: George Allen and Unwin, 1956), 107; Randall Stevenson, *The Last of England?*, Oxford English Literary History, v.12 (Oxford: Oxford University Press, 2004), 53–5.

4. Richard Chase, 'The Fate of the Avant-Garde', in Irving Howe, ed., *Literary Modernism* (New York: Fawcett World Library, 1967), 145. First published in *Partisan Review*, 24, no.3 (1957), 363–75.

5. Monroe K. Spears, *Dionysus and the City: Modernism in Twentieth-Century Poetry* (New York: Oxford University Press, 1970), 15.

6. Lionel Trilling, 'On the Modern Element in Modern Literature' [1960], reprinted in *Beyond Culture* (London: Secker and Warburg, 1966); Harry Levin. 'What was Modernism?' [1960], reprinted in Stanley Burnshaw, ed., *Varieties of Literary Experience* (New York: New York University Press, 1962), and in Levin, *Refractions* (New York: Oxford University Press, 1966); Graham Hough, 'Reflections on a Literary Revolution', in *Image and Experience* (London: Duckworth, 1960).

7. Karl Shapiro, *In Defense of Ignorance* (New York: Random House, 1960), ix.

8. Randall Jarrell, 'From the Kingdom of Necessity', in *Poetry and the Age* (1953; London: Faber, 1955), 194. First published in *The Nation* (New York), 164 (18 Jan. 1947), 74, 76.

9. Charles Olson, letter of 20 Aug. 1951, *Charles Olson and Robert Creeley: The Complete Correspondence*, ed. George F. Butterick, 10 vols. to date (Santa Barbara: Black Sparrow Press, 1980 onwards), 7. 115; Perry Anderson, *The Origins of Postmodernity* (London: Verso, 1998), 6–9.

10. I. Hassan, 'Postface 1982: Toward a Concept of Postmodernism', *The Dismemberment of Orpheus*, 2nd ed. (Madison: University of Wisconsin Press, 1982), 259–72 (pp.267–8). An earlier version appeared in Harry R. Garvin, ed., *Romanticism, Modernism, and Postmodernism* (Lewisburg, PA: Bucknell University Press, 1980).

11. Marjorie Perloff, 'Modernist Studies', in Stephen Greenblatt and Giles B. Gunn, eds., *Redrawing the Boundaries* (New York: Modern Language Association of America, 1992), 154–78 (pp.169–70). See also Matei Calinescu, *Five Faces of Modernity* (Durham, NC: Duke University Press, 1987), 139–44.

12. Charles Altieri, 'Objective Image and Act of Mind in Modern Poetry', *PMLA*, 91 (1976), 101–14 (p.101).

13. D. Perkins, *A History of Modern Poetry* (Cambridge, MA: Belknap/Harvard University Press, 1976).

14. M. Bradbury and R. McFarlane, 'The Name and Nature of Modernism', in Bradbury and McFarlane, eds., *Modernism* (Harmondsworth: Penguin, 1976) 31, 36.

15. C. Jencks, 'Late-Modernism and Post-Modernism' (1978), in *Late-Modern Architecture* (London: Academy, 1980), 188, note.

16. F. Jameson, 'The Politics of Theory: Ideological Positions in the Postmodern Debate' (1984), *Ideologies of Theory*, 2 vols. (London: Routledge, 1988), 2. 103.

17. F. Jameson, 'Afterword', in E. Bloch et. al., ed., *Aesthetics and Politics* (London: NLB, 1977), 209.

18. F. Jameson, *The Political Unconscious* (London: Methuen, 1981), 280.

19. F. Jameson, *The Political Unconscious*, 236.

20. Robert Kern, 'Composition as Recognition: Robert Creeley and Postmodern Poetics', *boundary 2*, 6, no. 3 (1978), 211–32. The earlier instance occurs in Jerome Rothenberg 'A Dialogue on Oral Poetry with William Spanos', *boundary 2*, 3, no. 3 (Spring, 1975), 509–48 (p.520).

21. Charles Jencks, *The Language of Post-Modern Architecture* (1977; revised enlarged edition, London: Academy, 1978), 8. See also Jencks, 'The Pluralism of Recent Japanese Architecture', *Journal of the Royal Society of Arts*, 127, no.5280 (Nov. 1979), 742–55 (p.743).

22. Alan Wilde, 'Modernism and the Aesthetics of Crisis', *Contemporary Literature*, 20, no.1 (1979), 13–50 (p.40).

23. Alan Wilde, *Horizons of Assent: Modernism, Postmodernism, and the Ironic Imagination* (Baltimore, MD and London: Johns Hopkins University Press, 1981), 120.

24. Fredric Jameson, *Postmodernism, or The Cultural Logic of Late Capitalism* (London: Verso, 1991), xvi, 305.

25. Michael Murphy, 'Neoclassicism, Late Modernism, and W. H. Auden's "New Year Letter"', *Cambridge Quarterly*, 33, no.2 (2004), 101–18; Jean Radford, 'Late Modernism and the Politics of History', in Maroula Joannou, ed., *Women Writers of the 1930s: Gender, Politics, and History* (Edinburgh: Edinburgh University Press, 1999), 33–45.
26. Wilde, *Horizons of Assent*, 9–10.
27. Wilde, *Horizons of Assent*, 122–3.
28. Rod Mengham, 'Introduction', *Vanishing Points* (Cambridge: Salt, 2004), p.xviii.
29. Andrew Crozier, 'Introduction', in Andrew Crozier and Tim Longville, eds., *A Various Art* (Manchester: Carcanet, 1987), 12.
30. Mengham, 'Introduction', *Vanishing Points*, p.xix.
31. For 'neo-modernist', see Neil Corcoran 'Varieties of Neo-Modernism: Christopher Middleton, Roy Fisher, J. H. Prynne', in *English Poetry since 1940* (Harlow: Longman, 1993), and Robert Bond, *Iain Sinclair* (Cambridge: Salt, 2005), 3–19.
32. Tyrus Miller, *Late Modernism: Politics, Fiction, and the Arts between the World Wars* (Berkeley: University of California Press, 1999), 5.
33. D. Attridge, *J. M. Coetzee and the Ethics of Reading* (Chicago: University of Chicago Press, 2005), 2–3, n.5.

Further Reading

Modernism and Postmodernism

Bradbury, Malcolm. 'Modernisms/Postmodernisms', in Ihab Hassan and Sally Hassan, eds., *Innovation/Renovation: New Perspectives on the Humanities* (Madison: University of Wisconsin Press, 1983), 311–28.

Bush, Ronald. 'Modern/Postmodern: Eliot, Perse, Mallarmé, and the Future of the Barbarians', in Robert Kiely, ed., *Modernism Reconsidered* (Cambridge, MA: Harvard University Press, 1983), 191–214. Looks at Eliot's engagement with the 'open' poetry of Perse and Mallarmé.

——. 'T. S. Eliot and Modernism at the Present Time', in Ronald Bush, ed., *T. S. Eliot: The Modernist in History* (Cambridge: Cambridge University Press, 1991), 191–204. By examining the reception of *The Waste Land*, Bush suggests that modernism and postmodernism might be best seen as two modes of reading.

Eagleton, Terry. 'Capitalism, Modernism and Postmodernism', *New Left Review*, 152 (1985), 60–73, repr. in *Against the Grain* (London: Verso, 1986), and in David Lodge, ed., *Modern Theory and Criticism: A Reader* (Harlow: Longman, 1988), 385–98.

Nevo, Ruth. 'The Waste Land: Ur-Text of Deconstruction', *New Literary History*, 13 (1981–2), 453–61.

Pitchford, Nicola. 'Unlikely Modernism, Unlikely Postmodernism: Stein's *Tender Buttons*', *American Literary History*, 11 (1999), 642–67. A careful and approachable examination of a writer particularly troubling for the conventional modernist/ postmodernist distinction.

Late Modernism

Attridge, Derek. *J. M. Coetzee and the Ethics of Reading* (Chicago: University of Chicago Press, 2005). Attridge's relevant reflections are mostly to be found in the introductory chapter.

Miller, Tyrus. *Late Modernism: Politics, Fiction, and the Arts between the World Wars* (Berkeley: University of California Press, 1999). As noted above, Miller sees the category as a transitional moment between modernism and postmodernism.

Nicholls. Peter. 'Modernising Modernism: From Pound to Oppen', *Critical Quarterly*, 44, no.2 (Summer 2002), 41–58.

Further Reading

Definitions of Modernism

Most critical accounts of modernism include some form of definition, so this selection is somewhat arbitrary, but includes works which clarify key issues.

Adams, Robert Martin. 'What was Modernism?' *Hudson Review*, 31 (1978), 19–33.

Anderson, Perry. 'Modernity and Revolution', *New Left Review*, no.144 (Mar.–Apr. 1984), 96–113.

Beebe, Maurice. 'Introduction: What Modernism Was', *Journal of Modern Literature*, 3, no.5 (1974), 1065–84.

Calinescu, Matei. *Faces of Modernity: Avant-Garde, Decadence, Kitsch* (Bloomington: Indiana University Press, 1977). Incorporated into his 1987 book.

——. *Five Faces of Modernity: Modernism, Avant-garde, Decadence, Kitsch, Postmodernism* (Durham, NC: Duke University Press, 1987). Though the history of the term 'modern' and the quarrel of the ancients and the moderns have been examined by many writers, Calinescu's is the most thorough account.

——. 'Modernity, Modernisme, Modernization: Variations on Modern Themes', in C. Barg, F. Durieux, and G. Lernout, eds., *The Turn of the Century/Le tournant du siècle* (Berlin and New York: Walter de Gruyter, 1995), 33–52.

Eysteinsson, Astradur. *The Concept of Modernism* (Ithaca, NY: Cornell University Press, 1990). Eysteinsson makes very little reference to modernist literature as such, but carefully analyses concepts of modernism in literary criticism.

Friedman, Susan Stanford. 'Definitional Excursions: The Meanings of Modern / Modernity/ Modernism', *Modernism / Modernity*, 8, no.3 (Sept. 2001), 493–513.

Kermode, Frank. 'The Modern' in *Continuities* (London: Routledge Kegan Paul, 1968).

Levin, Harry. 'What was Modernism?' (1960), in Stanley Burnshaw, ed., *Varieties of Literary Experience* (New York: New York University Press, 1962), 307–29.

Nicholls, Peter. *Modernisms: A Literary Guide* (1995). This seems likely to achieve the same status as Bradbury and McFarlane's 1976 volume. International in scope, it argues for the plurality of modernist movements.

Szabolcsi, Miklos. 'Avant-garde, Neo-avant-garde, Modernism', *NLH*, 3, no.1 (1971), 49–70.

Sheppard, Richard. 'The Problematics of European Modernism', in Steve Giles, ed., *Theorizing Modernism* (London: Routledge, 1993), 1–51.

——. *Modernism-dada-postmodernism* (Evanston, Ill.: North Western University Press, 2000). Chapters 1–3 are an expanded version of 'The Problematics of European Modernism'; the book examines continental modernism.

Collections of Essays on Modernism

Bradbury, Malcolm, and James McFarlane, eds. *Modernism 1890–1930* (Harmondsworth: Penguin, 1976). A classic collection of essays, notable for seeing modernism as an international movement. Though it has little to say about issues that rose to prominence in the 1980s (particularly the politics of modernism), it is still valuable.

Bradshaw, David, ed. *A Concise Companion to Modernism* (Oxford: Blackwell, 2003). Essays on the intellectual and cultural contexts for modernist literature, with a particular emphasis on the sciences, philosophy and other academic disciplines, as well as valuable essays on publishing and the concept of the state.

Bradshaw, David, and Kevin J. H. Dettmar, eds. *A Companion to Modernist Literature and Culture* (Oxford: Blackwell, 2005). At the time of writing, forthcoming. Includes thematic essays and essays on major modernist works.

Brooker, Peter, ed. *Modernism / Postmodernism* (London: Longman, 1992). Edited at the end of the period in which modernism was contrasted (to its disadvantage) with postmodernism; nevertheless, it collects some valuable essays.

Chefdor, Monique, Ricardo Quinones, and Albert Wachtel, eds. *Modernism: Challenges and Perspectives* (Urbana: University of Illinois Press, 1986).

Dettmar, Kevin J. H., ed. *Rereading the New: A Backward Glance at Modernism* (Ann Arbor: University of Michigan Press, 1992). Very much of its time, when the main debate concerned the relation of modernism to postmodernism, but it contains some valuable essays.

Giles, Steve, ed. *Theorizing Modernism: Essays in Critical Theory* (London: Routledge, 1993).

Thormaehlen, Marianne, ed. *Rethinking Modernism* (Basingstoke: Macmillan, 2003). Includes a valuable annotated bibliography of criticism (pp. 252–73).

Witemeyer, Hugh. *The Future of Modernism* (Ann Arbor: University of Michigan Press, 1997). In the light of political and postmodern criticism of modernism, argues for its continuing importance and vitality.

Anti-Semitism, Authoritarianism, Fascism, and Reactionary Politics

Carey, John. *The Intellectuals and the Masses: Pride and Prejudice among the Literary Intelligentsia, 1880–1939* (London: Faber and Faber, 1992).

Childs, Donald. *Modernism and Eugenics: Woolf, Eliot, Yeats and the Culture of Degeneration* (Cambridge: Cambridge University Press, 2001)

Ferrall, Charles. *Modernist Writing and Reactionary Politics* (Cambridge: Cambridge University Press, 2001). Argues that fascism was attractive to modernists because it promised the reintegration of art and society.

Harrison, John. *The Reactionaries* (London: Gollancz, 1966).

Jameson, Fredric. *Fables of Aggression: Wyndham Lewis, the Modernist as Fascist* (Berkeley: University of California Press, 1979). Influential in establishing a political agenda in modernist criticism, and, strangely, in making Wyndham Lewis a legitimate object of critical attention.

MacLeish, Archibald. *The Irresponsibles* (New York: Duell, Sloan and Pearce, 1940). Not a criticism of modernist writers for being fascistic, but for evading their political responsibilities.

Nixon, Cornelia. *Lawrence's Leadership Politics and the Turn against Women* (Berkeley: University of California Press, 1986).

Sultan, Stanley. 'Was Modernism Reactionary?', *Journal of Modern Literature*, 17 (1991) 445–62.

Tratner, Michael. *Modernism and Mass Politics: Joyce, Woolf, Eliot, Yeats* (Stanford, CA. Stanford University Press, 1995).

The Canon

DeKoven, Marianne. "'Why James Joyce Was Accepted and I Was Not": Modernist Fiction and Gertrude Stein's Narrative', *Studies in the Literary Imagination*, 25, no. 2 (Fall 1992), 23–30.

Kenner, Hugh. 'The Making of the Modernist Canon', in Robert von Hallberg, ed., *Canons* (Chicago: University of Chicago Press, 1984).

Parrinder, Patrick. 'The Strange Necessity', in Colin MacCabe, ed., *James Joyce* (Brighton: Harvester, 1982), 151–67. In the Kenner school, taking Woolf and West as a genteel dilution of 'international modernism'. See criticisms by Scott, below.

Scott, Bonnie Kime. 'A Joyce of One's Own', in Lisa Rado, ed., *Rereading Modernism* (New York: Garland, 1994), 209–30.

Colonialism

Booth, Howard J., and Nigel Rigby, eds. *Modernism and Empire* (Manchester: Manchester University Press, 2000). A response to Jameson's 1988 pamphlet (see below), which the editors criticize for being narrow in its canon and restrictive in its causality.

Esty, Joshua. *A Shrinking Island: Modernism and National Culture in England* (Princeton, NJ: Princeton University Press, 2004). On the relation of 'late modernism' (by which Esty means the period 1930–60) and the contraction of the British empire.

Jameson, Fredric. 'Modernism and Imperialism' (1988), in Terry Eagleton, Fredric Jameson and Edward Said, *Nationalism, Colonialism, and Literature* (Minneapolis: University of Minnesota Press, Frederic Janeson and Edward Said, 1990), 43–65.

Said, Edward. 'Representing the Colonized', *Critical Inquiry*, 15 (Winter 1989), 205–25. Mostly concerned with anthropology, but influential.

Harlem Renaissance and African-American Writing

Baker, Houston. *Modernism and the Harlem Renaissance* (Chicago: University of Chicago Press, 1987). A classic study, though see Pavlic (below) for some criticisms.

De Jongh, James. *Vicious Modernism: Black Harlem and the Literary Imagination* (Cambridge: Cambridge University Press, 1990). A cultural history of the district, more concerned with representations of Harlem than with the literature produced in the 'Harlem Renaissance'.

Douglas, Anne. *Terrible Honesty: Mongrel Manhattan in the 1920s* (New York: Picador, 1996). On communication between white and black writers and artists.

Ellison, Ralph. *Shadow and Act* (New York: Random House, 1964), 144–66. Particularly 'Hidden Name and Complex Fate' and 'The Art of Fiction', which touch on his response to high modernist works.

Friedman, Susan Stanford, 'Modernism of the "Scattered Remnant": Race and Politics in the Development of H.D'.s Modernist Vision', in Michael King, ed., *H.D.: Woman and Poet* (1986), 91–116, repr. in Shari Benstock, ed., *Feminist Issues in Literary Scholarship* (Bloomington and Indianapolis: Indiana University Press, 1987), 208–31.

Mishkin, Tracy. *The Harlem and Irish Renaissances* (1998). Particularly interesting on the identification of each group with the Jewish diaspora and their simultaneous anti-Semitism.

North, Michael. *The Dialect of Modernism: Race, Language, and Twentieth-Century Literature* (New York: Oxford University Press, 1999).

Pavlic, Edward M. *Crossroads Modernism: Descent and Emergence in African-American Literary Culture* (Minneapolis, London: University of Minnesota Press, 2002). Critical of Houston Baker's 1987 study for taking a narrow view of modernism, and of other scholars in the field for distancing African-American writers from European modernism, in spite of evidence of their positive interest.

Rampersad, Arnold. 'Langston Hughes and Approaches to Modernism', in Amritjit Singh, William S. Shiver, and Stanley Brodwin, eds., *The Harlem Renaissance: Revaluations* (New York: Garland, 1989), 49–68.

Wintz, Cary D., ed. *The Politics and Aesthetics of 'New Negro' Literature* (New York: Garland, 1996). An anthology of essays from c.1925 to c.1940.

Marxist Approaches to Modernism

Calinescu, Matei. 'Modernism and Ideology', in Monique Chefdor, Ricardo Quinones, and Albert Wachtel *Modernism: Challenges and Perspectives* (Urbana: University of

Illinois Press, 1986) 79–93. Emphatically not a Marxist approach, but rather, a blunt refusal to follow Fredric Jameson's lead on Wyndham Lewis.

Eagleton, Terry. 'Capitalism, Modernism and Postmodernism', *New Left Review*, 152 (1985), 60–73, repr. in *Against the Grain* (London: Verso, 1986), and in David Lodge, ed., *Modern Theory and Criticism: A Reader* (Harlow: Longman, 1988), 385–98.

——. *Criticism and Ideology: A Study in Marxist Literary Theory* (London: NLB, 1976)

——. 'The End of English', *Textual Practice*, 1, no.1 (1987), 1–9; repr. in *The Eagleton Reader*, ed. Stephen Regan (Oxford: Blackwell, 1998), 270–78.

——. *Exiles and Émigrés: Studies in Modern Literature* (London: Chatto and Windus, 1970).

——. 'Modernism, Myth and Monopoly Capitalism', *News from Nowhere* 7 (1989), 19–24; repr. in *The Eagleton Reader* ed. Stephen Regan (Oxford: Blackwell, 1998), 279–84.

Jameson, Fredric. *Fables of Aggression: Wyndham Lewis, the Modernist as Fascist* (Berkeley: University of California Press, 1979).

—— *The Political Unconscious: Narrative as a Socially Symbolic Act* (London: Methuen, 1981). Jameson develops to its full a Marxist methodology which combines consideration of the style and form of modernist writing with a high-level historical perspective.

Moretti, Franco. *Signs Taken for Wonders: Essays in the Sociology of Literary Forms*, tr. Susan Fischer, David Forgacs, David Miller (London: NLB, 1993).

Williams, Raymond. *The Politics of Modernism: Against the New Conformists*, ed. Tony Pinkney (London: Verso, 1989).

Science and Modernism

Albright, Daniel. *Quantum Poetics: Yeats, Pound, Eliot, and the Science of Modernism* (Cambridge: Cambridge University Press, 1997). Albright draws his basic metaphor from physics—he argues that modernists were searching for the fundamental particles of poetry—but does not engage with the science of the time more widely.

Bell, Ian F. A. *Critic as Scientist: The Modernist Poetics of Ezra Pound* (London: Methuen, 1981).

Cain, Sara. 'The Metaphorical Field: Post-Newtonian Physics and Modernist Literature', *Cambridge Quarterly*, 28 (1999), 46–64.

Hayles, N. Katherine. *The Cosmic Web: Scientific Field Models and Literary Strategies in the Twentieth Century* (Ithaca, NY: Cornell University Press, 1984).

Kayman, Martin A. *The Modernism of Ezra Pound: The Science of Poetry* (London: Macmillan, 1986)

Ryan, Judith. *The Vanishing Subject: Early Psychology and Literary Modernism* (Chicago: University of Chicago Press, 1991). On the impact of 'empiricist psychology', particularly William James and Ernst Mach.

Whitworth, Michael H. *Einstein's Wake: Relativity, Metaphor, and Modernist Literature* (Oxford: Oxford University Press, 2001)

Whitworth, Michael H. 'Physics: "A Strange Footprint,"' in David Bradshaw, ed., *A Concise Companion to Modernism* (Oxford: Blackwell, 2003) 200–20.

Social and Cultural Contexts

Bell, Michael. *The Context of English Literature, 1900–1930* (London: Methuen, 1980).

Bradshaw, David, ed. *A Concise Companion to Modernism* (Oxford: Blackwell, 2003).

North, Michael. *Reading 1922: A Return to the Scene of the Modern* (New York: Oxford University Press, 1999). Wide ranging cultural study.

Stansky, Peter. *On or about December 1910: Early Bloomsbury and its Intimate World* (Cambridge, MA: Harvard University Press, 1996). Takes its cue from Virginia Woolf ('on or around December 1910'), and examines British culture in wide range.

Trotter, David. *Paranoid Modernism: Literary Experiment, Psychosis, and the Professionalization of English Society* (Oxford: Oxford University Press, 2001). Does not contain a great deal of historical background, but pursues an interesting argument with regard to professionalization.

Index

abstraction, 14–15, 71–2
abstractions, 15
academicism, 198
Adorno, Theodor, 79, 122–31, 142–3,
    147–8, 155–6
  on Lukács, 113–19
  letter to Benjamin, 142, 156
  criticisms of his account of
    Lukács, 119
aestheticism, 129
Aiken, Conrad, 263
allegory, 79–80
allusion, 11–12, 167–8
  in Pound, 89–90
Altieri, Charles, 79, 274, 285–6
Anderson, Perry, 3, 197–8
annus mirabilis (1922), 24
anonymity, 203
anti-symbolist tradition, 80
architecture, critical terminology of, 275,
    276, 284
Aristotle, 93, 104
art, production and reception of, 131–5
artist, relation to audience, 10
artist, relation to art-work, 7–8, 34–5,
    135–6, 144–5
Athenaeum (periodical), 21–2
Attridge, Derek, 293
audience, mass, for modernist writers,
    172
aura, 190
authoritarianism, 177
  further reading, 298–9
autonomy of art work, 122, 124, 130–1

avant-garde, 122–39, 173–4, 238–9, 260
Axel's Castle (Wilson), 65–6

Baldick, Chris, 39
Barney, Natalie, 237
Baudelaire, Charles, 15, 23, 115, 189–97,
    200–3
  'A une passante', 206
  'Loss of a Halo', 190–7
  'Painter of Modern Life', 202–3, 206–7
  'The Salon of 1845', 202
  'The Salon of 1846', 202
Beckett, Lucy, 82
Beckett, Samuel, 110, 284
  Molloy, 109
belief, crisis of, 223–4, 239
  see also God *and* Christianity
Bell, Clive, 163–4
Benjamin, Walter, 79, 189, 191, 200
Benn, Gottfried, 110–11, 112
Benstock, Shari, 218, 220
  'Beyond the Reaches of Feminist
    Criticism' (extract), 220–7
  'Expatriate Modernism', 227
Bergson, Henri, 71, 76–7
Berman, Marshall, 189–90, 200–1, 205
  criticisms of, 197–8
  All That is Solid Melts into Air (extract),
    190–7
Bhabha, Homi, 234–6
bibliography, McKenzie's definition, 245
birth, dates of, 19–20
Bishop, John Peale, 248–50

Black Mountain College, 289
  see also Olson, Charles
Blair, Sara, 289
Blake, William, 67–70
Blamires, Harry, 100
blasé attitude, 186–7
Bloch, Ernst, 101
Blomfield, Reginald, 35, 40–1
Bloom, Harold, 82, 83, 84–5
book history, 244–67
book market, 261
boulevards, 192–3
bourgeois art, 132–3, 138
Bradbury, Malcolm, 230, 274–5
Brecht, Bertolt, 114, 228–9
Brighton, Andrew, 7
Brooks, Cleanth, 45, 46, 47
Brooks, Romaine, 237–8
Bunting, Basil, 281
Bürger, Peter, 173–5, 247, 260
  on Adorno 130–1
  Theory of the Avant Garde (extract)
    131–7
  historicist objections to, 138
'By the Watermelon Vine' (song), 166

canon, 50, 217–18, 221–3, 245–6
  creation of, 247–67
  further reading, 299
Cantos, The (Pound), 82–3
  as an 'open' text, 274
capitalism, 193 (*see also* commodity
    economy)
Carey, John, 14, 142, 172
caricature, 28, 30–1
Carlyle, Thomas, 17
Carne-Ross, D. S., 88–9
Casillo, Robert, 290
censorship, 15, 99
chaos, 11–12, 193, 196
character, 26–33, 277–8
Chase, Richard, 273
Chinitz, David, 159–60
  T. S. Eliot and the Cultural Divide
    (extracts), 160–4, 164–72, 173–6
Christianity, 220, 224
  see also belief *and* God
city, 181–214
  urban environment, 192–3
  urban life, 11
Cixous, Hélène, 217

class, 9, 231–2
  aristocratic classes, 198
  see also bourgeois art
classicism (Hulme's idea of), 27–8
clocks, 185–6
close reading, limitations of, 266–7
Cocteau, Jean, 162–3
collective action, 196
colonialism, further reading, 299
commerce, 6–8
commodity, art as, 124–5
commodity economy, 195
Compton-Burnett, Ivy, 280
Conrad, Joseph, 7
  Nostromo, 269
Conrad, Michael Georg, 149
constructionism, 94–5
consumerism, 210
contemporary society, writer's relation to,
    10
context, 5–6, 47–8
  further reading, 302
courtly art, 132–3
critical strategies, 5–6
criticism, art's relation to, 8–9
  psychoanalytic, 231–2
crowds, 151–2, 189
  see also masses
'Cubanola Glide' (song), 166
culture, 49, 134, 141–77
  high and low, 141–77
  mass, 7–8, 14, 49
  mass culture as feminine, 147–52
  terminology of, 147–8

dadaism, 131
dates, epochal, 23–4
Davenport, Guy, 89
Davidson, Donald, 43
Davidson, Harriet, 10
Davie, Donald, 89, 282
de Man, Paul, 79–80
DeKoven, Marianne, 143, 230–1
'delayed decoding', 7
depression, economic (1929 onwards),
    272
depth, 279
desanctification, 191–2
deviation, 109
Dial, The (periodical), 249–60, 266
difficulty, 11

discourse, free indirect, 13 (*see also*: monologue, interior)
discrimination, psychological, 186
distortion, 111
diversity, 20–1, 231–2
Donne, John, 70

Eagleon, Terry, 8, 137
eccentricity, 110
écriture féminine, 148–9, 220
editions, commercial, 261–2
    limited, 261–4
    of female writers, 219
editorial theory, 245
Eliot, T. S., 30–3, 94, 159–77, 247–67
    conservatism of, 174, 176
    The Dry Salvages, 7
    Hulme, T. E., and, 64
    Inventions of the March Hare, 164
    'The Metaphysical Poets', 43, 44
    Notes to *The Waste Land*, 263–4
    Sweeney Agonistes, 176
    'Tradition and the Individual Talent', 37–9, 65, 246
    '*Ulysses*, Order and Myth', 12–13, 99
    The Waste Land, 164–72, 246, 247–67
elitism, 14, 141–77
Elliot, Bridget, 237
Ellison, Ralph, 164
empathy, 14–15, 71–2
ephemerality, 18–19, 182–4, 200
exchange-value, 124
expressionism, 94–5, 101
Eysteinsson, Astradur, 113, 139, 175

fascism, further reading, 298–9
    see also Nazism
Faulkner, William, 106
Felski, Rita, 'Modernism and Modernity' (text of), 228–39
femininity, 143–4, 144–57
feminist approaches, 148–9
fetishism, 123–4
First World War, 19–20, 216, 224–5, 227
Firuski, Maurice, 262–4
flâneur, 189, 199, 203
    status of concept, 213
flâneuse, 199–213
    impossibility of, 213
Flaubert, Gustave, 15, 144–6

form, spatial, 12, 45–6
formalism, 8, 99–119
    critical preference for, 232, 236, 260
Forster, E. M., 276
fragmentation, 11
Frank, Joseph, 45–6
freedom, individual, 188–9, 193–4
Freikorps, 143
Freud, Sigmund, 109
Friedman, Susan Stanford, 224, 226
Frith, W. P., *Derby Day* (painting), 100
Fugitive, The (periodical), 42
Fuller, Ronald, 40
futurism, 9, 16, 28
    legacy of, 35–7

Gallagher, Catherine, 236
gender, 15, 143–4, 144–57, 216–40
genealogies of modernism, 22–3
generations, 19–20
geometry, 31–2
Gilbert, Sandra, 230
Gilbert, Stuart, 100
God, failure of, 191, 226, 230
    see also belief *and* Christianity
Gordon, Lyndall, 217
grand narratives, 9
Greenberg, Clement, 155–6
groups, 19–22
Gubar, Susan, 230
Guys, Constantin, 202–3

Hanscombe, Gillian, 217–18
Harlem Renaissance, 159
    further reading, 300
Hartman, Geoffrey, 83
'Harrigan' (song), 165
Harvey, David, 199
Hassan, Ihab, 273–4
Haussmann, Georges Eugène, 192–3
Heidegger, Martin, 105
Henke, Suzette, 217
hermeticism, 68–9, 286
Hesse, Eva, 290
heteronomy, 126
heterosexuality, 224
high culture, *see* culture, high
high modernism, *see* modernism, high
history, and New Criticism, 4
    in poetry, 86
    literary, 236

history, and New Criticism (*cont'd*)
  modernist obsession with, 247
  narratives of, 9–10, 238
Hogarth Press, 262
holocaust, 272–3
Hopkins, Gerard Manley, 23
Horkheimer, Max, 147, 148
Hough, Graham, 273
Hulme, T. E., 9, 14–15, 70–8
  errors in, 74
  historical theories of, 73
  'Modern Art and its Philosophy', 26–8
  'Notes on Language and Style', 78
  'Romanticism and Classicism', 63–4
  precedents for, 77–8
humanism and anti-humanism, 26–33
  Hulme, T. E., and, 73–4
Huyssen, Andreas, 142, 174–5, 260
  'Mass Culture as Woman' (extract),
    144–57
  on Bürger, 137
  on 'Great Divide', 158

ideology, 9, 102–13, 123
imagination, 70
Imagism, 24–6, 66, 70–8, 226
impersonality, 7–8, 43, 64–5
impressionism, 33–5
individualism, 135
individuality, 7–8, 35
innovation, 35
institution of art, 130–1, 247
instrumentalism, 127
  see also: reason, instrumental
internationalism, 16
inwardness, lack of in Pound's poetry,
    88–9
irony, 225, 276
Isherwood, Christopher, 277

Jacobs, Jane, 205
Jaffe, Aaron, 218
Jakobson, Roman, 50
Jameson, Fredric, 6, 101, 113, 275–6, 284
Jarrell, Randall, 273
Jarvis, Simon, on Adorno, 123–9
Jay, Gregory, 167
jazz, 160–73
  associations of, 160
  definition of, 160
  opposition to, 161, 162

Jencks, Charles, 275, 284
Jones, David, 281
Jonson, Ben, 31–2
journals, *see* periodicals
Joyce, James, 64, 115, 226, 251
  and feminism, 217, 220
  Mann, Thomas, contrasted with 103
  Ulysses, 12–13, 15, 24, 34, 100, 103,
    165–6
justification of art, 6–7, 95

Kafka, Franz, 108, 128–9
Kelmscott Press, 261
Kenner, Hugh, 81–82, 89
Kermode, Frank, 79–80, 83–4
  Romantic Image (extracts), 67–70, 70–8
knowledge, art as, 118–19, 123
Kracauer, Siegfried, 148
Kristeva, Julia, 148, 217, 228

Laforgue, Jules, 164
language, 28, 224, 226–7
  literary, 8–9, 93
  ordinary, 93
  scientific and poetic, 42–3
language poetics, 280
late modernism, *see* modernism, late
Lawrence, D. H., 15, 99, 142
  and gender, 217
  letter of 5 June 1914, 28–30
Le Bon, Gustave, 151–2
Leavis, F. R., 99, 142
Levin, Harry, 273
Lewis, Wyndham, 16, 216
life-praxis, 132–3, 173
Light, Alison, 219
Little Review (periodical), 255, 259, 266
Litz, A. Walton, 83
Liveright, Horace, 250–1, 257, 258–9,
    260, 262
logocentrism, 219
London Mercury (periodical), 22
low culture, *see* culture, low
Lukács, Georg, 100–1
  'The Ideology of Modernism'
    (extracts), 102–9, 109–13
Lyotard, Jean-François, 9

MacCabe, Colin, 50
'machine age', 6
machinery, 17

Madame Bovary (Flaubert), 144–6
magazine, little, 21, 261
magazines, *see* periodicals
magic, relation to symbolism, 68
magnetism, 30
man, definition of, 115
  as differentiating creature, 183
  as fallen, 9
  as solitary, 104
  as *zoon politikon*, 104
  'metropolitan man', 182, 183–8,
    199–200
  'public man', 204
manifestation, 134–5
manifestoes, 20–1, 28
Mann, Thomas, 102–3
Marcuse, Herbert, 134
Marinetti, F. T., 28
Marx, Karl, 191, 195
Marxist approaches, further reading,
  300–1
masculinity, 143–4, 144–60, 224
mass culture, *see* culture
masses, 14
McAdam, John, 194
McDonald, Peter D., 269
McElderry, B. R., 169–70
McFarlane, James, 230, 274–5
McGann, Jerome, 245
McKenzie, D. F., 245
media, mass, 141
Mellors, Anthony, 281
  Late Modernist Poetics (extracts),
    281–6, 288–91
'men of 1914', 217
Mengham, Rod, 280
metaphor, 44, 50
metonymy, 50
Miller, Henry, and gender, 217
Miller, J. Hillis, 86
Miller, James E., 217
Miller, Tyrus, 281, 282–5, 288
Millett, Kate, 216–17
mimesis, 34–5, 122
mind, complexity of, 13
minstrel show, 168–9
'modernism', the term, 39–41, 227, 233,
  274–6
  in Lukács, 102
  further reading 295–6
modernism, 'coordinates' of, 198
  defences of, 99–100

empty category, 3
  reaction against, 40–1
  retrospective construction, 39, 41
  characteristics of, 10–16, 45–6, 153–4,
    230
  chronological limits, 4, 229, 272–3
  high, 274–5
  late, 272–93
    emergence of the term, 275–6
  modernity, contrasted with, 3–4
  non-existent, 3, 82
  non-literary forms, 281–2
  postmodernism, antithetical to, 285
'modernist', the term, 39–41
'*modernité*', the term, 233
'modernity', the term, 228, 233
modernity, 16–19, 169
  and the city, 181–214
  and women, 227–40
  nonsynchronicity within, 234
'modernization', the term, 233
modernization, 155–6, 194
money economy, 184
monologue, interior, 13, 102–3, 117
Montherlant, Henry de, 111
Moody, A. David, 167
Moore, George, 252–3
Morgan, David, 208
Morris, William, 261–2
Muir, Edwin, 36–7
Murry, John Middleton, 21–2, 30
Musil, Robert, 110, 113
'My Evaline' (song), 166
myth, 12–13, 285
mythical method, 176

naturalism, distinguished from realism,
  112
Nazism, 142, 272
neo-Romanticism, 288
Nerval, Gérard de, 68
networks of writers, 19–22, 217–18
New Criticism, 41–9, 66
  decline of, 49–50
  shortcomings of, 47–9
Nietzsche, Friedrich, 26, 150, 183, 186
normality, 110
North, Michael, 167
novelist, *see* artist

obscurity, 11
occultism, *see* hermeticism

Olson, Charles, 79, 273, 275–6, 282, 284, 285, 289

pantheon, 22
paraphrase, heresy of, 43
Paris, 227
parody, 168–9
Parsons, Deborah, 213
past, the, 9–10
  as orderly, 11
Pater, Walter, 8, 18–19
patronage, limits of, 253
patrons, journals as, 254
periodicals, 20–2
Perkins, David, 274
Perloff, Marjorie, 10–11, 16, 80, 94, 260
  on Hassan, 274
  'Pound/Stevens' (extracts), 81–92, 92–4
personality, disintegration of, 108
perspective, 111–12
perversity, 110–11
Pinkney, Tony, 217
plurality of experience, 235
poet, *see* artist
poetry, redemptive power of, 47
  relation to prose, 75–6, 93
  sound structure, 85
  verbal medium of, 87
politics, 48–9, 51
Pollock, Griselda, 236
popular culture, *see* culture
postmodernism, 156–7, 220, 223, 228–9, 273–4
  relation to modernism and avant-garde, 137
post-structuralism, 50, 217
potentiality, abstract and concrete, 106–7, 114
Pound, Ezra, 30, 34, 35, 65, 99–100, 249–52
  dismissive of Stevens, 81
  influence of, 289–90
  see also Cantos
praxis, *see* life-praxis
primitivism, 13, 111, 117–18, 285–6
professions, exclusion of women, 208
projectivism, 79–80
prose, relation to poetry, 75–6, 93
prostitute, 205–6
Prynne, J. H., 280, 289
psychology, 109

psychopathology, 109
public sphere, exclusion of women, 200–1, 205–6, 207–8
publishing history, 15, 244–67
  key questions in, 246
punctuality, 185–6

quantification, 6, 184–5, 187

Rainey, Lawrence, 247, 283
  Institutions of Modernism (extracts), 247–67
Randall, A. E., 35–6
Ransom, John Crowe, 41–2, 46–7
rationality, *see* reason
rationalization, 199–200, 234, 238
Read, Herbert, 41
reader, 10, 12
  role of, 46
realism, 99–120
  in women's writing, 219
reality, art's relation to, 116–18
  definitions of, 33–5
reason, instrumental, 6–7, 8–9, 95, 127
referentialism, *see* representationalism
Renaissance, Hulme on, 72–3
representationalism, 8, 219
  neglect of, 231–2, 237
reserve, personal, 187
revolution, 197–8
Reznikoff, Charles, 281
rhythm, poetic, 25
Richards, I. A., 43
Richardson, Dorothy, 216
Roberts, Michael, 23, 44
Rogers, Bruce, 262
Romantic Image (Kermode), 79–80
romanticism, 63–97
Rousseau, Jean-Jacques, 9
rural life, 183
Ruskin, John, 17, 186
Russell, Bertrand, 142

sacral art, 131–33
sages, Victorian, 17–18
Sand, George, 205
Sartre, Jean-Paul, 145
science, 35, 42–4
  contrasted with magic, 68
  demonized, 46–7
  further reading, 299–300

Scott, Bonnie Kime, 217–18
Second World War, 272–3, 289
Seldes, Gilbert, 161, 249
self, ideas of, 7, 30, 26–33
  see also subjectivity
Sennett, Richard, 204
Shakespeare, William, 31
'Shakespearian Rag' (song), 167–72
Shapiro, Karl, 273
Sheppard, Richard, 5–6
Showalter, Elaine, 221–3
Sieburth, Richard, 138
Simmel, George, 181–2, 200–1, 204–5
  'Metropolis and Mental Life' (extract),
    182–9
Smith, Stan, 39
Smyers, Virginia, 217–18
socialism, 183
sociology, 207–8
sociology of texts, 245
solipsism, 117
solitariness, 104
song, popular, 165–6
space, social construction of, 198
Sparrow, John, 41
spatial form, *see* form
Spears, Monroe K., 8
specialization, 7, 183
Spender, Stephen, 11, 18
Stein, Gertrude, 219, 222–3
Stevens, Wallace, 81, 83–8, 89, 161
  Notes toward a Supreme Fiction, 83–8
stream of consciousness, 13–14
  see also monologue
structuralism, 50–1, 217
structure, 91
  poetic, 44–6
subject-matter, 15, 44
subjectivism, 107
subjectivity, 182–9
suffrage, 216
surface, 31–2, 89–90, 278–9
surrealism, 131
symbol, 79–80
symbolism, 67–70
  Pound's move out of, 89
Symons, Arthur, 67–8

Tanselle, G. Thomas, 245
Tate, Allen, 41–9
technique, 118
  poetic, contrasted with content, 86–8

technology, novelty of, 198
Tennyson, Alfred, 261
terminology, 233, 274–6
  further reading, 295–6
  history of, 39–41
text, centrality of, 236
  irrelevance of, 266
Thacker, Andrew, 199
Thayer, Scofield, 249, 251–3, 254–60
Theweleit, Klaus, 151
  influence on Huyssen, 143
time, 185–6
  experiments with, 12
  Imagism and, 25–6
  women's, 235
Time and Tide (periodical), 219
Tomlinson, Charles, 282
tradition, 9–10, 35–9
transcendence, 12, 47
transvestism, 205
Trilling, Lionel, 273
tropology, 50

Ulysses, *see* Joyce
unconscious, 13
Unkeless, Elaine, 217
Untermeyer, Louis, 164
urban, *see* city

value, 8
Vanity Fair (periodical), 259–60, 265,
  266
Veblen, Thorstein, 209
Vendler, Helen, 83, 86
vers libre, 25
Victorian era, 16–19
Virago Press, 219
Vogue magazine, 159

Wagner, Richard, 150
Wallace, Jo-Ann, 237
war, *see* First World War, Second World
  War
Waste Land, The, *see* Eliot, T. S.
Watson, James Sibley, 255–6
Weber, Max, 7, 208
West, Rebecca, 100
Wilde, Alan, 276, 284
  Horizons of Assent (extract from),
    276–9

Williams, Raymond, 79, 141
Williams, William Carlos, 79, 275–6, 281
Wilson, Edmund, 65–6, 160, 162
Wilson, Elizabeth, on Janet Wolff, 213
Wolf, Christa, 145–6
Wolff, Janet, 'Feminism and Modernism', 213
    The Invisible *Flâneuse*' (extract), 199–210
women, exclusion from accounts of modernism, 230
    exclusion from high culture, 148
    exclusion from professions, 208
    experience of, 209–10
experience of the city, 200, 204–6
ignored by sociology, 207–9
networks, 217–18
writers, neglected, 221
writers, reprinted 219
Woolf, Virginia, 33–5, 216
Worringer, Wilhelm, 26–7, 71–2

Yeats, W. B., 68–70, 251
    on Blake, 70
    publishing practices, 261–2

Zukofsky, Louis, 281